A critical history of
modern Irish drama
1891–1980

A critical history of modern Irish drama 1891–1980

D.E.S. MAXWELL

York University, Toronto

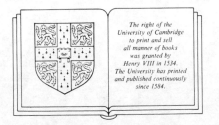

The right of the
University of Cambridge
to print and sell
all manner of books
was granted by
Henry VIII in 1534.
The University has printed
and published continuously
since 1584.

CAMBRIDGE UNIVERSITY PRESS

Cambridge
London   New York   New Rochelle
Melbourne   Sydney

Published by the Press Syndicate of the University of Cambridge
The Pitt Building, Trumpington Street, Cambridge CB2 1RP
32 East 57th Street, New York, NY 10022, USA
296 Beaconsfield Parade, Middle Park, Melbourne 3206, Australia

First published 1984

Printed in Great Britain at
the University Press, Cambridge

Library of Congress catalogue card number: 84–5801

British Library Cataloguing in Publication Data
Maxwell, D.E.S.
A critical history of modern Irish drama,
1891–1980.
1. English drama – Irish authors –
History and criticism   2. English drama –
20th century – History and criticism
I. Title
822'.912'099415   PR8789
ISBN 0 521 22532 9 hard covers
ISBN 0 521 29539 4 paperback

Contents

List of illustrations   *page* vii

Chronology   ix

Acknowledgment   xvii

Introduction   1

1   Dreams and responsibilities: 1891–1904   8

2   Possible forms: the early plays   20

3   Difficult, irrelevant words: W. B. Yeats and J. M. Synge   33

4   An art of common things: 1905–1910   60

5   A painted stage: 1911–1929   79

6   Plays and controversies: Sean O'Casey   96

7   The mill of the mind: Denis Johnston   114

8   The plays, the players and the scenes: 1930–1955   131

9   Explorations 1956–1982   158

10 The honour of naming: Samuel Beckett and Brian Friel   188

Notes   213

Select bibliography   225

Index   241

Illustrations

1 The stage of the old Abbey Theatre, Dublin, during rehearsal (Photo: G. A. Duncan) *page* 2

2 The stage of the new Abbey Theatre (Photo: G. A. Duncan) 5

3 Exterior of the old Abbey Theatre, 1951 (Photo: G. A. Duncan) 15

4 Scene from Yeats's *At the Hawk's Well*, part of the *Cuchulain Cycle* at the Lyric Theatre, Belfast, 1968–9 (reproduced by permission of the Lyric Theatre, Belfast) 35

5 Scene from Yeats's *The Death of Cuchulain*, part of the *Cuchulain Cycle* at the Lyric Theatre, Belfast, 1968–9 (reproduced by permission of the Lyric Theatre, Belfast) 44

6 Synge's *Playboy of the Western World*, with Sara Allgood, Fred O'Donovan and Brigit Dempsey, during the Abbey's American tour 1911–12 (Photo: G. A. Duncan) 63

7 T. C. Murray's *Birthright*, with Fred O'Donovan and Eileen O'Doherty at the Abbey, 1910. (Photo: G. A. Duncan) 74

8 George Shiels's *The Passing Day* at the Abbey, 1981 (Photo: Fergus Bourke) 87

9 O'Casey's *Juno and the Paycock* at the Abbey, 1979. (Photo: Fergus Bourke) 99

10 O'Casey's *The Silver Tassie* at the Abbey, 1972. (Photo: Fergus Bourke) 104

11 Denis Johnston's *The Scythe and the Sunset* at the Abbey, 1981. (Photo: Fergus Bourke) 115

12 Denis Johnston's *The Old Lady Says 'No!'*, at the Peacock Theatre, 1929, with Micheál MacLiammóir and Meriel Moore 119

13 Brendan Behan's *The Hostage*, Abbey, 1970. (Photo: Fergus Bourke) 154

vii

List of illustrations

14 Thomas Murphy's *The Sanctuary Lamp* at the Abbey, 1975.
    (Photo: Fergus Bourke)   163

15 Thomas Kilroy's *Talbot's Box* at the Abbey, 1977. (Photo:
    Fergus Bourke)   173

16 Graham Reid's *The Death of Humpty Dumpty* at the Peacock
    Theatre, 1979. (Photo: Fergus Bourke)   184

17 Beckett's *Waiting for Godot* at the Pike Theatre Club,
    Dublin, 1955 (reproduced by permission of Carolyn Swift)   192

18 Synge's *Riders to the Sea* at the Abbey, 1971. (Photo: Fergus
    Bourke)   193

19 Beckett's *Happy Days* at the Peacock Theatre, 1973. (Photo:
    Fergus Bourke)   195

20 Brian Friel's *Philadelphia, Here I Come!* at the Abbey, 1981.
    (Photo: Fergus Bourke)   202

21 Brian Friel's *Translations* at the Abbey, 1980. (Photo:
    Fergus Bourke)   208

Chronology

1878   Standish O'Grady's *Bardic History of Ireland*

1879   Michael Davitt founded the Land League

1880   Charles Stewart Parnell elected leader of the Irish Parliamentary Party

1890   Parnell/O'Shea divorce case, Parnell lost control of the Irish Parliamentary Party

1891   Death of Parnell; Irish Literary Society initiated in London

1892   Irish National Literary Society founded in Dublin; Douglas Hyde's lecture, 'The Necessity for de-Anglicising Ireland'

1893   Gaelic League founded; Hyde's *Love Songs of Connacht*

1894   William Butler Yeats's *The Land of Heart's Desire* at the Avenue Theatre, London

1899   Arthur Griffith founded the *United Irishman*. Irish Literary Theatre's first season, at the Antient Concert Rooms, Brunswick (now Pearse) Street, promoted by Lady Gregory, Edward Martyn, George Moore, and W. B. Yeats: Yeats's *The Countess Cathleen*, Martyn's *The Heather Field*

1900   Irish Literary Theatre's second season, at the Gaiety Theatre: Moore's *The Bending of the Bough*, Martyn's *Maeve*

1901   Irish Literary Theatre's third season, at the Gaiety Theatre: Moore and Yeats, *Diarmuid and Grania*, Hyde's *Casadh an tSugáin* (*The Twisting of the Rope*)

1902   The essay by John Eglinton (W. K. Magee), 'The de-Davisisation of Irish Literature' printed in the *United Irishman* 31 March. First productions of W. G. Fay's Irish National Dramatic Company, at St Theresa's Hall, Clarendon Street: AE (George Russell), *Deirdre*, Yeats, *Cathleen ni Houlihan*; and in October, at the Antient Concert Rooms: James Cousins's *The Sleep of the King* and *The Racing Lug*, Fred Ryan's *The Laying of the Foundations*, Yeats's *The Pot of Broth*, and P. T. McGinley's *Lizzy and the Tinker*

1903   Foundation of the Irish National Theatre Society: president Yeats, vice-presidents Maud Gonne, Douglas Hyde, AE; stage-manager W. G. Fay; secretary Frank Fay. First season, at the Molesworth Hall: Yeats's *The Hour Glass* (prose), *The King's Threshold*, Lady Gregory's *Twenty-Five*, John Millington Synge's *In the Shadow of the Glen*, Padraic Colum's *Broken Soil*. In May, at the invitation of the Irish Literary Society, London, the Irish National Theatre Society presented in the Queen's Gate Hall, South Kensington: Yeats's *The Hour Glass*, *The Pot of Broth*, and *Cathleen ni Houlihan*; Lady Gregory's *Twenty-Five*; Ryan's *The Laying of the Foundations*

1904   Second season, at the Molesworth Hall, of the Irish National Theatre Society: Yeats's *The Shadowy Waters*, Seamus MacManus's *The Townland of Tamney*, Synge's *Riders to the Sea*. On 11 May the Society accepted the offer of Miss A. E. F. Horniman to give them the use of 'the hall of the Mechanics' Institute in Abbey Street and an adjoining building in Marlborough Street . . . to turn into a small theatre'. On 20 April, Patent in the name of Lady Gregory was granted, and on 27 December the Society presented in the Abbey Theatre Yeats's *On Baile's Strand* and Lady Gregory's *Spreading the News*. Foundation of the Ulster Literary Theatre

1905   Sinn Fein founded. Formation of the National Theatre Society Ltd, directors Lady Gregory, Yeats, and Synge; stage-manager W. G. Fay; secretary Frank Fay. Productions included: Synge's *The Well of the Saints*, William Boyle's *The Building Fund*, Colum's *The Land*. G. B. Shaw's *John Bull's Other Island* rejected

1906   Theatre of Ireland formed by dissident Abbey members, president Edward Martyn. Abbey productions included: Yeats's *Deirdre*, Boyle's *The Mineral Workers*

1907   Synge's *The Playboy of the Western World*, George Fitzmaurice's *The Country Dressmaker*, Yeats/Gregory *The Unicorn from the Stars*, Colum's *The Fiddler's House*, *Playboy* riots

1908   Resignation of the Fays. Yeats's *The Golden Helmet*, Fitzmaurice's *The Pie-Dish*, Lennox Robinson's *The Clancy Name*. Rutherford Mayne's *The Drone* (Ulster Literary Theatre at the Abbey)

1909   Death of Synge. Robinson appointed play-director; his *The Cross Roads*, Shaw's *The Shewing-Up of Blanco Posnet*

1910   Withdrawal of Miss Horniman's subsidy. Synge's *Deirdre of the Sorrows*, Yeats's *The Green Helmet*, Colum's *Thomas Muskerry*, Robinson's *Harvest*, T. C. Murray's *Birthright*

1911 St John Ervine's *Mixed Marriage*. Moore's *Hail and Farewell* published

1912 Robinson's *Patriots*, Murray's *Maurice Harte*, Ervine's *The Magnanimous Lover*, Yeats's *The Hour Glass* (verse)

1913 Irish Citizen Army and Irish Volunteers founded. Dublin lock-out and strike. Fitzmaurice's *The Magic Glasses*

1914 Robinson's resignation as play-director

1915 Ervine appointed Abbey manager. Ervine's *John Ferguson*

1916 Easter Rising. Ervine's resignation. Robinson's *The Whiteheaded Boy*. Yeats's *At the Hawk's Well* in Lady Cunard's London home

1918 George Morshiel (George Shiels) *Under the Moss*, Ulster Literary Theatre, Belfast. Robinson's *The Lost Leader*

1919 Anglo-Irish War (to 1921). Robinson re-appointed to the Abbey. Dublin Drama League founded. Yeats's *The Player Queen* by The London Stage Society at King's Hall, Covent Garden. *The Only Jealousy of Emer* published in *Poetry* (Chicago) January

1921 Anglo-Irish War: Truce. Yeats's *Calvary* in *Four Plays for Dancers*

1922 Anglo-Irish Treaty ratified, Irish Free State established, outbreak of Civil War. Six northern counties retained British connections as Northern Ireland. Shiels's *Paul Twyning*, Murray's *Aftermath*

1923 Civil War ends. Robinson appointed to the Abbey Board of Directors. Yeats awarded Nobel Prize. Sean O'Casey's *The Shadow of a Gunman*

1924 O'Casey's *Juno and the Paycock*, Murray's *Autumn Fire*

1925 Abbey granted Government subsidy. Shiels's *Professor Tim*

1926 de Valera founded Fianna Fail. Radio Eireann begun. Construction of the Abbey's Peacock Theatre. O'Casey's *The Plough and the Stars* caused riots at the Abbey. Yeats's version of Sophocles' *King Oedipus*, *The Cat and the Moon*

1927 Abbey rejection of Austin Clarke's *The Son of Learning*. Yeats's Sophocles' *Oedipus at Colonus*, Shiels's *Cartney and Kevney*

1928 Abbey rejection of O'Casey's *The Silver Tassie*. The Edwards/MacLiammóir Gate Theatre began performances at the Peacock

1929 Censorship of Publication Act. Abbey rejection of Denis

Johnston's *The Old Lady Says 'No!'*; produced by the Gate Theatre at the Peacock. *The Silver Tassie* produced in London. Dublin Drama League dissolved. Yeats's *Fighting the Waves*

1930 Gate Theatre opened in its own premises. Yeats's *The Words upon the Window Pane*

1931 Johnston's *The Moon in the Yellow River*, Yeats's *The Dreaming of the Bones*

1932 de Valera's Fianna Fail party formed government. Murray's *Michaelmas Eve*, Paul Vincent Carroll's *Things That Are Caesar's*

1933 Robinson's *Drama at Inish*, O'Casey's *Within the Gates* published, Johnston's *A Bride for the Unicorn* (Gate Theatre)

1934 Robinson's *Church Street*, Mayne's *Bridgehead*, Yeats's *Resurrection*, *King of the Great Clock Tower*, Johnston's *Storm Song* (Gate Theatre)

1935 Ernest Blythe joined the Abbey Board. Hugh Hunt succeeded Lennox Robinson as play-director. Yeats's *Full Moon in March*, *Poetry* (Chicago), March. O'Casey's *The Silver Tassie*

1936 Division of Gate Theatre into Gate Theatre Productions (Edwards/MacLiammóir) and Longford Productions (Lord Longford). Shiels's *The Passing Day*, Johnston's *Blind Man's Buff*

1937 New Constitution for the Irish Free State. Hyde elected first President of Ireland. Carroll's *Shadow and Substance*

1938 Resignation of Hugh Hunt. F. R. Higgins appointed Abbey managing director. Yeats's *Purgatory*. *The Herne's Egg* published

1939 Death of Yeats. *The Death of Cuchulain* in *Last Poems and Two Plays*. Ulster Group Theatre founded. Johnston's *The Golden Cuckoo* (Gate Theatre)

1940 Dublin Verse-Speaking Society founded by Austin Clarke and Robert Farren. Shiels's *The Rugged Path*, O'Casey's *The Star Turns Red* (Unity Theatre, London), Johnston's *The Dreaming Dust* (Gaiety Theatre), O'Casey's *Purple Dust* written

1941 Death of Higgins, succeeded as Abbey managing director by Blythe

1943 O'Casey's *Red Roses for Me*

1944 Lyric Theatre Company founded by Austin Clarke. Shiels's *The Old Broom*, (Group Theatre), Belfast

1945 Shiels's *Tenants at Will*. Arts Theatre Studio founded in Belfast by Hubert and Dorothy Wilmot

1946 M. J. Molloy's *The Visiting House*. O'Casey's *Oak Leaves and Lavender* published

1948 Defeat of Fianna Fail government, Coalition government formed under John Costello. Molloy's *King of Friday's Men*

1949 Irish Free State declared independent Republic of Ireland. Death of Hyde and Shiels. O'Casey's *Cock-a-Doodle-Dandy* published

1950 Seamus Byrne's *Design for a Headstone*

1951 Abbey burned down. Lyric Theatre inaugurated in Belfast by Mary and Pearse O'Malley

1953 Alan Simpson and Carolyn Swift opened the Pike Theatre. Molloy's *The Wood of the Whispering, The Paddy Pedlar*

1954 Brendan Behan's *The Quare Fellow* (Pike Theatre)

1955 Controversy over Cyril Cusack's Dublin production of O'Casey's *The Bishop's Bonfire*. Samuel Beckett's *Waiting for Godot*, Pike Theatre and Arts Theatre Club, London

1956 Johnston's *Strange Occurrence on Ireland's Eye*

1957 First Dublin Theatre Festival. Alan Simpson prosecuted for his production of *The Rose Tattoo*. Hugh Leonard's *A Leap in the Dark*, Beckett's *Endgame* at the Royal Court Theatre, London

1958 Dublin Theatre Festival cancelled after ecclesiastical disapproval of the inclusion of work by James Joyce and O'Casey's *The Drums of Father Ned*. Death of Lennox Robinson. Johnston's *The Scythe and the Sunset*. Behan's *The Hostage* at the Theatre Royal, Stratford E., London. Beckett's *Krapp's Last Tape* at the Royal Court

1960 Sam Thompson's *Over the Bridge* independently produced after its censorship by the Group Theatre. Irish television service begun

1961 Thomas Murphy's *A Whistle in the Dark* at Stratford E., James Douglas's *North City Traffic Straight Ahead*, at the Dublin Theatre Festival. Opening of Arts Theatre's permanent house in Belfast

1962 Brian Friel's *The Enemy Within*, J. B. Keane's *Hut 42*, Beckett's *Happy Days* at the Royal Court

1963 Brookborough succeeded as Prime Minister of Northern Ireland by Terence O'Neill

Chronology

1964 Friel's *Philadelphia, Here I Come!*, Eugene McCabe's *King of the Castle* at the Dublin Theatre Festival

1965 Terence O'Neill and his southern counterpart Sean Lemass met, without success, to improve cross-border relationships. Beckett's *Film* at the Venice Film Festival

1966 The new Abbey Theatre opened. Friel's *The Loves of Cass Maguire* at the Helen Hayes Theatre, New York

1967 Friel's *Lovers* (Gate Theatre)

1968 Civil Rights Movement gains strength in Northern Ireland. Murphy's *Famine* (Peacock), Tom Kilroy's *The Death and Resurrection of Mr Roche* (Dublin Theatre Festival). Friel's *Crystal and Fox* (Gaiety Theatre). Probably the first production of the entire cycle of Yeats's *Cuchulain* plays, Lyric Theatre, Belfast

1969 British troops drafted to Northern Ireland to control violence. Beckett awarded Nobel Prize. McCabe's *Swift*, Murphy's *A Crucial Week in the Life of a Grocer's Assistant*, Friel's *The Mundy Scheme* (Olympia Theatre)

1970 IRA campaign of violence begun in Northern Ireland. Beckett's *Breath* (Oxford Playhouse)

1971 Internment introduced in Northern Ireland. Synge's *The Tinker's Wedding* first produced, Murphy's *The Morning After Optimism*, Friel's *The Gentle Island* (Olympia Theatre), John Boyd's *The Flats* at the Lyric Theatre, Belfast

1972 Direct rule by Westminster instituted in Northern Ireland. Murphy's *The White House*, Tom MacIntyre's *Eye Winker, Tom Tinker*; W. J. Haire's *Between Two Shadows* (Royal Court; Lyric, Belfast), Beckett's *Not I* (Lincoln Centre, New York)

1973 Friel's *Freedom of the City*, Leonard's *Da*, Haire's *Bloom of the Diamond Stone*

1974 Power-sharing Executive formed in Northern Ireland, brought down by Ulster Workers' Council strike. Death of Clarke

1975 O'Casey's *Purple Dust*, Friel's *Volunteers* and *Living Quarters*, Murphy's *The Sanctuary Lamp*, Stewart Parker's *Spokesong* (Dublin Theatre Festival)

1976 Leonard's *Time Was*, Beckett's *That Time*, *Footfalls* (Royal Court), *Ghost Trio*, BBC Television, *Radio II* BBC Radio

xiv

1977 Parker's *Catchpenny Twist*, Kilroy's *Talbot's Box* (Dublin Theatre Festival)

1978 O'Casey's *Cock-a-Doodle-Dandy*

1979 Graham Reid's *The Death of Humpty Dumpty* (Peacock), Friel's *Aristocrats*

1980 Reid's *The Closed Door*. Field Day Theatre Company founded by Brian Friel and Stephen Rea, Friel's *Translations* (Derry Guildhall)

Note: All plays performed at the Abbey Theatre unless otherwise indicated.

Acknowledgment

I wish to express my gratitude to the Humanities Research Council of Canada for their generous assistance with travel and other expenses. Grateful acknowledgment is made to authors for all quotations from their work; and for quotations from W. B. Yeats to Michael Yeats, Macmillan, London Ltd, and Macmillan, New York Inc.

Introduction

(1)

In 1897 Lady Gregory, Edward Martyn, and W. B. Yeats, founders of the Irish Literary Theatre – which in 1904 was to become the Abbey Theatre – met in Lady Gregory's house in Co. Galway to discuss the venture. Their letter of intent, addressed to prospective guarantors, proposes 'to build up a Celtic and Irish school of dramatic literature'.[1] As we shall see, the founders, shortly to be joined by George Moore, had different understandings of the character which this theatre should assert. Clearly, however, they regarded it as having neither native precedent nor instructive model in the general run of contemporary English drama. Commentators, from the earliest studies by Ernest Boyd (1918) and A. E. Malone (1929), concur on the truth at least of these premisses.

Boyd quite briskly dismisses 'the work of Irishmen whose spirit is as remote from their country as the scene in which their plays are laid'.[2] This principle excludes from consideration as Irish dramatists G. B. Shaw and Oscar Wilde. Malone regards more fully both these two playwrights and the issue they exemplify. He sees in them, placing them with William Congreve, George Farquhar, Oliver Goldsmith, and R. B. Sheridan,

a perfection of dialogue which is quite distinctively Irish; and they all have that wit which is no less a distinguishing mark of the Irishman. They are all satirists, viewing English life with a somewhat disapproving smile. In all their comedies it is the life of the English people that is satirised, there is nothing of Ireland in them but the pert dialogue and the ironic wit which are characteristic of their countrymen at large. Comedies by English writers tend to be humorous and sentimental, while comedies by Irishmen tend to be witty and ironic. Had it not been for the line of Irish writers from Farquhar to Shaw English comedy would have been almost entirely deficient in that satiric content.[3]

Malone's points are well taken and worth some development. When he talks of Shaw and Wilde 'viewing English life with a somewhat disapproving smile', he implies a stance at an eccentric angle to their (mainly) English objects of satire. Both are curious, detached observers of a scene only exotically familiar to them. The attitude harks back, for instance, to Goldsmith's inventing a Chinese as the voice of his alien status in his *Citizen of the World* essays; and to the cryptic variations which Swift imposes on Gulliver's accounts of his 'own dear beloved country'. Part of this distinguishing blend of intimacy and division comes from a peculiarly but not uniquely Irish acknowledgement of a sovereignty of words. Malone recognises in Shaw and Wilde the perhaps excessively advertised 'pert dialogue and ironic wit which are characteristic of their countrymen'. More deeply, this delight is in a language which competes with life rather than running imitatively alongside it; creates a rival world which may either displace factual reality or in quite practical ways alter it.

Many of the dramatists considered in this study assert that words, if they are not paramount, are the equal of reality, possibly its creator, when words affect the way we see things. The assertion is central to the dramatic tension in Synge, and in the expatriate tradition is plainly evident in Wilde. Nevertheless – and as Malone also concludes – despite these resonances from their national background, the emigrant playwrights belong to the lineage of English theatre. They are rovers, marauders even, but within an English heredity. The great exception is Samuel Beckett, who declares his separation from that heredity by exile in France. An important part of his artistic genealogy is traceable to the tradition of Irish writing in English, and

1　The stage of the old Abbey Theatre, Dublin, during rehearsal

2

more particularly to the movement initiated by the Irish Literary Theatre. It was in French that he began to evolve his own dramatic language; there can be no doubting the profound part in Beckett's experience of French companionships, French society and culture. Its unevicted host is his Irish background. Though a single, it is a closely informing, aspect of his work. It is to that aspect that the consideration of Beckett in this study is directed.

In attempting to find cause for the flight of the playwrights who might have established an Irish drama, Malone cites the total absence of any Irish equivalent to the venerable European–English tradition which took drama from the *tropes* of the mediaeval Church through the miracle and morality plays to the secular stage.[4] Eventually, theatres were built in Ireland, in Dublin and in provincial, mainly garrison, towns.[5] They and for the most part their repertoire were imports, the property of the Anglo-Irish, descendants of the original English invaders, who supplied their major patronage. English touring companies presented English plays, and this was the fare available to popular audiences in, for example, Dublin in the nineteenth century, where our story really begins.

The Irish dramatist Dion Boucicault (1820 or 1822–90) is of a rather more indigenous nature, though essentially he was a very practical man of the English and American theatre of his time, turning his hand to its fashionable melodrama and French comedy. His celebrated Irish plays are *The Colleen Bawn* (1861), *Arrah na Pogue* (1864), and *The Shaughraun* (1874). The interest of these lively and well-crafted plays, enjoyed by Shaw and Sean O'Casey, is their inverting the stupid and unreliable Stage Irishman into the charming and patriotic Stage Irishman, a reversal which Dublin took to its heart. Though their subjects and settings are Irish and their characters sentimental versions of Irish people, they are doing nothing more fundamental than adapting Irish matter to the prevailing theatrical formulae. These were not the plays to germinate a theatre expressive of lives and sensibilities whose reality had been so far unregarded by the drama.

(II)

Various chronicles carry the tale beyond the point where Malone stops: Peter Kavanagh's *The Story of the Abbey Theatre* (1950), Lennox Robinson's *Ireland's Abbey Theatre* (1951), Gerard Fay's *The Abbey Theatre* (1958), Hugh Hunt's *The Abbey, Ireland's National Theatre* (1979). These record the Abbey's history and with that to all intents and purposes the chronological progress of Irish drama. Other theatrical enterprises there have been and are but the Abbey is comprehensively dominant. The books mentioned contain little extended criticism of the playwrights. Kavanagh's has the strongest thesis. He is concerned to demonstrate, prematurely as it turns

3

out, that '[the Abbey's] collapse entitles one to the conclusion that the Abbey Theatre did indeed die with Yeats'.[6] In addition to these, Robert Hogan and various collaborators are producing their invaluable *Modern Irish Drama*, beginning at 1899, drawing largely on contemporary accounts.

More purely critical studies are Una Ellis-Fermor's *The Irish Dramatic Movement* (1939, 1954) and Katherine Worth's *The Irish Drama of Europe from Yeats to Beckett* (1978). These commentaries agree with Kavanagh in seeing Yeats, little thought of as a dramatist in his own time and in Ireland, as the presiding genius, and not only as a capably ruthless administrator. They judge his plays to be the model for and example of a modern verse drama; the dramatic theories dispersed throughout his writings an exciting programme for theatrical experiment – dance, music, and visual effects involved in a speech heightened and rhythmical yet appropriate to the stage. In Una Ellis-Fermor's opinion Yeats's plays reach an 'immediacy . . . achieved as the Jacobean and Greek dramatists achieve it, not by the quenching but by the exaltation of the poetic imagination'.[7] Much of this power she attributes to its origins in the speech and folkways of Irish peasants. For Katherine Worth Yeats's plays are a product more of his response to the *avant-garde* European drama of his formative years – notably Maeterlinck – than of an Irish inspiration. He looks back to the stark effects of the moralities and in his 'total theatre' of song, instrumentation, stylised movement, lighting, anticipates O'Casey, Beckett, Harold Pinter, Edward Bond – indeed the modernist–contemporary stage as a whole.

This is the highest praise for Yeats's dramatic achievement and influence. It is easiest to agree on the magical persuasiveness of his theorising. Certainly his example has not led to a renaissance of verse for the stage: the inconsiderable verse plays of John Masefield, John Drinkwater, and Lascelles Abercrombie come far short of Ellis-Fermor's claim that they realise 'the possibility of poetic drama as a working theatre form'. T. S. Eliot, a more plausible contender, fitted his verse for the stage by making it increasingly like prose, without ever accepting prose as the medium for poetic drama in this century. The value of Yeats's plays is still a contentious matter. The academic consensus, it is true, approves them. There are dissenting voices. Robert Hogan in *After the Irish Renaissance* (1968) whose main concern is to survey the course of Irish drama since Yeats, argues that they are rather eloquent verse exposition than dramatic enactment.[8] James Flannery, on the other hand, with substantial experience of producing them, sees in Yeats's plays exactly the virtues apparent to Katherine Worth, poetic drive and stageworthiness combined.[9] The plays, astonishing sketches for a verse drama that never attained full being, do not seem to me to warrant this enthusiastic discipleship.

Nonetheless, judge Yeats the dramatist how we may, he remained for

Irish drama an enduring memorial to an idea of poetic drama, active in later imaginations in quite other ways than Yeats's. Irish theatre in its heydays advances Yeats's intents; in its doldrums at least pays lip-service. In the common interpretation the Abbey turned to realist theatre and everyday matter: the 'peasant' plays of Padraic Colum, William Boyle and T. C. Murray. The fantasy plays of George Fitzmaurice were a brief aberration in this progress. Yeats said of the Abbey's development in these years (1903–10), 'its success has been to me a discouragement and a defeat'.[10]

Synge's plays might be argued on either side. It was their passionately poetic language, their 'astringent joy and hardness'[11] that commended them to Yeats. They also invited scrutiny as realist representations of peasant life. Synge took pains over the accuracy of clothing and domestic interiors, he used the realist proscenium stage, he claimed that his language was faithful to peasant speech. His audiences looked for this conformity to truth but objected that his unflattering portrayal of country people falsified Irish life. Synge, mistakenly, defended himself largely on those terms. His plays in fact escape the nineteenth-century realist convention which is their frame.

2   The stage of the new Abbey Theatre

Introduction

Their effect – and it is an effect of language, its elaborate stylisation, and the
rôle given to it of interfering with life – is to disturb the apparent solidity of
his stage's material accessories, to fantasticate and mythologise character
and action.

Between them, Yeats and Synge propose a view of drama within which
we can discern an outline of the Abbey's evolution. Yeats, looking at the
balance of verse/prose/poetic/realist theatre, saw his expectations miscar-
ried. He did not recognise designs fulfilled in the realistic style which his
prospectus rejected in favour of renewing 'the theatre of Shakespeare or
rather perhaps Sophocles'.[12] He does not altogether discount the virtues of
dramatic prose, but his overruling belief is that verse more readily commands the full amplitude of poetry. Among his contemporaries he delighted
in Synge's 'highly coloured musical language', and praises – above its due –
the 'vivid speech' of Lady Gregory's plays. The prose of their successors
was too remote from his preconceptions for his ear to catch its poetry:

Mr. Colum and Mr. Boyle . . . write of the countryman or villager of the East or
centre of Ireland, who thinks in English, and the speech of their people shows the
influence of the newspaper and the National Schools. The people they write of, too,
are not the true folk. They are the peasant as he is being transformed by modern life
. . . There is less surprise, less wonder.[13]

The comments, true enough as far as they go, cut off possibilities.
Elsewhere Yeats argued that the only greatness achievable by a realist play
must 'arise out of the common life' and its language – meaning the language
or the kind of language available to Synge. He goes on to ask, 'Is it possible
to make a work of art, which needs every subtlety of expression if it is to
reveal what hides itself continually, out of a dying, or at any rate a very
ailing, language and all language but that of the poets and the poor is already
bed-ridden.'[14]

Yeats is enforcing the answer 'no'. The answer really is that common
speech, however different from – one might even concede inferior to – the
hibernicised English on which Synge drew, is amenable to the metamor-
phosis of art. Contemporary theatre – Beckett or Harold Pinter, in Ireland
Thomas Murphy or Brian Friel – absorbs its poetry from registers of speech
which by Yeats's criteria are limited to giving 'the sensation of an external
reality'. Yeats's theory, in his own restriction of it, is partial. If we extend it
in a way which Yeats disallows, and take Synge's stylising of spoken
language as a model for other forms of colloquial speech, we have a draft, so
to speak, which anticipates the governing practice of the Abbey drama.

The work of the Abbey Theatre, of Irish drama, is a long experiment,
sometimes descending to stretches of mechanical self-duplication, with the
boundaries of realist theatre. On its heights it engages realist theatre in

6

poetic transformations, subdued in Colum, extravagant in O'Casey, beyond the mere traffic with, in Yeats's phrase, 'the sensation of an external reality'. It is remarkable in the tradition that it is essentially the flowering of an indigenous experience and imagination. It develops manners of presentation which are not discursive or sequential, which move away from literal portrayal: towards, in short, modernist attitudes and methods.

The experimental drama of Europe and Ibsen particularly were known in Ireland at the turn of the century. In Ireland it was suggestive not dominant, impressionable not prescriptive. Synge rejected it. It interested Yeats, but his feelings, about Maeterlinck for instance, were mixed. He drew upon Europe, as he did upon the Japanese Noh plays, quite arbitrarily to confirm or satisfy his own propositions. Denis Johnston, the Irish dramatist perhaps most consciously receptive to the drama abroad, gave to his borrowings from German expressionism a peculiarly Irish character. It is a self-sufficiency within cavalier alliances which continues to the present, informed by the sense of language as both reflecting and supplanting reality. There is a metaphor of this in the comment by the Irish painter Patrick Collins on his own work: 'you don't believe in the things you're painting, you believe in the thing behind what you're painting. You destroy your object yet you keep it.'[15]

The conclusions formulated here state the general argument of this study of Irish drama since the time of the Irish Literary Theatre – in effect the Irish dramatic tradition. Within world drama it is a brief chronicle, some eighty years, its achievement the more extraordinary for that. As far as possible the account given here both of its main events and its major dramatists sets them in their joint chronology. The inevitable and reluctant omissions, especially in the richly endowed present, when time has not yet passed sentence, represent personal judgments. At the heart of the matter, and so attracting the emphasis, are the playwrights rather than the theatres and players whose part is to supply the necessary stage, at their most enterprising when they beckon to a continuing line of dramatists. 'If we can pay our players,' Yeats said to the Royal Academy of Sweden, 'and keep our theatres open something will come.'[16] The players paid and the theatres kept open justified his faith. Its inheritance is the subject of this book.

1. Dreams and responsibilities: 1891–1904

I had had from the beginning a vision of historical plays being sent by us through all the counties of Ireland.

Lady Gregory

the peasant's primitive mind is too crude for any sort of interesting complexity in treatment.

Edward Martyn

the example can be set by the production every spring of an original dramatic work like the *Heather Field*, and by the production every autumn of a European masterpiece, like Ibsen's *Vikings of Heligoland*.

George Moore

I hope to get our Heroic Age into verse, and to solve some problems of the speaking of verse to musical notes.

W. B. Yeats

(1)

At the turn of the century, the Irish Literary Theatre took form amidst the conflicting intentions of its main sponsors: Lady Augusta Gregory, Edward Martyn, George Moore, and W. B. Yeats. Yeats was the chief agent. In 1891 he played a large part in organising the Irish Literary Society in London and the next year in Dublin the National Literary Society, which heard the lecture by Douglas Hyde, the celebrated Gaelic scholar, 'The Necessity for de-Anglicising Ireland'. Both Societies were part of a vigorous movement to encourage a literature which, whether in the English or the Irish language, would have a distinctly Irish character. Yeats had always been interested in drama – his play *The Countess Cathleen* was published in 1892, *The Land of Heart's Desire* performed in London in 1894 – and began to seek a special place for it in the movement.

In 1897 he discussed with Lady Gregory and Edward Martyn, two landowners in the west of Ireland, the possibility of setting up a literary theatre in Dublin. A proposal, in the form of a letter signed by the three of them, was sent to various prominent Irishmen. It set out their plans:

We propose to have performed in Dublin in the spring of every year certain Celtic and Irish plays, which whatever be their degree of excellence will be written with a high ambition, and so to build up a Celtic and Irish School of dramatic literature. We hope to find in Ireland an uncorrupted and imaginative audience trained to listen by

8

its passion for oratory, and believe that our desire to bring upon the stage the deeper thoughts and emotions of Ireland will ensure for us a tolerant welcome, and that freedom to experiment which is not found in theatres of England[1]

and solicited funds to keep the experiment going for a season in Dublin in each of the three years 1899–1901. Support for the Irish Literary Theatre was forthcoming. Opposition from commercial theatres and difficulties over licensing alternative buildings for theatrical performances were overcome. The detailed planning began for the first presentation in 1899, at which point George Moore was invited to join the original trio.

The four founding members made up an odd combination of social correspondences and divisions. Lady Gregory was a Protestant landowner. Martyn and Moore were landlords too. Both were Catholics, Martyn agonisingly devout, Moore ostentatiously lapsed. Martyn was a near neighbour of Lady Gregory in Galway, the Moore estates were in Mayo. All were humane proprietors, though Martyn had had a patrician hostility to the demands and depredations of the tenants' Land League in their campaign against the system of land tenure. Moore was a permanent absentee. Yeats, through his Sligo family, also had strong connections with the west of Ireland. At least tribally he was a Protestant, though not of the landowning gentry.

Moore claimed a greater practical experience of the stage than any of his partners, with some reason. Apart from his celebrity as the author of *Esther Waters*, and as a self-advertised 'bohemian', he had conducted a vendetta against the conservatism of the English theatre critics (*Impressions and Opinions*, 1891). He was an active supporter of J. T. Grein's Independent Theatre, which in 1893 staged his *The Strike at Arlingford*. Even so, Moore's credentials were not overwhelming. They were sufficient to allow him to condescend to Yeats and even more to Martyn. The Irish enterprise gave him the opportunity to instruct his colleagues and to display himself to advantage. *Hail and Farewell*[2] is his satirical account of events. Somewhere between history and fiction, it inclines the facts to magnify Moore.

Moore took credit for the construction of Martyn's *The Heather Field* (1899). During rehearsal he disrupted the casting of it. He was similarly autocratic with Yeats's *The Countess Cathleen*, in the same season, being particularly severe with the histrionics of Florence Farr, whose 'most perfect poetical elocution' Yeats greatly admired.[3] Moore also collaborated – acrimoniously – with Yeats on *Diarmuid and Grania* (1901); and, assisted by Yeats, with Martyn, whose *The Tale of a Town* became Moore's *The Bending of the Bough*, favoured over the Martyn play for the theatre's 1900 season. Martyn did not relish this high-handedness. In the end he refused his name to any joint version: 'Moore would put in what he liked', Yeats reports him as saying.[4]

9

There was plainly cause for the quartet to be at temperamental odds. When Yeats remarked, with how much sincerity we do not know, that Moore had his good points, Martyn answered: 'I know Moore a great deal longer than you do. He has no good points.'[5] Among their contending displays Lady Gregory played an indispensable rôle as entrepreneur. It was she who organised the financial guarantees. Because Martyn defrayed expenses these were never taken up, but the backing they represented was essential. She had not yet begun to write plays and so did not challenge the self-regard of anyone else, nor did she have cause to defend her own. Perhaps for this reason she was the better able to placate Martyn and restrain Moore. She enjoined a fortnight's silence on Moore when, in the Irish Literary Theatre's first season, *The Countess Cathleen* came under suspicion of heresy. Lady Gregory assembled enough clerical opinion to quieten Martyn's pious misgivings – Moore was spoiling for a fight – and so retain his patronage.

Altercation and conflicts of personality took place on a certain common, if shifting, ground. The Irish Literary Theatre arose partly – as its original proposal implies – from its founders' shared contempt for the English commercial theatre: for its parade of spectacle; its cluttered realism of stage décor; even for its serious playwrights, acclaimed for inferior imitations of their betters, particularly of Ibsen. The condition of English theatre was indeed deplorable. The London stage was occupied – as was the Dublin commercial theatre – by melodrama, romance, farce, and versions of Shakespeare monstrously 'revised' to suit the demands of fashionable players. In Dublin the main theatres – the Royal, the Gaiety, the Queen's – were given over to imported companies whose productions of English popular successes combined, with few exceptions, the modish and the slipshod.[6] Plays of simple faith and mindless patriotic sentiment, of which Dion Boucicault's were the most estimable, recognised an Irish audience but held to the prevailing style. They planted a hardy growth whose vulgarities were to flourish in more high-minded plays, like Maud Gonne's *Dawn* (1904), free from commercial motive.

It is an indication of the standard mediocrity that audiences regarded the 'well-made' plays of Henry Arthur Jones (*The Silver King*, 1882) and Arthur Wing Pinero (*The Second Mrs. Tanqueray*, 1893) as substantial theatre. Purporting to address social problems, they are a kind of genteel melodrama. Pinero had a slight gift for epigrammatic dialogue; his serious plays never penetrate beyond the conventions of the fashionable life which is their subject. Technically, the plays resort to such innocent devices as letter-writing and peripheral 'conversations' to allow two front-of-stage actors to expound the plot.

Between 1888 and 1898, when he was in turn drama critic for *The Star*,

The World, and *The Saturday Review*, George Bernard Shaw enthusiastically belaboured this delinquent English theatre. True inspiration, it seemed, had settled abroad, for Shaw, decisively with Ibsen, more widely in the experimental theatres of France and Germany: André Antoine's Théâtre Libre, founded in Paris in 1887; Otto Brahms's Free Stage society in Berlin (1889). Their object was to further the work of their young nationals, to introduce the *avant-garde* drama of all countries, and to create their own companies of players.[7]

Nominally at least, the Irish Literary Theatre subscribed to the same ideals, though the thought of training its own locally recruited actors did not, in its beginnings, occur to its organisers. The first issue of the journal *Beltaine*[8] included a laudatory essay by C. H. Herford on the Scandinavian dramatists. Martyn and Moore spoke consistently of the virtue of staging Continental in association with Irish drama. In *Beltaine*, Moore recommended a double season, 'in the autumn of great plays by Ibsen, Maeterlinck and Tolstoi'. Martyn believed, 'Our foreign influences should come from the continent'; and in *Samhain* projected for the theatre 'native works, also translations of the dramatic masterworks of all lands . . . that dramatists may be inspired to work in the great art tradition'.[9] Yeats, on the other hand, was interrogative about Alfred Jarry's *Ubu Roi*, the first performance of which he had seen in Paris in 1896; about Antoine sceptical,[10] and, contrary to the intellectual consensus, hostile to Ibsen.

He had seen *A Doll's House* in London in 1889, and later recalled having 'hated the play'. He could not 'admire dialogue so close to modern educated speech that music and style were impossible'.[11] Yeats persistently identified Ibsen with the 'social drama': Lady Gregory's diary for 1898 reports his belief that 'there will be a reaction after the realism of Ibsen, and romance will have its turn'.[12]

Yeats's view was partial. He identified in Ibsen, as he did in Shaw, an 'inorganic, logical straightness'.[13] Some of the constriction in his attitude was due to the English emphasis, which was also Shaw's, on Ibsen's caustic treatment of social issues in plays like *The Pillars of the Community* (1877), *A Doll's House* and *An Enemy of the People* (1882). William Archer's translations did not much contribute to delivering the poetic Ibsen, the Ibsen who declared that poetry interested him more than social reformation.[14] Yeats, also, was in search of a dramatic verse. He acknowledged that there could be a 'prose drama that is remote from real life like my *Hour Glass*'; and that a play might use 'rhythmical prose'.[15] But prose, however highly charged, did not admit his purposes. In Ibsen's he was aware of 'a stale odour of spilt poetry'.[16] Nevertheless, there was in Ireland opinion and evidence enough to enlarge Yeats's reading of Ibsen and to question his antipathy.

George Moore drew neatly on Ibsen to decry an aversion: 'Do they not all think that Mr. Pinero has been influenced by Ibsen? As well might you talk of the influence that Michelangelo exercises upon the pavement-artist.'[17] Frank J. Fay's dramatic criticism in the *United Irishman* twice commended to Yeats the example of Ibsen, whom Fay associated with Shakespeare and Molière: all three had practical stage experience and could put poetry, in a wholly beneficent sense, in its place.[18] Martyn was a proselytiser for the new Continental drama, most of all for Ibsen, whose 'exquisite music' and 'symphonic beauty' inhabited 'the most direct realism of speech'.[19] In 1900 James Joyce praised the disturbing latencies of Ibsen's dialogue: 'at some chance expression . . . long reaches of life are opened up in vista'.[20] The next year Joyce rounded upon the Irish Literary Theatre. He castigated its failure to 'look abroad'; and 'Mr. Yeats's treacherous instinct of adaptability'.[21] In response, between 1900 and 1904, Yeats was tempering his judgment on Ibsen with occasional praise in *Beltaine* and *Samhain*. If not an honoured guest, Ibsen was at least admitted to the house.

The expectations were enticing and ambitious. Martyn wrote of 'a great intellectual awakening in Ireland'; Yeats of a stage of Irish history 'when imagination . . . desires dramatic expression'; Moore of the Irish Literary Theatre as 'a new outlet for the national spirit and energy'.[22] Outside this euphoria, dream had to negotiate with fact; cosmopolitan with local; art with politics; an élite with an audience; versions of nationality with each other and with the diverse options that might express them. More immediately, at the end of its three seasons the Irish Literary Theatre had to consider its future.

(II)

The third and last issue of *Beltaine* in 1900 noted the coming 'end of our three years of experiment, which is all we proposed to ourselves at the outset'. In 1901 in *Samhain* Yeats amplified this brief announcement that a phase had ended. He was writing as of a stage gone by and scrutinising the choices that arose from it. He had been counselled against the Irish Literary Theatre's practice of importing English actors, notably by Frank Fay in his *United Irishman* articles. It was to the busy talents of Frank and his brother Willie that Yeats's attention narrowed.

By profession Frank was a clerk–secretary and Willie an electrician. Their real calling was the theatre. Between 1891 and 1899 they formed a succession of companies giving farcical sketches, recitations and songs. Their more serious ambitions began to flower in W. G. Fay's Irish National Dramatic Company. Its first performances in April and October 1902 included Yeats's *Cathleen ni Houlihan* and *The Pot of Broth*. Martyn, already affronted by the Irish Literary Theatre's defaulting on its pledge to international drama, criticised the style of acting. It was of a kind inimical to the social and psychological drama he most prized. Yeats agreed that the acting was alien to the drama Martyn preferred. 'But that,' he added, 'is as it should be.'[23] By this time Moore had tired of the venture and gone back to England. Yeats was adamant that any 'return to the theatre is out of the question. He represents a rival tradition of the stage.'[24] The frail alliance had ruptured.

'I am myself,' Yeats wrote in *Samhain* in 1903, 'most interested in the Fays' "The Irish National Dramatic Company," which has no propaganda but that of good art.' In the same year the Company was re-constituted as the Irish National Theatre Society, with Yeats as President. The Fays were a welcome replacement for Martyn's demurrals and Moore's attitudinisings. They were also the inspiration of the style which had displeased Martyn. It was their coaching which prepared the best Irish actors of those early days. For this the credit goes mainly to Frank Fay. He was an elocution teacher and had schooled himself in the history and theory of drama. Very much to Yeats's taste he urged the primacy of distinct, melodious speech; and called for the training of Irish players – after the precedent of Antoine – through whom he wished, in Yeats's phrase, 'to restore words to their sovereignty'.

Yeats's precepts for the stage followed his general aesthetic turn. Jarry's *Ubu Roi* threatened the cast of his imagination, that of Mallarmé, Verlaine, Moreau: 'our subtle colour and nervous rhythm . . . the faint mixed tints of Condor'.[25] Suggestion, symbol, distance of effect were proper also to the stage, and most endangered there by the temptations of gesture, 'business', and all the apparatus of conventional theatre. These were the distractions which Yeats wanted to depose in favour of speech, restoring simplicity to restless movement and cluttered space. Poetic drama particularly should be 'staged with but two or three colours', often with 'nothing more than a single colour, with perhaps a few shadowy forms to suggest wood or mountain'.[26] Movement should be thrifty, the actors 'free to think of speech'.[27] Yeats had complex directions for the musical pitching of the spoken word, certainly too elaborate for the actors he had, perhaps for any audience but himself.[28]

Fay agreed on the simplifications advocated by Yeats and with a realistic valuation of the resources he could draw upon for premises, properties and players. His patriotism did not hinder his admonishment of the amateurs who gave Douglas Hyde's *Casadh an tSugáin* (*The Twisting of the Rope*):

they must be prepared to face a lot of hard work, and to remember that an artist is never done learning. And let them take great care to be distinct in their speech; an audience will do a great deal of the acting itself if it only hears the words.[29]

It was a simpler therapy for speech than Yeats's. Fay stated it repeatedly in the *United Irishman*. His advocacy, after Coquelin, the French classical actor whom he had seen in Dublin, of a clearly spoken verse and articulateness, won ground over the kind of chant sought by Yeats. Max Beerbohm in his review of the company's performance in London in 1904 commended their 'simple recitation' of *The King's Threshold*.[30] In the previous year the *Times* critic had given a friendly description of the company's techniques:

The speaker of the moment is the only one who is allowed a little gesture . . . The listeners do not distract one's attention by fussy 'stage business' . . . Add that the scenery is of Elizabethan simplicity and you will begin to see why this performance is a sight for eyes made sore by the perpetual movement and glitter of the ordinary stage.[31]

Between them Yeats and the Fays gave Irish theatre its essential domestic body. They were building a stock of Irish players, renewable from the proliferating amateur societies; and they were building a repertoire of Irish plays by new writers: by James Cousins (*The Racing Lug*) in the Fay Company's 1902 season; in the first season (1903) of the Irish National Theatre Society, by Lady Gregory (*Twenty-Five*), Padraic Colum (*Broken Soil*), and most important of all, by J. M. Synge (*In the Shadow of the Glen*). The new enterprise had a more secure basis than that of the Irish Literary Theatre, to whose intentions, as they understood them, Moore and Martyn were giving a galvanic afterlife. In June 1903 Martyn sponsored a revival by the Players' Club, an amateur group, of *The Heather Field*, along with *A Doll's House*, stage-managed by Moore. In April 1904 the same company presented Martyn's *An Enchanted Sea*. Yeats did not fear the rivalry, writing to John Quinn that his own theatre would 'always be best in poetical drama or in extravagant comedy or in peasant plays'.[32] However, apart from the rivalry, affairs were not proceeding easily.

As Yeats wrote to Frank Fay, 'All theatrical companies make rows but ours seem to have more than the usual gift that way.'[33] Their cause was the national conscience and its fastidious guardians. Arthur Griffith, editor of the *United Irishman* and a supporter of the Society, invigilated its programmes with an eye to impure moral and political doctrine. Internally, the Society was vulnerable to its own democratic rules. The performance of a play required, after approval by the reading committee, consent of three-quarters of the membership, which in 1903 numbered seventeen and included actors. In that year Willie Fay, according to him for artistic reasons, withdrew Padraic Colum's *The Saxon Shillin'*, a play opposing Irish enlistment in the British Army. Maud Gonne, a vice-president, and Colum took it as censorship of patriotic art. For the politically doctrinaire faction of the Society this skirmish anticipated the major engagement over Synge's first play.

The Republican objection to *In the Shadow of the Glen* was that it was immoral and anti-national. The wife who leaves her older husband for the enticement of a tramp was taken to demean the purity of Irish womanhood and to feed anti-Irish prejudice. Maud Gonne and Arthur Griffith resigned from the Society, together with Douglas Hyde, as did two of its best players, Dudley Digges and Máire Quinn. James Cousins also defected. The seceding players joined a theatre company established in 1903 within the Gaelic League to give occasional performances. Enlisting from the Irish National Theatre Society, its challenge seemed more serious than Martyn's. Yeats and the Fays remained fixed in Synge's support: first because there is 'no propaganda save that of good art'; more empirically because a Synge is harder to come by than a Digges.

During all these alarms the Society was vagabonding insecurely from site to site. When a permanent home came, it was a gift from Annie Horniman, a

3 Exterior of the old Abbey Theatre, 1951

wealthy English eccentric and admirer of Yeats. Her only interest in Irish nationalism was her detestation of it. The object of her philanthropy was to promote Yeats and his plays, not Irish drama. Miss Horniman was not a compliant patron. She despised the Fays; vied with Lady Gregory to be Yeats's protector; and held a veto on any play she might consider propagandist: once again, an alliance tense with internal strains.

Still, the Society now had living quarters, a building in Abbey Street converted to a theatre and readied for occupancy by the Irish National Theatre Society – from now on commonly known as the Abbey – in December 1904. It was modestly appointed. It seated under five hundred. Its stage was small and shallow – sixteen feet deep. Having exited from one side an actor had to use an outside lane to enter on the other. The lighting was 'perfectly simple standard stage lighting'.[34] It permitted none of the refinements that had captivated Yeats in the productions of Gordon Craig (1872–1966), the unorthodox and inventive English stage designer. The Abbey nevertheless established itself as the home of Irish drama.

Yeats did, however, declare encouragement for 'dramatic enterprise apart from our own company'.[35] The most substantial offshoot outside Dublin had its tentative beginnings in 1902 – without any authorisation from the (then defunct) parent it claimed – as the Ulster Branch of the Irish Literary Theatre. Bulmer Hobson and David Parkhill had travelled from Belfast to Dublin for the Dublin season of 1902. In November of that year they staged *Cathleen ni Houlihan* and *The Racing Lug* in Belfast, with Dudley Digges and Máire Quinn from the Dublin company; and according to Hobson without much encouragement from Yeats.

Hobson and his companions had been 'running a small group trying to spread the ideas of Wolfe Tone and the United Irishmen and met with little noticeable success. So we decided to try the drama as a vehicle of propaganda.'[36] The productions of the Ulster Literary Theatre, eventually founded in 1904, did not discover any major dramatist, though two farcical comedies, Rutherford Mayne's *The Drone* (1908) and Gerald MacNamara's *Thompson in Tir-na-nOg*, achieved wide popularity. The company remained entirely amateur to the end, which came in 1934. It never had a house of its own, but it did sustain dramatic life in Belfast, seeking in kitchen comedy and kitchen tragedy a regional variant of the realist style which its parent was acquiring.

This growing bias towards realism is heralded even between 1899 and 1904 in the balance of the Irish National Theatre Society's repertoire. The balance was clearly not of the Martyn persuasion. It included none of the new Continental work. Only his own *Heather Field*, more marginally his *Maeve*, and Moore's *The Bending of the Bough* leaned to Ibsen's social–psychological drama. The remaining plays were working towards independent formulations of Irish themes, set increasingly in a mundane, contemporary world – in Synge's plays enchanted by the power of his language. The poetic treatment of heroic legend, largely through Yeats's contributions, was still holding a place, and was represented in almost all the individual programmes of 1899–1904. But there was no sign of its practice extending, whereas the realists multiplied.

(III)

Despite the Ulster Theatre's declared intention 'to try the drama as a vehicle of propaganda' its programmes do not indicate a strong political leaning, nor did they lead to rancorous political controversy. The Southern movement, on the other hand, quickly found that there was to be no purely aesthetic rendering of accounts. An Irish theatre, for its audience, unavoidably impinged on politics, which Yeats called 'the most vital passion and vital interest of the country'.[37]

Yeats's own desire to make the theatre an Irish one was plain. He might have defined it, after Hyde, as 'the de-misrepresentation of Ireland': replacing the caricatures of the popular stage with faithful images of heroic legend and peasant life. But Yeats's ideas of fidelity to truth were an irritant to the political orthodoxies, Unionist and Nationalist. In many of the theatre's productions neither the *Irish Times* nor the *United Irishman* could find an Ireland they were willing to recognise. Yeats was too ready to claim 'for our writers the freedom to find in their land every expression of good and evil necessary to their art'.[38] Evil, other than the evil of English political oppression – or its converse, Republican subversion – did not figure in the sentimental insistence on Irish piety.

An understanding of the dispute between the political and the aesthetic codes of judgment calls for a look at its history. In the late 1880s Yeats was at least gesturing towards extreme Nationalist positions. Two relationships led him perhaps rather beyond the limit of his own convictions. One was his veneration for John O'Leary, a founder in 1873 of the Irish Republican Brotherhood, whom Yeats met in 1886. The other attachment was his love for Maud Gonne, whom he met three years later.

Maud Gonne, a rebel against her well-to-do, Protestant upbringing, unequivocally demanded art for politics' sake. Yeats's *Cathleen ni Houlihan*, with its evocations of patriotic war, met her stipulations. The bloody metaphors of her own play, *Dawn*, even more explicitly exalt the supposed purification of blood-letting.[39] Not surprisingly, she chided Yeats for his defence of Synge because Yeats was asking 'for freedom for the theatre . . . I would ask for freedom for it from one thing more deadly than all else – freedom from the insidious and destructive tyranny of foreign influence'.[40]

Arthur Griffith was of Maud Gonne's mind, arguing that when 'art ceases to be national, it will also cease to be artistic, for nationality is the breath of art'.[41] Griffith's is a tenable wording, but to be 'national' in his understanding was to hold that any adverse representation of Ireland and the Irish denied the necessities of the political struggle.

The example of John O'Leary was more edifying. His revolutionary politics had some of their genesis in the writings in the *Nation* of Thomas Davis and the other Young Ireland propagandists during the mid 1840s. Their poetry trafficked in bellicose and weltering metaphor, lamenting the loss and invoking a resurrection of the Gaelic past and its defeated heroes. Their fervour aroused O'Leary's patriotism but did not impair his literary judgment. Yeats tells us that O'Leary 'no more wished to strengthen Irish Nationalism by second-rate literature than by second-rate morality'. Yet whatever one might censure in the vulgarities of Davis's style, its potency was indisputable, and O'Leary 'wished for some analogous movement'.[42] So, wanting to relieve it of Davis's blatancies, did Yeats.

There was a theoretical alternative to the use of English, whether or not drawing on the model of Davis, to serve both political and artistic ends: to reverse the erosion and the threatened total extinction of Irish as the national tongue. Throughout the country there was support for, though far from general participation in, the Irish language revival. Its main agent was the Gaelic League. This was founded in 1893 by Douglas Hyde. Its aims were cultural: to retrieve the Irish past, its language particularly. It sought political neutrality, but here too cultural nationalism was not easily separable from the economic and political, and from the comprehensive ideal of breaking the union with England. The dramatic movement from its beginnings espoused the revival, certainly in its cultural aspect. But even Frank Fay, uncompromising in principle that a truly national theatre was impossible 'except through the medium of the Irish language'[43] settled for the reality that, while one might attempt to hold the two languages in conference, English had in fact secured mastery.

In Ireland, moreover, the long intercourse with Gaelic had given English a distinctively hibernicised character, to that extent redeeming its function as a colonising usurper. Yeats saw it as a suitable indigenous medium and, for want of a native dramatic tradition, was willing to place Davis in its heritage. Politically, he was among the names from the Anglo-Irish past of which Yeats approved. He defended Davis against the imputation that he, Wolfe Tone, Robert Emmett, Charles Stewart Parnell, all Protestants, all leaders of rebellion, 'were but anglicised Irishmen at best'.[44] Conversely, he was wary of the possibility that Davis's Nationalist inwardness might provincialise the Irish imagination.[45]

To the issue of Davis's literary merit Yeats paid such tribute – 'many a fine war song', 'a battle call' – [46] as would not flagrantly betray critical honesty. Honesty did have its say, that Davis was 'the maker of three or four charming songs that were not great, and of much useful political rhyme that was not poetry'.[47] But however imperfectly, Davis was habituating Irish subjects to the English language, as Yeats wished to do. Hyde also, conceding that Irish would reach only a minority, admitted Davis as an interpreter of the Irish inheritance. His own *Love Songs of Connacht* (1893) and Lady Gregory's translations continued to propagate through English the Gaelic culture it had superseded. So too had Standish O'Grady's enormously influential *History of Ireland* (1878–80), less a history than an evocative recounting of heroic legend.

The clamours and divisions of Irish politics pressed upon the founders of the dramatic movement demands as obstinate as the aesthetic dissensions between its founders. A movement guided by an élite was encountering populist ardours and a growing Catholic middle class of Victorianised respectability. The letter soliciting guarantees for the original theatre had looked towards 'a Celtic and Irish school of dramatic literature'. This theme, national autonomy and the nature of a national culture, obtruded on the more rarified issues of verse-poetic/prose-realist, cosmopolitan/native theatre. The judgment of the audiences, however wrongheaded, was a corrective to any Platonic model imposed from above. Yeats was fully aware of these demands, and of the extent to which the theatre could honourably satisfy them. By 1904 his arbitrations were bearing upon a growing number of Irish playwrights, and to their work we shall now turn.

2. Possible forms: the early plays

Much of the work of the movement's first five years is of slight worth. It nevertheless collectively, even excluding the plays of the major figures, merits more than passing remark. However tentatively, it was entering a dramatic void and making possible its fuller occupancy. The lesser writers may by their example, however imperfect, indicate the circumstances that are particularly ready for the artist's imagination.

Synge acknowledged a generative excitement from seeing the performance of Douglas Hyde's *Casadh an tSugáin*, along with *Diarmuid and Grania*, in 1901.[1] In 1902, the year when Synge completed *Riders to the Sea*, he attended the December performance of James Cousins's *The Racing Lug*, which was also attempting the creation of dramatic legend from the elemental disasters of the sea. Of Alice Milligan's *The Last Feast of the Fianna* Yeats said that 'if it were acted without scenery it would resemble a possible form of old Irish drama'.[2] Whatever the value of the conjecture, it shows another superior imagination collaborating with a lesser to designate 'possible forms'. These interchanges, in short, were establishing a necessary body of work: 'part of an attempt to create a national dramatic literature in Ireland'.[3]

Frank Fay's review received Hyde's play enthusiastically, partly because amateur native actors had performed a play in Irish, and, unlike their English counterparts in *Diarmuid and Grania*, with conviction. Lady Gregory's translation catches a vigour in the play. It concerns the trick by which the guests at a farmhouse dance rid themselves of Hanrahan, poet, adventurer, and caster of fierce spells. He must leave of his own accord, for if ejected he might 'make a rann', one of his curses 'that would split the trees and that would burst the stones'. Flattery and amusingly elaborated deceit persuade him that only he can twist a rope of hay from inside to outside the house to extricate an imaginary 'coach upset at the bottom of the hill'. The play is good enough fun, a slight but agreeable romp. *Casadh an tSugáin* belongs in a minor vogue of one-act folk comedies: P. T. McGinley's *Eilís agus an Bhean Deirce* (*Lizzy and the Tinker*), and Seamus MacManus's *The Townland of Tamney* are also of the genre. *The Racing Lug* is of altogether greater consequence.

It is set in the respectable Presbyterian home of a Northern fisherman Johnny, his wife Nancy and daughter Bell. Bell is attracted to a young fisherman, Rob; her father urges on her – 'you that are fit to be the mistress of a manse' – the claims of the local minister, who exits 'looking hungrily at Bell'. Johnny discovers Rob and Bell in each other's arms, a quarrel follows and, inferring an accusation of cowardice, he takes out the racing-lug on a stormy night. The second scene announces the wreck of the lug and Johnny's death. Both suitors propose, almost wordlessly, to Bell, who accepts, by embracing, Rob. Nancy dies, the minister kneeling beside her, in another ambitious stage-direction, 'with self-renunciation on his face'. Bald summary diminishes this, as it does any play.

The Racing Lug escapes its naïvetés into a forcible simplicity of word and gesture: the minister movingly signalises Nancy's death in a ceremony of stopping the wall clock; the only linguistic flourish is Johnny's simile for Bell, 'with your big words that run on as many feet as a lobster'. The play closes with the biblical image which opens it – ' "And there was no more sea" ' – no more separation – repeated at the end by anticipations of security threatened, a reality crumbling:

NANCY. What's that? Did you call me, chile?
BELL. The gulls are wheeling and crying, that's all.
NANCY. There it's again, it's your father; he wants me to kiss him now he's finished with the net. Tell him I'm comin' in a minute.
BELL. Don't mind, mother; he'll come himself very soon.
NANCY. There he is. Wasn't that his step on the garden walk?
BELL. Not yet, not yet. It's only the waves making a trampling on the shingle.

Domestic settlement yields to the sea and its laments; the humans make their choice and re-assert their lives in a suddenly altered state.

In Alice Milligan's *The Last Feast of the Fianna* the heroic past, recalled, disturbs the obvious perception of a commonplace present, the present throws its shadow back on that questionably heroic past. The pallor of Miss Milligan's prose fails to match the interesting shades of contrast and likeness which this, and her vision of the event, require. But its failure has ambitions which invite re-phrasing of a 'possible form'; in the broadest terms to make English amenable to Irish subjects.

All these minor plays make tentative overtures to a seizure of dramatic power, suggesting subtler approaches to Yeats and Synge. Lady Gregory, who was fifty when she came to write plays, fastened upon these models in more direct ways. Between 1907 and 1927 she turned out thirty-seven plays: folk comedy, folk tragedy, history plays, translations. All came alike to her, and earned Yeats's astonishing tribute that the 'first use of Irish dialect, rich, abundant, and correct, for the purpose of creative art was in J. M. Synge's *Riders to the Sea* and Lady Gregory's *Spreading the News*'.[4] The literal 'correctness' of Synge's dialogue is disputable; Lady Gregory's, while 'correct', does not move much beyond accurate transcription of how people spoke towards a theatrical rhetoric.

Her intention, like Synge's, was revivalist. Both believed that effectively Gaelic Ireland had lost its language as a social and literary resource. The hibernicised English of demotic speech, still linguistically vital, had a new potency. Through it, imagination might repair its disinheritance and return to popular converse the ancient legends, the folklore, the vocabulary for an Irish sense of self, of place, of nationhood: 'work . . . in English that is perfectly Irish in essence, yet has sureness and purity of form'.[5]

Lady Gregory's contributions to these 'purposes of creative art' were ambitious but impaired by defects of sensibility. Praising Lady Gregory's love for 'the peasant', A. E. Malone nevertheless observes in her 'an attitude towards the people, and in some of her most popular plays, that touch of patronage and unconscious snobbery which is expected from the "county" landowning families'.[6] The colonial eye diminishes its subjects to the fetchingly odd. Local colour remains damagingly local and 'colourful', contesting the claim that the fantasies which Lady Gregory's characters typically indulge in 'grow into the universal through the saving glory of their individual imaginations'.[7] Lady Gregory's earliest plays, *Twenty-Five* (1903) and *Spreading the News* (1904), do not represent the scope of her aspirations. They do reflect her continuing preoccupation with illusion and delusion and the dramatic manoeuvres by which she tried to deliver it. Both plays depend upon a trick, the kind of situation which Hyde used in *Casadh an tSugáin*.

The deception in *Spreading the News* is involuntary. Rumour spreads and multiplies around a village, helped by a deaf stallkeeper. A farcical Ascendancy magistrate is misled, along with the villagers, into thinking that a murder has taken place – in this way:

TIM CASEY. Listen, Shawn Early! Listen Mrs. Tulley, to the news! Jack Smith and Bartley Fallon had a falling out, and Jack knocked Mrs. Fallon's basket into the road, and Bartley made an attack on him with a hayfork, and away with Jack, and Bartley after him. Look at the sugar here yet on the road! . . .
MRS TARPEY. What did you say she was doing?
SHAWN EARLY. Laying out a sheet on the hedge.
MRS TARPEY. Laying out a sheet for the dead!

Lady Gregory described this as comedy. In the simplest meaning of the term it is: it gained laughs. But the laughter it won was for exclamatory farce, with entirely vacuous characters and some gift for vernacular imitation. 'No trade at all but to be talking', says Mrs Tarpey of the villagers: the talk does not engage and calculate reality as the language of Synge's characters does. Nor do the self-deceptions cast a shadow into any depth of meaning beyond their own buffoonery: Bartley, who is merely fatuous, fails even to approach Lady Gregory's intent, 'the lasting glory of that great and crowning day of misfortune'.[8]

The pretensions of *Twenty-Five* to profundity of metaphor are more apparent. Christie, returned from America, implausibly unrecognised by anyone but his old love Kate, now married to Michael, is the Stranger, the Redeemer of dreams – other than his own. He engineers the card game twenty-five to lose the fifty pounds Michael needs, and leaves, the Saviour of the house. The play ends in a ritual of dance, invoked by Christie in words heightened to intensify the moment of his departure:

CHRISTIE. You wouldn't refuse the greatest stranger in the house. Give me a dance now and I'll be thinking of you some time when I'm dancing with some high up lady having golden shoes, in a white marble court by the sea. Here Fiddler give us a reel. (FIDDLER *strikes up.* CHRISTIE *takes* KATE's *hand. Dance for a minute. Stops. Kisses her and flings over to the door. Turns round and waves his hat.*)
CHRISTIE. Good-bye neighbours, that was a grand evening we had.

Twenty-Five does not realise its pretensions. The dreams are extraneous to the reality: the 'white marble court by the sea' to the cards, the need for Christie to explain away his third-class return ticket to the 'grand evening'.

It is unjust to consider Lady Gregory in the company of Synge's genius. Synge's was the uniquely complete realisation of the purpose they shared, to sustain vernacular echoes in the cadences of a dramatic prose. Lady Gregory's achievement does not call for the seriousness she devoted to discussing it; removed from Synge's dominance it makes a modest place for itself in her 'theatre with a base of realism'.[9] Synge paid tribute to her instruction, as did Yeats. Flawed though they are, her plays consolidated a style, modulating vernaculars, which developed into the Abbey staple, and their popularity helped to keep a theatre in being. Perhaps most far-reachingly, her work existed within the philosophy enunciated by Synge:

I am prepared to stake everything on a Creative movement even if we all go to the work house at the end of the four years . . . Yeats speaks of making our theatre a copy of continental [theatres]. That is exactly what for the next ten years at least we should avoid. National dramas have never been created by theatres. Goethe at the end of his life said that he and Schiller had failed to make a German drama at Weimar because they had confused their audiences with, one day, Shakespeare, one day Calderon, one day Sophocles and another Racine. If we do the same we are doomed. An occasional foreign play that illustrates our own work should be done, as we have played *The Doctor*, and are going to play *Oedipus* . . . Our supply of native plays is very small and we must keep our company very small so that this little store of native work will keep it occupied.[10]

The plays of Edward Martyn come from a simple and dogmatic opposition to Synge's view, but labour into caricatures of his idea of Ibsen's psychological drama:

Oh-ha-mad. How can she say such a thing? Mad – who is saner than I am? Ha-ha – I suppose people of her type thinks everyone who differs from them, mad. How curious! Ah, we have not a single sympathy. That is what it is. (*With a look of terror*) Merciful heaven, is it possible, though, she may be right? Can there possibly be a doubt which is the reality and which is the dream? Oh, horror – horror!

The speaker is Carden Tyrrell in *The Heather Field*. A landlord, he has embarked at ruinous expense on the reclamation of a heather-infested field. He has ceased to love his wife, who thinks him, as his mother was, insane and is plotting to have him certified. His friend Barry Ussher announces the symbolic parallel. Of Tyrrell's marriage he says, 'Oh, I foresaw all. I knew this change could not last. The old, wild nature had to break out again when the novelty was over . . . the latent, untamable nature was not to be subdued'; and of the field, 'If heather lands are brought into cultivation for domestic use, they must be watched, they must have generous and loving treatment, else their old wild nature will avenge itself.'

These portentous anticipations come to their readily foreseeable end. The heather re-appears and Tyrell lapses into fugue, memories of a romantic past, a journey in Europe and a choir singing Palestrina – 'Fit music for those bright young days', the 'mystic highway of man's speechless longings'. The exposition of the lurches in the plot takes on a less clamorous but no more winning accent:

The chief mortgagee was most pressing, and threatens to foreclose immediately. I have implored of him again and again to wait until I can let the heather field, but in vain. Miles, whom I expect home this evening, was to have made a final appeal to him in Dublin last night. I can only hope for a favourable result.

The Heather Field is not a modest proposal. Martyn was a perceptive enough reader of Ibsen and recognised in him, in Joyce's words, the flashes by which 'long reaches of life are opened up in vista', the phrasing which 'tells a chapter of experience'. Tyrell is the Ibsenite hero, borrowing from the diseased heredity of Osvald in *Ghosts* and from John Gabriel Borkman's grandiose projects. *The Heather Field* situates him uneasily somewhere between the 'social problem' of his indifference to his tenants' welfare, his estrangement from his wife, and the private corruptions of his imagined voices 'singing of youth in an eternal sunrise'.

Una Ellis-Fermor credited Martyn with having 'opened up new country only to lose his way in it'.[11] It would be truer to say that he had an understanding of Ibsen's cartography but never designed the projection for a map of his own. Martyn's is the sad case of a talent unequal to its schemes, and certainly incapable of diverting Irish theatre from the growing assurances of a native landscape, one of whose earliest interpreters was Padraic Colum.

In 1903 the Irish National Theatre Society presented Colum's first major play, *Broken Soil*. In 1907 a revised version, *The Fiddler's House*, was published, and produced by the Theatre of Ireland. Conn Hourican, the fiddler, lives with his two daughters, Anne, the younger, and Maire, in the cottage left to Maire by her grandmother. Brian MacConnell, a young farmer, is paying court to Maire, James Moynihan, a farmer's son, more successfully to Anne. The play has little action and no intrigue in the conventional sense. It is the kind of play which Martyn wanted, a drama whose plot is in psychological recognitions and misapprehensions divulging themselves within and between the characters.

The settled cottage life, in which Maire is the family manager, holds Conn tenuously, the household chores he is forever undertaking charmingly avoided. Maire is annoyed by yet understands her father's spasmodic escapes to the pub and an audience for his fiddle: 'You have only the fiddle, and you must go among people that will praise you.' The relationships are evasive and oblique. Maire's protestations of attachment to the cottage, her conditioning with Brian, are part of her truth. It does not deny Conn's perception that while Anne is 'the pet that doesn't fly and keeps near the house', Maire is 'the wild pigeon of the woods'.

Brian, Maire and Conn are in search of a whole truth for themselves whose disclosure will carry injury with it. Brian is poised between wanting possession of Maire and a tenacious will to be his own man. Maire too is determined for her selfhood – but what is that self? She can say both 'We couldn't let him go off like a rambling fiddler', and to her father 'If you took to the roads I'd think I ought to go with you, for we were always together.' The Ardagh Feis decides Conn. He goes off to play at it, and back to the roads. Maire rejects Brian and joins her father, leaving the cottage to Anne and James. The roads have won, it seems, but Anne and the cottage remain, and the Maire who leaves them is not the same as when first she travelled with her father. Her last words, on leaving, are 'Tell Brian MacConnell that when we meet again maybe we can be kinder to each other.'

Conn Hourican, the peasant musician, is a type of the Artist. His 'gift' is an assumption, its analogies discreetly implied in fleeting metaphors of birdsong, companionship, independence and dominion, by unloaded symbol. Colum, certainly, has more title than Synge to be called realist. But his prose is deceptively plain. The dialogue, despite its local idiom, has a strangely modernist shaping, bothersome to the critic who is thinking in terms of orthodox plot. The repetitive formalities of phrasing, and elliptical transitions, at times seem aimless. In the same year as Synge's *In the Shadow of the Glen*, Colum was drawing towards the obliqueness of a twentieth-century dramatic syntax. Maire is coming to renounce Brian. Their exchanges circle around images of subjection, departure and return, song. The rapid transitions move towards knowledge and definition:

BRIAN. Sure you'd leave them all to come with me.
MAIRE. Ay, I think I would. Do you know where I saw you first, Brian?
BRIAN. When was it, Maire?
MAIRE. In a field by the road. You were breaking a horse.
BRIAN. I was always a good hand with a horse.
MAIRE. The poor beast was covered with foam and sweat, and at last you made it
   still. I thought it was grand then. (*She sings.*)
     I know where I'm going,
     I know who's going with me,
     I know who I'll love,
     But the dear knows who I'll marry.
  Are your brothers with you, Brian?
BRIAN. Is it building with me?
MAIRE. Building with you? (*She sings.*)
     Some say he's dark,
     I say he's bonny,
     He's the flower of the flock,
     My charming, coaxing Johnny.
BRIAN (*with sombre passion*). No. My brothers are not with me . . . The house is
   left desolate, and they are all again me.
MAIRE. The house is left desolate?
BRIAN. I'm heart-broken for what I did.
MAIRE. Ah, Brian MacConnell, I don't know what to say to you at all.
BRIAN. You'll give me your promise, Maire?
MAIRE. Promise. I've no promise to give to any man.

Maire, the real centre of the play, is to an extent the manipulator, controlling the talk, which does not reveal, but makes revelation possible. The main characters all reach an issue, but it is problematical, not final. Maire's choice may be seen to be a sacrificial act, an offering of part of herself, homage to Conn. What this entails remains an open question. *The Fiddler's House* rebuts Martyn's dismissal of 'the peasant's primitive mind', requiring for its expression a genuinely novel translation of common speech to a language for theatre.

Oliver St John Gogarty, defending *Broken Soil*, argues against it that because it dealt with the folk its situations 'cannot be as great and comprehensive as a heroic subject'.[12] Yeats, who also praised Colum's success, agreed. Colum's people were 'the peasant as he is transformed by modern life', lacking 'surprise and wonder', their speech discoloured by 'the newspaper and the National Schools'. The subdued poetry of Colum's

prose did not reach Yeats's ear. The dialect prose which for Yeats epitomised encroachments upon poetry – a 'highly coloured musical language',
'vivid speech'[13] – was that of Synge. Though Yeats's continuing pursuit was
of a dramatic verse for heroic tales, poetic prose still enticed him. Lady
Gregory collaborated in *Cathleen ni Houlihan* and the farcical *The Pot of
Broth*. *The Hour Glass*, first presented in its prose version in 1903, was
Yeats's own.

Based on an Irish story, *The Hour Glass* tells of a Wise Man who, having
corrupted the land into scepticism, is given an hour to find a believer. It is a
parable of intellectual arrogance and its voluntary submission to an exalted
mystical force, of this world and 'the one invisible', separate and yet
communing, divided from each other and, mysteriously, within themselves. Each is understandable by intellect, or by its sensual delights, or by
its glimpses of a reality beyond itself; Heaven is powerful – 'I am the Angel
of the Most High God' – and desolate – the 'threshold is grassy, and the
gates are rusty, and the angels that keep watch there are lonely'.

Defects in the transmission of the parable are evident, for example a
repetitiveness in the Wise Man's search for a believer. More important,
while a fable need not require a naturalistic psychology, this one does
require disturbances of tone to phrase its choices. The prose lacks a range of
suggestive voices to compel belief in the threats and the promises of this
world's and the other world's enigmas, in the Wise Man's overbearing logic
and its sudden dereliction. The multiplicities of the kind from which
Yeats's poems make their riddling architecture, do not pass from lyric to
dramatic expression.

Yeats felt some dissatisfaction with the play and set store by his revisions
of it, which led to the 1914 poetic version. He incorporated a number of
songs. Much of the prose he cast into verse – with some uncertain
metaphors for a major poet:

> But what their mothers dinned into their ears
> Cannot have been so lightly rooted up

does not improve upon 'Surely what you learned at your mother's knees has
not been so soon forgotten.' At the end the Fool, in front of the closed
curtain, has the last word, inviting the audience to join in his arcane
knowledge of angelic beings, which he refuses to share. This new ending,
thrusting the disregarded Fool into his cryptic challenge, does better satisfy
the paradoxes with which Yeats surrounded the heroic gesture, the proud
'wasteful virtues' of *Responsibilities*. But in general the alterations do not
redress the essentially verbal failings of the original.[14]

Yeats's early plays are interesting when they allow mockery, an intimate
of his poetry, to attend the 'beautiful lofty things' of Irish legend; when the

celebration of heroic deeds and figures incorporates the ironic detachment he admired in Synge. A striking instance of this in Yeats is a Prologue to *The King's Threshold*, published in the *United Irishman* on 9 September 1903 but not performed. An old man in *déshabillé* and with a flickering candle gives a rambling, deflationary account of the confrontation between King Guaire and the poet Seanchan. He talks of the play as a play, an illusion, and of the characters as emblems both of splendour and of a world heedless of life's tribulations: 'the stage there will be filled with great ladies and great gentlemen . . . as if there was no such thing in the world as cold in the shoulders, and speckled shins, and the pains in the bones and the stiffness in the joints . . .' This arresting voice does not persist into the play, though Yeats, in the early version and in the later where Seanchan dies, did try to convey some of its parody. A pompous Mayor and two querulous cripples bumble around the dying bard.

These conflations of heroic and absurd exhibit in Yeats, as Katherine Worth claims, the modernist *dérèglements* of form and viewpoint. Similarly in *The Shadowy Waters* (1904) the ship houses the dreaming Forgael with a crew of worldly rogues; and the play's many revisions, as S. B. Bushrui proposes,[15] are partly to give an everyday body to ethereal vision: 'yellow and brown ale' on the searoad to 'mystic marriages / Impossible truths'. Yet these plays are open to the same objections as *The Hour Glass*. The repetitious efforts to dissuade Seanchan from his fast parallel the Wise Man's repetitious search for a believer. The lyric and the parodic do not coalesce. The verse is more complicated than complex. With *On Baile's Strand* Yeats's gropings towards verse for a modern theatre began to find a hold.

Its earliest version (1903) has the same structure as the revised (1906). Fintain and Barach – the Blind Man and the Fool as the revision has them – frame the action in a consciously undignified opening and ending. It is a far from perfect play and Yeats's revisions bring some remedies. The assembly of kings is given a reason to meet, the wilful Cuchulain's disloyalty to Conchubar. The dispute gives their debate a point. The verse, and even more the prose of the Blind Man and the Fool, are sharpened. Their opening scene, entirely rewritten, both conveys and masks its information: it does not conclusively identify the Young Man as Cuchulain's son, the expositors are more cryptic, more reductive, as in the Fool's disentangling the Blind Man's tale with his feet, his bag, and his cap as its characters. But even in the early version there are auguries of a dramatic experience growing in Yeats. The verse, in exchanges and in longer speeches, has tighter control and a colloquial edge:

> I think that a fierce woman's better, a woman
> That breaks away when you have thought her won,

For I'd be fed and hungry at one time.
I think that all deep passion is but a kiss
In the mid battle, and a difficult peace
'Twixt oil and water, candles and dark night
Hill-side and hollow, the hot-footed sun,
And the cold sliding slippery-footed moon

The metaphors of opposites stir into a life that insists on the feeling, not, by some distracting embellishment, on themselves – though the moon might have been left less adorned.

Although, as the following chapter argues, Yeats affirms 'the sovereignty of words' in drama, all the possibilities of animating the stage fascinated him. The 1911 production of *The Hour Glass* used Gordon Craig's screens, lighting effects, costumes, and masks. The *Irish Times* critic approved:

The scenery is a mere arrangement of neutral-tinted screens . . . The arrangement of the screens is designed with perfection to permit of the most effective . . . groupings of the characters, and also to admit of those variations in the lighting of the stage which supplied [a powerful] aid to the expression of the emotional progress of the plays . . . The new arrangements served to strip away everything that would distract from the emotional and dramatic unfolding . . .[16]

Such excursions may be interpreted, in Yeats's words, as forwarding 'a decoration of the stage almost infinite in the variety of its expression and suggestion'; or as Katherine Worth puts it, 'his radical break with the naturalistic convention'.[17] The course of Yeats's flirtations between words, and in a broad sense, décor, was an errant one. However, he was consistent enough in seeing the words as the elemental substance: lighting, settings and the rest, whatever their potential for enhancement, need something to enhance.

There can be no doubt that Yeats was directed to these novel potentialities in part by his experience of Continental theatre in the eighties and nineties. With Arthur Symons, the influential translator of the French symbolist poets, as his mentor, he found in France a theatre that appealed to him, alternatives to Antoine, whose naturalistic style had nothing to offer. In February 1894 Yeats attended the performance in France of Villiers de l'Isle Adam's symbolist play *Axël*. As his review indicates, he was entranced: 'it brings us a little nearer the heroic age'; 'the Sacred Book that I longed for'.[18]

Yeats is less enamoured of the plays of Maurice Maeterlinck. His mysticism produced characters whom Yeats described as 'faint souls, naked and pathetic shadows'.[19] He was averse to their disposition to 'tremble and lament'. Nevertheless, when Aurélien Lugne-Poe's *Le Théâtre de l'Oeuvre* presented *Pelléas et Mélisande* in London in 1895, Yeats recognised the importance of the event: 'of immense value in helping to understand a more ideal drama'. Lugne-Poe devised settings, 'symbolic and decorative scenery',[20] appropriate to Maeterlinck's 'interior' drama: instead of melo-dramatic sexual passion or martial adventures 'an old man, seated in his armchair, waiting patiently, with his lamp beside him, giving unconscious ear to all the external laws that reign about his home'.[21]

These impressions germinated in Yeats's mind with his own theories of dramatic verse and its ideal staging. He was in search for his dramatic verse of the effects which he described in the poem 'A Coat' (*Responsibilities*) as 'walking naked'. He wanted, that is, to diminish verbal embellishment and merely decorative trappings, to cast upon a noble mythology the 'cold eye' of his epitaph: as, indeed, when not bowdlerised, did the mythology itself. The transference to Yeats's drama of the foreign stirrings has its interest. Continental theatre occupied the part of Yeats's imagination which saw possible answers in non-realist theatre, in methods that the norms of contemporary English theatre did not supply. More important were the use of Irish themes and subjects, the example of his Irish contemporaries, the private commuting between his dramatic and non-dramatic verse. Yeats was an interpreter, not an imitator, of the exotic European dramaturgy. His question, as it were, was, 'how do I write plays about Cuchulain?' not, 'how do I write plays in the method of the French symbolists?'

Synge's only treatment of legend, *Deirdre* (1910), imbues the tragic story with the mordancy of his prose in the kind of compact which Yeats sought. Even in Synge's peasant plays Micheál MacLiammóir has remarked, at a distance, 'the unearthly life of those ancient figures of mythology',[22] – brought down to earth. The first of these plays, *In the Shadow of the Glen*, declares Synge's interest in a language which may endow anecdote with the authority of legend.

Here the anecdotal basis – a trick as in *Casadh an tSugáin* – is that an aged husband, Dan Burke, pretends to be dead in order to trap his young wife, Nora, in the infidelities which he suspects. When he rises from his supposed death bed Michael Dara, Nora's fancy, reneges on their understanding, and Nora goes off on the roads with the tramp who has called in for shelter:

you've a fine bit of talk, stranger, and it's with yourself I'll go. (*She goes towards the door, then turns to* DAN.) You think it's a grand thing you're after doing with your letting on to be dead, but what is it at all? What way would a woman live in a lonesome place the like of this place, and she not making a talk with the men passing? And what way will yourself live from this day, with none to care you? What is it you'll have now but a black life, Daniel Burke, and it's not long, I'm telling you, till you'll be lying again under that sheet, and you dead surely. *She goes out with* THE TRAMP. MICHAEL *is slinking after them, but* DAN *stops him.*

Much of the talk in the play is about talk: 'I heard a thing talking – queer talk'; 'saying a prayer for his soul'; 'a voice speaking on the path'; 'saying a good word for a dead man'; 'talking with someone'; 'the like of that talk'; 'a talk of getting old'; 'you'll be saying'.

The tramp's 'fine bit of talk' divides the characters. It wins Nora, is 'blather' to Dan – 'for it's too much talk you have surely' – to Michael is the yarning of an itinerant in 'a poor coat'.

Nora and the tramp, the absent Patch, another outcast, together leave the world where to marry for a 'bit of a farm and cows on it' leads to 'lonesomeness', embittered age, and youth with no prospect but to age – 'the young growing behind me and the old passing'; 'you'll be getting old, and I'll be getting old'. The roads seem to offer a liberation of sorts, to be elevated from harshness by the words which in the glen are mute, or resigned to circumstance:

TRAMP. We'll be going now, I'm telling you, and the time you'll be feeling the cold and the frost, and the great rain, and the sun again, and the south wind blowing in the glens, you'll not be sitting up on a wet ditch the way you're after sitting in this place, making yourself old with looking on each day and it passing you by. You'll be saying one time, 'It's a grand evening by the grace of God,' and another time, 'It's a wild night, God help us, but it'll pass surely.' You'll be saying –

Synge's contraries are not as patent as between a constricted small-holding and becharmed vagabondage; nor between crabbed age and youth, as if all these existed each in its own unalterable right. We are not being led to wonder about a plausible motive for Nora, nor about the 'real' world which she and the tramp will inhabit. The play is suggesting how percep-tions of reality may transmute reality. When Lady Gregory wrote to Synge about his *The Aran Islands* she advised him to add 'some more fairy belief' and to quote from the keens and fairy songs.[23] Synge ignored the advice. He was not after guidebook anthropology any more than he was out to duplicate the way people spoke. The origin of Synge's characters and places is in 'a reproduction of external experience', which he leads to 'the deeper truth of general life in a perfect form'.[24] The shadow of the glen lengthens into other fields, echoing with the life of words.

In *Riders to the Sea* (1904) the brief scene where Bartley appears has him virtually indifferent to Maurya's lamenting her fears for him. He speaks to Cathleen and Nora and 'won't hear a word from an old woman and she holding him from the sea'. Cathleen supports Bartley: 'who would listen to an old woman with one thing and she saying it over?' The words are ominously prophetic, almost prescribing a destiny, as Bartley leaves 'with an unlucky word behind him, and a hard word in his ear'. The destiny is fulfilled. Bartley, like his brothers, drowns, his body brought on stage. Words and ritual now are 'making lamentation for a thing that's done'. Words may enunciate a peace as they have foretold disaster:

MAURYA . . . (*She pauses, and the keen rises a little more loudly from the women, then sinks away. Continuing.*) Michael has a clean burial in the far north, by the grace of the Almighty God. Bartley will have a fine coffin out of the white boards, and a deep grave surely . . . What more can we want than that? . . . No man at all can be living for ever, and we must be satisfied.

More apparently than in *In the Shadow of the Glen*, the cottage of *Riders to the Sea* is host to the seasons and the creatures of Irish life and legend, 'the long nights after Samhain' and 'the black hags that do be flying on the sea'. Though there are only the two such references, they bring the play's tragedy into a pagan as well as a Christian cosmology, where human suffering identifies itself beyond its time and setting. Synge's province, at once local and placeless, is not of the kind which Yeats dismissed as creating 'kilts and bagpipes and newspapers'. Synge disengages it from region and history, stating it as Yeats described: 'Only that which does not teach, which does not cry out, which does not condescend, which does not explain, is irresistible.'[25]

With this body of work achieved the Abbey entered its permanent home. The possibilities were both attractive and disheartening. Politically and in terms of the theatre's artistic development, what was to come was still unsure. The definitions were to clarify around Yeats and Synge.

3. Difficult, irrelevant words: W. B. Yeats and J. M. Synge

I have left the words of the opening and closing lyrics unchanged, for sung to modern music in the modern way they suggest strange patterns to the ear without obtruding upon it their difficult, irrelevant words.

W. B. Yeats

We had the *Shadowy Waters* on the stage last week, and it was the most *distressing* failure the mind can imagine – a half-empty room, with growling men and tittering females . . . No drama can grow out of anything other than the fundamental realities of life which are never fantastic, are neither modern, nor unmodern, and as I see them rarely spring-dayish, or breezy, or Cuchulanoid!

J. M. Synge[1]

(I)

Although his plays may be the most doubtfully dramatic of the major work of the movement, Yeats attracts a mass of recondite theoretical discussion, in the past quarter century mostly eulogistic.[2] As they so persistently occupied a great poet, the plays need to be accounted for. Yeats himself, meditating purpose and method, proposes an heretical understanding, for which he found neglected precedents, of the theatrical hierarchy of words, movement, gesture, music. There is a beckoning, that is, to alternative compositions of the verbal and the non-verbal, the revision of a stage accustomed to the domination of speech, psychological realism, and a carefully circumstantial imitation of social particulars. Yeats's dissatisfactions began with the place of the word, degraded, he believed, by an 'ailing' common speech and subordinate to mere 'tricks of the theatre'. Throughout his career, though as the Introduction to 'Fighting the Waves' indicates not with entire consistency, the word retained its supremacy, certainly its status as an irremovable item, whatever its degree of participation, in the stage activity surrounding it. The course of Yeats's judgments on the authority of language is worth pursuing. It negotiates the boundaries within which the other elements may settle.

'The theatre began in ritual', he wrote in 1899, 'and cannot come to its greatness again without recalling words to their ancient sovereignty.' *Samhain* reiterates the claim; 'if we are to restore words to their sovereignty we must make speech even more important than gesture'.[3] Already, Yeats is extending the role of language beyond the informative, the expository. He

33

takes it as an agent, at this time *the* agent, to reinstate ritual, leading drama 'to inhabit as it were the deeps of the mind'.[4]

Language cast into verse is traditionally appropriate to the purpose, but in Yeats's time, dramatic verse, blank verse particularly, was theatrically listless, intimidated by the Elizabethan heritage and deprived of continuing precedent by its narrative use in the nineteenth century. Drama itself had a certain subservience, as had the nineteenth-century narrative poem, to the dominant manner of the dominant literary form, the novel: social, realistic, story-telling, sequential. Proust, Joyce, Virginia Woolf deliberately thwart those conventions. The imperative for Yeats was some comparable dislodgement of theatrical orthodoxies. Looking back twenty years from 1937, he recalls the language he considered fit to carry it off – 'not, as Wordsworth thought, words in common use, but a powerful and passionate syntax, and a complete coincidence between period and stanza'.[5] His deciding upon a stylised, oracular speech did not, in principle, exclude simplicities of speech, whose 'enterprise / in walking naked' he had acknowledged in 'A Coat' (1912).

Between 1902 and 1919 the employment of useful accompaniments to speech increasingly exercised Yeats, gesture included. It is a part, for example, of sacred ritual – of conjuring, blessing, malediction. Its purpose, then, is to reinforce the nature of the language – strongly rhythmical, incantatory, abstracted from 'average common speech'[6] – in proposing drama as a sacrament, not an entertainment or a social document. Thus gesture assists language in the defiance of the proscenium stage, which, deprived of its projecting apron, essentially pictorial, reproduces an external scene, and keeps its audience at a distance. *At the Hawk's Well* (1916) recommends ordinary room lighting to avoid 'mechanical means of separating [the masked players] from us'; the Old Man and the Young Man enter through the audience. In *Samhain* Yeats constantly deplored the naturalistic impositions, attributing the Abbey's duplication of them to 'the necessities of a builder'. 'We must submit', he added, 'to the picture-making of the modern stage. We would have preferred to be able to return occasionally to the old stage of statue-making, of gesture.'[7] Sculpture and gesture may seem odd companions. But gesture develops into dance, dance ends in stillness, a sculpted shape reminiscent of movement: the handiwork of Callimachus in 'Lapis Lazuli', 'draperies that seemed to rise / When sea-wind swept the corner'. Movement and stillness combine in action of a kind distinct from the mindless traipsing back and forth of the conventional stage. The total effect of the compound was to be 'a mysterious art' – and the mediaeval Mystery Plays are relevant texts – 'doing its work by suggestion, not by direct statement, a complexity of rhythm, colour, gesture, not space-pervading like the intellect, but a memory and a prophecy'.[8]

The caveat remains – 'speech is essential to us'. In the early years Yeats was chary of any but minimal stage movement. He once expressed a wish to rehearse his players in barrels, that they might think only of the words; and recalled his satisfaction in the audience's acceptance of Synge's *The Well of The Saints* (1905), 'though the two chief persons sat side by side under a stone cross from start to finish'.[9] Nevertheless, ideas were germinating in his mind of a self-contained theatrical logic, a drama which would not be *about* something, which would take as its premiss an empty stage whose space would dictate a proper means of filling it, 'as a decorator of pottery accepts the roundness of a bowl or a jug . . . a true art because peculiar to the stage'.[10] At that time, 1904, it was an embryonic aesthetic. In 1919 it had burgeoned: 'we have to prepare a stage for the whole wealth of modern lyricism, for an art that is close to pure music, for those energies that would free the arts from imitation, that would ally art to decoration and to the dance'.[11] In this accounting language yields – though not finally – to images of dance and music. The stage is a place for motion, for sounds other than

4 Scene from Yeats's *At the Hawk's Well*, part of the *Cuchulain Cycle* at the Lyric Theatre, Belfast, 1968–9

35

speech, experiences different from those expressible in words, so implying that in theatre, words alone are not enough. Not relinquishing its demands, language looks towards movement and music at least as collaborators.[12]

It was around the Japanese Noh plays, to which Ezra Pound introduced Yeats in 1915, that all these dispersed ideas cohered. To catch their reflection in Yeats's drama, there is no need for an exhaustive study of the Noh tradition. Yeats's knowledge was confined to the plays 'translated by Ernest Fenollosa and finished by Ezra Pound'. As he had with symbolist drama, Yeats seized upon the features which confirmed his own prospectings; and upon an ancient artistic lineage – 'artistocratic' as he saw it – to validate them. Pound's Introduction describes it as 'a symbolic stage, a drama of masks'.[13]

There at once is a figure close to Yeats's lifelong fascination with the mask in human behaviour – the pose or attitude assumed as an antithesis to and concealment of the interior nature, the mark of a 'rebirth as something not oneself, something . . . created in a moment and perpetually renewed'.[14] He had already, in 1910, planned to use masks in *The Hour Glass* and *On Baile's Strand*. Worn by actors, the masks were a metaphor of the human duality, and represented, like the Noh actors' movements which were copied from marionette shows, a convention remote from realistic theatre. The Noh plays were set in 'some holy place or much-legended tomb', often the site of a meeting with god or spirit revealed, with the divesting of the mask, behind an apparent mortal: tales of dead lovers, of visions, phantoms. They were settings, stories, and a *dramatis personae* compatible with Yeats's resuscitating Irish legend 'to bring again to certain places their old sanctity or their romance'.[15] Words, dress, and dance, integrated in a 'rhythm of metaphor', did away with 'character' – the domain of comedy, a superficial individualising – and for Yeats's purposes made possible the expression of 'personality'. The distinction, as with many distinctions Yeats makes, is inconsistently explained. Broadly, however, personality in Yeats's usage is to be found in dramatic characters who are defined not by personal idiosyncrasies, though those they do have. Their nature is legendary, mythic, expressing the depths of an essential spirituality in human action.

To clarify its outlines, the formal theory is here for the moment abstracted from Yeats's practice in the plays. It might justify a theatre – of whose logical extremes Yeats in fact stopped short – in which speech defers to acts without words. The verbal and the non-verbal consort, in fluctuating command to be sure, but never conceding a natural, final authority to words. Dance, music, the singing voice are not merely an enhancement or paraphrase of words. They are there of right to make the statements which are in the nature of their language and untranslatable into speech. They can lead, ultimately, to a theatre prepared to do without words. Beckett's *Film* uses only visual images. A man, muffled up, shambles through city streets to a room where he makes absurd efforts to avoid being seen: some victim, perhaps, of psychic despair, seeking refuge and pursued by the implacable camera, which is the relentlessly observing world. Whatever the 'meaning', it exists wholly in the enclosure of the images. We are to regard them for their own sake. They are not there to endorse the report of a speaking voice.

These farther shores were not for Yeats. Language remained paramount, 'vivid speech', 'syntax that is for ear alone'. Plays are not narcissistically expressing just their own form. They are about something. Their habitation, though they must distance it, is the world. In the poetry, 'Sailing to Byzantium' and 'Byzantium' tell us so. There is a necessary 'contact with the soil'. In the Noh plays the 'sign of a great age' is 'the continual presence of reality'.[16] While for the tragic hero the action is interior, 'in the depths of his own mind', the play must show us its surrounds, both 'the reality that is within our minds, and the reality that our eyes look on'.[17]

Yeats's was not a purely aesthetic philosophy. His plays vigorously assert the quality of the tragic hero, of action called upon to resolve the conflicts on which thought will merely speculate. The title 'Meditations in Time of Civil War' sets out the opposition, and the poem does not give meditation the better of it. 'Observed facts', Yeats said, 'do not mean much until I can make them part of my experience.' Alluding to Marx, he agreed that 'History is necessity'; but only 'until it takes fire in someone's head and becomes freedom or virtue . . . such a conflagration is about us now' (1930).[18] At least part of Yeats's mind consented to the decisive initiatives of action. Such action is the hero's part:

The heroic act, as it descends through tradition, is an act done because a man is himself, because, being himself, he can ask nothing of other men but room amid remembered tragedies; a sacrifice to himself, almost, so little may he bargain, of the moment to the moment.[19]

Yeats's plays mirror this heroic pose, passionate and wilful, placing them in one respect with Robert Brustein's Messianic drama, as a rebellion against God, the hero/priest absorbed in his own image, defiant of any but his own law, moved by passion that 'asks no pity, not even of God'.[20] The outcome of tragedy is 'tragic joy', a celebration of the spirit confronting terror and loss. It is the property and gift of a hero distinguished by arrogant pride, yet submissive to his destined end. He surrenders only to self-imposed demands. Yeats's accounts of the heroic temper admit ironies of the sort he admired in Synge's 'curious ironical plays', his 'bitter condiments'. Self-regarding, the hero invites, from without, hostility, incomprehension, parody which mock his pretensions. It goes to modify, in Synge's derisive

37

use of MacKenna's term, any 'Cuchulanoid' excesses. Yeats soon abandoned the simple propaganda of romanticising an Heroic Age, 'the deliberate creation of a kind of Holy City in the imagination, a Holy Sepulchre, as it were, or Holy Grail for the Irish mind'. The 'touch of something hard' in Cuchulain disallows pure reverence. Yeats brings to it an 'impartial imagination, a furious impartiality'.[21]

(II)

In the later version of *On Baile's Strand*, the Blind Man and the Fool are grotesquely masked. There is little else out of the ordinary to embellish or transcribe the words; perhaps the Fool's game with feet, bag and cap, though it doesn't silence the Fool. Indeed the song of the Women is all but drowned by the conclusion of the Cuchulain/Conchubar argument. The play is amenable to interpretation carried in its dialogue, and by the implications of an uncomplicated set of contrasts in character and rôle. Cuchulain is the tragic hero, indifferent, not very appealingly, to Aoife and his son, except for their part in his destiny. His actions must confirm this as his own, 'full of glory, and heart-uplifting pride'. Whether or not he meets his death at the end, in his frenzy – tragic joy or tragic rage? – he assaults the sea, an antagonist fitter to his stature than the cautiously bureaucratic Conchubar, bent on serving out his time. Reduced, their *alter egos* are the quarrelling Fool and Blind Man, privy to the facts, but not to their meaning. Cuchulain/Conchubar; Fool/Blind Man; Cuchulain/Fool; Conchubar/Blind Man: these are the dualities.

In *At the Hawk's Well*, the first of Yeats's plays directly influenced by the Noh, he moves away from conveying his meaning essentially through words:

As [two of the Three Musicians] unfold the cloth, they go backward a little so that the stretched cloth and the wall make a triangle with the first Musician at the apex supporting the centre of the cloth.

The triangle is a sustained visual motif, composing and breaking its symmetries. The Musicians, standing at the side, make up one. The Third, silent Musician corresponds to the Guardian of the Well, who is at the apex of another, completed with the entrance of the Old Man and the Young Man (Cuchulain in youth). It is the latter which disintegrates: with the dance, and the exit, of the Guardian; then with the departure (seen) of Cuchulain, to 'the clash of arms'; and of the Old Man (concealed by the unfolded cloth) with his knowledge, 'The accursed shadows have deluded me.' The trio of Musicians remains, to sing of heroic and mundane fates: 'Wisdom must live a bitter life'; 'the comfortable door of his house'.

This is a possible reading of what might happen on stage, saying little overtly of the play's narrative or theme. The movements described are intended in themselves to please the eye, shaping the stage. They are dramatically functional too. Their changing outlines and relations act out crucial divisions and correspondences between the worlds of the two mortals, their mortal Chorus – the Musicians – and the otherworldly Guardian. Although the play cannot be discussed wholly in terms of a balletic structure, that is indispensably part of its unity. When the characters are mute, movement and the sounds of gong, drum and zither take up the burden.

The two plays represent a division in Yeats's programme for drama. *On Baile's Strand* belongs, or at least was intended to belong, to the popular theatre as Yeats originally envisaged it, creating an audience for verse, and a sense, which had a political motive, of 'the Irishry'. The most obviously political, *Cathleen ni Houlihan*, is a patriotic call to arms. *The Countess Cathleen* in one aspect contributes to Yeats's romance of the Anglo-Irish Big House. Selling her soul to the Devil to relieve the starving poor, the Countess wins the hearts of the peasants, who come 'crowding around her and kissing her dress'. In *The King's Threshold* the poet has his place among the king's lawmakers, obdurately sticking to his rights, successfully in the first version. The Cuchulain of *On Baile's Strand* – 'I whose mere name has kept the country safe' – is the heroic leader, resolute but in the end confounded, risking the 'wasteful virtues', in his *hubris* loftier than the politic Conchubar: who survives.

The plays of Yeats's 'Abbey period' (1898–1912) are within a programme for turning a history of political defeat into a history of artistic triumph.[22] Parnell's disgrace and death were the emblems of the defeat. The fate of Parnell has a corrosive presence in *Dubliners*, which Joyce began in 1904. *The King's Threshold*, first seen the year before was, like the movement generally, a remedial work, an attempt to reanimate the Irish imagination, which might then generate political energies. Yeats the aesthete, the mystic, was admitting some of the simpler requirements of the *pièce à thèse*. They forced the plays into a platitudinous opposition of two argumentative viewpoints or attitudes, with parties to argue them: the saintly Cathleen, the demonic merchants; Seanchan, the King; Cuchulain, Conchubar. Quite realistic interpretations of character, motive, behaviour – Ibsenite or Shavian as Yeats would have it – can explain their role in the dramatic plan, a piece of diligent but unexacting carpentry. Their elevated, even apocalyptic, language is the utterance of an altogether different quality of experience.

In his impassioned waking vision, Seanchan inhabits Yeats's mystic half-world, where mortal and divine paths cross:

There had come a frenzy into the light of the stars,
And they were coming nearer, and I knew
All in a minute they were about to marry
Clods out upon the ploughlands, to beget
A mightier race than any that has been.

Cuchulain debating with Conchubar in the world of politics is also a subject
of the country of the Sidhe, 'The Shape-Changers that can put / Ruin on a
great king's house.' What is Cuchulain's nemesis, witchcraft or political
ineptitude? The play does not want to ask that question: the fracture
between its two worlds insists on it. The worldly engagements obscure the
otherworldly. These plays lie uneasily between arguable disputes and
magical revelation, benign like Seanchan's or malevolent like Cuchulain's.

Yeats was clear enough on the nature of tragic experience and its divorce
from 'character'. It was an 'ecstasy, which is from the contemplation of
things vaster than the individual and imperfectly seen, perhaps, by all those
that still live. The masks of tragedy contain neither character nor personal
energy. They are allied to decoration and to the abstract figures of Egyptian
temples.' The tragic moment is 'a moment of intense life . . . The
characters that are involved in it are freed from everything that is not a part
of that action . . . an activity of the souls of the characters, it is an energy, an
eddy of life purified from everything but itself. The dramatist must picture
life in action, with an unpreoccupied mind, as the musician pictures it in
sound and the sculptor in form.'[23] Yeats isolates: the single incident that
yields a vision of self; the purging of human complexity into a purification of
the soul; the dramatic forms – abstract figures, musical sounds are the
examples – which will take the place of and so become the experience itself.
Sturge Moore praised *Deirdre* for 'the rare distinction of its self-imposed
limitations'.[24] The limitation Yeats specifies – 'the intense moment' –
implies some dramatic equivalent of the lyric poem, like the compression in
'The Cold Heaven' of past and future into its brief epiphany. The Abbey
plays hesitate between that and missionary parables of political redemption.

At the Hawk's Well decisively abandons the impurities – excrescences at
least – to enforce the elements of song, movement and ritual in an episode of
lyrical ecstasy. Their place is in a single, dominating cluster of images. The
narrative is simple, invented by Yeats, not taken from the legends:

He who drinks, they say,
Of that miraculous water lives for ever.

The two seekers after immortality are Cuchulain, on his one pilgrimage to
the place, and the Old Man, a suppliant for fifty years, always lulled to sleep
as the dry well briefly fills. So he is again, as Cuchulain, distracted from his

purpose at the well by the Hawk-Guardian's dance, rushes out, as the dance leads her off stage, to capture her. She has 'roused up the fierce women of the hills, / Aoife and all her troop', with whom Cuchulain will do battle: 'I will face them.'

The Old Man is malcontent, passive, too cowardly to confront the Guardian's 'unfaltering, unmoistened eye', suitor for reward unearned. Cuchulain, haughty, martial, amorous, meets her gaze: 'I am not afraid of you, bird, woman, or witch.' The immortals, the Sidhe, delude them both: Cuchulain recognises that a greater betrayal would have been the mere extension of life conferred by the miraculous waters. His, too, is the swift resolution of a single encounter, not the Old Man's protracted agony of disappointed hopes.

There is more to the contrast between them than might appear. A third term, entered by the Musicians, disturbs the basic antithesis: the peace of domesticity, 'a pleasant life / Among indolent meadows', 'Where a hand on the bell / Can call the milch cows / To the comfortable door of his house.' As early as 'The Stolen Child' the gifts of fairyland are full of duplicity: only at the end of the poem, too late for the child, does 'the world full of weeping' reveal its allure:

> He'll near no more the lowing
> Of the calves on the warm hillside
> Or the kettle on the hob
> Sing peace into his breast.

It is not a life for Cuchulain, but nor is it for the Old Man. Nor is it to be. He has 'waited / While the years passed and withered me away':

> I have snared the birds for food and eaten grass
> And drunk the rain.

Like Cuchulain, the Old Man is a type of outcast, a Quester; unlike Cuchulain a Quester ignorant of his right vocation, the modest, unheroic fulfilment of settled life.

These meanings are contained in the words of the play's songs and dialogue, which also set the scene. The folded black cloth of the Musicians, a square blue cloth for the well, a patterned screen with a hawk motif: the simple properties represent satisfactorily in 'the eye of the mind' the barren actuality of 'three stripped hazels', 'a well long choked up and dry', 'heaped up leaves at her side. / They rustle and diminish.'[25] The verse is full of dying falls which the music may pick up, and at the climax hand to the menacing energies of the Hawk-Guardian's dance. The dance is important. In it the Guardian becomes the active agent of the Sidhe, 'the unappeasable shadow', as she has earlier in her hawk-cries:

Modern Irish drama

It was her mouth, and yet not she, that cried.
It was that shadow cried behind her mouth. . .
                    the terrible life
Is slipping through her veins.

The dance should draw Cuchulain into its orbit. His will joins the spirit will as the dance claims him, tranced. He will suffer the curse of which the Old Man warns him:

Never to win a woman's love and keep it;
Or always to mix hatred in the love;
Or it may be that she will kill your children. . .
Or you will be so maddened that you kill them
With your own hand.

Against the Old Man's expectation, he will retain 'that proud step / And confident voice'. Submitting to the hypnotic dance Cuchulain makes the Sidhe a part of him, as he is of them: 'Grey bird, you shall be perched upon my wrist.' Cuchulain's immortality is to be won through hardy endeavour, after death. The action set in the mind, Cuchulain's arriving at that knowledge, flows into the theatrical forms.

Yeats had found a form adaptable to his vision and for the rest of his drama adhered to it, though *Purgatory* (1938) has none of the Noh borrowings. It is a miniature form, the short playing time the same as its 'real' time, and it is asked to accommodate the action of an epic, stretches of Irish legend, abstruse brooding on fate, heroic virtue, transactions between life and the after-life. The necessary compression is rich not in radiant ambiguities but in sibylline obscurity.

Now, even the most teasing of Yeats's lyrics, whether read aloud or on the page, gives lucid directions for the passage to its 'fruitful uncertainty'. 'The Cold Heaven', whatever its full import, leads us unimpeded from 'rook-delighting' to 'riddled with light', to the quickening ghost. In 'Sailing to Byzantium' we can hold 'begotten, born, and dies' at the beginning with 'what is past, or passing, or to come' at the end; and gradually respond to the poem's equilibrium between 'monuments of unageing intellect' and 'the mackerel-crowded sea'. In 'The Second Coming', 'Things fall apart', 'the worst are full of passionate intensity'. The 'fall' and the 'full' set in motion an inevitable fulfilment. A cycle of two thousand years enters 'its hour'. There is no need to go to *A Vision* to follow what the words tell us. We are overhearing in the poem a single voice which unifies its hesitancies, reservations, contradictions even. The most arresting of Yeats's confrontations take place not in the dialogue poems but in the poems which, in Donne's phrase, are 'a dialogue of one'.

That kind of tension is a peculiar felicity of Yeats's poetry, and his drama is weakened by its absence. In the lyrics the conflicts, which delighted Yeats, fuse. As Denis Donoghue puts it, the poem is the master, experience the servant.[26] But transfer the conflicts of motive and response to Yeats's theatre, give them to different characters in an unfolding action, and they tend to remain in disarray.

The Only Jealousy of Emer takes place, we are told by Emer, Cuchulain's wife, at some time after the events of *On Baile's Strand*. The play has a triple Cuchulain: the hero bewitched by Fand of the Sidhe, wearing an heroic mask, neither living nor dead; the same figure, in distorted mask, through which speaks Bricriu of the Sidhe; the Ghost of Cuchulain, masked as the first. *Godot*'s bowler hats are more dextrously handled. The Cuchulain transmigrations, especially in performance, are bewildering crises in the plot. The Ghost in pursuit of Fand is halted, presumably, by Emer's altruistic renunciation of his love, and, it must be, re-occupies the disenchanted body – vacated by Bricriu. He wakens in the arms of his mistress, Eithne Inguba, who with some gall takes credit for his restoration.

Emer assents, for her own reason, to Bricriu's behest that she deny her love: better Cuchulain alive with Eithne, it would appear, than possessed by the Sidhe. Her renunciation must be profoundly sacrificial, an abandonment of her 'hope that some day, somewhere / We'll sit together at the hearth again.' Bricriu tells her that that will never be, knowledge which makes the outcome apparent to the audience and thus diminishes the tension of the sacrifice. But perhaps Bricriu is not to be trusted. His own motives are murky. He declares himself 'Fand's enemy' and wants to frustrate her. He is also vaguely credited with some desire that Eithne should submit to his 'power', why we do not know. There are difficulties over Fand too. It is she whose power has entranced and still holds Cuchulain – unless Emer intervenes. Yet Fand is reduced to inveigling Cuchulain, adding some fishwifely abuse over his past lecheries, into the binding kiss: dancing goddess, 'more idol than human being', but petitioner too. Who is the Prospero of the affair? Fand, come to claim her prize, or Bricriu, who conjures up the Fand/Cuchulain encounter for Emer's benefit? Or both, playing out an off-stage drama of their own?

These questions are not dismissed by appeal to the unnaturalistic style of the play. They are embedded in its narrative, confusions befogging the myth it is intended to impart. The characters are being made in their brief lives to represent too much – given human personalities acting as they do for reasons we are to take as being of this world, while also symbolising archetypes of experience. Stirring in the play are Yeats's ideas about beauty, 'A strange, unserviceable thing / A fragile, exquisite, pale shell', and about desire. We may take Fand to be the Muse, Ideal Beauty. Emer and Eithne are kinds of Mortal Beauty, Love domestic and illicit. Humans and gods

5 Scene from Yeats's *The Death of Cuchulain*, part of the *Cuchulain Cycle* at the Lyric Theatre, Belfast, 1968–9

(except for some of Fand's cryptic lyrics, somehow diminutive), will and destiny, contend. The opening and closing songs imagine these contraries in tension 'within / The labyrinth of the mind'. To see the whole play in these terms demands an act of faith oblivious of their denigration in the characters' squabbles, content with the absence of any clear action to register the pressure they have in the lyrics.[27]

44

This is not to deny Yeats's plays their moments of drawing the audience into a stage action which is synonymous with, not just reporting, mood and feeling. Song, words, and dance move together in the *Hawk's Well* as easily as Yeats ever made them. In parts of the meeting between Fand and Cuchulain, Yeats resists the temptation to lyrical expansiveness – 'O Emer, Emer!'. In *The Dreaming of the Bones* perhaps the dance of Diarmuid and Dervorgilla, 'traitors' seven hundred years dead, and Dervorgilla's desolate parting, achieve the same impact, though the wordiness of their rejection by the young patriot of Easter 1916 dissipates the spell. The indignity of Cuchulain's death, invented for him by Yeats in *The Death of Cuchulain*, casts a mordant final eye on the heroic legacy; whether or not it is repudiated is left in doubt. The sceptical ironies are fully restored. T. S. Eliot remarks of *Purgatory* 'the extraordinary theatrical skill with which [Yeats] has put so much action within the compass of a very short scene of but little movement', and commends the play as 'a masterly exposition of the emotions of an old man'.[28]

Eliot's praise is not entirely positive. He talks of action, but also of exposition and a static quality, presumably not merely physical. Intentionally or not, the comment hints at a theatrical vacuum. The ancestral house – dark, illuminated, dark – and the galloping hoof-beats are nice theatrical effects, but they interrupt expository discourse on 'what is past, or passing, or to come', and their devious workings. The old man's bitter heart informs his speeches, endlessly revolving his resentments and pretensions – 'Go fetch Tertullian.' His querulous passion is more likely to hold him in that circle, a parody of bardic vision, than move him to the savage murder of his son, his auditor. The momentum of Yeats's plays is typically this, not so much action imminent, inevitable, and completed as action suspended in a lyric deliberation of its choices.

For all the modish invocation of Beckett as Yeats's heir, his plays occupy a different continuum. Yeats's legendary kingdoms make O'Gradyish historical claims. Even at their most bitter – Yeats in despair, unlike Beckett, rages – they purport correspondences, direct and indirect, with present realities – 'something to keep the "Irishry" living'.[29] Their idealising, abstracting purposes, greatening 'character' into divine, magical forms, summon 'rhythm, balance, pattern, images that remind us of vast passions, the vagueness of past times, all the chimeras that haunt the edge of trance'.[30] Yeats's ironies depend on that 'once-upon-a-time'. Beckett's derelicts, talking to keep their void intact, have no such memories.

There is no evidence that Yeats set theatre upon the courses he advocated in the enticing prose of his theorising. The practice of his own drama validates it only in rare moments. Yeats created for his verse – always sovereign – an aesthetic made up of borrowings from Irish legend and

European and Japanese drama. The verse remained intractable. It is the unmistakable, single voice of the lyric poet, imposed on all the characters, withdrawn, neglectful of the inhabited, waiting stage.

(III)

In Yeats's field of vision Ibsen's theatre was peopled by 'little whimpering puppets', judged, as they were created, by a narrowly correctional moral code, not the 'higher court' of godlike contemplation.[31] The run of conventional theatre so insistently limited the kinds of perception it was admitting that the form itself seemed at fault. Yeats had reason to assail the idling imaginations that had settled in it. He was a revolutionary not a reformer: verse for prose, economical stylising not lavish representation, the divine not the social being. Ibsen's lesson, it was Chekhov's too, escaped him: that is, the impressionable nature of realist theatre, the flexibility of boundaries within the proscenium. Realist theatre was in fact responsive to a poetic symbolism which in stories of bourgeois apartments and drawing-rooms creates figures of ageless desires, frustrated and fulfilled.

Synge had no higher regard for Ibsen than had Yeats. 'Analysts with their problems', he wrote in the Preface to *The Tinker's Wedding*, 'and teachers with their systems, are soon as old-fashioned as the pharmacopoeia of Galen – look at Ibsen and the Germans'. In the Preface to *The Playboy* he argued that the 'intellectual modern drama' of Ibsen and Zola failed because its urban speech starved 'the reality of life' into 'joyless and pallid words'. 'For the present the only possible beauty in drama is peasant drama.' Its vitality resided in an 'English that is perfectly Irish in essence, yet has pureness and surety of form'.[32] Synge's theatre is certainly not Ibsen's. Yet it resembles Ibsen's to the extent that it too invades the basically realist form to enrich the literalism forced on it.

Synge's plays did not come, in his own phrase, like 'the blackberries on the hedge'. Their overflowing life is a composition of drafts revised to the year of his death. The chronological span of their composition shows his continual labour and its intensity in the last three years of his life: *Riders to the Sea* (1900–5); *In the Shadow of the Glen* (1902–5); *The Playboy of the Western World* (1905–7); *Deirdre of the Sorrows* (1907–9). The work, in short, was intimately part of him, the more consumingly because it is a miraculously objectified transmuting of his own haunted personality.

Synge was robust, but his body harboured Hodgkins disease, which killed him. He was abnormally preoccupied with his health, premonition or neurosis one cannot tell. David Greene, his biographer, relates Synge's morbid obsession with death to a family disposition and to his mother's fundamentalist religious teaching. His life was one of alienation from his

46

class and personal background: bourgeois Protestant, well-to-do, respectable, clerical, landowning. All his doings were, for his upbringing,
eccentric: the study of Irish, of music, itinerant in Europe, living in Paris,
an aura of professed Bohemianism. His love for the Abbey actress Máire
O'Neill (Molly Allgood) was illmatched and frustrating. Synge was a silent,
introspective man, reclusive with his colleagues, even his friends, yet on his
Western Irish travels convivial. His 'Etude Morbide' is perhaps, in part, a
Byronic gesture: 'Every day some new morbid idea strikes through my
brain like the thrust of a poisoned dagger. How long can it continue? I have
no delusion, no definite mania, yet I watched myself day and night with
appalling apprehension.'[33] The tone is unconvincing but its affected expression is of feelings genuinely part of Synge's nature.

As the failure of style signified, there was an aimlessness in Synge's
pursuit of a vocation, until, after their meeting in Paris in 1896, he saw the
force of Yeats's advice to go to the Aran Islands. On his first visit in 1898 he
found in the island talk what Yeats called 'more than speech, for it implied
an attitude towards letters, sometimes even towards life'.[34] Ignoring or
rejecting the upheavals in European culture, Synge's creative urge
responded to the Aran scene, desolate and magnificent, and to a tragic joy, it
is fair to call it, in the islanders' endurance of a hard and dangerous life.
'Isn't it a sad story to tell?' one of them wrote to him about a death in the
family. 'But at the same time we have to be satisfied because a person cannot
live always.' In the Preface to his *Poems and Translations* Synge commended
poets who 'used the whole of their personal lives as their material'. The Aran
experience was the catalyst which precipitated his own private despairs into
the impersonal, healing lament of his tragi-comic art. It glorifies his
morbidity and reticence beyond an inert pessimism. The organised
churches, which he abominated, are replaced by an almost pantheistic
nature, earthy, innocent, demonic, translated into a dance of words.

'No drama', as Synge wrote to Stephen MacKenna, 'can grow out of
anything other than the fundamental realities of life,' and he had himself
quite a literal standard of authenticity. For the production of *Riders to the
Sea* he asked a friend on Inishere for samples of Aran flannel and pairs of
pampooties. His cottages and shebeens are precisely transferred to the
stage: 'nets, oil-skins, spinning wheel . . . pot-oven'; 'counter on the right
with shelves . . . many bottles and jugs . . . a settle . . . a table . . . a large
open fireplace; with turf fire'. They are the particular furnishings of
particular places, but with exits 'through the Meadows of Ease, and up the
floor of Heaven to the Footstool of the Virgin's Son'. Pegeen Mike, 'in the
usual peasant dress', commonplace to the Widow Quinn, has 'poetry talk
for' her too, 'the light of seven heavens in your heart alone'. The 'real' time
of *The Playboy* is an evening and a day, its passage is through 'the elements

and stars of night'. Synge's idea of the beauty he invoked for peasant drama reflected a darkness in his sensibility. In *The Playboy*, dualities immediately engage us, of the romantic, or romanticising, and the mundane; and of a stage form familiar, recognisable, and subtly disturbed.

He left nothing like the volume of Yeats's dramatic theory. There are nevertheless two general questions to be discussed as a preliminary. These are his affiliations with the work of other dramatists, and his use of Anglo-Irish dialect. The contemporary Europeans he rejected. Maeterlinck, like Mallarmé in a different camp from Ibsen and Zola, was equally reprehensible. His 'poet's dream which makes itself a sort of world, where it is kept as a dream', was as detached from 'the profound and common interests of life' as Ibsen was too much of them.[35] The preface to *The Tinker's Wedding* praises Jonson and Molière, and Synge's plays do have precedents in classical comedy where journeys might or might not end in lovers' meeting. Yeats's belief in Synge's knowledge of Racine appears to have more foundation than Synge's biographer allows: 'there are among his papers scene analyses of both *L'Avare* and *Phèdre*, and he attended lectures of French literature by Petit de Julleville, whose monumental *Histoire du Théâtre en France* he knew well'.[36] From the Abbey he learnt practicalities of stagecraft. It did not reshape his composition. He wrote, revised, shuffled balances of structure at his typewriter.[37] The proscenium stage he accepted presumably because it was to hand. Synge, like William Faulkner, was largely impervious to the literature around him. When he sought example at all, he sought it in the past. His genius was individual, secret, making its own mirrors for Wicklow glens and Western shores.

David Greene quotes the conclusion of the philologist A. G. Van Hamel, that the language of Synge's plays is 'a very realistic and vigorous Anglo-Irish'.[38] Padraic Colum was of much that opinion, perceptively qualified: 'Synge's dialogue reproduces the energy and extravagance of the people's speech . . . It is true that Synge's dialogue is a splendid convention . . . Nevertheless, I feel as much reality in Synge's as the speech of that acknowledged master of Irish life and manners – William Carleton.'[39] Such testimony refuted the frequent charge that Synge's language, like his picture of Irish peasant life, was a debasing invention. In his own defence, Synge 'claimed no more than that nearly every word and phrase he used was genuine Anglo-Irish'.[40] Alan Bliss's 1971 paper is an important study. By rigorous linguistic analysis it establishes, it seems irrefutably, that Synge's use of Anglo-Irish syntax contains inaccuracies and improbabilities, diminishing in the later plays but persistent; and that this is irrelevant to Synge's art:

It was part of Synge's greatness that he realised . . . that the future of poetic drama did not lie within the limits of the traditional blank-verse form – that a new poetic medium needed to be forged, one which would combine the vigour and intensity of poetry with the flexibility and naturalism of prose. He found the makings of such a medium in the Anglo-Irish dialect, and he exploited them to the full.[41]

'Forged' has Joyce's appropriate ambiguity.

(IV)

The Playboy of the Western World and *The Importance of Being Earnest* are equally artificial, and in comparable ways. Flickering through both are glimpses of a reality outside their own action. Synge's glimpses are of a nightmare, peopled by monstrous and threatening shapes: squint-eyed Linahan, crippled Patcheen, the mad Mulrannies, 'the broken harvest and the ended wars', 'the thousand militia walking idle', 'the loosed khaki cutthroats, or the walking dead'. From the urbane flat and the country mansion of *The Importance*, Wilde looks disparagingly at 'the Fall of the Rupee', 'the University Extension Scheme', 'The Radical papers', 'acts of violence in Grosvenor Square', 'revolutionary outrage'.

The plays decide how this reality is to be admitted. They hold it, so to speak, in abeyance, proposing instead their own experiences, which are more amenable to control. The agent of control is words, in both plays exercising at least temporary sway. Cecily conducts Ernest/Algernon's courtship of her in her diary, and it comes to be, though not exactly as the words foretold. More lethally, Jack says of Ernest, the brother whom he has invented, 'If Gwendolen accepts me, I am going to kill my brother, indeed I think I'll kill him in any case.' Algernon can similarly eliminate the imaginary Bunbury: 'Oh! I killed Bunbury this afternoon . . . he was quite exploded.' The dénouement resurrects Ernest – doubly, in fact. Once more, fiction has become reality, once again in altered form. Wilde brings to the cross-purposes of drawing-room comedy (and tragedy) a distinctively Irish tradition of fantasy, of words that match their reality against literal facts.

Similarly in *The Playboy*: Christy murders his father only rhetorically, not in fact. He thereby gains his heroic status. His triumph in the races confirms it. Old Mahon turns up, wounded by Christy's loy, but alive. Christy panics at the sight of him. The village girls try to dress Christy in women's clothes. Pegeen brands him with the turf. Humiliated, he is as we have seen him first, 'a Munster liar and the fool of men'. In the final reversal he rounds upon and masters his Da, by words – 'Go on, I'm saying . . . Not a word out of you' – a hero again, to go 'romancing through a romping lifetime'. For Christy it is a comic victory, for Pegeen something of a tragedy: '(*breaking out into wild lamentations*) Oh my grief, I've lost him surely. I've lost the only playboy of the western world.' We are constantly aware of gaps, opening and closing, between the statement of words and what we see: transparent lies, fictions that come true, are exposed, find a new truth. The drama relies upon this interplay of correspondences and incongruities between language and the facts it purports to describe. The onus is on language. It must be, as it is, both consciously flamboyant 'high talk' and plain speech – Pegeen 'handling merchandise' – 'in the heavens above'.

Within that general obligation, the speech keeps up the impetus of dramatic interchange among its voices: the mosaic of six voices in Act I (Saddlemyer ed., *Plays*, p. 117); the switching dominances in the Christy/Pegeen dialogue (pp. 132–4) as Pegeen, briefly jealous, taunts him and succumbs again. For Pegeen, Christy is an exotic alternative to the miserable Shawn Keogh and a marriage blessed by 'Father Reilly's dispensation from the bishops or the Court of Rome'. He is the antithesis not only of Shawn's respectability but of his father's earthbound grossness: snoring by the dunghill and 'shying clods against the visage of the stars', a denial of Seanchan's poetic union of clods and stars in *The King's Threshold*, and of Christy's panegyric to Pegeen: 'the love-light of the star of knowledge shining from her brow'.

The imaginative fiction is on the verge of enthralling the community (whose encouragement was part of its creation) and its – relatively – settled ways of church, family, local boundaries: 'That's a grand story'; 'He tells it lovely'; 'any girl would walk her heart out before she'd meet a young man was your like for eloquence or talk at all'. The beautiful love scene between Christy and Pegeen in Act III is a delicate, fragile communion of their longings. All the talk of their 'lonesomeness', of dark and fear, which echoes through the rest of the play, has vanished. Michael James, drunk, interrupts them and accepts Christy – with a final prayer superbly out of place:

I'm a decent man of Ireland, and I'd liefer face the grave untimely and I seeing a score of grandsons growing up little gallant swearers by the name of God, than go peopling my bedside with puny weeds the like of what you'd breed, I'm thinking, out of Shaneen Keogh. (*He joins their hands.*) A daring fellow is the jewel of the world, and a man did split his father's middle with a single clout should have the bravery of ten, so may God and Mary and St. Patrick bless you, and increase you from this mortal day.

For the villagers, eloquence alone is not enough. 'There's a great gap', Pegeen says bitterly, 'between a gallous story and a dirty deed.' The pragmatic community rejects poetry for its former ways – 'By the will of God, we'll have peace now for our drinks.' Unlike Nora of *In the Shadow of the Glen*, Pegeen desolately chooses 'lonesomeness', either in wretched marriage to Shawn, or spinsterhood. For the artist Christy, the forger of other worlds, society has no room. Off he goes, not only without the lady, but with the crazed, ugly father. Romantic comedy could not arrive at stranger ends, nor more forcefully dramatise the dangerous therapies of art, liberating and deceptive.

By its vitality, *The Playboy's* language resists – it is the most self-assured resistance in Synge's plays – the knowledge that romantic love is mutable, even, in a society of bartered brides, a freak, as the artist is irredeemably an alien and fugitive. The plays revolve around small communities and fugitives of one sort or another: in *The Tinker's Wedding* a district clustered round a church, a tinker's camp; in *The Well of the Saints* a similar district, and two blind beggars precariously on its fringes. All are a stage for the antagonisms between private freedom and agreed conventions, anarchic imagination and calculating prudence, dream, actuality and their compromises. The themes are consistent, their synthesis varied. *The Tinker's Wedding*, riotously irreverent, but a little shrill, assuming too much of what it should establish for us, is the least satisfactory. It frightened the Abbey at the time, and was not produced until 26 April 1971.

Sarah Casey capriciously wants to marry Michael Byrne, with whom she has lived for years. Michael's mother, Mary, steals the cup which is part of the priest's fee. When he refuses to marry them and threatens to report their thefts and assaults, they tie him in a sack until he swears 'to leave us in our freedom, and not talk at all'. Released he shouts a Latin malediction. The tinkers flee. We are to understand that an iconoclastic pagan hedonism, having re-asserted itself, properly falls back – though it looks craven – on its own territory. The open licence of heathen bacchanalia and canting priestly authority must reject each other. Sarah did wrong to look at all to religion and is restored to her unorthodox but natural properties.

The priest, greedy and hypocritical, blusters. The tinkers win the battle of words. They have stories of 'the great queens of Ireland' – fallen into the tinkers' world, a great deal more brutal than pastoral or heroic: the great queens with 'fine arms would hit you a slap the way Sarah Casey would hit you'; 'a great clout in the lug'; 'she'll knock the head of you'; 'lonesome and cold'; 'two rocks and rain falling'. Here almost entirely vicious, language is vituperative with the power of ugly miseries, which it extols as much as it does the tinkers' lawless freedoms and 'the fine life' of Jaunting Jimmy. Bold words, the bright colours of Sarah's red and green handkerchiefs, insolent bravado, outdo the priest's black garb and the grasping, prohibitionary, Christianised life. The tinkers become, or are intended to become, more than public nuisances to be 'moved on'. As Synge suggests in the Preface, they are a more primal force, 'the Satanic element in man' – and in laughter.

Synge does not quite persuade us to that mythic level. He originally entitled it *The Movements of May*, and perhaps intended a rite of Spring.

There is a hollowness at the centre of the play. It lacks an event, a coming together of circumstances, compatible with its rhetoric. 'All art is a collaboration', Synge said. In *The Tinker's Wedding*, there is a discrepancy between the language and its factual situation. Unlike the pretended death in *Shadow of the Glen*, or *The Playboy's* hypothetical parricide, the occasion fails to respond to its exaltation by the language. Sarah's whim, the squabble over the marriage fee, the priest's threat and the tinkers' reprisal do not lead us to the expansive claim for a free dignity sanctified in its own tradition of 'a long time . . . going our own ways – father and son, and his son after him, or mother and daughter, and her own daughter again – and it's little need we ever had of going up into a church and swearing'. In *The Well of the Saints* the blind beggars, Martin and Mary Doul, inhabit a real world where miracle and squalor, at home together, do work to a melancholy heroism.

The play extends the ironic fairy tales in which a wish is longed for, granted, and regretted. The Douls are content in the illusion of their good looks, fostered by the country folk, 'not mournful at all, but talking out straight with a full voice, and making game with them that likes it'. But they hanker, Martin particularly, after sight to confirm their own beauty and that of the natural world, which fills their other senses. A wandering Saint bestows it on them with holy water, revealing them to each other, 'a pair of pitiful shows'. Martin sees in the world only their own likeness, ugly, comfortless. As their sight dims again they come to a reconciliation, with life and between themselves, 'a beautiful white-haired woman', an old man to be dignified by 'a beautiful, long, white, silken, streamy beard'. The world is tolerable in their now conscious limitation of it:

Isn't it finer sights ourselves had a while since and we sitting dark smelling the sweet beautiful smells do be rising in the warm nights and hearing the swift flying things racing in the air till we'd be looking up in our own minds into a grand sky, and seeing lakes, and broadening rivers, and hills are waiting for the spade and plough.

They refuse the Saint's offices. Saint and people expel them to the roads: to 'a soft wind turning round the little leaves of the spring and feeling the sun, and we not tormenting our souls with the sight of the grey days, and the holy men, and the dirty feet is trampling the world' (Martin); and to 'a slough of wet on the one side and a slough of wet on the other, and you going a stony path with a north wind blowing behind' (Mary).

In the play's three acts, autumn is the bestowal of sight, winter its meaning, spring the acceptance of blindness. Each season in the dramatic action culminates in a developing tension and its impassioned release of feeling. The Chorus of the people, shifting from compassion to mockery as the sighted Martin takes one girl after another for Mary, is the prelude to their devastating recognition – 'wizendy hag', 'crumpled whelp' – abuse of each other, physical menace. The immanence of God, to which the Saint directs their thoughts, is far off. At the end of Act II, his advances to Molly Byrne repelled and their dream abandoned, Martin's dolorous vision of life bursts into a vengeful hell in which he suffers and lusts:

Molly Byrne and Timmy the smith, the two of them on a high bed, and they screeching in hell . . . It'll be a grand thing that time to look on the two of them; and they twisting and roaring out, and twisting and roaring again, one day and the next day, and each day always and ever. It's not blind I'll be that time, and it won't be hell to me I'm thinking, but the like of Heaven itself, and it's fine care I'll be taking the Lord Almighty doesn't know.

Act III, with Martin and Mary reunited, resumes their bickering, as before, in growing tenderness and knowledge of the need they share. Martin strikes the holy water from the Saint's hand. The rejection affirms commitment to life reduced and solaced by the blindness which can work its imaginative miracle 'in the mind'.

The folk see none of this. The Saint inspires in them uncomprehending reverence. Entirely in another world, he hardly impinges on their lives and livelihoods. Acceptably dependent when blind, object of fickle charity, when he defies those understandings and his 'queer, bad talk' upsets the community's self-satisfaction, Martin Doul is denied any place. His only penance would be to resume his subservience. When he will not, the mockery of Act I turns to manhandling, expulsion, a desire for his punitive death: 'I'm thinking the two of them will be drowned together in a short while, surely.' Again, the community rallies against the transforming intruder to defend its conventions.

The Well of the Saints is a fable of the shaping human spirit at work within a necessary but malleable human entrapment. Martin Doul, and Mary more passively, particularise a condition of life. They are creatures of the senses, peculiarly aware of that state of being, making whatever more they can of sensuous perception. The play's multiplying images, directly of sight, sound, touch, smell, by implication of taste, represent the reality on which imagination must work. Freedom, to apply the Marxist axiom, is the knowledge of that necessity. The Saint's call to abstract supernatural truths is the ultimate, defeatist illusion. Martin's fearsome hell exists only as the obverse of the Saint's equally delusive 'splendour of the spirit of God'. Heaven and hell are within the sensuous world, the bare, and barely endurable, recognition of 'feeling the sun' and 'a stony path'. Martin is the artist, Mary his responsive audience, as he works through his experiences for a meaning in the material supplied by his senses. His resolution is not an escape from actuality. It is an acceptance of its dualities, fair and foul, and of the wholeness to which they may be brought.

The meaning of the play is in the activity of its stage and verbal images, not in one or other of the big speeches. They do, however, crystallise determining moments, as Martin's in Act II:

I was the like of the little children do be listening to the stories of an old woman, and do be dreaming after in the dark night it's in grand houses of gold they are, with speckled horses to ride, and do be waking again, in a short while, and they destroyed with the cold, and the thatch dripping maybe, and the starved ass braying in the yard.

The imaginative effort is to hold in balance the gold houses and the dripping thatch, things, as Yeats puts it in 'The Curse of Cromwell', that 'both can and cannot be'.

It is easy to decode the stories of the plays into the events of Synge's life and its psychic properties: the alienation of Christy and Martin; the doomed loves of Pegeen and Deirdre; the mood of transience; the countervailing powers of imagination. These masked, depersonalising correspondences between the private life and the form of its expression are important mainly as a sign of the privacy of Synge's path to his aesthetic. He was detached from the most influential contemporary writing of Europe. His own sensibility, his knowledge of classical theatre, and an exotically local scene and dialect fused in a drama whose purpose is beyond the superficial novelty of local colour. Synge's work can be partly understood within, and was the finest achievement of, the aims and principles of the Irish movement. He must also be seen as a solitary pioneer taking his images of Ireland into an art which asserts itself in ways characteristic of modernist practices. His plays have the impersonality, precisely the distance between 'the man who suffers and the mind which creates', to be advocated by T. S. Eliot: a far cry from the 'Etude Morbide'.

Yeats was clear on the emerging ethos of modernism – his doctrine of the Mask is a version of impersonality – and on Synge's affinity with it. His interpretation of a dictum of Goethe was that 'to a writer creation is action'. Of Synge he said that he 'elaborated style and emotion, an individual way of seeing'; and that his art 'shows us the world as a painter does his picture, reversed in a looking-glass'.[42] In the modernist understanding, art is an action whose end is to create artistic forms which are not a decorative wrapping for ideas to be extracted and judged, nor a 'likeness to life', but in themselves a means to knowledge about life. So, while modernism does not insulate art from life – may indeed, as in Brecht, insist upon a social obligation – its emphasis is on the autonomy of art, its independent life within the disorienting mirror-world 'where logic is reversed', bound only by its own rules.

Behind Synge's local settings we are aware, in Thomas Kilroy's words, of 'a radical, anarchic spirit . . . one which invokes the kind of aesthetic values that inform the best of modern writing. I try to describe this sensibility as private, intensely preoccupied with the nature of human freedom . . . radically subversive of the established morality of middle-class society.'[43] The idiom of Synge's plays answers to these values. They do not offer programmes for living: more designs, in Yeats's phrase, for 'a way of seeing' things. Their prose poetic in its strong rhythms and cadences as in its diction, is a quirkish, radical usurpation of naturalist theatre. Christy Mahon and Martin Doul are spokesmen for, actors in, the 'secondary world' of the artist, in Chesterton's words, 'the landscape of his dreams; the sort of world he would like to make or in which he would wish to wander; the strange flora and fauna of his own secret planet'. As we have seen, the secondary world of Synge's plays is not a prelapsarian Eden. Rage, lust, envy, greed are part of it, substance just as much as innocence or exuberant joy for the act of poetic creation. Holding reality always in its regard, the language of the plays, and the actions, oppositions and harmonies it develops, express an edifying meaning in experiences that might in themselves be merely disheartening. Christy, and in this he is typical of Synge's dramatic method, is both the artist and the creation of his own art. The meaning of the play is its enacting the process which brings Christy into being. Synge's 'local habitation', retaining its regional identity, formulates the propositions of twentieth-century aesthetics.

Synge's effort, having secured his material, was to find its expressive form. His models, Romantic and Jonsonian comedy, classic French and realist theatre, he moulded to shapes of his own, like R. L. Stevenson's 'true artist', who 'with each new subject will vary his method and change the point of attack'. No play was finally satisfactory. So, writing to Máire O'Neill in December 1906, Synge was looking beyond Christy Mahon: 'My next play must be quite different from the *P. Boy*. I want to do something quiet and stately and restrained.' This final venture was *Deirdre of the Sorrows*. It turns to the 'saga people', of whom he said, they 'seem very remote; one does not know what they thought or what they ate or where they went to sleep, so one is apt to fall into rhetoric'.

Deirdre of the Sorrows is a play of autumn leading to winter intercepted, a threnody which makes celebration of life part of its lament. Time is its motif – a present time of love, as we see it in the play, intensely but briefly satisfied, with shocking rapidity a thing of the past, an object of nostalgic memory which posterity inherits in the telling of it. Deirdre's and Naisi's is an erotic love. Synge made for it a tough rhetoric that blends carnal, natural, and ecstatic. It earths 'flame and bright crown' in the tangible reality of woods and rivers, mud, the tracks and pathways of the glens, 'a gamey king', and Deirdre seven years 'spancelled' with Naisi. Heroic myth, un-

Cucholanoid, acquires a body of words which familiarise, while honouring, legendary grandeur.

'A cycle of experience', Synge wrote in one of his notebooks, 'is the only definite unity, and when all has been passed through and every joy and pain has been resolved in one passion of relief, the only rest that can follow is in the dissolution of the person.'[44] The tone is of Shakespeare's 'Ripeness is all', 'the readiness is all'. Synge's words affirm the spiritual force made animate in the Deirdre legend as his play interprets it: a willed alliance with destiny, not mute submission. Although never finally revised, *Deirdre of the Sorrows* achieves a unity which enfolds the 'cycle of experience' it records: the ageing Conchubar's love for Deirdre; her escape to Scotland with Naisi and his brothers, Ainnle and Ardan, the sons of Usna; the seven years of Naisi's and Deirdre's love; their return to Ireland on Conchubar's promise of immunity and privilege; Conchubar's treachery, the killing of Usna's sons, Deirdre's suicide: all but Deirdre's fate foretold before her birth.

Synge firmly incorporates the prophecy. Lavarcham – Deirdre's companion – Conchubor, Deirdre herself repeatedly advert to it. It is not developed as in the legend, where magic and portents assist it to its fulfilment. Here, humans alone determine the outcome of love. In Act II, dismissing Lavarcham's warnings against return to Ireland, Deirdre appeals to the force of destiny: there's 'little power in what I'd do Lavarcham, to change the story of Conchubor and Naisi and the things old men foretold'. But Deirdre is composing her own version of its concluding harmony. The offer of Fergus, come as Conchubor's messenger and guarantor, causes indecision. To go or not to go? Now no, now yes. At last, in the prospect of betrayal – Naisi dead and Deirdre Conchubor's – and despite the intercession of Ainnle and Ardan, they agree to go:

DEIRDRE. It may be we do well putting a sharp end to the day is brave and glorious, as our fathers put a sharp end to the days of the kings of Ireland . . . or that I'm wishing to set my foot on Slieve Fuadh where I was running one time and leaping the streams, and that I'd be well pleased to see our little appletrees Lavarcham, behind our cabin on the hill, or that I've learned Fergus, it's a lonesome thing to be away from Ireland always.

AINNLE. There is no place but will be lonesome to us from this out and we thinking on our seven years in Alban.

DEIRDRE. It's in this place we'd be lonesome in the end . . . Take down Fergus to the sea . . . He has been a guest and a hard welcome and he bringing messages of peace.

FERGUS. We will make your curragh ready and it fitted for the voyage of a king . . .

DEIRDRE. Go you too, Lavarcham. You are old and I will follow quickly.

LAVARCHAM. I'm old surely, and the hopes I had my pride in are broken and torn.

DEIRDRE. Woods of Cuan, woods of Cuan . . . It's seven years we've had a life was

56

joy only and this day we're going west, this day we're facing death maybe, and death should be a poor untidy thing, though it's a queen that dies.

Deirdre has the initiative in her sight of young love's mortality. We see only the last day, winter beginning, of their seven years. All conspires to corroborate her instinct: Naisi's misgivings that 'a day'd come I'd weary of her voice . . . and Deirdre'd see I'd wearied'; Fergus's hearty alternative of stately fame; Lavarcham's history and resigned old age; the grotesque Owen's brutish truths of passion languishing and youth humiliated in age – 'are you well pleased that length with the same man snorting next you at the dawn of day?'; queens with 'their backs hooping'.

In the upshot, self-betrayal threatens Deirdre's pact for a death that will idealise love before the attrition of time breaks its completeness. She pleads with Conchubor and almost succeeds. Her last words to Naisi are cold and bickering. Again, the catastrophe is suspended, cast in doubt, the inevitable questioned and deferred. Fergus, outraged, fires Conchubor's palace. Deirdre's suicide re-affirms her fidelity in a death that looks beyond the end of life. She acts not out of calculation, clear motive, but a sense of epic occasion:

because of me there will be weasels and wild cats crying on a lonely wall where there were queens and armies, and red gold, the way there will be a story told of a ruined city and a raving king and a woman will be young forever . . . It was sorrows were foretold but great joys were my share always, yet it is a cold place I must go to be with you, Naisi, and it's cold your arms will be this night that were warm about my neck so often . . . It's a pitiful thing to be talking out when your ears are shut to me. It's a pitiful thing, Conchubor, you have done this night in Emain, yet a thing will be a joy and triumph to the ends of life and time.

The play proceeds by dramatically spaced changes of movement to its destined end, willed by Deirdre, checked by events, resuming its course. Unlike Shakespearean tragedy, it ends in wars and chaos just begun. As in *The Plough and the Stars*, lovers die in a burning, collapsing world. The salvation is an entirely personal, and paradoxical one, a dignifying death in which even Conchubor shares. The lovers defy time by consciously making events over into legend – 'a story', as Deirdre foretells within the prophecy, 'will be told forever'. Again, facts become art, in Joseph Conrad's words, 'a form of imagined life [which] puts to shame the pride of documentary history'.

(V)

Synge averred that he raged against 'people who go on as if art and literature and writing were the first things in the world. There is nothing so great and sacred as what is most simple in life.[45] The point is a sane and welcome one. In Synge's art the counterpart to this point is the principle that 'on the stage one must have reality'. He adds that 'one must have joy', relating it to speech in the drama, the 'sureness and purity of form' he wrote of elsewhere.[46] Both Yeats and Synge felt Yeats's 'Savage God' in a world fragmented and profoundly discouraging to the artist; the community, the locally recognisable, the craft broken, or at any rate its loss epitomised, by urbanisation and industrialism – Marx's 'alienation'.

The present urged the past upon the poet, either as an evasion – with some honourable exceptions, Georgian pastoral – or as a stabilising force: Eliot's 'civilization of Europe', or Dante's Christianity; Yeats's Irish mythology or his Byzantium. Eliot's and Yeats's pasts were to an extent confections, but intelligent, animated, and felt in, not detached from, the disintegrating societies to which they are summoned, emblems of both contrast and coincidence between present and past. Eliot's 'These fragments I have shored against my ruins', Yeats's 'smithies of the Emperor' that 'break the flood' make high claims for art. But the poem which is the claim is a human artifact. The self-contained integrity of its art is an act of defiance against whatever in life is demeaning, torpid, bureaucratic. 'Sailing to Byzantium' is part of, not just about, 'whatever is begotten, born, and died'. Christy Mahon's, 'I a proven hero at the end of all' is of the same order. Synge was fortunate to find his source of resistance, his model of language and of a quality of life for which the language spoke, in a present, not a past. They existed in a remote area in whose present a vanishing past was still preserved.

In the history of the Abbey, Yeats and Synge dominate their scene, despite the inescapable fact that Yeats did not realise his ambition to foster a verse drama. Synge too is seen as lacking a posterity. His poetic peasant drama gave birth, in the common account, to a realist, documentary peasant drama, which whatever its virtues was not poetic. His language, though admired, attracts obituary notices. It 'is not available', Eliot concluded, 'except for plays set among that same people'[47] – nor even, it might plausibly be added, for them, since that people no longer exists.

The lesson of Synge is more complex and more encouraging than that. His stage language used a local source, which in itself had enormous vivacity, to create a quite artificial dramatic rhetoric. Synge's example is the use he made of his model. One might think of Eliot's own, sadly abandoned, experiment in *Sweeney Agonistes*. One would certainly think of Beckett's, even of Pinter's, variations on a wholly different vernacular – equally formalised in a repetitive, circling diction and syntax. The majority of Synge's local successors, it may be said at once, are not in any direct line of descent. Yet as will be seen, they can arrive at a poetry of their own minor key, and at some of the anti-realist effects of modernism.

4. An art of common things: 1905–1910

I think we have seen an end of the democracy in the Theatre, which was Russell's doing, for I go to Dublin at the end of the week to preside at a meeting summoned to abolish it. If all goes well, Synge and Lady Gregory and I will have everything in our hands.[1]

All went well. The Irish National Theatre Society became the National Theatre Society, Limited, governed by a board of directors made up of Yeats, Synge, and Lady Gregory. Willie Fay was stage-manager and Frank Fay secretary. The players, now salaried employees, were disenfranchised. Again, the disgruntled resigned. In 1906 Máire Nic Shiubhlaigh (Mary Walker), her brother Frank, George Roberts, Máire Garvey, and Padraic Colum founded the Theatre of Ireland. Martyn became its president. The Abbey faced this challenge in disunity. The autocracy of the new constitution of the National Theatre Society, Limited did not still the constituent autocrats. It gratified the Fays, seemingly now in control of their own domain. Miss Horniman had no objection to it. She did not, however, read it as conceding to the directors any of her own prerogatives.

Dispute was incessant. An arrangement allowing the Theatre of Ireland some use of the Abbey stage and a settlement from Abbey funds angered Miss Horniman. She asserted the right, unacceptable to the directors, to deny the theatre to any play she considered propagandist. Her main and persistent irritation was with Willie Fay. Letters and memoranda uttered her growing distaste. According to them, Willie's stage management was 'slovenly' – a recurrent word; he failed to discipline the company, whose rowdy behaviour on an English tour distressed Miss Horniman; his rendering of accounts was feckless. Miss Horniman had ground for her complaint. Willie Fay was overworked, irascible, and erratic. The players resented his disciplinary caprices. Yeats doubted that he was fitted to run a theatre – whose fate, besides, was much more in Miss Horniman's than in Fay's gift. Her solution was to replace Fay, allowing him to direct only Irish peasant plays.

In 1907 this came about. A young Englishman, Ben Iden Payne, was appointed managing director. The compromise was unworkable. No one was sure what was meant by 'Irish peasant plays', nor how Willie Fay was to be paid. Miss Horniman continued to intervene, advising against Payne's playing Oedipus. Payne resigned in June. Willie Fay was reinstated, though not on a clear understanding of his position, and presented a set of proposals which would enlarge his powers. The directors refused him. In January 1908 he and Frank resigned their engagements, Frank retaining his membership of the Society. Frank was expelled in March amid the rancour of public fighting. The directors had a case. The main players sided with them; on an American appearance the Fays had pretended to an association with the Abbey that was then at best tenuous; and their account of the break was disingenuously in their own favour. The Fays too had a case. They had served the Abbey well and for small enough reward. Behind them they left a group of distinguished players: Sara Allgood, Arthur Sinclair, Máire O'Neill, Fred O'Donovan; and a theatre yet closer to Yeats's proprietorship.

The Fays' departure did not reduce Miss Horniman's distempers. The renewals of the Patent and of her subsidy were due in 1910. She vacillated, but events on the whole confirmed her doubts. In November 1908 she excluded the Theatre of Ireland from the Abbey. In 1909 she took exception to Sara Allgood's participation in a meeting of sympathisers with women's suffrage. The offenders, guilty in Miss Horniman's mind by commission or association, included Yeats, Lady Gregory, and Mrs Patrick Campbell. Apology did not eradicate the injury. The final disrespect was the Abbey's failure to close on the death of King Edward VII in May 1910, a farce of delayed telegrams between the new manager, Lennox Robinson, and Lady Gregory.

Explanation did not placate Miss Horniman, then negotiating to hand over the theatre to the directors on sufficiently generous terms: it had cost her a great deal of money. She withdrew her subsidy. The Society bought the leases and set about raising funds to endow the theatre. The new Patent was granted. Arbitration dragged demeaningly on until May 1911, when Miss Horniman was required to make a retroactive payment of her final year's subsidy, although the Abbey in the end did not accept the money.

By 1911 – effectively in 1910 – Yeats was indisputably master in his own house. No vestige remained of democratic rule, nor of dissension in the leadership. Synge was dead; the Fays had gone; Miss Horniman had severed her connection; Lady Gregory, established as a playwright, deferred to Yeats; the players who insisted on a voice had deserted in other directions. The satisfied managerial desire, however, did not mean the arrival of Yeats's poetic theatre. His own dramatic work suffered. Between 1904 and 1910 the only plays he wrote were *Deirdre*, the revision of *The Shadowy Waters*, *The Unicorn from the Stars* (with Lady Gregory), *The Golden Helmet*, and its verse adaptation as *The Green Helmet*. The Abbey was a controversial institution, Yeats was active in its defence – against critics, the public, rival companies.

Three major rows kept outrage alive in the years that led to Yeats's securing control: the failure to mark King Edward's death, the much chronicled riots over *The Playboy of the Western World*[2] in 1907, and the presentation in 1909 of Shaw's *The Shewing-Up of Blanco Posnet*, which had been refused the Lord Chamberlain's licence for performance in England. Synge was a constant offender of nationalist and pious opinion. *In the Shadow of the Glen* and *The Well of the Saints* had established his plays in the popular judgment as caricaturing the Irish folk into a licentious, foul-mouthed peasantry. Synge appealed to nature and his observation of it: 'I have used very few words that I have not heard among the country people, or spoken in my own childhood before I could read the newspaper.'[3]

The appeal did not exonerate Synge in the mind even of some of the company. Máire Garvey had objected to the language of *The Well of the Saints*. *The Playboy* caused more widespread misgivings. Yeats, Willie Fay, and Lady Gregory all wanted cuts in 'objectionable sentences'. The play went on much as he had written it. The critics were almost unanimous in condemnation. A relatively small but sufficient section of the public demonstrated nightly in the theatre to deny it a hearing. The directors kept the play on in defiance of the familiar armoury of abuse.

The Playboy was fresh evidence not only against Synge. It corroborated a general and reiterated antipathy to Yeats and his aesthetic. He was arguing at a level quite different from that of the detractors. Their assertion was simply that the play was an inaccurate representation of Irish life and indecent in its language, exaggeratedly squalid, not truly realistic – and so, for the nationalist critics, a disservice to the political cause. As we have seen, Synge answered such objections in terms of the realism around which the debate centred. So went the accusations, so went the replies. Yeats's speculations went further. They range before and after *The Playboy*, but *The Playboy* gave them, in every sense, a theatrical enactment.

After *The Playboy* Yeats was still advocating 'Art for Art's sake'. Of *Cathleen ni Houlihan* he said that 'he did not write it to make rebels . . . "Art for Art's sake" meant art for the sake of sincerity, for the sake simply of natural speech coming from some simple, natural child-like soul.'[4] There is a great deal more to it, in Yeats's understanding, than either child-like simplicity or greenery-yallery dandyism. In a strikingly dramatic image, and alluding specifically to *The Playboy*, Yeats asserted the bleak, demonic power in the enquiries of art into life:

A picture arose before my mind's eye: I saw Adam numbering the creatures of Eden; soft and terrible, foul and fair, they all went before him . . . We . . . are Adams of a different Eden, a more terrible Eden perhaps, for we must name and number the passions and motives of men . . . There is no laughter too bitter, no irony too harsh for utterance, no passion too terrible to be set before the minds of men.[5]

The Playboy, Synge commented,

is not a play with 'a purpose' in the modern sense of the word, but although parts of it are, or are meant to be, extravagant comedy, still a great deal more that is behind it, is perfectly serious when looked at in a certain light. That is often the case, I think, with comedy, and no one is quite sure to-day whether 'Shylock' and 'Alceste' should be played seriously or not. There are, it may be hinted, several sides to 'The Playboy'.[6]

Extravagant comedy there is, but with a black regard towards Yeats's 'terrible Eden'. 'There was I one time screeching in a straitened waistcoat', says Old Mahon, acceding to the rôle of a madman foisted on him by the Widow Quin; and at the end returning to it: 'Glory be to God! (*With a broad smile*) I am crazy again!' Christy survives his victories and his humiliation to 'go romancing through a romping lifetime'. The play closes in a celebration

6 Synge's *Playboy of the Western World*, with Brigit Dempsey, Fred O'Donovan and Sara Allgood, during the Abbey's American tour 1911–12

of Christy restored to his 'poet's talking, and such bravery of heart'. But that is not the whole tale.

The ending leaves Pegeen with her loss of the playboy. It returns her to the 'lonesomeness' which is a constant motif in her and Christy's courtship. She is again 'a girl you'd see itching and scratching, and she still with a stale stink of poteen on her', no longer Christy's 'the Lady Helen of Troy, and she abroad pacing back and forward with a nosegay in her golden shawl'. Christy's triumph keeps the abjectness to which he has been reduced by 'games made of him': by Pegeen – 'you swaying and swiggling at the butt of a rope, and you with a fine stout neck, God bless you! the way you'd be a half an hour, in great anguish, getting your death'; by his roping and burning in the last act. The passions and motives, while laughable, intimate terror. The feelings, and the words, which overcome Christy's defeats, encompass irony, bitterness, violence within the comic frame.

Synge's occupation here is with 'variations from the ordinary types of manhood . . . and in this way only the higher arts are universal'.[7] In *The Playboy* Christy is tramp, coward, hero, saviour, victim, finally bard: a nucleus around which lives find identities. He creates a world, magnificently comic, in which, true, he conquers, but which also contains loss and desolation, and questions the realities it calls into being. It is for these considerations, not the clamours and outcry of its reception, that *The Playboy* is important.

Shaw's *The Shewing-Up of Blanco Posnet*, which has no comparable weight, stirred the Abbey to resist the Lord Lieutenant's attempt to suppress the play. Ireland had no censorship office with the right to advance scrutiny and approval of a play. The Lord Lieutenant, however, did have the power, long unexercised, to ban a play after its first performance and, under the Patent, to revoke the theatre's licence. As Yeats saw, the administration's purpose, though perhaps hardly the sinister and far-reaching policy he made out, was indirect enforcement of the Lord Chamberlain's authority where it did not extend, in Ireland. The Abbey won its point. *Blanco Posnet* went on – in a disconcerting mélange of insecurely American and inappropriately Irish accents. There were no reprisals. Tactically, Yeats had fought a successful case; strategically he had demonstrated the Abbey's confidence in itself.

Its resolve was strengthened by its successful British tours. The critics received it on the whole favourably, though not with unmodified raptures. The London *Sunday Sun* review described *The Well of the Saints*, however, as 'an affair of European importance'.[8] These tours established the Abbey, despite the existence of its rivals, as the representative of Irish drama.

Even at home its rivals, judged retrospectively, posed no real threat. The Cork National Theatre Society, established in 1904, foundered and did not re-emerge until 1908, as the Cork Dramatic Society. In 1909 it gave the first play of T. C. Murray, *The Wheel of Fortune*, and one by Lennox Robinson, *The Lesson of Life*, who thereafter associated themselves with the Abbey. The Theatre of Ireland had some experienced players and the support of critics who used it to belabour the Abbey. But it led a spasmodic life, subsisting mainly on revivals, and a few new plays, such as Seamus O'Kelly's *The Shuiler's Child*, whose occasional success has not outlived their occasion.

The Ulster Literary Theatre, soldiering on in Belfast, was acquiring a reputation for imaginative staging. In 1907 it made its first appearance at the Abbey, visiting there again in 1908 and 1909. The Dublin notices were generally friendly, a whit condescending, and took new opportunity to condemn the Abbey for the contrast between its 'decadent sophistries' and 'Ulster sanity'.

(II)

In the North itself there was substantial discussion of the Ulster Literary Theatre's work and its place in the dramatic revival. The province's liberal minds commended the company for its enunciation of a provincial identity in 'its raciness, its tang of the soil, its fine, vivid phrases';[9] and for its criticism of mean-spirited values. 'Energy, tenacity, and thrift', wrote J. W. Good, 'are considerable qualities in the making of a people . . . but when thrift verges on meanness, when tenacity becomes obstinacy, and energy finds its only outlet in a frantic struggle for wealth, it is time for those who care for life and the beauty and graciousness of life to protest.'[10] The theocratic Catholicism of the South had its protestant counterpart.

The plays which prompted these expectations were, as the Abbey's were coming to be, on a domestic scale, with none of Yeats's vistas of a poetic barony. Even the historical plays were reduced in circumstance. Seosamh MacCathmaoil's *The Little Cowherd of Slainge* is more typical of them than Bulmer Hobson's heroic *Brian of Banba*. Gerald MacNamara's *Thompson in Tir na nOg* deposits an Orangeman in the world of legend. Lewis Purcell's *The Pagan* is a comedy of ancient Ireland. All these plays were first presented in Belfast, as was Rutherford Mayne's *The Drone* at the Abbey by the Ulster Literary Theatre. The hero of this, Mayne's most popular play, is an antic placed among the orthodoxies of hard work and respectable marriage. Daniel Murray is the drone, battening on his brother John's home on the strength of his imaginary prospects as an inventor. In a basically simple plot, complicated by a breach of promise suit against John, and the romantic dallyings of his daughter, Daniel by strokes of luck triumphs over a sceptical Scots engineer and emerges as the family's saviour. The play's engaging advice is that virtue may err and fortune smile on folly. *The Drone* falls short of its own undemanding pretensions. It is a failure that Daniel nowhere lives up to his reputation as 'a great talker'. A tongue-tied knave lacks conviction.

Synge's is the indisputably lasting achievement of these years. The moulders of the Irish theatre's personality, however, were Padraic Colum, William Boyle, Lennox Robinson, and T. C. Murray, with a quirkish turn briefly given by George Fitzmaurice. Lady Gregory was the most prolific playwright of the period. Including translations, she gave the Abbey some seventeen plays. Most of them were one-act comedies, sometimes amusing like *Hyacinth Halvey* and *The Workhouse Ward*. They continue in the, as it now seems, rather wearisome, easy way of their predecessors. These plays contain little to arouse hopes for the more grandiose schemes of Lady Gregory's Irish history plays. Of these *Kincora* (1905) and *Dervorgilla* (1907) were received with respectful attention. They are laboured, wordy, and appear now historical curiosities themselves.

Amongst contemporary opinion of them, we may infer from Joseph Holloway's report that George Fitzmaurice was not one of Lady Gregory's admirers. It was his 'opinion that *Dervorgilla* without Sara Allgood in the title role would be excessively tedious'.[11] Austin Clarke alleges, and Carol Gelderman denies,[12] that Fitzmaurice's rapid progress from acclaim to obscurity was a result of Yeats's jealousy. Be that as it may, Yeats certainly was not officious in advancing Fitzmaurice, the nearest approach to another Synge the Abbey was to have.

Both were at work with the difficulties of a hybrid language. English as spoken in Ireland was an indigenous creation as well as a colonising imposition. Less palatably, in the nationalistic regard, it was an enticement from native ways and adopted solely in the hope of material benefit. Hibernicised English had other broadly political implications. In its wilder flights of 'big words' and misunderstood meanings it was ludicrous. It romanticised, but however magical could not alter, 'the idiocy of rural life' – a phrase Synge underlined in his reading of Marx's *Capital*; and it dressed up the atrocities of violence, like the 'dirty deed' tricked out as the 'gallous story' in *The Playboy*. All these wider implications occupy Synge's plays. They concern Fitzmaurice too, but Yeats was strangely blind to the claims of Fitzmaurice's language as a successor to the poetic prose of Synge.

An English reviewer of *The Pie-Dish* (1908), did Fitzmaurice fuller justice:

In Mr. Synge, Mr. Fitzmaurice has gone to school with a good master. He has caught the secret of the greatest pieces that the Abbey Theatre has staged: that is to say, he has that imaginative reach which gets deep down into the elementary terrors and desires, and hopes and fears, of the world: that insight which pierces through the surface of common life and sees into the great forces beneath.[13]

Fitzmaurice's first play, *The Country Dressmaker*, went on at the Abbey on 3 October 1907. Yeats, writing to Synge about charges that the Abbey was suppressing popular plays, had this to say of it: 'How can we make [the audience] understand that *The Playboy* which they hate is fine art and *The Dressmaker* which they like is nothing?'[14] *The Country Dressmaker* is indeed a good deal more formally conventional than Fitzmaurice's one-act fantasies, *The Pie-Dish*, and *The Magic Glasses* (1913). The Dublin critics, while admitting its success, entered it with Synge in their register of political heresy: 'it displays the Irish peasant of Kerry in a light scarcely less loveable than Mr. Synge's "Parricide" . . . He might, without straining beyond the borders of accuracy, have introduced a few more lofty and more Irish types than appear in his conception.'[15] The Abbey presented *The Magic Glasses* on 24 April 1913, also the year when Fitzmaurice wrote *The Dandy Dolls*, which after Yeats's discourteously managed rejection of it remained unproduced until 1945. Like *The Pie-Dish*, *The Magic Glasses* reaches 'deep down into the elementary terrors and desires'. The Dublin critics regarded it as 'a clever little joke' and a 'farce', though it concerns witchcraft at once quack and sinister, diabolic possession, and the killing of the fey Jaymony Shanahan, by his enchanting, murderous magic glasses.

Jaymony is the son of Padden and Maineen, thirty-eight years old, a 'natural'. Secluded in the loft he escapes from 'the slush – same old thing every day – this an ugly spot, and the people ignorant, grumpy, and savage', into the fantasies made visible to him by the magic glasses:

in the red glasses:

the purtiest women was ever seen on the globe . . . And in the glass I could see myself and the one I was doting on, and we together for the six days of the week. Times we'd be talking and times there wouldn't be a word out of us at all, our two mouths in one kiss and we in a sort of a daze.

and in the blue –

'tis myself I see on a noble horse, spangled and grey; I seen my own bright sabre flashing and I leading the army on, and we driving the Saxon invader before us – through the plains of Desmond, and on and on, even to the Eastern sea.

So Jaymony tells the choleric Mr Quille, miracle-worker, charlatan, feared, mistrusted, reverenced, summoned to cure him. Quille prescribes a bewildering régime, strides off, and Jaymony returns to the loft. Abruptly, the devil possesses the house:

PADDEN. Don't I see the horns and the horrid hoofs?
AUNT JUG *and* AUNT MARY. We see the horns and the horrid hoofs.
PADDEN. Brimstone I smell!
AUNT JUG *and* AUNT MARY. Brimstone we smell!

Jaymony is found, 'his jugular cut by the Magic Glasses!'

The Dandy Dolls, with even easier liberties of assumption, enters the human and the legendary, pagan and Christian, domestic and marvellous, in a single world. Roger Carmody, stealer of the priest's geese, obsessed in the making of dandy dolls, becomes a prize in the mysterious feud between the three Grey Men of Doon and the Hag of Barna and her son. 'So sure', Roger's wife, Cauth, tells the Grey Man, as he 'makes a doll, so sure will the Hag's Son, soon or late, come at it, give it a knuckle in the navel, split it in two fair halves, collar the windpipe, and off with him carrying the squeaky-squeak.' The Grey Man has come partly to buy, partly to warn, partly, it may be, to sacrifice: he will purchase unblemished dandy dolls; the Hag and her son will come that night at ten o'clock; if the Hag's son steals the windpipe from the newest doll, 'the finest I ever made', Roger must drink the full of the bottle given him by the Grey Man.

The Carmody child, Roger's creation in another kind, sits for the most part mute, bridging the play's two scenes with a snatch of song and riddling games:

CHILD (*playing marbles on the floor*). Into my first of nothing, into my second of nothing, into my last of thaw-game! (*chalks a circle on floor and plays another game*) Pinked! That's a button won. No! By J, I'm fat! (*singing*) 'Oh then, buttercups and daisies, etc.'

The Hag's son enters, then the Hag, and in a darkened scuffle capture the doll's windpipe. Roger drinks from the bottle and is later seen dragged off by the Grey Man and the Hag. 'Galloping like the wind they were through the pass of the Barna mountains sweeping him along with them, forever and ever, to their woeful den in the heart of the Barna hills.' Roger has known the Grey Man in some previous time – 'was it', he asks ambiguously, 'about the time I was turning into a man?': adult, that is – or human?; maker of children or of bewitching dolls?; fated, in the end, to be spirited from the world to a tormenting otherworld, divided and overlapping.

In Fitzmaurice's 'folk-world', Jaymony, Roger and the rest live, where it is real, among grotesques; where it is legendary, with the diabolic, menacing and seductive. Jaymony's parents report a district peopled by the sick and crippled. The devil is nearby, Mr Quille his intermediary. Roger and Cauth squabble and miscall each other, as might any ill-assorted couple, but here about wonders – the dolls, the Hag, the Grey Men – equally with Roger's idleness: 'that leaking oven', 'that hole in the thatch'. It is a world with a sight of, yet transcending, Lady Gregory's folk realities. It employs a language even more stylised than Synge's, more remote from, but still touching, its peasant sources along the bleak Atlantic coast: 'a rhythmic, gibing speech', in Austin Clarke's words, 'in which [characters] catch up each other's talkativeness . . . rhythms of speech, rhythm of movement and grouping – the unity which one finds in ballet'.[16]

It might be argued, though unfairly, that where Synge was a Pygmalion, Fitzmaurice was something of a Frankenstein. His genius was eccentric and risky; Yeats was an unreliable judge of other people's experiments, hence his rejection of *The Dandy Dolls*. When Fitzmaurice abandoned, or was discouraged from, the theatre, Irish drama lost an impulse which might have complemented the dominant strain of realism.

(III)

Yeats's remark is correct enough, that Colum's plays reflect 'the peasant as he is transformed by modern life', his talk subdued by 'the newspaper and the National Schools'. The disparaging tone is Yeats's quirk. That changing life of Ireland and its dialect can be adapted for the stage as readily as any other. In *The Land* (1905) and *Thomas Muskerry* (1910) Colum proves this conclusively.

'Standing in the rain with our hats off to let a landlord – ay, or a landlord's dog-boy – pass the way!'; Murtagh Cosgar, in *The Land*, recalls the oppression of landlordism. Now he has the right and he has the means to buy his farm. His sense of property is obsessive. Partly it is an acquisition for himself, partly an inheritance to pass, on his own terms, to his remaining son, Matt, to whom he says bitterly, 'In the houses that are now, the young marry where they have a mind to.' For all his sores, angers, Murtagh has secured his land. Others are less fortunate. His neighbour, Martin Douras, is resigned to being too poor to buy. His clownish son, Cornelius, childishly enamoured of big words – 'There are things in that paper I'd like to be saying' – fancies Murtagh's daughter, Sally. Martin's daughter, Ellen, a teacher, and Matt, love each other. She had no dowry to satisfy his father's ambition.

The young look to other prospects than bondage to the land. New lands, America, offer new welcomes which may balance loss:

A GIRL. They say that a turf fire like that will seem very strange to us after America. Bridget wondered at it when she came back. 'Do civilized people really cook at the like of them?' she said.

A BOY. It's the little houses with only three rooms in them that will seem strange. I'm beginning to wonder myself at their thatch and their mud walls.

ANOTHER GIRL. Houses in bogs and fields. It was a heartbreak trying to keep them as we'd like to keep them.

A GIRL. Ah, but I'll never forget Gortan and the little road to Aughnalee.

Matt prefers to win over his father to accepting Ellen:

MATT. Ellen, Ellen, I'd lose house and land for you. Sure you know that, Ellen. My brothers and sisters took their freedom. They went from this house and away to the ends of the world. Maybe I don't differ from them so much. But I've put my work into the land, and I'm beginning to know the land. I won't lose it, Ellen. Neither will I lose you.

ELLEN. O, Matt, what's the land after all? Do you ever think of America? The streets, the shops, the throngs?

MATT. The land is better than that when you come to know it, Ellen.

ELLEN. Maybe it is.

It comes close to being so. Under the threat of Matt's emigrating, Murtagh concedes. Ellen, offered all, refuses: 'It's my freedom I want.' The farm will come to Sally, who marries Cornelius. Matt goes to America, Ellen to a new school, with a distant undertaking of reunion.

The characters through whom Colum represents his view of Ireland are Con Hourican the artist, Murtagh Cosgar the man of the land, and finally the official, Thomas Muskerry. In its 1963 publication, *Thomas Muskerry* is quite extensively revised. It introduces a new character, brings on stage another only mentioned in the 1907 text, and compresses the final scene. The changes, though more than just tinkering, do not improve upon the play's original statement of Muskerry's decline and the back-biting small town life which surrounds it. As the revisions confirm, Colum quickly established a dramatic style whose assurance none of his later experimental work commanded. *Thomas Muskerry* continues in the stark, suggestive idiom of its predecessors.

About to resign as Master of Garrisowen workhouse, Muskerry is caught up in his son-in-law's commercial misadventures, and an impending scandal in the workhouse. He dies in the workhouse infirmary, resented by his family, stripped of the small authority both dear to him and, narrow though it is, giving some outlet for his glimpses of an ampler life. On stage, the workhouse's cheerless office and drab uniforms are a view into a part of Muskerry; and upon Garrisowen, its shutters going up. The figure of Myles Gorman, the blind piper, denies these constricting indignities: a workhouse inmate, cheated of his land, freed in spirit 'like the woodquest flying away from the tame pigeons'. In Gorman is another part of Muskerry, of his unrealised longing for the remoteness of his cottage, his recognition of his departure as belonging to a departing Ireland. His job, his family's mercenary jealousies, a town whose relationships are between debtors and creditors dispossess him of a minor grandeur and degrade the workings of love in him.

Colum's three plays subdue their power in a composition of scenes and dialogue which, without baldly pointing its features, keeps in sight the individuals and their particular situation. An historical moment exacts

responses from characters peculiarly sensitive and vulnerable to its changing forces. Ostensibly, the dialogue emerges from choices definable within a
set of personal relationships. It holds both that and broader social dissolu-
tions and revisions largely beneath what is actually spoken. When Maire
sings 'I know where I'm going', in *Fiddler's House* it echoes beyond her own
resolves, and laments a new desolation on the roads. The 'time' of the
conversation between Matt and Ellen in *The Land* has many meanings. It is
'a great day for the purchase'; a day with 'great gladness and shine' in it;
behind that are the 'twenty years for the purchase'. 'There's something
here', Ellen says, and also 'something going'. She turns to her own
condition, 'a long time waiting' for Brian – as Murtagh has been for the
land. Time is the time to settle a personal destiny and the time too of an
epoch. The personal choice, which will entail loss, reflects an era no longer
uttering familiar assumptions.

This delicacy of manoeuvre is Colum's distinction as a 'realist'
playwright. Its subtleties elude William Boyle, chronologically Colum's
nearest successor. In Boyle's *The Building Fund* (1905) a grasping old
woman leaves her money to the church, thus disappointing her equally
grasping son. Her granddaughter, hitherto a rival for the inheritance, joins
fortunes with her uncle in their common frustration: 'He knows how to
make money.' In *The Mineral Workers* (1906), an Irish version of the
Edwardian 'problem play', an engineer returned from America sets out to
exploit his uncle's farm as an iron mine: 'wealth laid by and folded
underground, which energy might bring forth'. Some unprepossessing
locals oppose him as alien, vandal, sharp dealer: 'The independent heart of
Ireland won't stand it.' He outsmarts them, secures his industry, the then
'progressive' choice and, in the process, the love of the right woman, Kitty,
who has played him astutely: 'You're a girl worth the knowing.'

Boyle, though as popular in his time as Colum, is now virtually unknown.
He was produced, and well received, in England and America as well as in
Ireland. Some of the contemporary reviews make strange reading. Boyle
appears as an uproarious comic: 'a diverting comedy'; 'a bright comedy';
'punctuated by bursts of laughter'; 'peals of the heartiest laughter'. One
wonders what the Abbey style can have been to produce this response. With
the exception of *The Eloquent Dempsey* (1906), a farce, the plays are desolate
enough.

In *The Building Fund*, Sheila, the granddaughter, finally turns out to be
moved by avarice, and is intriguing to satisfy it. Uncertainties in her are
hinted: some genuinely pious emotion, some care for her grandmother's
decline. She may be compelled, reluctantly, by isolation in a friendless
world: 'I have no one else to do it for me.' The play does not pursue these
possible divisions in her self, which remains a stock, explicable being.

Meanings, as with the grandmother, are in the end made perfectly explicit:

SHEILA. Gone without a priest, a word of holy comfort! Gone with her two arms clasped about the world!
GROGAN. Wanting to take it with her.

Boyle works, essentially, not in mysteries of behaviour but in trickeries of plot. The characters of his plays, with reasonable plausibility, enact a peculiarly Irish anti-pastoral. He recognised a seamy materialism in the fierce attachment to land; and in the peasant an understanding of the translation of values from possessing land to dealing in money. Boyle did not move, in phrases from a defence by Colum of *Thomas Muskerry*, into the 'universal', the 'typically human', from intimate knowledge of 'his own time and locality'.[17]

Lennox Robinson's management of the Abbey was hospitable to this domestic drama of rural and small-town life. In 1909 Yeats offered him the job of, as it would now be called, artistic director, reportedly because he thought his head looked interesting from behind. Disagreements with Lady Gregory led to Robinson's resignation in 1914. In 1919 he returned, and was the Abbey's main director of plays until 1935, when Hugh Hunt took over from him. He was appointed to the Abbey's board of directors in 1923, and remained on it until his death in 1958. His angular figure and interesting head became as familiar in the house as Yeats had been. The replacement of Yeats by Robinson signified Yeats's recognising his theatre's bent: it was in 1919 that he described it to Lady Gregory as 'a discouragement and a defeat'.[18] Robinson's policies and his own plays secured 'realism' its place as the kind of work expected from and done well by the Abbey.

One of Robinson's later and most popular plays, *Drama at Inish* (1933), recounts the disastrous effects produced in a small seaside resort by a touring company's portentously sombre repertoire. The suggestible inhabitants of Inish begin to plan suicides and infidelities. The comedy perhaps embodies a rueful backward look at Robinson's own early plays, which have the gloom of youth fresh upon them. In the first of them, *The Clancy Name* (1908), a murderer's timely death saves a family reputation, in the mother's ill-judged sense of it. *Harvest* (1910) rests on the idea that their superior education has profoundly corrupted the children of a farming family. It is a situation which seems right for comic development. However, Robinson envelops it in a bitterness and despair which overburden their preposterous cause. He admitted a rather facile modishness: 'We were very young and we shrunk from nothing. We knew Ibsen and the plays of the Lancashire school, we showed our people as robbers and murderers, guilty of arson, steeped in trickery and jobbery.'[19] Ibsen may have been an inspiration. He is certainly not the criterion for measuring Robinson's early achievement. It has indications of craftsmanship, though Robinson puts this skill to evading the issues he raises: hence in *The Clancy Name* a convenient accident removes John and his problems. The English well-made play is a nearer imaginative compatriot than is Ibsen. Robinson's early plays, like Boyle's, define their problems with a bluntness that writes them into the fixities of a time, a place, a group of people. Motives are perspicuous and arguable. The language which argues them debates propositions, implying no parables beyond the 'problem' within which it is sealed.

Robinson's next set of plays turns, in politically turbulent times, to political subjects, and begins a diversification of matter and treatment with which Robinson continued throughout his career. *The Dreamers* (1915) leaves the present for the history of Robert Emmet's futile uprising of 1803, and his love affair with Sarah Curran. Denis Johnston has said of the rebellion that in its popular interpretation it retains 'all of the elements that make for magic. It was very high-minded, and completely unsuccessful.'[20] *The Old Lady Says 'No!'* is Johnston's own satiric version of the events. Robinson's inspection of them is in part deflationary too. It shows Emmet's followers uselessly drinking and brawling among themselves. The enthusiastic Clitheroe and the carousing mobs of Sean O'Casey's *The Plough and the Stars* come to mind. Essentially, however, Robinson takes the story into serious regard, particularly in the exchanges between Emmet and Sarah. The dream has not prepared itself for the assault on reality, though in Robinson's account it leaves a residue of faith which is more than illusion.

The hypothesis of *The Lost Leader* (1918) is that Parnell may be alive and living in the west of Ireland as Lucius Lenihan. In the final scene, before he is accidentally killed, Lenihan appeals for a uniting of factions. The closing stage direction is left unanswered: 'A great dignity and peace brood over the face of Lucius Lenihan or is it the face of Charles Stewart Parnell?' Whether he is really Parnell, or speaking as a figment of his own imaginings, Lenihan diminishes the squabbling politicians of 1918. Fantasy may perpetuate truths obscured in the sensible world. William Archer described *The Lost Leader* as 'one of the most imaginative plays of our time'.[21] It is an exaggerated claim. The psychiatrist and the journalist who investigate Lenihan belong in a play where his doubtful identity is a problem, not a mystery and a symbol; and Lucius's rhetoric does not meet its obligations.

These plays do lessen Robinson's confinement, so to speak, in a stage-set whose solidity imposed itself on any fantasy or abnormality in its imitation of the real. But illusion may supplant reality, may be made to reflect reality by distorting it. Robinson's overt borrowings from modernist theatre were an unhappy venture, like extensions built on to a conflicting architecture. *The Round Table* (1922) and *Ever the Twain* (1929) indulge in brief expressionist flourishes which are totally at odds with the nature of the plays.[22] Only *Church Street* (1934) repays its debt, here to Pirandello in *Six Characters in Search of an Author* (1921). Hugh Riordan is a young dramatist, apparently mediocre, certainly unsuccessful. Home after a London failure, he is contemptuous of life in and around Church Street. Aunt Moll hints at secret dramas which he has been too imperceptive to see. She challenges him to make a play of them. Reassembled, the characters we have seen in their real lives enact the situations Hugh has invented for them: peculation, abortion, penury and starvation concealed – all with some foundation in his aunt's gossip. Once again in reality, Hugh draws back from finding what truth there may be in his invented tragedies. 'Is it a game?' his father asks, and we are left to wonder how the play and the play within the play, metaphors of the real and the imaginary, all relate to each other and to truth.

Church Street makes more than superficial decoration of its modernist

7   T. C. Murray's *Birthright*, with Fred O'Donovan and Eileen O'Doherty at the Abbey, 1910

conjuring with the stage illusion. The play's form betokens its meaning. In the end, reminiscent of parlour tricks, party charades, it fails to create an unease that will sabotage the confidence of representational, mimetic drama. Robinson's experiments are sports which he could enter effortlessly, a natural games player capable but never master of a novel skill. In 1916, *The Whiteheaded Boy* had indicated the direction he could pursue with more modest but more certain expectation, placed between comedy and farce, character and caricature.

Robinson's plays do not reach, nor do they aspire to, the heights of high comedy. They entertain by situations ingeniously turned, never elaborating their premiss into fanciful extravagance, always comfortingly in control. Thus he continued in the *genre*, with *Crabbed Youth and Age* (1922), *The Far-Off Hills* (1928), and the four Inish plays from *Drama at Inish* (1933) to *The Lucky Finger* (1948). Robinson was a maker of estimably well-made comedies and represents the kind of play with which, when genius was absent, 'the Abbey did well during the first decades of its history'.[23]

T. C. Murray is a dramatist much of that kind. *Birthright* (1910), his first play, again has the artist, the free spirit, suspect to and defeated by his own people. A trunk, coffin-like, occupies the stage. It is for Shane, the younger Morrissey son, emigrating because his elder brother, Hugh, will inherit the farm. Hugh is the darling of the townland – 'there isn't the beating of Hugh Morrissey in Ireland for anything'. But to his father, Bat, Hugh, though hardworking, is 'in every twist and turn of him' his mother Maura's son, and not 'with the true farmer's blood' in him. Blaming Hugh for the death of a valuable mare, Bat disinherits him.

In the dully candlelit set of Act II – Maura 'stands in the shadow of the doorway', Bat 'on the doorstep outside', 'the kitchen very dimly lit', Hugh 'in the shelter of the deep fireplace' – the father renounces the son. The brothers join more violent issue:

HUGH. You're a liar, and I will say it again, and I'll say it till I'm hoarse, for there was never a dirtier grabber in all Ireland than yourself – grabbing a brother's land.

SHANE. That's a lie for you. What right had you to this place – you that never did an honest day's work in your life?

HUGH. What right had I?

SHANE. Yes, yes, what right? Is it because you were born a year or two before me? 'Tis the man's work an' not the reckoning of his years that makes the right! So it is!

Old resentments at the son favoured by his mother crowd in on Shane. The two fight, and Shane fells, has perhaps killed, Hugh.

Shane strikes the blow. Its genesis lies beyond the hesitancies of his envy and the rage of a sudden occasion. Its origin is in the morose inclination of

Bat's toil with 'a cold, poor place, with more o' the rock, an' the briar, an' the sour weed than the sweet grass'. Improved, the land stays harsh, resisting the labours it endlessly demands. Bat is the land's synonym. He broods through half-attended dialogue, following not the words spoken but the compulsion of his thoughts, imposing his own bile: 'the black darkness', 'the black look-out', 'a black flood covering the world', 'a dark dream', 'the black trouble', 'the black rage', 'black shame', 'the black hatred'. Maura's gentleness, Hugh's gaiety, are impotent against the murk of landscape and feeling. The place possessed narrowly possesses. Toil becomes greed, not for land alone but, in Shane, to perpetuate Bat's ruinous devotion to it: ' 'tis the small farm we'll all be wanting when we're dead', a neighbour says to Bat, and, 'That's no talk at all', Bat replies. *Birthright* is a tightly constructed tragedy of love confined and destructive, its possible openings intercepted.

As *Birthright* demonstrates, Murray's was a sombre enough vision of Irish life, and his pacing to a strong climax deliberate, carefully prepared. His considerable later plays are *Aftermath* (1922), *Autumn Fire* (1924), and *Michaelmas Eve* (1932). The titles suggest sequels which give an ending to events left between possible conclusions. The plays in fact do disclose, over an unstaged span of time, the meaning of the 'present' with which they begin. The first two acts of *Aftermath* have Myles O'Regan, a humane, idealistic young teacher, falling in love with Grace Sheridan, a teacher too. His mother wants him to marry Mary Hogan, who 'haven't fine poetry talk and nonsense', but 'could buy and sell them that talk like angels'. A light, comic sequence in more urbane, sophisticated language – unusual in Murray – between Grace and her married sister, confirms Grace's detestation of Mrs O'Regan. She abandons Myles. Act III, four years later, finds Myles, a remarkably aged thirty, married to Mary, embittered, a tyrant at school. A visit from Grace, also married, with two children, finally turns him from Mary to a nebulous destiny elsewhere: 'there's a Voice crying to me at all hours, "Go! Go!" and I dare not disobey'.

Aftermath is more finely shaded than its empurpled curtain lines. The shadows of the first two acts fitfully threaten, but until Act III do not eclipse, the chance of edifying unions. In the sequel the main actors have to live with choices where will has resigned to the force of circumstances: Grace to the affectations of provincial society, Myles and his mother to his mother's 'seed, breed, and generation' of the soil. Old ways are moving uncertainly to new adoptions. No one wins, no one is to blame. The antagonists are the characters that their inherited, unreliable backgrounds have shaped them.

Murray is at his best in *Autumn Fire*. Owen Keegan, boringly gratified by his health and athletic prowess in late middle age, marries Nance, thirty years younger. Nobody approves. His daughter Ellen, thwarted by an unhappy love affair, sees in Nance a giddy 'dolly face', in her father 'our own labouring man'; the difference in age disconcerts his brother; his son Michael has an eye to Nance:

NANCE. And myself is wondering more is it Michael Keegan I'm listening to. Such queer riddling talk an' nonsense – and you to be such a rock o'sense always.
MICHAEL. Is that what you say?
NANCE. What else could I say, Michael?
MICHAEL. You've a short memory, Nance.
NANCE. Why so?
MICHAEL. Have you no memory of that wet evening I came on you sheltering under the bushes from the rain?
NANCE. 'Tisn't so much that happens here that I'd be likely to forget it. But, honest, Michael, I thought 'twas only a boy's wild romancing talk to pass the time in a shower.

In Act III, nine months later, Owen is bedridden by a stroke, Michael and Nance are thrown closer together, tenderness stronger than the evasions. Ellen foments her father's jealousy: Michael is to leave home. Late back from the market – ''Tis the summer-time, and they're young sure', Ellen comments waspishly – Michael and Nance kiss farewell, overseen by Owen. He rejects Nance's protests of innocence, loyalty. The lights dim, he is left alone: 'They've broken me . . . son – wife – daughter.' The sequel, in Murray's way, has no beneficiaries, nor virtue rewarded, nor a sure finality. The marriage will persist uselessly, Nance bereft of Michael, Ellen loveless, without place in a loveless house.

Here Murray subdues the dialogue within his range, responsive to its situations. The action is simple, and coherent with character: Owen's stroke precipitates but does not essentially cause the catastrophe. He is a reduced, small-farm Othello, flattered by attention – 'a kind soft voice is pleasant in a man's ear'. His confidence is misplaced in an ill-perceived reality. The idyll of Michael and Nance, in Murray's world, can only be tentative, guilty: one wonders if Murray saw an irony or a genuine solace of faith in Owen's last words, 'I've no one now but the son of o'God.' His work was of its time, but like Colum's with a life beyond its contemporary relevance.

(IV)

The first of the new plays in 1910 was Synge's posthumous *Deirdre of the Sorrows*, the last was Lady Gregory's *Coats*. The gap between Synge's tough magnificence and Lady Gregory's tomfoolery exempts them from any sane common standard of judgment. It is not, however, to be taken as the measure of a decline in the theatre. Yeats's kings, poets and peasants had made way for teachers, priests and small farmers, observed with Synge's candour, without his dignifying comedy or the enlarging rituals of his language. The editorialising naturalist theatre – Galsworthy not Ibsen – proposed answers for which it could with some conviction formulate problems. That was not Synge's theatre, nor for that matter Fitzmaurice's. Their plays did not have ' "a purpose" in the modern sense of that word'. Their localities, like Beckett's, are in tones of voice, not regional topography or a point in linear history.

Synge's successors are closer to 'realism'. The three realist walls of their stage circumscribed its fourth, invisible wall. The plays of Colum, Boyle, Robinson, Murray are circumstantially placed on a map and in a period, dramatically paraphrasing the documentation of newspapers, government reports, parish records. Their subjects, indeed, solicited editorials: the fate of younger sons, of unmarried daughters, the young and old at a loss amidst changing expectations, the land made available for purchase, with new emotional penalties. Yet the locations and the characters – Maire in the midlands, Muskerry in Garrisowen, Nance in County Cork – advance towards Synge's extremities of fable. Colum's dialogue, and at his best Murray's, added to their fictions a metaphorical command. Its emphasis is more that things happen than that we can hear explanations of them. Explanations, motives, consequences lie beyond words that can only allude to them. America is America, Ardagh is Ardagh. No one articulates the further meaning that in the plays adheres to them.

'Lennox Robinson', Yeats wrote to Lady Gregory, 'represents the Ireland that must sooner or later take the work from us.'[24] The work was an 'art of common things',[25] the final usurper of verse in Yeats's theatre. Synge's prose is the dramatic poetry of these years. The prose of Colum and Murray – which is certainly not Yeats's verse, nor the miraculous, the miracle-working incantations of Synge either – has an attenuated poetry of its own. The variety represented by Synge, Fitzmaurice, Colum, and Murray, homogeneous in its Irish starting-points, constituted a suggestive achievement. It suggestion was of a theatre nominally realist but demonstrating possible amplitudes in realist conventions. The years that followed these initiatives held the possibility of developing these achievements.

5. A painted stage: 1911–1929

Continually, in the contemporary theatre, the painted shadow is out of relation to the direction of the light, and what is more to the point one loses the extraordinary beauty of delicate light and shade. This means, however, an abolition of realism, for it makes scene-painting, which is, of course, a matter of painted light and shade, impossible.[1]

(I)

In 1929 the Abbey rejected Denis Johnston's *The Old Lady Says 'No!'*. In 1928 it had refused Sean O'Casey's *The Silver Tassie*. One excuse advanced has been that the Abbey's technical resources and its players could not do justice to the peculiar demands of either play.[2] A more likely explanation is a failure of judgment and perhaps of daring, a fault in the managerial central nervous system. It is certainly hard to account charitably for Yeats's rejection in 1927 of Austin Clarke's *The Son of Learning* (later re-named *The Hunger Demon*). Yeats would have done better to encourage this attempt to bring verse to the stage.

In those three years, the Abbey stuck to new works by Lennox Robinson and T. C. Murray, now old hands; by George Shiels, who with six plays since 1921 was entrenched as a favourite with audiences; and by Brinsley MacNamara, also a popular success from the time of his first comedy, *The Glorious Uncertainty*, in 1923. It was all, though not humdrum, very familiar. The only novelties were Denis Johnston's direction of *King Lear* in 1928, and Yeats's return from the drawing-rooms of London to the theatre:[3] his two Sophocles translations in 1926 and 1927, and his dance play, *Fighting the Waves*, in 1929.

The natural strains of management, it is true, were aggravated by the lack of guaranteed funding, aggravated in its turn by much greater events: the Dublin lockout and rioting of 1913, the First World War, the Easter Rebellion of 1916, the subsequent Anglo-Irish War, curfews, the Civil War of 1922–3. From all this came the Irish Free State of the twenty-six southern counties and the six-county Northern Ireland, established by the Anglo-Irish treaty of 1921 and left each to its factional turmoils.

In its own little world, the directorate cast about for administrative easement. Lennox Robinson's first appointment lasted for five years from 1909. Robinson was closely shadowed by Lady Gregory and by Yeats, who despite his brave words on the 'abolition of realism', and however weary he was of the 'people's theatre', recognised its command. Between 1914 and 1919 four managers were successively in charge, if so it may be called, three of them intent on advancing their own careers: Yeats's deliberating presence did not induce hopes of permanence. The fourth, St John Ervine, who served for a year from July 1915, was an imaginative and disastrous choice. He was from Belfast, cantankerous, it would be fair to say, and given to answering back. He never desisted from passionate and derogatory comment on Irish affairs, political and dramatic.

Ervine was in fact a gifted and intelligent man, caught up in the necessity of placing himself in the eccentric design of Northern Protestantism, nothing so simple as 'Anglo-Irish'. It was on the one hand 'British' – a politically convenient collective term; on the other it was of Ulster, in, but not nationally at home in, Ireland; nor in its cross-channel regard fully of England either. The Northern parish was an inherited and unresolved conglomerate of options. The options could hold together only so long as they were not pushed to a final choice. Within them, a large Catholic minority asserted an entirely Gaelic – and Catholic – monopoly of virtue. In a period when the choice appeared a mere duality, British or Irish, Ervine took his stand.

In 1900, when he was seventeen, he went to live in London. He met Shaw and took an interest in Fabianism. His play *The Orangemen* (1914) is a comic study of a bigoted Northern Protestant, his wife in whom the same faith takes on a serene tolerance, and his son, defiant of his father's hand-me-down prejudices. It was first produced in England. So too was *Jane Clegg* (1913), set in the lugubrious, penurious lower-middle-class suburbs of London. Jane in her scene is something like Nora in Ibsen's *Doll's House*. She contends with a comic/pathetic mother-in-law, two dramatically irrelevant children, a philandering, peculating husband, and in the upshot clings to the generous integrity of a New Woman.

Such liberal triflings did not long survive Ervine's passage back to Ireland. The First World War, the Republican conviction that Albion was perfidious still, awakened Ervine's indigenous Unionism. A few months before the Easter Rising he described Ireland as 'very nearly a lunatic nation'. During it, his sympathies were entirely with its suppression. The Abbey he regarded as a not particularly distinctive member of the British repertory system. None of this sat well with the Abbey actors. They disagreed politically with their manager, who had also been severe with a growth of crass staginess in their playing. Defied on his demand for extra rehearsals, Ervine fired the whole company; and shortly afterwards resigned from the theatre where he had begun his career with plays on

Northern Irish subjects: *Mixed Marriage* (1911), *The Magnanimous Lover* (1912), *John Ferguson* (1915). He returned to both theatre and subject with *Boyd's Shop* (1936), *William John Mawhinney* (1940), and *Friends and Relations* (1941).

Ervine's early plays for the Abbey completed, so to speak, the national geography of its drama. More fully than his Northern predecessors – Cousins, Mayne – he was the cartographer of his province, Co. Down particularly. He knew its vernacular and was accustomed to its convivialities as well as its 'dull angers and ancient rages'.[4] Ervine satisfied the current understanding of originality, which was taken to mean a choice of controversial subjects and their treatment in a dramatic speech figured upon popular idiom – of whatever social class.

Ervine chose contentious subjects. In his Irish bearings he was much in the style of Colum and Murray, neither of whom was innovative in any strictly formal sense. Nor was Ervine. They all worked within 'the division into clear-cut acts with an unfolding of the plot and a dénouement'.[5] In Colum's plays, language strains against these impositions. Working-class Northern speech, which has the same potential, is the idiom of Ervine's *Mixed Marriage*:

MICHAEL. A tell ye, Mr Rainey, the employers have used religion to throw dust in our eyes. They're eggin' us on to fight one another over religion, so's we shan't have time til think about the rotten wages they give us. They set the Cathliks agin the Prodesans, an' the Prodesans agin the Cathliks, so's ye can't git the two to work thegither for the good o' their class . . .
RAINEY. There's a differs.
MICHAEL. Only a very little. Look at me. A'm like yerself. A'm a workin' man. A want t' marry an' have a wife an' children an' keep them an' me dacently, an' a want t' sarve God in the way A was brought up. You don't want no more nor that.
TOM. Ay, indeed, that's true. People are all the same the wurl' over. They jus' want t' be let alone.
HUGH. Man, da, whin A'm out wi' Mickey, A sometimes think what a fine thing it'ud be if the workin' men o' Irelan' was to join their hans thegither an' try an' make a great country o' it. There was a time whin Irelan' was the islan'o'saints. By God, da, if we cud bring that time back again.
RAINEY. It's a gran' dream.

The dialogue is declarative. It brusquely ushers the characters into the advocacies which their situation will make untenable: the Brotherhood of Man *versus* the Prejudice of Faction; Male Ideology *versus* Female Sentiment. Rainey argues by blank statement of opinion. Partly from vanity, he agrees to support a Catholic-led strike in Belfast, holding together a tenuous coalition of workers of both faiths. He withdraws his support on discovering

that Nora, a Catholic, is secretly engaged to his son Hugh. Michael too
wants the engagement to be broken. It endangers the strike – even, as he
appeals to Nora with more passion than credibility, threatening 'the
destruction o' a nation', denying 'the wurl's needs'. Michael has Parnell in
his mind, and the eternal Temptress who 'wheniver a man's come near
deliverin' Irelan' . . . stepped in an' destroyed him.' Nora stands firm.
Rioting breaks out, and when the British Army opens fire on a mob outside
the Rainey house, she is shot. 'A was right', is Rainey's epitaph for her.

Ervine's women are, as was his way, the play's voice of reason, compassionate, practical. Mrs Rainey sees life in extensions from her own
'unemancipated' feelings and experience – 'A'm thinkin' it's more important fur a wumman t' be able t' make a good dinner for her man nor t' be able
t' pray in the same church'; and can tell Michael that Hugh and Nora 'are
bigger than the wurl', if ye only knew it'. Nora, more passively, judges
beliefs by her own dilemma, unwished and unexpected, which is outside the
abstractions the men prefer to judge. Nora refuses the parts of the
Temptress, and of all the female personifications of Ireland, Kathleen ni
Houlihan and Dark Rosaleen; and dies, to no purpose.

The play entertains these ambitious discriminations, not the simple-
hearted liberalism it might seem to pronounce. Its weakness is that the
discriminations are lost in their vulgarisation. 'The scene is the same as in
Act I', we are told of Act II. So is the conversation that is the substance of
both acts. It lengthily opposes bigotry and tolerance, casts Rainey as
uniquely the villain; and fills in with the laughs of Belfast vernacular and its
articles of faith:

RAINEY. Aye, ye can make fun, but it was the gran' day fur Englan' an' Irelan' that
    wus, when William O' Orange driv Popery out O' Irelan'.
TOM. He didden drive it far. Sure, there's plenty o' Papishes in Bilfast . . .

The jokes and domestic prattle take the place of transitions within the
dialogue. A treatise shapes every major sequence. Conversations are in
isolated blocks of debate, not growing into conjunctions between themselves. They take their place in a form, we are made conscious, imposed and
finally obtrusive; and give way to random interludes. The play is not at all
unplanned; the plan too easily declares itself.

In *John Ferguson*, Ervine took up the subjects of sex and property. John
Ferguson is a once well-to-do farmer now fallen upon evil days. Illness, an
unscrupulous mortgager, Henry Witherow, and a son (Andrew) not cut out
for labour have brought him to this pass. James Caesar, previously a victim
of Witherow, is now a grocer, prosperous and despicable. He is paying
unwelcome court to John's daughter, Hannah, on whom Witherow has
lustful designs. Off stage in America, John's brother is procrastinating on

the payment of money which will release the mortgage. Much of the play depends upon the frailties of the transatlantic post.

Caesar offers to pay off the mortgage. On this understanding, Hannah accepts his proposal of marriage. Having walked home with him she goes back on her word and sets off to tell Witherow that he must still foreclose (Act I). Witherow rapes her. Caesar swears vengeance (Act II). Witherow is found murdered, Caesar is arrested (Act III). At this point John receives the mortgage money from his brother, Andrews admits that it was he who shot Witherow, and against his father's persuasion to flight goes off to confess his guilt, accompanied by Hannah (Act IV):

SARAH FERGUSON. Where are they? They're not gone?

JOHN FERGUSON. Ay, they've gone. Sit down, wife.

SARAH FERGUSON. Oh, why did you let them go? I can't let him go, John, I can't let him go!

JOHN FERGUSON. You must, Sarah. God has some purpose with us, and there's no use in holding out against God, for He knows, and we don't;

upon which he reverts, as he has begun, to the Bible:

And the King was much moved, and went up to the chamber over the gate, and wept: and as he went (*his voice begins to break as he reads the following passages*), thus he said, O my son Absalom, my son Absalom! Would God I had died for thee, O Absalom, my son . . . my son.

'An eye for an eye, da, and a tooth for a tooth', says Andrew of the murder of Witherow. 'That's not the spirit that lives now, son!' his father replies. 'That's the spirit that was destroyed on the Cross.' Thus the play grounds the issues of that moral debate. Hannah's duty attracts a more secular terminology: to satisfy her leanings, or to sacrifice them and save the farm. Her father leaves the decision to his daughter; her mother urges the marriage of convenience. In both its main situations, *John Ferguson* shifts the participants to one or other of the two choices it permits.

Ervine's characters have a liveliness suffocated by a plot which circumscribes their destinies. Their feelings turn within predictable alternatives, not towards less fathomable responses. The only vagrant in *John Ferguson* is an itinerant whistle-player, the half-witted 'Clutie' John Magrath: 'I'm no hand at proving things. That's why I haven't got any sense.' It is nevertheless he who incites Andrew to action. With his delayed exits and entrances, 'Clutie' hovers upsettingly somewhere between an active and a choric part, out of place on a stage expectant of divisions that are based on rigid principles; and absent from the last act. Thus Clutie can have no part in the end of *John Ferguson*. *Mixed Marriage*, both in its language and its sceptical typology, has some promise of a less obvious moralising. Ervine could not keep, probably was unaware of, such a promise. His later plays honour realism in the observance of its simplest commands.

Yeats was not alone in regretting the consolidation of realist practice. Others took it as signifying the mortality of the Abbey's ideal: cosmopolitan experiment within a national, non-commercial theatre. It had in fact always been more national, as distinct from the easier 'nationalistic', than cosmopolitan. Though it was at the time often churlishly received, the repertoire of the years which culminated in Synge's plays appeared now the monument to a golden age. 'The Abbey is exhausted', Brinsley MacNamara wrote in the *Independent* on 9 May 1913; and on 4 March 1916 *New Ireland* pronounced, 'The Abbey is mortally sick.' Its successes, MacNamara's among them, and failures were alike of a predictable kind. The new dramatists with talent of any substance persisted, like Ervine, with realism, and mainly, like George Shiels, with comedy.

Shiels too was from Northern Ireland, from Co. Antrim, to which he returned after some years in Canada, permanently disabled after a railway accident. His first two plays, *Under the Moss* and *Felix Reid and Bob*, written under the name George Morshiel, were given in Belfast by the Ulster Literary Theatre in 1918 and 1919. In 1921 the Abbey presented two further one-act plays, *Bedmates* and *Insurance Money*. *Paul Twyning* (1922) and *Professor Tim* (1925), also at the Abbey, established his enormously popular style of kitchen comedy, maintained over some twenty plays and more than thirty years.

Shiels, again like Ervine, was self-taught, but without Ervine's intimacy with the world of theatre. Shiels's was a world limited by his disablement. From it he observed human behaviour in a society, in his view of it, painfully occupied with concealment, at pains not to 'give itself away'. This secretiveness darkens the comic progress of his plays to morally satisfying rewards and punishments. Behind familiar situations – arranged marriages, domineering mothers, repressed children – there is a suspension of judgment that makes Shiels's plays disturbing. Shiels supplies good music-hall laughs, as when, in a farcically emotional climax, Paul Twyning cries, 'Water! Water! And brandy for me!' The laughter does not, or should not, conceal the ironic reserve apparent to and disliked by Yeats. Of *Cartney and Kevney* (1927), he wrote: 'It displayed a series of base actions without anything to show that its author disapproved or expected us to do so.'[6]

We need not share Yeats's uneasiness to allow the justice of his comment. Shiels's first two plays satisfy the taste for the broadly comic. That is only part of a subtly deceitful world. Seeming altruism has private ends, advantage not principle determines action, pure mischief rejoices its practitioners. In *Paul Twyning* the Lord of Misrule is Paul himself, an itinerant labourer. Situations inspire him to improvisations for the charm of their unpredictable outcomes. Like Mosca in Ben Jonson's *Volpone*, though more benevolently, he can

> be here,
> And there and here, and yonder, all at once;
> Present to any humour, all occasion;
> And change a visor, swifter than a thought!

Paul's dupe is James Deegan, a Magistrate of the Crown, owner of ninety-five acres, one of the new Catholics, in the North as in the South, risen to bourgeois prosperity.

In an imbroglio of family connivings Paul initiates action, witnesses, offers to testify and refuses. He supports in bewildering turn sons against father, father against sons, this against that suitor for a bride-to-be, that trickster against this. Events lead to a fairly conventional sorting out of partners, even Paul furnished with a sweetheart. But the curtain falls on mischief still concealed. Deegan, thinking, 'all has turned out well', remains ignorant that Paul's puckish tinkerings have sequels yet to be revealed. His version of the happy ending will not be, for him, the end at all. Shiels stands by, waiting.

The best of Shiels's later comedies even more rigorously exclude any moral arbitration by their creator or a genial intruder. *The Old Broom* (Group Theatre, Belfast, 1944; Abbey 1946) is a typical history of unremitting avarice. The characters appeal to whatever code of behaviour may fit their purposes – or hide one within another – with no sense of contradiction between them. Hubert Dobie talks to Ben Broom about marrying Ben's daughter:

HUBERT. It's about Barbara.
BEN. Yes, what about her?
HUBERT. Well, she and I are friendly – indeed, something warmer than friendship.
BEN. I suspected something warmer. What age are you?
HUBERT. Not quite twenty-four.
BEN. Barbara is quite forty.
HUBERT. I know, sir.
BEN. Now, if your ages were reversed I'd very gladly encourage you. Your sister Rachel has made Austin an excellent wife. I like Rachel very much.
HUBERT. And she's awfully fond of you, sir.
BEN. Is she in favour of this romance?
HUBERT. Yes, sir, she's very keen on it.

and later – 'Well, the position is quite clear and logical. You evidently want to dispose of yourself to the best advantage.'

Liking, friendship, warmth, romance are counters with unvoiced synonyms in the vocabulary of mortgages, bank loans, calculation.

Nothing in the play chastises this duplicity. Similarly in *The Caretakers* (1948) the rapscallions contesting a will improve their lot indifferently by slander, threats, legal quibbles, and lachrymose sentiment. The schemers who come off best gain their reward by favourable chance and adroit chicanery, never virtue. It is by such designs that Shiels's language, whose inflections hold close to common speech, states the dramatic conflicts which Shiels, at his worst, moves to sentimental escapes; and more usually confines to precise, non-committal report, secreting a bitterness more 'like that of Swift', according to Frank O'Connor, 'than of any other Irish writer'.

Shiels's idea of comedy was a grim one, apparent even in his calling his *Tenants at Will* (1945) 'a comedy in three acts'. Set in 1844, on the brink of the potato blight and the Famine, *Tenants at Will* is hardly a comedy at all. Its period is the declining years of Daniel O'Connell, whose populist movement led to the Catholic Relief Act of 1829. This act removed most of the restrictions on Catholic participation in public life. It did little for the peasants, who continued to subsist precariously close to starvation and under laws that made them their landowner's creatures.

Tenants at will remained tenants at will. The will in question was that of their landlords, whose fields they worked for whatever wage was offered, and who were free to dispossess them of their tiny holdings. 'I won't allow anything for tenant-right', says Rock, the rising farmer in Shiels's play. 'They've no rights to sell.' It was for the peasants a world of hard labour, hand-to-mouth dependence on the potato, their only crop, of landlords' agents and under-agents, bailiffs and under-bailiffs, of charity dispensed by proselytising 'moral agents' from the Big Houses, of the police and the army, of paying rents, tithes to the Protestant Church of Ireland, poor rates, and a county cess. The fable of Shiels's play draws with considerable skill of compression on this history, and dramatises the vocabulary of its 'Gruesome hypocrisy':[7] land and families, dead and living, rents and duty – all measurable:

DYSON. How many children have you?

PATRICK. Five living, sir, and two dead. The oldest boy is twelve and the youngest four.

NORAH. They're in bed, your honour. Where they'll sleep tomorrow night, God knows.

DYSON. How much land have – or had you?

PATRICK. Two acres and a garden, but the road is in the measurement.

DYSON. You paid rent for the road?

PATRICK. We did, your honour, and had to keep it in repair. Three days' duty work every year.

DYSON. Did you pay no county cess?

86

PATRICK. Five shillings a year we paid, and another shilling of poor rates. The tithes were added to the rent.

Michael, Patrick's brother, is a skilled platelayer who has worked in France and picked up both the rhetoric of revolution and its activism – 'the only cure for greed and tyranny: down it!' He kills his father's landlord and his son, who have made a few hardheaded concessions to the tenants they are dispossessing. Patrick is reprieved from their impositions: 'there will be no evictions and the arrears of the rent are forgiven'. But the 'happy ending' has transience written on it. Neither oratory nor deed has removed 'his Lordship Sir Andrew, and he at the Manor House', the play's last words.

Shiels derived Michael from a Sean Keating drawing – 'three men in a currach, the hand of one gripping the gunwale, his thumb expressing courage, confidence, independence. Out of that thumb grew Michael Sheegan.'[8] Michael exhibits these qualities in the play, but in the world devised by Shiels. It leaves us regarding human beings move towards the

8 George Shiels's *The Passing Day* at the Abbey, 1981

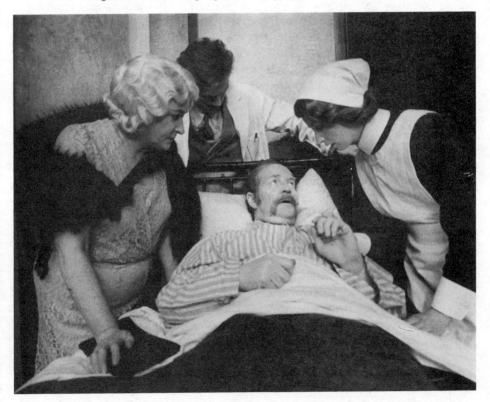

ends they envision, the equity of their failure or success 'not the playwright's business'.[9]

The Irish director Tyrone Guthrie was Shiels's surest interpreter. His 1951 production of *The Passing Day* (1936) expressed the core of Shiels's chilly world. In this corner of it, as John Fibbs lies dying in hospital, the scene moves back to his last day in his general store. Wife, doctor, lawyer, customers, acquaintances pass through, soliciting favours and the wealth he has to bestow. The play's narrative concerns Fibbs's will. Is it to reward his intolerable wife, his nephew, meanly treated and hard enough in himself, or neither? The real manipulation is emotional. The characters, in this or that grouping, profess without qualm or even overt recognition, totally opposed loyalties, to tactical advantage.

Feelings are discussed, but outside contempt, ambition, avarice, not felt. 'Love?' the nephew's girlfriend asks him, 'What do you mean?' From both uncle and nephew a repressed sexuality flickers towards her. Images of death accumulate. A gravedigger, denied relief of a debt, hopes, while he mimics digging a grave, that Fibbs will 'pay the balance aforenight'. Fibbs's dead parents appear to him, past replicas of his own money-grubbing sterility. On his last day of life dissatisfactions surface. He proposes to his lawyer a holiday to the Amazon, 'the longest cruise in the world'. It is not the cruise he is to go on. On his death, his will still turning in his mind, the outcome is hardly even rough justice. *The Passing Day* is comedy stripped, in David Kennedy's words, 'of its muffling laughter to reveal a hard and bitter world'.[10]

(II)

When Shiels began to write, some twenty years after the Irish Literary Theatre's first season, the Abbey had acquired a distinguishable character.[11] Robert Hogan's *The Modern Irish Drama*, volume IV, calls the years 1910–15 'The Rise of the Realists', and the title might be fairly applied to the longer span covered by this chapter. One must discriminate, however, amongst the practices of the dramatists generally assembled within that category: Colum, Boyle, Murray, Ervine, Shiels. Synge too might be included: he performed his marvels within the form of an essentially realist stagecraft. Critical opinion, after Synge's death, tended to see this line not as one of descent in a neutral, genealogical sense, but as a deterioration.

Two essays in *The Irish Review* advanced this proposition.[12] Walter Mennloch sees Yeats and Synge as 'the two "explosions" that carried the Irish theatre so far up the hill'. Of the two, Synge was without doubt dramatically the greater. Mennloch acknowledges a greatness in Yeats's plays but has reservations about a transparency in his characters and predicts that he will make no new explosion. 'There is need of another', Mennloch concludes, to 'clear the theatre of its impending lumber of dead conventions and traditions.' G. Hamilton Gunning would have agreed that the Abbey was thus lumbered. His essay argues that the decline apparent to him in 1912 has some hope of a prosperous sequel. It is bad in such garish ways that it must die of its own disabilities.

Yet it is not entirely clear what is the model which the critics saw its inheritors as debasing, nor in precisely what their fault lay. Gunning lumped together as 'Literary Plays' (approved) the work of Yeats, Synge, and Colum, the 'three dramatists of genius' who opened the Abbey.[13] The three have little in common. They all wrote about 'peasants' but in utterly dissimilar ways. The poetry of Yeats's language is not that of Synge's. Synge was 'realist' but in an individual and eccentric way. Yeats saw this. He said that Synge's characters were not replicas of Irish country people. The person in the audience seeing them 'has added to his being, not to his knowledge'.[14] Other dramatists arrived at this effect from a more closely documentary fidelity, and in less figured and elaborate speech: the manner of Colum – circumstantial, plainer spoken.

Insofar as the critics were arguing simply that Synge's plays were immeasurably better than those of his successors, the case is indisputable. But it contains a wider assumption, ascribing to Yeats, Synge, and Colum a non-existent community of vision and manner, a 'literary' treatment of themes and subjects either heroic in themselves and thus conveyed, or elevated above an origin in the commonplace: some formula accountably lost, but recoverable. The argument was, at least, on a rather higher level of intelligence than charges of immorality and lack of patriotism. Now, however, at that higher level, it would seem reasonable to set Yeats and Synge aside, as in their different ways special cases, and to see Colum and his successors as exercising, without undertaking any radical sabotage of, the potentialities of realist theatre.

They were not, certainly, prospecting the wilder shores of theatrical experiment. Yeats aside, the work of Irish dramatists just before and for most of the 1920s shows no trace of the messianic attack upon the orthodoxies of stage form popular in Europe and America, where expressionism was the *avant-garde* fashion. Derived from Strindberg's *The Dream Play* (1901) and *The Ghost Sonata* (1907), its intention was to depart from representing surface reality, doing away with plot, sequential narrative, discursive accounting of cause and effect, with localised place and character, breaking the solidity of the proscenium stage into phantasmal 'dissolves' of scene: a theatrical equivalent of T. S. Eliot's *The Waste Land*. In Germany the architects of the Bauhaus (1919) envisaged 'a great keyboard for light and sound, a flexible building capable of transforming and refreshing the mind by its spatial impact alone . . . The playhouse itself, made to dissolve into the shifting, illusionary space of the imagination, would become the scene of action itself'[15] These contrivances were more than a purely technical methodology. They were to enact the disjunctions and elisions of states of mind and politically were 'symbolic of the revolution against the bourgeoisie'.[16]

These heady freedoms had their excesses. They were often put to the service of melodrama, strident message-mongering, and a simple desire to shock. The hero of Ernst Toller's *Transfiguration* (1917) exhorts the mob: 'you could go forward with winged feet, while today wherever you go you trail after you iron chains. Oh, if only you were men and women – men and women unqualified – free men and women!' In Georg Kaiser's *Gas* (1920) an officer commits suicide as a conveniently pacifist symbol. Characters urinated – Brecht's *Baal* (1918) – and vomited – E. E. Cummings's *Him* (1927) – on stage. Formal licence was no guarantee either against a ponderous solemnity. Kaiser's *From Morn to Midnight* (1916) turns upon a journey undertaken by a clerk who has stolen money from the bank where he works. Without discernible wit, scenes at a racetrack, a private room at a cabaret, a snowy field (with a tree that becomes a skeleton), satirise a decadent, rapacious, fragmented society. The hero dies (apparently) in the last scene, the lights go out, and the play ends with the blatantly metaphorical line, 'There must be a short circuit in the main.'

Expressionism has much more to its credit than the turgidities cited above. It is a convention, and as with all conventions its success depends upon what its exponents make of it. Luigi Pirandello's *Henry IV* (1922) and *Six Characters in Search of an Author* (1921) brought expressionism to its fullest imaginative release. It was entirely appropriate to his concerns: the conflict of values between destructive truth and solacing illusion; between appearance and reality; madness and sanity; the designs of art and the controls possible to life; the actor, his part, and their relationship to actuality. Thus, intellectually, one may explain Pirandello's themes. The plays embody them in the agonies of individual lives. The characters of *Six Characters* belong to 'A Play in the Making'. They insist, arrived on a bare stage, upon determining the destinies which the dramatist who created them has left unfinished. The narrative they invent, a parody of nineteenth-century melodrama – to which the actors who will take the parts contribute amendments – leaves two of them dead – perhaps 'really' dead. It is a play – both drama and pun – on philosophical paradoxes translated into startling emblems of feelings shared between life and theatre: 'Heart-mysteries there'.[17]

Without reaching these heights, American playwrights who turned to the idiom practised it on the whole more circumspectly than most of their

European mentors. Elmer Rice's *The Adding Machine* (1923) manages it with humour, and E. E. Cummings's *Him*, though chaotic even for an expressionist play, has some nicely surrealistic dialogue. Three Fates talk:

FIRST. George says he doesn't see why guinea-pigs can't have children if children can have guinea-pigs.
THIRD. A clean tooth never decays.
SECOND. Do children have guinea-pigs?
FIRST. Oh yes, more's the pity. Mine often have it.
THIRD. Your nails show your refinement.
SECOND. Badly?

The dialogue of John Dos Passos' *Airways Inc.* (1928) and *The Moon is a Gong* (1923) entertainingly contrives both to echo and to mock the oratory of radio announcers and the cynical propaganda of 'big business'. None of this is great drama. Expressionism was a dangerous guide. It lured Eugene O'Neill, whose genius finds itself in the naturalism of *Desire under the Elms* (1928), into the tortured pretensions of *The Hairy Ape* (1922), with its heavily symbolic cage, and *The Great God Brown* (1926) with its ultimately silly masks. Yet expressionism, for all its grandiose failures, left a durable inheritance, delicately effective, for example, in Tennessee Williams's *The Glass Menagerie* (1945), Arthur Miller's *Death of a Salesman* (1949), and Tom Stoppard's *Rosencrantz and Guildenstern are Dead* (1966). It also registers on contemporary Irish drama, in the work of Brian Friel, Tom Murphy and Tom Kilroy; even, perhaps, in Shiels, who first wrote *Tenants at Will* as a vast chronicle play (rejected by the Abbey), having the Devon Land Commission of 1845 'sitting on the stage with the whole cavalcade of misery passing before it'.[18]

In its heyday, however, expressionism made no impact on Irish drama, though Lennox Robinson, as already remarked, in mid-career and past expressionism's prime, tinkered with it. Apart from the towering figure of James Joyce, who anyway, in a sense, never left Dublin, and Yeats's intellectual excursions, the Irish imagination, especially in theatre, lived with its creative insularity: with qualified exceptions to be noted. The Abbey had never done much to invade that insularity. It was as a corrective to it, and as a tardy honouring of the theatre's early professions of cosmopolitanism – still in Yeats's mind – that in 1919, with Yeats's support, Lennox Robinson founded the Dublin Drama League. Robinson described the aims of the venture, which was managed by subscribing members:

Here in Ireland we are isolated, cut off from the thought of the world, except the English world, and from England we get little in drama, except fourth-rate. I ask you, for the young writer's sake, to open up the door and let us out of our prison. Seeing foreign plays will not divorce our minds from Ireland . . . but brought into touch with other minds who have different values of life, suddenly we shall discover the rich material that lies to our hand in Ireland.[19]

Despite Lady Gregory's disapproval, the League was allowed to use the Abbey on Sundays and Mondays, when the Abbey did not play. The Abbey Company was free to take part in League productions and most of them – including F. J. McCormick, Barry Fitzgerald, Eileen Crowe and Arthur Shields – did so. Many of them also had their first experience of directing for the League.

Expressionism, as the dominant European form, was well represented. The League gave Pirandello's *Henry IV* in 1923, his *The Game as He Played It* in 1927, Toller's *Masses and Men* in 1925, *Hoppla!* (directed by Denis Johnston) in 1929, Strindberg's *Ghost Sonata* in 1925. It also presented Chekhov, Leonid Andreyev, O'Neill, Claudel, Euripides, and Yeats's dance plays, *At the Hawk's Well* in 1924, *The Only Jealousy of Emer* and *The Cat and the Moon* in 1926. The League, a part-time operation and never a rival to the Abbey, gave Dublin its first sustained exposure to a range of serious drama which the Abbey excluded. It was in its own right, a worthy, responsibly managed, and exuberant enterprise. It challenged the Abbey to reconsider its self-reproducing conformities; and young writers to absorb a variety of forms. In the event the Abbey, though it did take over half-a-dozen of the League's productions, stuck to its ways, as did the young writers. Sean O'Casey attended sixty per cent of the League's plays;[20] the form of his brilliant Dublin trilogy (Mennloch's third 'explosion') – *The Shadow of a Gunman* (1923), *Juno and the Paycock* (1924), *The Plough and the Stars* (1926) – owes nothing formally to the *avant-garde* work he saw there. It is perfectly compatible with the dramatic – not always the moral and political – orthodoxies of the Abbey. While more was to come of O'Casey's contacts with the League, they did not shape his beginnings. His first plays in fact affirm the gusto and the subtleties still to be evoked from the realist convention.

One of the great interests of the Irish dramatic movement's first twenty-five years is indeed almost as a case history of a form, naturalist theatre, forever being pronounced dead and forever reviving. Yeats's observation of 'the painted shadow out of relation to the direction of the light' is one such notice of its decease, or execution. By it he meant, literally, the conflict between static, two-dimensional representation and the swathing perspectives of lighting on a stage whose boundaries may endlessly divide and blend. By extension he also meant, as opposed to the use of symbol, ritual, dance, music, verse, the realist theatre's crude approximations of reality – in scene, language, character – simply coded signals in which the audience could easily decipher superficial resemblances to life. The décor of realist theatre, in short, was for Yeats a metaphor of its general sacrifice of depth and complexity, subduing the freedom of the dramatist to draw from the shape of daily facts the contours of legend and of archetypal experience.

There is no doubt that realist theatre is capable of the kinds of stereotyping which Yeats criticises. Realist theatre, however, also had capabilities well beyond the allowance of Yeats's repeated strictures on it. It too can make its terms with the nature of dramatic fiction as Pirandello describes it:

The problems presented in a work of art are always problems of life . . . Take 'To be or not to be' out of the mouth of Hamlet, treat it as a philopshical problem, and you can solve it according to your own sweet fancy. But leave it there forever on Hamlet's lips, uttered out of his torment, and the question 'To be or not to be' will never be solved in all time. These life problems and emotions are imprisoned in a perfect form by a Shakespeare or a Dante, become fixed for eternity. Emotions embedded alive.[21]

At their own levels, the plays of Boyle and Ervine are closer to the 'philopshical problem', organised to reach a solution among prescribed options; those of Colum and Shiels closer to a form which 'embeds emotions alive', defined by the world of the characters, but restlessly posing their questions beyond it.

The dramatic world's insistence on its own reality gives it its status in the world of the audience. Though their form is traditional, of the nineteenth century, Colum, and Shiels particularly, share in the chilly ironies and objectivity of Joyce's *Dubliners* – or of Swift. The author's beliefs, or thoughts, or attitudes are announced, if they are announced at all, by inducing the reader/audience to make particular associations of words, images, episodes. It is this, for example, rather than Shiels's use of motorbikes in *The New Gossoon*, that makes Colum and Shiels 'modern'.

The Abbey's purely realist tradition – not to make extravagent claims for it – had an honest (sometimes dishonest) skill, and at its best gave the 'painted stage' a dimension beyond documentary paraphrase. The completion in 1926 of O'Casey's trilogy, a work whose self-confidence defies its imperfections, was in a way a completion of the tradition in these years. It gave the Abbey exactly the artistic and popular success it needed. The theatre was in good fettle. Its finances, too, had taken a permanent turn for the better. In 1925 it received a government subsidy of £850, increased in the next year to £1000 per annum. This was largely due to the influence of Ernest Blythe, a member of the new Free State Executive Council, a Northern Protestant and an enthusiast both for the Irish language revival and the Abbey – the latter seen mainly as an agent of the former.[22] The subsidy enabled the directors, in 1926, to convert part of their premises into a little theatre, christened the Peacock. It was rented to outside groups, and gave a home to the Drama League, the Abbey School of Acting, and from 1927 the Abbey School of Ballet.

There was every reason to feel satisfied. Whatever Yeats's reservations about the naturalist form, the Abbey had fostered it to a triumph; and the League accommodated other kinds of plays, supported by but not threatening its parent. The anti-heroic version of the Easter Rising in *The Plough and the Stars*, its indecent language and low-life characters, after a quiet opening night, provoked riotous objections in the theatre. 'You have disgraced yourselves again', Yeats told the audience. Even this controversy bespoke the revivalist spirit, bringing back the brave days of *The Playboy*.

The Abbey's future did not go at all as on this evidence of renewal one might have predicted. O'Casey's next play, *The Silver Tassie*, submitted to the Abbey in 1928, had a boldly expressionist second act, which was a major cause of its rejection. Denis Johnston's *The Old Lady Says 'No!'* was a superbly localised variant of the expressionist style. Both plays were undoubtedly inspired by the Drama League's activities, which also gave rise to the foundation of the Dublin Gate Theatre, the first professional, permanent, and substantial alternative to the philosophy and practices of the Abbey.

It was created in 1928 by Micheál MacLiammóir and Hilton Edwards, renting the Peacock for its first seasons. MacLiammóir – actor, designer, director, playwright – was born in Cork, had studied art at the Slade School, acted in England with Beerbohm Tree, and in 1927 joined the Company formed by Anew McMaster to tour mainly Shakespeare's plays in rural Ireland.[23] In it he met Edwards, an Englishman who had played in the Old Vic and having come to Ireland stayed there: two men of great talent, energy, and imagination. They hired the Peacock initially to put on MacLiammóir's *Diarmuid and Grania*, and taking up from the Drama League developed their more ambitious project. The League recognised its successor's legitimacy by dissolving itself in 1929.

The Gate's aim, says MacLiammóir, was 'a new sort of theatre in Ireland . . . something more than a national theatre which interpreted but a portion of the national life'. The Gate hoped to improve 'the lack of visual sensibility of a nation whose ears had always been its strongest point of aesthetic perception'; and to contribute to 'methods of acting, production, design and lighting'. The material for these endeavours was to come not from the nurturing of new writers, but from 'ancient and modern plays from all sorts of places'.[24] The story of the Gate and what it made of its intentions is of the nineteen-thirties and after. In the late twenties it without question vibrantly diversified Irish theatre, which O'Casey abandoned after *The Silver Tassie* row. Its earliest seasons presented Wilde's *Salomé*, Evreinov's *Theatre of the Soul*, Tolstoy's *Powers of Darkness*, O'Neill's *The Hairy Ape* and *Anna Christie*, Karel Capek's *R.U.R.*, *The Adding Machine*; and on 3 July 1929 *The Old Lady Says 'No!'*.

The simplest understanding of this new situation was that the Abbey/Irish plays were on trial against the Gate/international theatre. MacLiammóir's recollection does not present it so:

'The Abbey's dead', people would say to us gleefully, knowing quite well it was nothing of the kind, and letters to the newspapers on the subject became a fashion. We at the Gate were seized upon in this campaign to beat the old traditional house, and that we were neither flattered by this move nor willing to be so used counted little, and a few enemies were made for us in the senior theatre – a silly, distressing business it all was that should never have begun.[25]

But begun it had. With all its ups and downs, the first quarter century of the movement, marked in its beginnings by the greatness of Synge and at its end by the greatness of O'Casey, now apparently faced at last, in two theatres, the conditions of its original prospectus, a co-existence of national and international drama.

6. Plays and controversies: Sean O'Casey

Sean O'Casey was the youngest of the thirteen children, eight dead in childhood, of a respectable, lower-middle-class Dublin Protestant family. Its fortunes declined when his father, Michael Casey, died in 1883, but never to the point of the family's having to live in the appalling tenements where O'Casey's first three plays are set. O'Casey knew the tenements intimately, but from a chosen life, not perforce. Although he took up a series of hard, manual jobs – docker, stone-breaker – one suspects that had he wished he could have done better. Without doubt he turned early, of his own accord, to cultural nationalism, to the labour movement, to left-wing Republicanism. In the Gaelic League he learned Irish. He was a member of the Irish Republican Brotherhood, helped Jim Larkin, the labour leader, in the 1913 strike, and was for a time secretary of the Irish Citizen Army.

Both movements advocated separation from England by force of arms, a policy which became increasingly repugnant to O'Casey. Before the Easter Rising in 1916 he had dissociated himself from both groups. His militancy was essentially of the mind. He was sceptical of and passionate against the orthodoxies of Gaelic nationalism, the Catholic puritanism of the new state, the myth and the rhetoric of violence – 'a cleansing and sanctifying thing'[1] – and the random suffering it inflicted. O'Casey was a deeply compassionate man, but belligerent as well, sensitive to slights, at times unjustly venomous. In a sad paradox, proclaiming himself 'a proletarian Communist', his eyes never opened to the perversions of Stalinism.

By his own account he came uninstructed to writing for the stage. In Dublin he saw a few plays, including Shaw's *Androcles and the Lion*, read many more – Strindberg, a little Ibsen, Boucicault, the Elizabethans; and 'let all the older literature of England into my soul'.[2] O'Casey's painfully weak eyesight made his programme of self-education a burden. He persisted with it, and with occasional appearances in amateur groups run by his brother, giving excerpts from Shakespeare and Dion Boucicault at charity concerts and other occasional entertainments.[3] By 1918 he had begun to publish: humorous songs, ballads, histories – the *Story of the Irish Citizen Army* brought him fifteen pounds in 1919; and to submit plays to the Abbey. In 1923 *On the Run* was accepted, and presented as *The Shadow of a Gunman*. It is set in 1920 at the time of the Anglo-Irish war which led to the Settlement of 1921. *Juno and the Paycock* (1924) and *The Plough and the*

Stars (1926) followed. *Juno* takes place during the Civil War between those who accepted the Settlement, the 'Free-Staters', and those who resisted its partitioning of the country, the 'Die-hards'. *The Plough* goes back to the Easter Rising.

These plays we may for the moment categorise as 'realist', though the term needs qualification. After *The Silver Tassie* (1928) with its expressionist second act, O'Casey's later work is in its attitudes propagandist and in its forms symbolic, stylised, experimental: *Within the Gates* (1934), *The Star Turns Red* (1940), *Red Roses for Me* (1943), *Purple Dust* (1945), *Oak Leaves and Lavender* (1947), *Cock-a-Doodle Dandy* (1949), *The Bishop's Bonfire* (1955), *The Drums of Father Ned* (1958). (The dates are those of first productions.) It is on the relationships between the early and the later plays that any assessment of O'Casey must turn.

O'Casey's life and background have an intrinsic fascination, and in both a general way and in particulars – the originals of this or that character – are transferred to his plays. There is a temptation to biographical source-hunting. However, as Micheál O hAodha has wisely remarked, 'there is the danger that the genius of O'Casey the dramatist . . . may be obscured by an approach which pays due attention to everything but the plays themselves'.[4] One important structural device in the plays does come from O'Casey's personal experience of 'more than forty years' immersion in the everyday life and ways of thought of Dublin working-class people, of more than a quarter of a century's acquaintance with the oral resources and copious writings associated with the nationalist and labour movements centered in Dublin'. That is, his drawing upon, usually for ironic effect, 'a massive store of patriotic writings, ballads, speeches, and fables . . . popular with a wide cross-section of Irish society . . . an astonishing richness of local associations and national folklore'.[5] Beyond that connection between the man and the plays, the biographical approach considers O'Casey's early plays, damagingly, as naturalistic 'slices of life', his own particularly. Its judgment is of social, historical, linguistic verisimilitudes, and of the life-likeness of the characters.

If the 'slice of life' is a category that will account for these plays only in a limiting way, then what category will accommodate them more generously? As his first commentators – A. E. Malone, Walter Starkie – took them, in the traditional genres of tragedy, comedy and tragi-comedy? Or are they, in Robert Hogan's argument, 'complicated modern versions' of Pastoral Tragi-comedy?[6] The political 'epic theatre' of Brecht? Symbolism? Expressionism? Absurdism anticipated? Criticism has variously tested O'Casey within each of these frames of reference, usually concluding that none of his plays fully satisfied, and may even actively frustrate, the opportunities of the form. Some of this dispute might find a purchase even in so straightforward a sequence as the following, early in O'Casey's work, early in the action of *The Shadow of a Gunman*. During it, Seamus Shields, hours late rising from his bed, is ambling about, dressing, and packing his pinchbeck goods. It launches the endless, inconsequential argument between an idle pedlar and a pretentiously sentimental poet.

SEAMUS. What's the use of having everything packed and ready when he didn't come? No wonder this unfortunate country is as it is, for you can't depend upon the word of a single individual in it. I suppose he was too damn lazy to get up; he wanted the streets to be well aired first – Oh, Kathleen ni Houlihan, your way's a thorny way.

DAVOREN. Ah me! alas, pain, pain ever, for ever!

SEAMUS. That's from Shelley's *Prometheus Unbound*. I could never agree with Shelley, not that there's anything to be said against him as a poet – as a poet – but. . .

DAVOREN. He flung a few stones through stained-glass windows. . .

SEAMUS. . . .I think I'll bring out a few of the braces too; damn it, they're well worth sixpence each; there's great stuff in them – did you see them? . . . They're great value; I only hope I'll be able to get enough o' them. I'm wearing a pair of them meself – they'd do Cuchullian, they're so strong. (*Counting the spoons.*) There's a dozen in each of these parcels – three, six, nine – damn it, there's only eleven in this one . . . Now I suppose I'll have to go through the whole bloody lot of them, for I'd never be easy in me mind thinkin' there'd be more than a dozen in some o' them. And still we're looking for freedom – ye gods, it's a glorious country! (*He lets one fall, which he stoops to pick up.*) Oh, my God, there's the braces after breakin'.

Farce is forever poised to break in on their claims: the breaking braces, the counting of the spoons, in the line of some of the arithmetical routines of the Hollywood comedians, Abbott and Costello, or Samuel Beckett's Molloy disposing his collection of stones around his pockets.[7] The aimlessness is in itself to the point: it is the quality of their lives. The dialogue also looks towards what is to come. There will be deaths – neither Davoren's nor Shields's. The 'he' of Seamus's first sentence is the rebel Maguire, killed on his foray to Knocksedan where, he whimsically tells Seamus, he is going 'to catch butterflies'. Minnie Powell is shot dead, mistakenly protecting Donal, the supposed gunman on the run. Language, allusion and 'business' all work to express energies and exhaustion of feeling. Kathleen ni Houlihan and Cuchulain are glibly invoked by the very unheroic Seamus; Shelley's quoted lament acquires the sudden vigour of flinging 'stones through stained-glass windows', its value already disputed: 'You can't depend upon the word of a single individual.'

Seamus Shields's braces are a comic, indeed a farcical, sign of a world whose structures will never live up to their promise. They are of a piece with the clock in *Juno and the Paycock*: 'the least little thing sets it astray', or the gramophone that 'wants to be properly played'; with the 'twarthing' collar that defies Peter Flynn in *The Plough*; with the entangling telephone wire in the last act of *The Silver Tassie*. These gambits require a finesse and a judgment of timing which they do not always have, even as the text presents them, let alone what a director or actor may make of them: the playing with the telephone wires is not very good vaudeville to begin with, and can easily get out of hand. The abounding verbal traps and malapropisms belong to the same world, the world, as Samuel Beckett has described it, of music-hall knockabout.[8] Again, some are better than others. A substantial instance is Captain Boyle's total incomprehension, in *Juno and the Paycock*, of Bentham's deriving Juno's name from classical myth: 'You see', says the Captain, 'June was born an' christened in June; I met her in June; we were married in June, an' Johnny was born in June, so wan day I says to her, "You should ha' been called Juno", an' the name stuck to her ever since.'

9   O'Casey's *Juno and the Paycock* at the Abbey, 1979

This speaks beyond the level of repartee to the play's whole system of anti-heroic ironies.

For all their occasional excesses, these routines and this kind of patter prepare the way for the same idiom to make consequential statements: as at the end of *Juno*, when Captain Boyle's situation, in his drunken description of it, applies beyond what he intends:

Wan single, solitary tanner left out of all I borreyed. (*He lets it fall.*) The last of the Mohicans. The blinds is down, Joxer, the blinds is down. . . . The counthry'll have to steady itself. It's goin' to hell. Where'r all the chairs . . . gone to . . . steady itself, Joxer. Chairs'll have to steady themselves. . . . I'm tellin' you, Joxer, th' whole worl's in a terrible state o' chassis;

or at the end of *The Silver Tassie*, Mrs Foran's 'there's nothing I love more than the ukelele's tinkle, tinkle in the night-time'. It is a world of pratfalls that collect into an image of a disintegrating society, a world whose nature is to fall apart. Its habitation, oddly, is the insistent, seedy solidity of O'Casey's prescriptions for his stage: walls, chairs, tables, fireplaces, precisely detailed, whose point is that they are unreliable and vulnerable. The directions are novelistic to the extent of describing items which are no longer, but have been, there – in *The Plough* the fireplace 'of wood, painted to look like marble (the original has been taken away by the landlord)'; so detailed, so visible to O'Casey's imagination, that, like the pub scene in the same play, they leave little to the stage designer's initiative. All, in the end, are merely precarious refuges. Here it is that the political voice must make itself heard.

A common interpretation of O'Casey is that his world is held together by its humane, pragmatic, apolitical women, not the motive of any alleviating system of ideas. Juno sustains the household, and stands by Mary in her pregnancy, while the Captain reviles her. Mrs Tancred is given the plea, 'take away our hearts o' stone an' give us hearts o' flesh!' – of which O'Casey thought well enough to have Juno repeat it. Bessie Burgess in *The Plough* saves Nora Clitheroe's life at the cost of her own. In *The Shadow*, Minnie Powell courageously sacrifices herself for Donal. Yet these virtues, though O'Casey quite evidently admires them, are qualified. For all Juno's caring, the household sunders. Mary prattles as glibly about politics as any of the men. Mrs Tancred 'in wan way . . . deserves all she got; for lately, she let the Die-hards make an open house of th' place'. Bessie Burgess, fanatical Unionist, as she dies, turns on Nora in the shocking outburst, 'I've got this through you, you bitch, you!'

Love, compassion, fellow-feeling, it would seem, are the prime virtues; but they are unreliable, and likely to be their own reward. Perhaps, at best, they may deliver an improving moral to the self-indulgent, the heartless, the imperceptive? Thus David Krause sees Davoren's response to Minnie's death: it 'makes Davoren see himself and his world with terrifying clarity.'[9] But Donal has learned nothing. He speaks at the end, mocked by the dialogue around him, as he does at the beginning. Immediately after his final speech comes Seamus's prosaic curtain line, 'I knew something ud come of the tapping on the wall.'

The women, despite their humanitarian sentiments, are not quite the rectifying force in whom Krause, for instance, sees 'the brutality of war through the realistic eyes of working-class Irishwomen instead of through the haze of sentimental patriotism'; or O hAodha, more subtly, 'the courage of women and the cowardice of men when faced with a tragedy which overwhelms them. But the cowards are gay and human, and the brave only crave a home or a husband.'[10] The women are not espousing exclusively home and husband. Their emotions direct them to political stances: Mary, Mrs Tancred, Minnie, Bessie. It is the men, however – when they are not simply layabouts – who represent political attitudes at least ostensibly a result of analytic consideration of ideas; and they are derided.

So far as the politics concern the liberation of Ireland by force, O'Casey's personal disillusionment with that whole programme accounts for its sardonic, negative treatment: of Pearse's mystical rhetoric of blood-letting, the bombast of Peter Flynn, Tommy Owen and all the other hangers-on. Jack Clitheroe has joined the Citizen Army out of vanity. Johnny Boyle, badly wounded in Easter Week, turns informer and coward during the Civil War. Donal Davoren is not a gunman at all. Only the engaging Maguire seems to have substance, and a belief, for which his fleeting entrance gives him no reasons. He is largely a plot device, leaving behind the bombs which will produce *The Shadow*'s catastrophe. The failures and braggarts, the absence of any hero or of a serious political thinker reflect O'Casey's cynicism. The question is whether it leads the plays into a series of culs-de-sac, admitting possible answers only to dally with and retreat from them. If the women, as guides to an ameliorating domestic, private sanctuary, in the end default, so too do Nationalist politics as a route to society's discovering a coherent sense of itself. Everything, it might be argued, ends in 'chassis' because set to work in a dramatic world dishonestly constructed to admit no real adversary. The question arises even more pressingly when we look at how the plays deal with ideas which O'Casey did actually profess.

James Simmons wonders at the plays' failures to include a large part of O'Casey's experience:

the work of trades unions, strikes, the Citizen Army . . . these things only appear obliquely whereas in Brecht's dramatisation of Gorki's *The Mother* you see serious socialists at work. . .
You may say that *Red Roses for Me* deals with a railway strike; but this is a very

romantic play, where all the attention is focussed on the individual talent and charm of Ayamonn. The big transformation scene is a sort of mystical vision of how one man's sympathy and fluency can inspire the downtrodden to dance for an hour. . . . There is no sense of how actual workers organise, which O'Casey knew all about, or what it is like to be politically active.[11]

Very little work is done, or even talked about, in O'Casey's working-class drama. Seamus Shields counts out his wares. Fluther Good fixes a door. Captain Boyle has the marvellous fantasy of his 'days at sea', 'fixed to the wheel with a marlin-spike, an' the win's blowin' fierce an' the waves lashin' an' lashin', till you'd think every minute was goin' to be your last, an' it blowed, an' blowed – blew is the right word, Joxer, but blowed is what the sailors use': words again; and that is about all there is of work. Two characters might seem to be, prospectively, spokesmen for positions supported by O'Casey: Jerry Devine, the socialist Trades Union organiser in *Juno*, Young Covey, a communist advocating the international class war above the national struggle in *The Plough*. But Devine is as interested in becoming union-secretary at £350 a year as in his 'principles', and rejects Nora in her plight. The Covey calls everyone 'Comrade' and has a line in platitudes from 'Jenersky's *Thesis on the Origin, Development, an' Consolidation of th' Evolutionary Idea of the Proletariat*'. Yet O'Casey did believe, 'There's only one freedom for th' workin' man: conthrol o' th' means o' production, rates of exchange, an' th' means of distribution' – and gives the words to a windbag.

It was this political nihilism, as one might call it, which, crudely perceived, provoked the demonstrations over *The Plough*. Audiences which had flocked to *The Shadow* and *Juno* now took violent exception. *The Plough* was a blatant attack on the purities of the nation's patriotism and sexual habits. Irish people did not, as the play showed them doing, loot and pillage. Rosie Redmond was an impossible character: according to Joseph Holloway, there were no streetwalkers in Dublin.[12] Critical opinion too, outside local pieties, found the nihilism a difficulty, most simply stated by Joseph Wood Krutch. 'His plays lack form, lack movement, and in the final analysis lack any informing purpose . . . To this day I do not know just where the author's sympathies lie'; again, 'O'Casey offers no solution; he proposes no remedy; he suggests no hope.'[13]

Seamus Deane offers a more sophisticated, detailed analysis[14] of, as he sees it, a bad faith, at least an illogic, 'an imperfectly conceived moral system', in O'Casey's way of dramatising his hostile critique of politics. Essentially, Deane argues, O'Casey is condemning politics by measuring it through an ideal of home, of family, from which politics is artificially excluded, and whose humane values ought to supplant the abstractions of politics. Yet we are constantly being shown – Johnny Boyle's execution,

Sean O'Casey

Molly's death, Clitheroe's death, Nancy Clitheroe's madness – that the family and its ethos cannot resist the intrusion of politics. O'Casey envisages 'a complex dramatic situation, conceived of ideologically in primarily political and economic terms'. But, on the one hand, the plays cannot adequately inspect the complexities. They are obscured by the medium through which they are seen, 'the apolitical family unit'; and on the other hand, the family offers only 'a simplistic and deforming kind of moral consolation'. Within this framework, the 'political' men – 'stupid, vain, egotistical, jargon-ridden . . . to the exact degree that they are involved in politics' – confront the humane women.

The argument works, however, by suppressing actions, and a general quality in the plays, which do not endorse its conclusion: that O'Casey establishes a fake dilemma by sentimentalising one of its terms. In fact, the 'political' – or shiftless – men do on occasion act selflessly: the Covey and Fluther put themselves at risk for Mrs Gogan, and Mollser's funeral; the humanitarian women desert the feelings which are their virtue. The position – no matter if it is at odds with O'Casey's declared loyalties – is that the beneficent human energies are enfeebled once they are brought into an institution; and a movement, an ideology, a family are all equally institutions. It is in this matter that O'Casey and Dickens are often compared.[15] Dickens's novels have savage and frightening families enough, but it is in the family and its individual members that ultimately he rests his faith, a world of Cheerybles and reformed Scrooges. Consider, by way of contrast, his treatment of labour organising itself in *Hard Times*. The Union is only another outlet for self-seeking ambition.

There are similarities in this regard between the two writers. But O'Casey's is a more rigorous logic. His plays do not have a single achieved 'happy family'. The family is every bit as fragile as the political imperatives. The most comprehensive inference from the plays is that nothing works, or at any rate not all the time. The moral, if a moral is what we want, is not, 'love is all you need', but 'love is all you have – and you cannot depend upon it'. It is a perfectly tenable view, however the politically committed mind may judge it, and the plays give it consistent expression. The families fail not because politics invades humanitarian sentiments, but because humanitarian sentiments are in themselves unreliable. Nor does tenement life seem especially designed for or hospitable to the support of family life. 'Puttin' a new lock on her door', Bessie Burgess says angrily of Nora Clitheroe, 'afraid her poor neighbours ud break through an' steal.'

Tenement life in the plays is not, as Deane argues, family life. It is the life of a loosely organised commune, full of comings and goings, animosities and goodwill. Apart from Johnny, a refugee in his home, the most constant and the dominant inhabitants of the Boyle rooms are not the family but the

103

Captain and Joxer. Davoren's and Shields's room receives in quick succession Maguire, the landlord, Minnie, Tommy Owens, Mrs Henderson and Mr Gallogher. When *The Plough* opens the Clitheroe flat is occupied by Fluther, Peter Flynn, Mrs Gogan, and Bessie Burgess. They are each a collective, a unit between the claims both of the family and of society at large. It is not impregnable. It does have the best chance of survival as a unit manifold and with its own integrity.

Seamus Deane remarks that 'there is no point in applying labels (tragic, tragic-comic and so forth) to [O'Casey's] plays'. This is true, but of the possible labels, 'absurdist' is the most easily attachable. In an absurd universe, the universe of Shields's braces, the only community possible is a disorderly house. It is doubtful that O'Casey thought this out consciously as a moral system. The plays unmistakably enact it. 'The whole city', says Fluther, as the British bombardment of Dublin intensifies, 'can topple home to hell.' Toppling, city, home, and hell are the play's points of

10 O'Casey's *The Silver Tassie* at the Abbey, 1972

reference. They 'place' the tenement/commune, which in its fragmenting way stubbornly coheres, withstanding the manifestoes of romantic love and of the grand designs of politics: an aspect, worked through, of Yeats's 'Easter 1916': 'where motley is worn'.

John Arden's 'Ecce Hobo Sapiens' is a close and sympathetic study of O'Casey's ideas of stage design.[16] It supplements the reading of O'Casey given above. Arden draws attention to his constant and precise use of emblematic colours to set a mood, make visual a theme. One thinks of the life of Mary Boyle's green and blue ribbons, of Minnie Powell's 'tam o'shanter of a rich blue tint', of the 'cheap, glittering, jewelled ornament' in Rosie Redmond's hair: obvious enough suggestions, but carefully pointed. They anticipate the more complex naming and showing of colours as O'Casey moved from realism: the grotesque shadings of the battlefield in Act II of *The Silver Tassie* (1928), the church scene in *Red Roses for Me* (1943), lit by green-gold hedge, white rowan, yellow laburnum, purple lilac, the red lining of the Rector's cassock. Arden sees such explicit instructions as drawing elaborately on reminiscences of the heraldry of bronze-age Irish literature – the descriptions of the heroes' accoutrements in the *Tain*, for example; on Christian iconography; and on associations in 'the essential, and sub-conscious poetic core of humanity': a Rose for love, a Lily for sacrifice.

Verbally, the equivalent effects pick from 'mediaeval morality-play, Shakespeare, Bunyan, and Victorian popular melodramas . . . the jokes and word-play of the building site, the street-ballad'. The amalgam constitutes, in Arden's words, a 'mythological landscape of popular imagery'. Theorizing, Marxist or other, has meaning only insofar as it can make itself a part of that landscape, those images, a world, existing in its vernacular observation of itself, of 'flesh-and-blood human beings who do not necessarily run according to predictable rules'. O'Casey's first three plays might be seen as a lament for the failure of Marxism – in particular – to translate itself into the idiom of the slums and the community of the tenement, the most sizeable social unit perhaps capable of political enlargement. Somewhere outside may be a liberating voice. It remains inaudible, or in the Boyle world can be heard only as distorted echo, parody.

The popular view is right, that O'Casey's first three plays are his best. As Brian Friel has put it, until

he was 42 years of age O'Casey's subscription to the Urban Muse satisfied him. They worked hand-in-glove; a perfect coalition. He fairly quivered with excitement when she led him through the streets and tenements of Dublin; and when he transformed those painful experiences into art, he was writing at the very peak of his considerable power. Those remarkable plays were the result: city plays, vibrant with the immediacy and transience of the city, pulsating with accurate and affectionate perceptions.[17]

Eugene McCabe, with good reason, believes that '*Juno* is worthy to stand alongside *The Playboy* and that astonishing work ranks easily with the greatest.'[18] The subsequent plays flounder – in restless, fascinating experiment. O'Casey flounders, one may fairly surmise, because he abandoned his familiar Urban Muse, leaving himself for his landscape, to quote Friel again, 'the globe, his only spiritual nutrition a political creed'. The creed is Marxism, as embodied in O'Casey's views of Stalin's Russia, often conveyed in a crudely propagandist way. The message of the later plays is of hope, of social deliverance perhaps postponed, but inevitable. Still, there is more to be said of these plays than that they are politically more 'positive' than the earlier. Their interest is not their too easily paraphrasable message. It is in their effort to find a refining medium for it, impaired mainly by O'Casey's averting his gaze from 'the landscape of popular imagery', its speech particularly.

This removal was always a danger, perhaps compounded by O'Casey's leaving Dublin to live in England, and as Thomas Kilroy suggests, by 'the hazards of self-education', at least as risky as formal instruction. From the beginning, although then never ruinously, O'Casey was tempted by 'fine writing', around which he stepped with a growing and misguided self-confidence. His love scenes are embarrassing: Jerry Devine's, 'Have you forgotten, Mary, all the happy evenin's that were as sweet as the scented hawthorn'; Clitheroe's, 'little, little red-lipped Nora'. Even Mrs Tancred's grand 'hearts of stone' set-piece is barely convincing. Davoren's high style is parody, but O'Casey's judgment was shaky and did not warn him, for example, of his inflating the crippled Harry's reminiscence of the war in *The Silver Tassie*:

Red wine, red like the faint remembrance of the fires in France; red wine like the poppies that spill their petals on the breasts of the dead men. No, white wine, white like the stillness of the millions that have removed their clamours from the crowd of life.

In the first three plays, however, the Dublin argot remains free of that kind of affectation. It is intact and exhilarating, so extensive that it is difficult to choose from it; but the following is indicative:

FLUTHER (*trying the door*). Openin' an' shuttin' now with a well-mannered motion, like the door of a select bar in a high-class pub . . . It's better than a new one, now, Mrs. Clitheroe; it's almost ready to open and shut of its own accord.

NORA (*giving him a coin*). You're a whole man. How many pints will that get you?

FLUTHER (*seriously*). Ne'er a one at all, Mrs. Clitheroe, for Fluther's on th' wather waggon now. You could stan' where your stannin' chantin', 'Have a glass o' malt, Fluther; Fluther, have a glass o' malt,' till th' bells would be ringin' th' ould year out an' th' New Year in, an' you'd have as much chance o' movin' Fluther as a tune on a tin whistle would move a deaf man an' he dead.

The phrasings and their rhythms were, and still are, current in Dublin, reconstructed from O'Casey's memory. A very different literary use of Dublin cant is possible. As Roger McHugh has pointed out, O'Casey divests it of its banalities, whereas in Joyce's *Dubliners*, 'only the banalities are left'.[19] Each is a variant upon real speech. O'Casey's ascends to what one might call High Cant, incorporating but outsoaring normal usages like, 'You're a whole man'. Fluther cannot say merely that he has given up drink. His expansive denial, alliterative, assonantal, cadenced, retains, while concentrating, the rhythms and idiom of its original. It is an urban equivalent of Synge's language, though closer to an actual popular speech.

The only 'literary' flavour in the colloquial dialogue is in the stream of quotations from and allusion to patriotic oratory, ballads, the poems of Burns, Macaulay, and Thomas Moore, all part of Dublin folk-lore, most evident in Joxer Daly's tag-ends of verse, usually with entirely ironic application. 'Let me', he says of Mrs Tancred's loss, 'like a soldier fall – me breast expandin' to th' ball!' This is very different from the poeticising that in *The Silver Tassie* starts to beset not only more formal speeches like Harry's but the vernacular itself. It falls prey to a stylising urge that runs counter to its nature. The characters here who resemble Joxer and Fluther are Sylvester Hogan and Simon Norton. This is how they talk:

SYLVESTER. I can see him yet. (*He gets up, slides from side to side, dodging and parrying imaginary blows.*) glidin' round the dazzled Bobby, cross-eye'd tryin' to watch him.
SIMON. Unperturbed, mind you, all the time.
SYLVESTER. An' the hedges by the road-side standin' stiff in the silent cold of the air, the frost beads on the branches glistenin' like toss'd-down diamonds from the breast of the stars, the quietness of the night stimulated to a fuller stillness by the mockin' breathin' of Harry, an' the heavy, ragin' pantin' of the Bobby, an' the quickenin' beats of our own hearts afraid, of hopin' too little or hopin' too much.

The language is neither real speech nor a convincing elevation of it. On such grounds, Yeats could have made a case for questioning, though not rejecting, *The Silver Tassie*. It is indeed remarkable that 'a director who wanted poetry in his theatre would ever have turned a blind eye on O'Casey's [Act II] set and haggled about the playwright never having actually been to the front lines himself'.[20] O'Casey has the better of the exchange of letters between him and Yeats, but there was more to Yeats's objections than the foolish one that O'Casey was writing beyond his experience or genuine interest. The important section in his letter of rejection, particularly infuriating O'Casey, is this:

The mere greatness of the world war has thwarted you; it has refused to become mere background, and obtrudes itself upon the stage as so much dead wood that will not burn with the dramatic fire. Dramatic action is a fire that must burn up everything but itself; there should be no room in a play for anything that does not belong to it; the whole history of the world must be reduced to wallpaper in front of which the characters must pose and speak.[21]

Yeats is writing in a very mannered form of words: 'high-flown burblings', Arden calls them; O'Casey, 'the pretentious bigness of a pretentious phrase'; but Yeats is talking, presumably, about the impersonality of art, and O'Casey's failure to achieve it.

It is not clear from his letter that Yeats ever properly accounted to himself for his dissatisfaction. The reasons he gives are unconvincing. He complains that, 'there is no dominating character'. In *Juno* the badly written will supplies a traditional 'plot'. So do the bombs in *The Shadow*. Yeats seems uneasy about its absence in *The Silver Tassie*: Harry Heegan, the athletic hero of Act I, goes back to the front, returns home paralysed by a wound, and in Acts III and IV is (too lengthily) rejected by his girlfriend for the comrade who rescued him from the battlefield. None of this need matter. The real weakness of *The Silver Tassie* is its turgid language, close to self-parody at times. Unlike the songs in the earlier plays, Burns's 'The Silver Tassie' stands out because it is the most assured writing in Act I. The play also fails to ally the rule of farce with the new assertion of a defiant self-salvation: the ukelele's tinkle tinkle in the night-time with Harry's final, 'What's in front we'll face like men!' We disbelieve Harry because his words ring false.

If *The Silver Tassie* fails, it does so only relatively. It is an anti-war *pièce à thèse* whose passion can be made to occupy the stage. Paradoxically, it is at its best not in the familiar local scenes and idiom but in the nightmare landscape and liturgy of Act II and the semi-realistic chants of Act IV:

SIMON. The air'll do him good.
SYLVESTER. An' give him breath to sing his song an' play the ukelele.
MRS HEEGAN. Just as he used to do.
SYLVESTER. Behind the trenches.
SIMON. In the Rest Camps.
MRS FORAN. Out in France.
HARRY. I can see, but I cannot dance.
TEDDY. I can dance, but I cannot see.

Lady Gregory, having seen the 1929 London production, wrote in her *Journals*, 'we ought to have taken it and done our best to put it on'.

The double rejection – by the public of *The Plough*, by the theatre of the *Tassie* – damaged O'Casey. He was never again to offer the Abbey a play. Thus he deprived himself of access to a theatre, whatever its shortcomings, where he could regularly see his work from page to stage. The pattern continued. When the Abbey, after a temporary reconciliation between Yeats and O'Casey, finally produced the *Tassie* in 1935, it ran for a week and caused a public outcry, for the usual reasons. This was also the fate of *The Bishop's Bonfire*, produced by Cyril Cusack in 1955. In 1958 the Catholic Archbishop of Dublin objected to O'Casey's inclusion in the city's Theatre Festival, and *The Drums of Father Ned* was withdrawn. In retaliation O'Casey banned all productions of his plays in Ireland (though he made an exception of the Lyric Theatre, Belfast). His relationship with his home-land was a series of withdrawals on both sides. Mysteriously, he developed no association with any experimental theatre in England, though the leftwing Unity Theatre in London did *The Star Turns Red* in 1940, and The People's Theatre *Cock-a-Doodle Dandy* in Newcastle-on-Tyne in 1949. Equally mysterious, an imaginative analogy of his departure from Dublin, is his abandoning the tenement setting. Perhaps he felt that under the dispensation of the new State its life, like Synge's West of Ireland, was moribund.[22] The subject of *The Star Turns Red* is a proletarian uprising, somewhat resembling the Spanish Civil War, in a heavily allegorised Dublin. Most of the later plays, however, have entirely different settings. The overt allegory remains.

Within the Gates, described as a Morality play, is a parable of moral and political salvation, set in Hyde Park with a host of expressionistically stylised characters. *Purple Dust* takes two fatuous Englishmen to the renovation of a Tudor mansion in the Irish village of Clune na Geera. They symbolise, implausibly, both capitalism, and a foolish romanticism opposed to the heroic stuff of Irish legend; and die in the political and imaginative cleansing of a Deluge. The period of *Oak Leaves and Lavender* is the Battle of Britain, its setting an English manor. Again, it is an apocalyptic fantasy, with the message that the present will die into a new life, as the house is transformed into a factory: the stage equivalent of a propaganda poster. *Cock-a-Doodle-Dandy*, *The Bishop's Bonfire*, *The Drums of Father Ned* all return to Irish villages. They are symbolic celebrations of the Life-Force, sexual, liberated, defeating clerical repression.

All these plays burst into occasional energies of speech. All of them, eventually, die in a programmed didacticism. All of them attempt, O'Casey in his vaudeville, populist way, rather the kinds of staging which Yeats was working with in his more esoteric manner: effects of dance, music, costuming, lighting, and stage design. Both playwrights were perhaps distracted by the glamour of experiment from the essential problem of sustaining a dramatic language. O'Casey's nearest approach to coordinating the two is *Red Roses for Me*, based on the rail strike of 1911 in Britain and Ireland. The play also draws from the Dublin lock-out of 1913 the workers' demand for an extra shilling a week and the savage police attack on an assembly in O'Connell (then Sackville) Street, in which two men died and hundreds were injured. The hero, Ayamonn Breydon, railway worker, strike leader, amateur actor, is loosely modelled on O'Casey. To all appearance, his political activities fail. He puts them above his sweetheart, Sheila Mourneen, who is sceptical of them, and he is killed in the police baton charge. Practically, towards the end, Inspector Firglas holds the stage, almost wins over Sheila, and disperses the loitering mourners. Brennan o' the Moor remains, and to its lovely air sings Ayamonn's song:

> A sober black shawl hides her body entirely,
> Touch'd by th' sun and th' salt spray of the sea;
> But down in th' darkness a slim hand, so lovely,
> Carries a rich bunch of red roses for me.

The shawled figure is Sheila. She is also Kathleen ni Houlihan, Ireland oppressed and Ireland rich in hope. The play shows her transfiguration only in prospect – as, indeed, O'Casey never saw realised in de Valera's Free State the 'Ireland the poets have imagined'. It is a visionary goal, made visible on the stage when Ayamonn exhorts the beggars and homeless, listlessly gathered by a bridge over the Liffey, and the sunset becomes a miraculous panorama of light, touching the 'black an' bitther city' into bright colours, dance, and song. It fades as the sound of marching feet heralds the violence of the final act; but, with the memory of Ayamonn, its prophetic life survives:

2ND MAN. That's the last, th' very last of him – a core o' darkness stretched out in a dim church.

3RD MAN. It was a noble an' a mighty death.

INSPECTOR. It wasn't a very noble thing to die for a single shilling.

SHEILA. Maybe he saw the shilling in th' shape of a new world.

Politically, as before, the people who speak for O'Casey's own orthodoxies are satirised, yet also comic scene-stealers: Mullcanny, a scientific materialist, mouths the theories of his 'Jenersky', Haeckel's *Riddle of the Universe* – 'yous can't do away with the os coccyges'; Roory O'Balacaun is a narrowly Irish chauvinist: 'Ruskin. Curious name; not Irish, is it?'

Yet O'Casey has at last drawn an urban poor whose suffering finds an outlet in a directed and self-aware militancy – the two railwaymen; and in 'a mythological landscape of popular imagery' – the complaints and reclamation of the down-and-outs:

EEADA. Two tiny sixpences – fourpence a head. Oh, well, beggars can't be choosers. But isn't it a hard life to be grindin' our poor bums to powder, for ever squattin' on the heartless pavements of th' Dublin streets!

DYMPNA. Ah. what is it all to us but a deep-written testament o' gloom: grey sky over our heads, brown an' dusty streets under our feet, with th' black an' bitther Liffey flowin' through it all.

Brennan enters and sings a ballad, faintly salacious, of two young lovers. It offends the weary loiterers. Ayamonn defends it, and gradually the drabness gives way to the symbolic dawn:

AYAMONN. There's th' great dome o' th' Four Courts lookin' like a golden rose in a great bronze bowl! An' th' river flowin' below it, a purple flood, marbled with ripples o' scarlet; watch th' seagulls glidin' over it – like restless white pearls astir on a royal breast. Our city's in th' grip o' God!

They sing together, then Ayamonn and Finnoola

dance opposite each other, the people around clapping their hands to the tap of the dancers' feet. The two move around to this spontaneous dance, she in a golden pool of light, he in a violet-coloured shadow, now and again changing their movements so that she is in the violet-coloured shadow, and he in the golden pool.

It is not flawlessly done. The dialogue is embellished with a prodigality of colour that adds unnecessary words to the silent comments of the set. Sheila and Ayamonn too, earlier, fall into the same ornamentation. Her mother, says Sheila, 'chatters red-lined warnings and black-bordered appeals into my ears night and day'. The speech, in short, has not shed the over-reaching of O'Casey's later style. But it holds more securely to a collaboration between linguistic stylising, naturalistic idiom, and ritualistic song and dance. Here again, though now embracing O'Casey's experiments, is the politically turbulent Dublin of the first three plays. In the familiar decaying tenements and streets, we hear the tumbledown argument in Act II between Mullcanny, O'Balacaun and Brennan, also reminiscent of the early plays. A knockabout world, it looks out upon the lyrical hope of Brennan's words closing the play: 'a rich bunch of red roses for me'. For O'Casey, the '1913 strike was the high-water experience and provided the criteria that never left him. Essentially he went on judging all phases of political struggle that followed, in terms of that experience.'[23] *Red Roses* embodies that experience in a record of loss, defeat, and, though deferred, hope. It attempts to give dramatic form not to political analysis but to political vision, and is certainly the closest O'Casey came to achieving other than 'a final spasm of dislocation . . . surrounded by the doomed furniture'.

Yet it is for O'Casey's activating 'the principle of disintegration in even the most complacent solidities' that one remembers the plays.[24] Lady Gregory reiterated that his 'strong point is characterization'.[25] O'Casey had indeed the trick, very much in the way of Shakespeare and Dickens, of inventing characters who seem to resemble the people of our real, primary world. The resemblance is a seeming one. O'Casey's characters exist entirely within the boundaries of the play, whose language and circumstances make up their identity. Captain Boyle has no fore-life or after-life. He is eternally fixed in his 'chassis', made up of the tumbling words, the collapsing paraphernalia, a marvellously integrated theatrical language. It is of the nature of cartoon, of burlesque both in the literary sense and that of American 'burleque.'

Distinguishing between the comic and the ridiculous, between Hogarth and the Italian *caricatura* painters, Henry Fielding remarks, 'it hath been thought a vast commendation of a painter, to say his *figures seem to breathe*; but surely, it is a much greater and nobler applause, *that they appear to think*'.[26] Of O'Casey, as of Hogarth, we may say that while the element of *caricatura* is present, his characters move in a life which places them in a set of ideas, however instinctively realised. O'Casey's is an exaggerated version of life, life as farce with which tragic experience must come to terms. O'Casey's dramatic execution of it enters the values by which it proposes judgments: the frailty of ideals, of humane feelings institutionalised, the 'principle of disintegration'. Lady Gregory is right about the importance of characterisation in O'Casey, but in a way that obscures O'Casey's extensions of character. There is a similar inadequacy in Yeats's opinion that O'Casey falters when he writes 'about people whom he does not know'.[27]

Yeats appears to have meant that O'Casey should write about tenement dwellers in a representational, naturalistic way. As Shaw asked Lady Gregory, 'Why does W.B.Y. treat O'Casey as a baby?' The assumption, which has persisted, is that O'Casey had no means of conveying to the stage either ideas – if he had them at all – or the ways by which, in his own knowledge of political action, ideas inform and express themselves in deeds. The major plays, the Dublin trilogy, are the work of a man of ideas certainly, and of ideas that are fundamentally pessimistic, sceptical about institutions, well aware of the ideas that are supposed to animate them, but in the end imaginatively persuaded by the saving grace, organic and anarchic, of, in his own image, 'life's busy tree'. His humour is in Eric Bentley's understanding of the term, 'gallows' humour': 'The purpose is survival: the easing of the burden of existence to the point that it may be borne.'[28] O'Casey's use of 'the people whom' – and the things which – 'he knew' is to that end. His 'painted stage', like the flatness of Alice's looking-glass, unfolds into shifting dimensions beyond the flatness of naturalism, reflecting and disturbing the proportions of the sensible world. Oddly, the further O'Casey moved, formally, from realism, the more naive became the intellectual content of his plays, the less subversive his treatment of it, and

Sean O'Casey

the further removed from the intention to which the early plays give such compelling dramatic voice. It is the voice whose sceptical interrogation words of O'Casey himself describe:

The world needs more of them – Askers and Seekers and Knockers. Now take that word Knock, that's a fine word – Knock, Knock, Knock. There are many doors in the world that need a powerful Knock.

7. The mill of the mind: Denis Johnston

Denis Johnston, though with Northern Irish family connections, is as much of Dublin as is O'Casey, but his was the prosperous Dublin of a Supreme Court judge's son. He had both the formal education and the early experience of theatre which O'Casey lacked. He read law at Cambridge and, in 1924, at Harvard. In the following year he was called to the English, Irish, and Northern Irish bars. At Harvard, Johnston had become interested in theatre, reading Shaw, and attending all the Boston little theatres he could find. This interest persisted. Around 1925, with Sean O'Casey, he saw Claude Rains in Kaiser's *From Morn to Midnight* at the London Gate Theatre. In Ireland, while a practising barrister, he worked with the Drama League. He acted in Pirandello (1927), Strindberg (1928), and O'Neill (1928); and directed *From Morn to Midnight* (1927) and Toller's *Hoppla!* (1929).

In Johnston's later career, from 1936, he was a BBC script-writer for radio and pre-war television, BBC war-correspondent in Africa, Italy, and Germany; and after the war a professor of drama at various American colleges. Apart from his plays he has written an account based on his experiences as a war correspondent: *Nine Rivers from Jordan* (1953), a book whose richly experimental form is a meditative search for life in the desolation of mass violence. More recently, *The Brazen Horn* (1977) speculates around philosophical and scientific bearings upon a mystical vision of his own.

Johnston's plays – like his biography – offer a kind of mirror-image of O'Casey. Broadly speaking, O'Casey began with realism and turned to experiment. Johnston began with *avant-garde* expressionism and turned increasingly to much more realistic staging. The distinction makes a convenient enough frame of reference, but with Johnston as with O'Casey it requires qualification. His first play, *The Old Lady Says 'No!'* was unequivocally an adaptation of modernist theatre to an Irish subject. Excluding radio and television drama and two adaptations, he has written nine plays altogether. The others are *The Moon in the Yellow River* (1931), *A Bride for the Unicorn* (1933), *Storm Song* (1934), *Blind Man's Buff* (1936 – not included in *The Dramatic Works*), *The Golden Cuckoo* (1939), *The Dreaming Dust* (1940), *Strange Occurrence on Ireland's Eye* (1956), and *The Scythe and the Sunset* (1958). Of these only *A Bride for the Unicorn* and *The Dreaming Dust* continue in the formal experimentation of *The Old Lady*.

Denis Johnston

The Old Lady Says 'No!' was submitted to the Abbey under the title *Shadowdance*. Yeats told Johnston of his two objections to it, that the scenes were too long and – after a pause – that there were too many scenes. Lady Gregory expressed distaste.[1] The play came back to its author with the words that became its title as a notice of rejection. Thus it was the Gate which on 3 July 1929 brought to life Johnston's first play.

The playlet which opens *The Old Lady* is part of a non-existent melodrama about Robert Emmet, his failed rebellion of 1803, his memorable speech from the dock at his trial; and his love for Sarah Curran. The point of its language is its outworn grandiloquence, a way of speaking that no longer carries conviction. Johnston put the sequence together 'almost entirely from lines by Mangan, [Thomas] Moore, Ferguson, Kickham, Todhunter, and the romantic school of nineteenth-century Irish poets'.[2] He then sets it into a mosaic of manners of speech in his contemporary Ireland, Dublin mainly, literary, political, and colloquial.

11   Denis Johnston's *The Scythe and the Sunset* at the Abbey, 1981

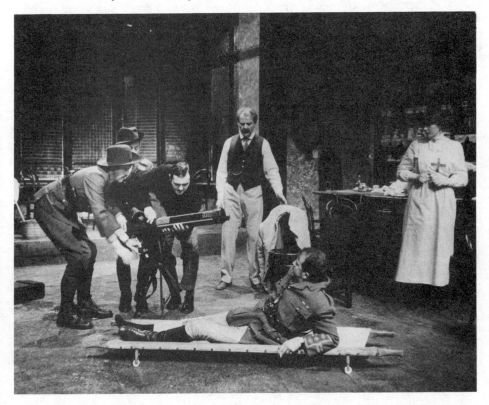

In the playlet, as Emmet and Sarah are taking a romantic farewell of each other, Major Sirr, the villain, enters to arrest Emmet, who is accidentally knocked out. We are admitted to what is going on in his unconscious mind, and the play proper begins. The Emmet-figure, now called the Speaker, makes a progress through twentieth-century Dublin. He is variously an actor – 'Perhaps he acts for the Civil Service Dramatics'; an actor who knows that he is cast as Emmet – 'I can't even remember my lines'; and believing that in fact he is Emmet – 'We know only one definition of freedom. It is Tone's definition; it is Mitchell's definition; it is Rossa's definition.'

These roles are not rigidly segmented. When, for instance, the Speaker sees the death of a young man whom he has shot, and says, 'I am only a play-actor', he is commenting in a sense on the real Emmet that he was merely posturing over ideals and their violent execution. Acting and the stage become a metaphor of self-indulgent politics exploited for their histrionic satisfactions. Not even the delusions/illusions are reliably stable:

OLDER MAN. He comes here and says he's Robert Emmet, and where are his boots? . . .
SPEAKER. I don't know . . . I thought they were . . . I see your point . . . I . . .
VOICES. Well?
SPEAKER. Perhaps I had better explain. You see . . . someone took them from me when I was playing Robert Emmet and . . .
OLDER MAN (*with heavy sarcasm*). Oh so you were *playing* Robert Emmet. A play-actor are you? Some of this high-brow stuff I suppose.

Absurdities multiply as the parody-quester encounters the banalities of 'liberated Ireland'. It presents both indifference to and debasements of his own ideals. The platitudes of modish life occupy a Flapper and her boyfriend: 'Do you like my nails this shade? Heart's Despair it's called' – compare, 'my heart bleeding for my country's woes'. All the talk of Bernadette and Carmel, in the accents of plebeian Dublin, is of 'the fellas'. The Flower Woman drinks, brawls, and, obliquely, pimps. Kathleen ni Houlihan is broken down into images of futility. The statue of Grattan, played by Major Sirr, is frustrated by the life he sees from his pedestal in College Green; and in an O'Casey-like tenement room, a young man still declaims, 'Up the Republic!'

This swirling collage does not represent glorious past *versus* squalid present, though there is perhaps a note of lament for squandered innocence, self-deception exposed. The play dramatises an instance of history's trick of repeating itself in an unprecedented, unforeseen idiom. The following excerpt epitomises something of the method:

Denis Johnston

SPEAKER (*commencing to act again, at the top of his voice*). Their graves are red but their souls are with God in glory. A dark chain of silence is thrown o'er the deep. (*. . . The gauze parts. Headlights of motor cars. A policeman with a white baton is directing the traffic, while behind him upon a pedestal stands Grattan with arm outstretched. He has the face of Major Sirr.*)
SPEAKER (*. . . fiercely accosts a Passer-by*). Do you hear? Awake!
PASSER-BY (*politely disengaging himself*). Sorry. The banks close at half two.

The passer-by's pursuit is entirely at odds with Emmet's ardour; as their manners of speech are at odds. *The Old Lady* is testing the mettle of Mangan-ese. The audience needs no intimate knowledge of its practitioners. While some allusions in the play draw upon local lore, Mangan-ese is standard nineteenth-century versifying, and the opening playlet fully exemplifies it. The subsequent action punctures it with contemporary Dublin vernacular, though that is not held up as an admirable model either. *The Old Lady*, in one formulation, is setting rhetorics against one another as a means of enquiry into the sentiments they are used to express.

Imitations of common speech occupy the stage. But some of Johnston's imitations are of other literary imitations. The Blind Man picks up his speech from Synge: 'Asking the way of an old dark fiddler, and him tip-tappin' over the cold sets day in and day out with never sight nor sign of the blessed sun above.' A tenement-room houses the dialect of the Boyles and Joxers. The play poises us between the Older Man's, 'bloody words. You can't change the world by words'; and the Younger Man's, 'What other way can you change it? I tell you, we can make this country – this world – whatever we want it to be by saying so, and saying so again.' As it began, the play ends with borrowed words, spoken by the Shadows, from 'some of Dublin's greatest contributors to the World's knowledge of itself';[3] and, in its final passages, draws upon Emmet's speech from the dock, the resurrection thesis of the Litany, and the Commination service of the Anglican church. Words have the last word, but they gesture towards positions rather than fix the play in a stance.

The Old Lady recognises that human discourse may include, 'you'll do the hell of a lot, ma . . . in me eye!' as well as, 'Was ever light of beauty shed on loveliness like thine!' The satiric intent and the designing of the language are inseparable. The characteristically modernist device of parody, linguistic burlesque, realises and embodies the satiric attitudes. *The Old Lady* is a remarkably effective blending of an invention which looks to cosmopolitan sources and a content which is parochial. The parochial, unlike the provincial, has an assured sense of its identity, and can more readily lead to universal implications.

For all its innovativeness, *The Old Lady* is the most Irish of plays. Unlike its ancestral *casus belli* (*The Playboy* and *The Plough*), it offended not just by attacking received 'Irishryness'. It was out to domesticate novel forms of statement. The new voice was Irish, but with, so to speak, a Continental accent. *The Old Lady* was shocking in its reversals of orthodox sentiment. It also, in ways more manifest than Synge's ritualisations of language, took up with a strange dramaturgy and made the stage itself an alien scene.

Some of Johnston's own statements about the play suggest a natural impatience about having it unequivocally labelled by genre. So in the Preface to the 1960 Cape edition of his plays, he refers to *The Old Lady*, as 'an expressionist gesture of dissent.' His Introduction to the play speaks of 'its expressionist tricks'. But the 'Note on what happened' (1929) includes a firm disclaimer: '*The Old Lady Says "No!"* ' is not an expressionist play and ought never to have been mistaken for one.'[4] Johnston has also claimed that the play's 'actual foster-parents are neither Evreinov, O'Neill nor Georg Kaiser. The two plays to which this experiment does owe something are, firstly, Kaufman and Connelly's *Beggar on Horseback* – a superb piece of American expressionism that I have always admired – and secondly, a Continental satire called *The Land of Many Names* by Josef Capek.'[5]

It is possible to reconcile these apparent discrepancies. A play drawing on 'expressionist tricks' need not be a thoroughgoing expressionist play. But *The Old Lady* is so charged with expressionist contrivances that the distinction may seem only a quibble. The technicalities of expressionist presentation, too, were more than a strictly methodological sabotage of conventional stagecraft. Like Joyce's and Eliot's underminings of traditional forms, they enacted the disjunctions, elisions, *dérèglements* of consciousness; and politically symbolised the revolution against bourgeois society.

These were, nonetheless, purely theatrical procedures, amenable to other imaginative dispositions: it is thus that Johnston applies the expressionist lesson. *The Old Lady* incorporates the fluidities, the disruptions, the intricacies of lighting effects, the phantasmal 'dissolves', of the expressionist stage, supplanting plot and sequential narrative. But Johnston transposes these to an unmistakably localised Dublin, far different from the indeterminate settings of expressionism. His divergence, essentially, is from the generally oppressive solemnity of the Ur-expressionists.

Johnston's renunciation of his imputed foster-parents comes out of this ambivalence. One would need an imaginative ear to pick up, in *The Old Lady*, even remote echoes from *From Morn to Midnight*, though both do indeed turn upon a journey. And despite Johnston's acknowledgment, *Beggar on Horseback*, a comedy with some not exactly tigerish satire, is no more likely a forebear. As most of *The Old Lady* may be taken to be the actor's/Speaker's/Emmet's hallucinations, so a large part of *Beggar on*

12 Denis Johnston's *The Old Lady Says 'No!'*, at the Peacock Theatre, 1929, with Micheál MacLiammóir and Meriel Moore

Horseback is the hero's dream. But the Kaufman/Connelly play works on a standard Broadway plot: struggling young composer finally gets the right girl. The elaborately staged dream anticipates the 'dream-sequences' of innumerable Hollywood movies, and has about as much substance. *Beggar on Horseback* is a straight 'romantic comedy' which its authors dolled up with a battery of, it is fair to say, 'expressionist tricks'.

Johnston's achievement in *The Old Lady* is to have secured a ground between Kaiser's stodge and Kaufman/Connelly's froth. In *The Old Lady*, comic deflation, rather than earnest Angst, identifies extravagances of serious concern. The structure, though intricate, is lucidly articulated. Associations of mood and theme, a consort of antiphonal forms of speech, a complex apparatus of stage design, replace naturalistic sequence or narrative. The reassurance of the solid and identifiable properties in the opening playlet recedes into expanses of light and shade, gauze, drumbeats, fugitive sounds and settings.

Johnston's next work, *The Moon in the Yellow River*, is to all appearances, and unexpectedly, a much more orthodox piece. It deals once again with the character of the new State, now in a manner agreeable to the realist style of the Abbey, which accepted the play. It had begun as a consciously undertaken parody of 'the Abbey play', creating parts identifiable with Abbey players, and echoing some celebrated dialogue: Captain Boyle's 'the last of the Mohicans'; in 'take away this cursed gift of laughter and give us tears instead', Mrs Tancred's 'take away our hearts of stone'; *The Plough*'s 'That's not playing the game.' But parody yielded to Johnston's subject.

In 1925 the Free State government authorised the construction of the Shannon hydro-electric power plant under German supervision. Its purpose was to speed industrial development, and more important to symbolise for the people the energies of independent Ireland, the herald of an end to the exhausting divisions of Civil War. There was widespread opposition. Republicans did not recognise the new government nor any of its undertakings. The foreign presence was unwelcome. The values of rural communities were being undermined.

In *The Moon*, Johnston looks at these contentions but shifts the power house to the mouth of the Liffey and has his feckless die-hard, Darrell Blake, organise an attempt to blow it up. The action takes place in a former fort, now occupied by Dobelle, a retired railway engineer; his sister, Aunt Columbia; Blanaid his daughter; Agnes, a servant, and her son Willie. Like an O'Casey dwelling, it harbours spasmodic visitors, notably George, an engaging and cultivated ne'er-do-well, and his Cockney friend, Potts. For some eight years they have been building in their quarters a cannon and the shells to fire from it: because, according to Dobelle, 'every time the people try to be free and happy and peaceful . . . somebody comes along and stops

Denis Johnston

them with big guns . . . [George] decided to make a big gun for himself so that the next time the people won't be so badly off'.

On the night planned for the attack, Dobelle is visited by Tausch, the German engineer in charge of the project, and by Blake and his band. Rain has damaged the Republicans' explosives, so they decide to use the cannon. It fails to work, but Tausch has summoned Free State soldiers, one of whom, Lanigan, a former comrade, shoots Blake dead. Act III revolves around a discussion of the morality of these events, until the drunken George and Potts, disposing of a shell, quite accidentally blow up the power house. Accompanying these political agonies are Agnes's concern, with which the play opens, over the three-day labour of Mrs Mulpeter, the birth of whose child is visually announced in Agnes's window opening of the final curtain; and Dobelle's reconciliation with Blanaid, whose birth had killed her mother.

The set, 'shockingly untidy', incorporating relics of the fort's war-like past – and a toy railway – is within earshot of the river traffic and the throb of the power house's 'mechanicalisms', suggesting, in Harold Ferrar's words, 'the clash of modernity with an Ireland clinging to her past . . . a central conflict of the play'.[6] Within this scene the actors deploy the moral commentary on the action. Tausch, representing inter-national industrialism, is a Teutonic mixture of pragmatism and sen-timentality, playing to himself at night, 'the melodies that we are fond of [to] bring back to us . . . the mountains, the lakes, the wife and children that one loves'; and defending the power house with quotation and statistic: 'As Schiller tells us, freedom cannot exist save when united with might. And what might can equal electrical power at one farthing a unit?' Dobelle, a cynic now, withdrawn from practicalities, warns Tausch in a powerful speech that the Irish nightmare will assail his tidy orderings of life:

DOBELLE. Have you ever heard of the bogey man, Herr Tausch? Well, here we have bogey men, fierce and terrible bogey men, who breathe fire from their nostrils and vanish in the smoke.
TAUSCH. You have what?
DOBELLE. And we have vampires in shimmering black that feed on blood and bear bombs instead of bats. And enormous fat crows that will never rest until they have pecked out your eyes and left you blind and dumb with terror.
TAUSCH. Come, come, Mr Dobelle.
DOBELLE. And in the mists that come down from the mountains you will meet monsters that glare back at you with your own face.

When the nightmare begins, it savours strongly of farce. George and Potts, amiable, inconsequential, drink to Potts's dead wife and quarrel idly about the technicalities of the gun. Willie is a blundering incompetent. The explosives are useless. So in its turn is the gun. Blake is to an extent playing with violence – 'tonight I am Dick Deadeye, the boy burglar!' He is flippant, but under the flippancy intent on his aims: 'Across the yard behind that parapet. And then you're to train the muzzle very carefully through one of these loopholes on to the roof of the turbine house. Now, do you understand me? Because say so, for God's sake, if you don't.' With the gun's failure and Lanigan's arrival, Blake reiterates his determination to destroy the works. Words turn to the effectual deed:

BLAKE (*as he plays*). Oh, Willie. Next parade will be the day I come out. And do see that the stuff isn't damp the next time. (*singing next verse*)
> And Li-Po
> Also died drunk
> He tried to embrace a Moon
> In the Yellow River.

TAUSCH. This is no country! It is a damned debating society. Everybody will talk-talk-talk-

BLAKE (*rising after a flurry of chords*). Died drunk! A pleasing thought. But needing a Nero to do it justice. *Qualis Artifex pereo.*

TAUSCH. But nothing ever happens.

(LANIGAN *without any demonstration shoots* BLAKE *dead. The latter falls with a little sigh of surprise. . .*)

Blake's death, Lanigan knows, will lead, in some future act of reprisal, to his own. The illusive moon will claim its victims. The cycle of murder and revenge will continue. Lanigan, all glamour gone, is a functionary, haunted by necessity, deprived of words to sanctify his actions. 'I'm not trying to explain', he tells the outraged Tausch, 'I don't know why;' but, 'it's my help you're always telephoning for before the end'. 'So', he says, 'shot in an attack on the works, is my report.' We might ask with Tausch, as he insists on having Lanigan arrested for murder, 'What joke is this?'; and ponder Dobelle's verdict: 'Lanigan is just yourself. He is your finger on the trigger . . . before you denounce him, I say you must give me an answer to what he has said. And you won't do that. Because there is no answer . . .'

The joke, the pun, the paradox, trick question, trick answer, by showing how easily accident may distort essence, outline the boundaries within which moral judgment must pick its way. Aunt Columba, a zanier Luddite than Blake, questions Tausch:

AUNT. Herr Tausch, if you call its tail a leg, how many legs do you say a cow has got? . . .

TAUSCH. If you call its tail a leg? Well, five, I suppose.

AUNT. Wrong, four. Because calling its tail a leg doesn't make it one;

and Tausch to Blake:

Revolution! What do you mean? That is just a word!
BLAKE. A beautiful word. So few people appreciate beautiful words nowadays;
and Blanaid to Tausch: '[my father] calls me a little slut, but I think it's
calling people things that makes them it, don't you?' The power of words:
words name objects and actions, either may validate the other. So who is
right, Blanaid or Aunt Columba?

The statement of the play is in part that words may be used to distort
rather than define actualities. For some, calling a tail a leg will make it
so. Words have a manipulative power, magic either black or white. In the
sphere of Tausch and Blake, deeds require the sanction of the words for
abstract ideas, however warped the connections between the two may
have become. Lanigan, although he is not himself an adept, is a product
of the words which have made him a gunman – Blake's words: 'It was he
that always had the wit to find the words for these things.' For Blake,
Lanigan, Willie, and Tausch the sequence of offence, retribution,
reprisal is unbreakable: as the toy train goes on its endless, predestined
circle.

The play does enshrine a small victory. Out of the deaths – of Blake, of
Blanaid's mother, of Potts's wife, prospectively of Lanigan – comes the
union between Blanaid and Dobelle. It is unsentimentalised. Blanaid asks
little; Dobelle retains his belief in the power of evil, the inevitability of
violence, suffering, the uncertainty of 'right' and 'truth'. What salvation
there may be is a personal one. The light of the new day, at the end, shines
upon Agnes and upon the sleeping Blanaid and her father. In the world
around them, nothing has been resolved. The brutalising energies of Irish
politics, and indeed of the European politics of that era, will take their
course. 'What', as Yeats asked, 'if the Church and the State / Are the mob
that howls at the door?'; and as appositely, 'More substance in our enmities /
Than in our love.' On the stage of *The Moon* conflicting political ideals can
reach no stable outcome. On the periphery of these ideals individuals may
arrive at a limited understanding. Ostensibly a realist play, *The Moon* brings
to eye and ear a delicate symbolism of décor and language.

Three of the later plays form a group of intelligent *pièces à thèse*. These are
Blind Man's Buff, loosely adapted from Ernst Toller's *The Blind Goddess*
and substantially reworked as *Strange Occurrence on Ireland's Eye*; and *The
Golden Cuckoo*. Based on law cases, they scrutinise the fragilities of the jury
system and the disasters which judgments satisfactory in law may inflict
upon individuals. The popular success of the first two owed much to their
well-timed dealings in revelations, their sardonic eye for the Dublin legal
profession, and the histrionic possibilities of a murder trial – familiar
ground to Johnston. None of these plays where the law supplies the
dramatic structure fully engages Johnston's curious blend of clearheaded-

ness and mystical questioning. Looking back on his travels from the River Jordan, he says, 'The milestones of this journey are like the footsteps of the race. In some odd and rather mystical way they seem to parallel the course of life itself, from childhood to maturity – a journey, maybe, in search of its own meaning.' The 'law plays' do not gain access to the 'odd and rather mystical way' of transfiguring solid actualities into symbols which under-mine the sufficiency of the physical, the circumstantial, the apparent. The last play of this kind, *The Golden Cuckoo*, again based on a real case, makes a closer approach.

Mr Dotheright, a harmlessly outstanding eccentric in a gallery of (mainly) harmless eccentrics, denied a fee he thinks is his due, stages a personal rebellion against injustice. He smashes the glass door of the local post office and declares 'a Commonwealth where men shall be given to dignity, and not Dignities to men . . . Revolution! Revolution!' He is arrested. The law acts, in its view, compassionately, but with no compre-hension of the real issues. Dotheright is sent, like Beckett's Murphy, not to jail but to a lunatic asylum, where, like Murphy, he finds a society he prefers.

Dotheright balances delicately on a fine line between delusion and sanity:

DOTHERIGHT. Indeed, you will be interested to hear that one of my closest friends is the Archbishop of Canterbury.
PADDY. You don't say? . . .
LETTY. Well perhaps – in a way –
DOTHERIGHT. Like the rest of your world, you believe that you can distinguish the real Archbishop from the false one. But it is harder than you think.
PADDY. By God, he's right. We're all imposters. Every one of us.
DOTHERIGHT. Excuse me, my friend is not an imposter, whatever the other gentleman in Canterbury may be.

It is deliberately made difficult to place Dotheright on a consistent set of premisses. 'He *is* crazy. It's the literal truth', Penniwise says of him. Among the powers *The Golden Cuckoo* brings to court are the 'literal truth' and the power of the words that play around its definition.

Dotheright, on whom the play depends, is a superb portrait of the saintly Fool. 'As a saint', he says himself, 'I am a failure. But as a Madman – ah, there at least, I am in the forefront of the field.' Either or both, he creates the circumstances of his own destruction, which he then, in his peculiar way, survives. Here the law is not satirised. It is made to seem irrelevant, and with it the institutions of State which it represents. Johnston's quest is among words and the sanctioning of institutions, by historical experience, almost obsessive Irish concerns. *The Golden Cuckoo*, much the best of Johnston's 'law' plays, takes them into a remarkable union of allegory and realism.

Where *The Golden Cuckoo* draws unobtrusively upon allegory, *A Bride for the Unicorn* is a fullblooded, modernised Morality, a kind of bride for *The Old Lady*. It uses similar expressionist/surrealist methods. Its twelve scenes – four in Part I, eight in Part II, played on two stage levels (a much more elaborate machinery is possible) – dissolve each into the next by means of lighting, movement, mood: a parodied College graduation to the mystical encounter of the hero, Jay, with a Masked Lady; cocktail bar to a nightmare onslaught by the Sins of the Fathers; a law court to a battlefield. Any particular Irish setting has vanished. These scenes present the humdrum purgations in reality of Johnston's Everyman: Jay. Through them, surviving them, he achieves the 'exultation' of reunion – is it in death? – with the Masked Lady. Joyfully, he sees her face, unrevealed to the audience.

Part I of the play draws in the scene with Psyche on light, romantic comedy, the Stock Exchange sequence on the drama of social conscience. The first scene of Part II is an O'Neill-like collage of non-realistic dialogue, interior monologue and stage directions, all spoken by the characters. The patrons of the cocktail bar talk a Noel Cowardly prattle. Johnston's collation of these theatrical styles, the intervention of his own varied diction, and the effects of mime, dance, song and music constitute his own quest for a form which would embrace a sacred drama lodged in a secular, temporal world.

A Bride for the Unicorn aims high, has enthralling moments, and remains a vexing play – to its audiences as to its author, who has constantly revised it.[7] Yet it has an audacity which carries its excesses, so that we persist in the quest to its triumphant Coda:

> Over the far horizon lies a cave,
> And in the mouth, a rock of massive stone
> Guarding the sepulchre in which he sleeps.
> There, all that has been is for evermore.
> Save us, O Phoebus, from the fear of Endings!

Like *A Bride for the Unicorn*, *The Dreaming Dust*, also in Johnston's experimental vein, makes play with interleaving theatrical forms. It opens with the players who have just presented 'The Masque of the Seven Deadly Sins', unmasking as they enter: Pride, Anger, Envy, and so on. The year is 1837, the setting St Patrick's Cathedral, Dublin, of which Jonathan Swift was Dean from 1713 to his death in 1745. His voice, an eerie whisper, begins to intrude upon the players' conversation, and at the instance of the 'present' Dean they enact scenes from Swift's life: seven actors in search of that enigmatic character.

Johnston's interest in it began with the puzzling relationship between Swift, Stella, and Vanessa. His controversial theory is that marriage between Swift and Stella was impossible because it would have been incestuous, a solution argued in his biography *In Search of Swift* (1959). Nineteen years earlier, the first version of *The Dreaming Dust* had dramatised the hypothesis, and by all acounts schemed it too mechanically around the revelation of 'the answer'. It explains much that otherwise seems very odd in the continuation of the Swift/Stella/Vanessa triangle. But as Johnston came to see, Swift is not bounded within that geometry, important though it is.

In the final version of *The Dreaming Dust*, the Dean takes the part of Swift and the Masquers those of members of his circle in England and Ireland, ranging 'over many years during the first half of the eighteenth century'. The doublings are intricate. Pride, for instance, is the allegorical figure, the actress who has played it in the Masque, and in the episodes from Swift's life takes the part of Stella. Anger similarly melts into Vanessa. They also stand back from their assumed roles to halt and comment upon act and motive.

Each of the actors advances an interpretation of Swift, dictated by the nature of the Sin he has represented. None is 'wrong'. Each is incomplete. Swift's protean shapes elude simplifying definitions. Somewhere between the players' views of him and his place among the Deadly Sins resides the whole, contradictory man. As Johnston presents him he is a tragic hero whose stature embraces both the corrupt grandeur of the allegorical Sins and the pettiness of human shortcomings. He is a hero who is also Everyman, his flaws a necessary part of his greatness, prey to all the ills that flesh and soul are heir to.

'Who is it that can tell me who I am?' asks Lear. At the end Swift makes his answer:

SWIFT. 'I am . . . that I am.'
(*He sinks back into his chair. The choir appears, passing in front of Swift's chair, where they pause and turn stage right*).
A VOICE (*chanting off*). May the words of our lips and the meditation of our hearts be always acceptable in thy sight, O Lord, our strength and our redeemer. The Lord be with you.
CHOIR. And with thy spirit.

It is a cry for acceptance, compassion, forgiveness, beyond biographical or psychoanalytic speculation.

The development of the *Dreaming Dust*, surreal, fragmented, multiplying roles, itself represents Swift, the consummate Masker: as Drapier, the political pamphleteer, behind Gulliver the ventriloquist of points of view, in *A Modest Proposal* the bland, bureaucratic voice advocating horrors. Above all he is to be seen, though harbouring genius, as the common clay, whose frailties and suffering touch the audience to fellow-feeling. Johnston's heroes must work their way through, and to the end retain something of, their doubts, irresolutions, imperfections of act and motive. The last play Johnston has written, *The Scythe and the Sunset*, returns to the theme, and to a realist presentation of it. The title is a parody of O'Casey's *The Plough and the Stars*, but the play is a counterpart to, not a debunking of, O'Casey's anti-war treatment of the Easter 1916 uprising.

Like O'Casey, Johnston admits an anti-heroic reading of the event – its incompetence (on both sides), its farce, and also its innocence: from the frivolous Dr MacCarthy's comment on the celebrated occupation of the General Post Office – 'Maybe they just want to buy some stamps' – to Roisin's description of her boyfriend Maginnis's contingent as 'the Flyboy Fusiliers . . . You'll be a gineral with that lot before yer brother's a serjeant in the Munsters.' Many Irishmen belonged to the Munsters, and other British regiments, and Ireland in 1916 on the whole supported the Allied cause. Tetley, the play's idealistic rebel, calls Dublin's derisive response to the uprising, 'that murderous Irish laughter'. This sardonic comedy characterises the first part of the play, which turns, however, as Joseph Ronsley has remarked, from the 'motley' to the 'terrible beauty'.[8]

The significance of the rebellion is elicited mainly from the interplay of feelings between Tetley and Palliser. The latter is an Anglo-Irish officer in the British Army, taken prisoner early in the action after an inept cavalry charge on the Post Office, and, diffidently, held prisoner in the squalid café hardby where the play unfolds. Palliser is an advocate of Empire, but insists equally on his Irishness. He prides himself on being a professional soldier, though as his own ludicrous sortie confirms, that need not mean much in the British Army of 1916. Tetley nevertheless feels a certain deference – 'a damned amateur' he calls himself, unable to assemble a captured machine-gun – 'I got my military training in the Board of Works.'

He is assured enough in Act I, when some kind of success is still possible. It is a short-lived hope. Tetley receives its disappearance with a realism and dignity which begin to move him and Palliser to a common respect, conceding to each other's point of view only a fuller recognition that it exists. As Palliser had been astute enough to advocate ridiculing rather than martyring the rebels, Tetley now, by degrees, sees his surrender and execution as a fruitful political act – 'What matters to me is that this week can be turned from a disgrace into a triumph – that all our mistakes and incompetence can be made of no importance whatever by giving ourselves up to some fool of a general.' Their martyrdom will transcend their follies. He suspects his fortitude – 'will the stomach turn to water?' – and is doubtful that his motive is 'for my country and for my people, and not just for my own satisfaction'.

Palliser recognises an historic inevitability in Tetley's death, which will herald the death of Palliser's world: 'I know what's coming, and there's no hard feelings so long as I don't have to be part of the audience. When we built an Empire . . . we had life and an interest in ourselves. Now we're tired of being what we are.' In acknowledgment of that, and in tribute, he waits to die in the collapsing building. So the lament for his passing, delivered by the mad Endymion, has a working pathetic force:

> The April wind blows cold on royalty,
> Swift, Grattan, Sheridan, Wellington and Wilde,
> Levees on Cork Hill,
> The tramp of crimson sentries in the colonnade.
> No more of Suvla Bay or Spion Kop.
> The bunting under which we spilled our colours on the globe
> Still hang in gaunt cathedrals
> Where no one goes.

Within the large antagonisms, Tetley and Palliser reach a new under-standing of themselves and of each other. Its occasion is a war and the abstract justifications that attend war. Johnston does not justify war. He accepts it as an ineradicable symptom of ineradicable human evil. He also denies that wars never settle anything. 'Of course they settle things. They settled American Independence, and they settled Slavery. They settled Tsarism, and . . . a hard-earned military defeat decided that the Boers should eventually have the whole of South Africa.'[9] The year 1916, in apparent defeat, settled some matters too. That is part of the play's concerns. More particularly, it is demonstrating that war, like any other human activity, may enforce not just suffering and the entrenchment of fanatical abstractions, but moments of spiritual deliverance.

The Scythe and the Sunset is not a Tetley/Palliser debate. Around them circulates a chorus of individual voices. Emer, a Maud Gonne or a Constance Markiewicz, provokes Palliser to setting up the machine-gun, which (an invented incident) she then uses to disrupt a peace parley across the street. Endymion, sometimes lucid, sometimes obscure, answerable to no one, interprets events and the sequels they prophesy. Reminiscent of the Fool in *Lear*, whose last words are, 'I'll go to bed at noon', his exit line is, 'Carriages at midnight'. A pattern of dramas encircles the central one, all encompassed by the public event. It is observed, clearly, with the benefit of hindsight. Yet the hindsight filtered into the play leaves the characters, Palliser and Tetley in particular, in their contemporary conclusions, tentative, not knowing.

The Scythe illustrates once again Johnston's ability to push the realist form to the very extremes of its boundaries. It manages with faultless discrimination, for example, the transitions from repartee, the practicalities of military command, to deeply touching feeling, from prose to economically placed verse. This quality raises the play quite beyond the legislative propositions of a drama whose problems look for redress by Parliamentary Bills. The 'problem play', though it has affinities with some of Johnston's lesser plays, is not a category to which even his realist work, at its best, conforms.

The comparison sometimes made between Johnston and Shaw has greater substance. Both have a high regard for the powers of reason; both write plays that derive from actual social circumstances; both assert comic, deflationary attitudes. Thomas Kilroy has argued, for example, the similarities between *The Moon* and *Heartbreak House*: 'Both plays have this mixture of conventional, mechanical domestic comedy of late Victorian theatre and a kind of visionary, apocalyptic writing, a forward looking consciousness which is however, in both plays, deeply cynical about contemporary progress.'[10]

These similarities exist. Important differences qualify them. Shaw's plays, and even more his Prefaces, have a Bullish air of encyclical infallibility. Shaw, in short, is much readier with answers than is Johnston. Johnston, too, has an unresting sense of not only human imperfection, but of a human imperfectibility – which must be taken into the 'everything' of Yeats's, 'We are blest by everything, / Everything we look upon is blest'. It was also Yeats who considered Poe superior to Whitman and Emerson, because they 'lacked the vision of evil'. We might feel something of the same lack in Shaw, for all his theatrical mastery, and his forward-looking consciousness; but not in Johnston.

A good deal of this casting about is due to a maverick quality in Johnston which resists categories, an irritation to directors and critics. They regret his endless revisings: 'no substitute for writing new plays'.[11] Questions abound: is he experimental or realist? sceptic or mystic? Irish or international? Any consideration of Johnston's career can hardly place him anywhere but in the Irish movement. If he is difficult to place in that, he is impossible to place in the much longer and more secure English tradition. From one point of view, in his variety, his command both of traditional and – very independently – experimental forms, he almost epitomises the aims of Irish Theatre.

That said, one must immediately qualify it. Johnston's experiments are not of the kind that Yeats desired – or at any rate, Yeats did not thus see them. Johnston does not write reverentially of Irish Heroic legend, nor of the peasant. But his subjects, almost without exception, are Irish subjects. He shares the temperamentally Irish double focus on the Irish inheritance and on its modern reshapings. He works within the Irish conviction that artistic imitation – by words, by theatrical enactment – is a defining part of the reality it imitates. Johnston's eyes are directed towards world theatre, and locally towards the scenes and voices which were declaring the social and spiritual morphology of the new Ireland, of which O'Casey said that Easter 1916 was 'the year One in Irish history and Irish life'.

Such pronouncements are within Johnston's parish. His plays evoke, and inspect, myth – not the inherited Irish sagas of Deirdre, Cuchulain, though their stories may supply a commentary. The myths which occupy him are myths in the making, those, consciously promoted, of the new Free State. Its attempt was to consolidate itself, to create images which would give it credence: of effective martyrdom, of an heroic, sacrificial pantheon culminating in Pearse; and drawing too on a bowdlerised version of the legendary warriors. It was a mythology designed to give body to a Gaelic, Catholic, Puritan identity for the new nation; and came close to creating a mirror-image of its Protestant counterpart in the six counties of the Northern state.[12] Johnston's continuing topic is these latterday myths, their distortions, the value of their distortions. Yet his attitude to them is not of easy disparagement. In Johnston's hands, the myths, however corrupt, retain an instructiveness. This immersion in the event as myth is among the most Irish of Johnston's mannerisms of imaginative appraisal.

8. The plays, the players, and the scenes: 1930–1955

(1)

Part of the building taken over by the Abbey had been a morgue. The Gate's permanent home, seating 400 and supported by public subscription, was a converted ballroom in the Rotunda Buildings, associated in Dublin with a maternity hospital. The Gate Company opened there with Goethe's *Faust* on 17 February 1930. The move to the Rotunda was a brave one, and the new arrival was made welcome. But Dublin is a small city. There is no sizeable body of theatre-goers interested in the kind of drama which the Gate's original manifesto proposed: 'To establish in Dublin an international theatre for the production of plays of unusual interest, and to experiment in methods of presentation free from the conventional limitations of the commercial theatre.'[1] As the novelty wore off, receipts declined. Holloway records many but not invariably large audiences for the Gate's first nights. The economics of theatre demands more than that. MacLiammóir remembers financial anxieties coming to a head in 1936: 'we were pouring out a series of productions in Dublin that nobody seemed to want, and the theatre was losing money and Edward was always writing cheques'.[2]

Edward was Lord Longford. Like Martyn before him he was a generous patron, and kept the Gate afloat. 'The lord will provide', said Mrs Hughes, the managing-secretary. Also like Martyn, Longford had artistic and managerial ambitions. On the Gate's artistic policy, essentially 'of producing Tchehov, Shakespeare, and Shaw',[3] he and the two founders agreed. The day-to-day relationship was unhappier. According to MacLiammóir, Longford interfered with casting, and blandly enforced his whim for hiring inexperienced and incompetent amateurs. As early as 1934, Holloway picked up a rumour of 'trouble behind the scenes in the Gate that is likely to destroy it. Those who made it and built it up are being cast aside. It was ever thus.'[4]

In 1936, MacLiammóir and Hilton Edwards were given reluctant permission to take the Company to Egypt. On their opening night in Cairo the irate entrepreneur told them that Longford – without their knowledge – had taken a company to London, where it too was billed as the Gate Theatre. The reunion of the disputing parties in Dublin led to compromise after 'days of fighting and voting, set to a stirring accompaniment of indictment and reproach'.[5] MacLiammóir and Edwards would use the Gate premises for six months of the year as Gate Theatre Productions, Longford for the other six as Longford Productions. The settlement, while amicable enough, intensified the financial difficulties of MacLiammóir and Edwards, which there was neither private patron nor government subsidy to alleviate. Necessarily, they turned increasingly to plays likely to be box-office successes.

The outbreak of the Second World War reinforced this policy. Foreign tours were impossible, and outside their occupancy of the Gate, MacLiammóir and Edwards gave several seasons at the Gaiety, a Dublin theatre of some 1500 seats. This involuntary modification of the Gate's original mandate to itself was not all to the bad. MacLiammóir and Edwards did not wholly default on it; and in any case a diet restricted to 'experimental' drama would be monotonous fare. The Gate's contribution to the Dublin stage was distinguished. Its productions offered an elegant and inventive, often dazzling, imagination to audiences indifferent, in MacLiammóir's view, 'to the pleasures of the eye, of the falling of light upon a beautiful object, of the high notes of two vivid colours in the austerity of a neutral setting, of the peaked and angular grouping in a massed pattern of movement'.[6] The Gate also, although it was not its main purpose, did encourage some new Irish writers, Denis Johnston foremost among them, and salvaged a few Abbey rejects.

Among the Irish plays which the Gate produced were several by MacLiammóir. The best of them, *Where Stars Walk* (1940) and *Ill Met by Moonlight* (1946), are a curious, entertaining mélange of Irish myth and Noel Coward's *Blithe Spirit*. Fairy creatures transported to the modern world meet, in *Stars* a romantic, in *Moonlight* a tragic, destiny. MacLiammóir's plays are an ingenious variant on the English social comedy contemporary with them, or of a decade gone by. They do not advance beyond a fragile charm and a rather preciously witty dialogue. As Robert Hogan has remarked, they were made to work 'on the stage precisely in the way that MacLiammóir wanted'.[7] The Gate, without question, displayed much more directorial panache than the Abbey, but one cannot escape the suspicion that for MacLiammóir in stage design and Edwards in direction, almost any play would serve their turn.

Not all Abbey refusals were ill-judged, and while Austin Clarke's poetic drama *The Hunger Demon* (1930) deserved the Gate's adoption, if only as continuing a rare species, neither it nor T. C. Murray's comedy, *A Flutter of Wings* (1929), is of any durable interest. Nor would either offend the most quivering timidity. At the Gate one would be as likely to see some such interesting new play, a solid classic, a West End success, or a jokey frolic, all equally well served, as 'plays of unusual interest'. MacLiammóir and Edwards chose plays with a wide enthusiasm for what might be made of them.

The Gate's other half, Longford Productions, also varied its offerings, mainly amongst Shakespeare, Sheridan, Shaw, Wilde, Ibsen and Chekhov. Apart from Lord and Lady Longford, it cultivated no new Irish dramatists. Not much need be said of the plays written by the Longfords. They passed their hour agreeably and urged no greater claim. Lady Longford's *Tankard-stown* is typical enough of their quality. Set in Ireland just after the Second World War, it brings together a new breed of managerial Irish whose Free State is justified by statistics, and a more familiar set of gombeen but charming Irish, manipulating the country's luxuries of food and drink, plentiful to English eyes. The English, some romantic some severe, see respectively, idyllic Ireland or the memory of a 'disloyal' neutrality. The Anglo-Irish Colonel Remnant's world is of 'ghosts, you understand. Ghosts of the Irish gentry. Ghosts of the extinct British Empire, sitting upon the grave thereof.' Amidst these conflicts, a young girl finds a resolution of sorts in love for a muck-raking Irish journalist, probably about to be brought into the commercial lures of the 'new Ireland'.

The dialogue ambles along pleasingly enough, neither it nor the intrigue defining a space where the varied themes might speak to each other. Exits and entrances mean that a line of talk has run out of steam. The Longford talents were much on the level of Lady Gregory's, though they took their work less solemnly than their predecessor did hers. The plays are an upstaged version of the Abbey's derided 'kitchen comedy'. They were not of a kind to create a theatrical identity, and although they had a following it was not enough to resist hard economic times.

The mid-fifties brought renewed problems. Dublin Corporation demanded a major and costly renovation of the theatre, bringing Longford Productions effectively to an end. In the sixties the Arts Council paid the theatre's debts, but by then MacLiammóir and Edwards were producing only a couple of shows a year, and no longer maintained a permanent company. A few years before MacLiammóir's death in 1978, a government subsidy was granted. The seasons began again, but the Gate was no longer a shaping force. Perhaps it had raised the expectations and the standards of its audiences. Its praiseworthy achievement is more a concern of stage history than of drama. It was still to the Abbey that audiences looked, frequently discontented, for new Irish playwrights.

(II)

During the Abbey Festival of 1938, the theatre presented Yeats's *Purgatory*. Yeats, much enfeebled, appeared on the stage from which he had vigorously hectored former audiences. At the end of the next year, after Yeats's death, Frank O'Connor complained in the *Irish Times* that by neglecting 'to commemorate the death of the greatest lyric poet of the age . . . the directors have disgraced themselves again'. The two occasions mark not only the end of Yeats's life. They are emblems of the theatre's failure, let alone to generate a verse drama, to become a home for Yeats's own work. Lady Gregory had said that his plays 'will always be, if I have my way, a part of our year's work'.[8] The years just before her death in 1932 had seen the Abbey acknowledge Yeats with *The Dreaming of the Bones*, *The Cat and the Moon*, *The Words upon the Window Pane*, and *Fighting the Waves*. But increasingly the Abbey found small place for Yeats. His last play, *The Death of Cuchulain*, was not staged until 1945, when it was presented by Austin Clarke's Lyric Theatre Company in Dublin.

The very fact that there is dispute over the dramatic merits of Yeats's plays is in itself evidence enough that the Abbey should have been keeping them alive. O'Connor had reason to be critical. Yet as Micheál O hAodha argues, the criticism which he represents was becoming of a 'niggling and negative' kind. Such criticism there had always been. Now, in the enclave of the Free State, it had about it no aura of Great Debate, made passionate by substantial cause, by plays that cried out their own defiance. The forties intensified the decline begun in the thirties:

After Yeats's death, Ireland's neutrality in the Second World War made Irish drama of the period not only neutral but indifferent. This same indifference can be more deadly than the puritanism which usually precedes it . . . There were fewer protests and no riots in Dublin theatres.[9]

The only dispute in the thirties at all reminiscent of past controversies was indeed reminiscent, not new matter: over the 1935 production of *The Silver Tassie*. The critics, the clergy, and religious organisations slated it. O'Casey wrote to the papers. The Directorate split, but with none of the sweep of general principle which Yeats could invoke from particular incident. Brinsley MacNamara resigned, having failed 'to make his fellow Protestant governors, Higgins and Blythe [elected to the Abbey Board earlier in the year], see *The Silver Tassie* with his Catholic eyes'.[10]

O'Connor had been consistently hostile to the Abbey. In 1934, with Sean O'Faolain, he wrote to the *Irish Times* complaining that the theatre was defaulting on its responsibility to discover new Irish playwrights. Its intention to produce new and classical Continental plays was a betrayal of its national being:

In the first place, we doubt that there has been any real slackening of activity among Irish dramatists, and we cannot, therefore, agree that the theatre was compelled to fall back on the revival of old plays . . . In the second place, we consider it bad policy on the part of a National Theatre to set out on a scheme for the production of Continental plays. This is, surely, a pitiable confession of defeat.[11]

O'Connor's argument is interesting and questionable. So was his opinion that novelists might be put to the writing of plays. He wrote some himself. Two were successful, *The Invincibles* (1937) and *In the Train* (1937), the latter based on his own short story. O hAodha attributes their merit to the collaboration of Hugh Hunt, then the Abbey's play director, and regards O'Connor's unaided efforts as 'episodic and undisciplined'.[12] Hunt describes *In the Train* as his 'adaptation of O'Connor's short story'.[13]

O'Connor's dramatic work is certainly a negligible part of his reputation, which rests securely on his short stories. His active interest in theatre was relatively short lived. But he was a man of strong views and determination, and joined vigorously in the Board's endless bickerings, at the time partly devoted to ousting Robinson. However, he did nothing – and in those fallow years it is probably the bleak truth that no one could have done much – to create any new renaissance of dramatic talent. His judgments were erratic. In 1938, in one of the whirligigs of time's revenges, the Board rejected Yeats's *The Herne's Egg* on the nonsensical grounds that it was obscene. In the same year it rejected Paul Vincent Carroll's *The White Steed* because it might offend the priesthood. O'Connor protested, but later agreed with the decision for aesthetic reasons. Carroll, whose previous play, *Shadow and Substance* (1937), had been acclaimed in both Dublin and New York, was understandably incensed. Shortly afterwards, the Abbey turned down a play by O'Connor. What with that and an enthusiasm much abated by continuous and unproductive in-fighting, O'Connor resigned in May 1939.

Details of the Abbey Board's machinations in the period covered by this chapter are of small interest. They arose from a discord of personalities lacking any visionary purpose. The Board was contriving expedients from desperation, not enacting a clear policy, to say nothing of an ideal. The Abbey was in a limbo of insisting on peasant plays (and in its actors on the so-called 'P.Q.' – Peasant Quality), increasingly less well done; and of seeking to augment this repertoire in view of the 'slackening of activity among Irish dramatists'.[14] Between 1931 and 1938 four prestigious Abbey tours of North America were financially gainful, and solved none of the theatre's real problems.

In 1934 Yeats proposed the creation of an advisory committee to the Board. Instead, the number of directors was increased, and assumed 'collective management', that is, consensus by disagreement. A Continental season was bruited, as was the advantage of importing a play director. Bladon Peake, a protégé of Nugent Monck, was appointed in 1934 and his contract terminated in January 1935. Hugh Hunt succeeded him in August of that year. He established good relations with the players, did the theatre considerable service, and resigned, disheartened by constant struggle with the Board, in November 1938. In September of the same year, on Yeats's final departure from Ireland, F. R. Higgins became managing director, a position assumed by Ernest Blythe when Higgins died, at the age of forty-four, in January 1941.

Properly judged, the decline of these years is not to be measured in an absence of new work. There was neither vision nor visionary to dominate the Board. Its malaise affected discipline and enthusiasm in players and directors. Hunt's tenure brought some revival of spirit, and the work of his nominee as designer, Tanya Moiseiwitch,[15] enlivened the Abbey's mournful succession of cottage kitchens. But there was no enduring inspiration, and in the war years no pressure to do more than satisfy large, popular audiences with undemanding entertainment, casually produced. The 'Abbey style' now was to reduce all plays to a common denominator of farcical comedy. It was this complacent shoddiness, not a dearth of plays, which provoked Valentine Iremonger, supported by Roger McHugh, to interrupt a performance of *The Plough and the Stars* in November 1947:

Ladies and gentlemen, just before the show proceeds, I would like to say a few words. When the poet Yeats died, he left behind him to the Irish nation as a legacy his beloved Abbey Theatre, then the first theatre in the world in acting, in production and in the poetic impulse of its tradition. Today, eight years after, under the utter incompetence of the present directorate's artistic policy, there is nothing left of that fine glory. Having seen what they did to O'Casey's masterpiece tonight in acting and production, I, for one, am leaving this theatre as a gesture of protest against the management's policy.[16]

Iremonger's complaint identifies the playing, not the plays.

In fact there were new plays enough. Between 1930 and 1940, 104 new plays were produced. Many were by the older and the more recently established dramatists: T. C. Murray, *Michaelmas Eve* (1932), *Illumination* (1939); St John Ervine, *Boyd's Shop* (1936), *William John Mawhinney* (1940); Lennox Robinson, *Drama at Inish* (1933), *Church Street* (1934); George Shiels, *The New Gossoon* (1930), *The Passing Day* (1936), *The Rugged Path* (1940). Even this much curtailed selection is adequate testimony to a theatre's continuing existence, however inappropriately the theatre dealt with it. It was to the Abbey that aspiring writers continued to send their scripts, and it is unlikely that rejections silenced talent. While there was no new dramatist at the level of *The Irish Review*'s 'explosions', the truly remarkable fact is that noteworthy dramatists did emerge: Teresa Deevy, *The Reapers* (1930), *The King of Spain's Daughter* (1935), *Katie Roche* (1936),[17] Paul Vincent Carroll, *Things that Are Caesar's* (1932), *Shadow and Substance* (1937), *The White Steed* (1939), *Farewell to Greatness* (1966). In this decade Carroll's is the new talent best worth examination, a rebellious, ambitious imagination that never wholly sought itself out.

Carroll was born in 1900 in Co. Louth, the son of a schoolmaster. He trained as a teacher in Dublin and after a brief return to Dundalk emigrated to Glasgow in 1921, where he taught in state schools until 1937. His experience of Irish provincial life was of clerical autocracy and bourgeois pietism and vulgarity. His response to them informs his plays, an outpouring of 'this rebel heart of mine',[18] powerful, but, one feels, halted somewhere between a simple and selective anti-clericalism and the more fundamental questioning of Catholic fidelities which they seem to promise. 'I'm a good Catholic', he has said, 'even if I have little time for the army of little boyish Irish curates who believe in the shamrock and the harp.'[19] The standpoint, a perfectly valid one, never entirely secures itself in the plays against a sentimentalising of their antagonisms. His first play, *Things That Are Caesar's*, comes closest to a persuasive development of its own premisses.

Eilish Hardy, another Ibsenite Nora, is trapped in an odious 'suitable' marriage, engineered by her grasping mother and approved by the local priest, Father Duffy. Father Duffy is the spokesman for the sacraments, more weightily than his delight in 'a good jolly wedding' suggests; and Eilish's father for the humanity which is Eilish's real ethic. As the marriage goes wrong, Eilish picks up the vocabulary of her father, who has said to the priest that he will be 'no party to his huxtering', 'this marriage bargaining'. Leaving her husband and child, she rounds upon her mother: 'She caught us both like mice in a penny trap, robbed us of our heritage that she now prostitutes, put us in a cage, made us mate – .' She is allowed to escape, as in the first version of the play she was not:

FR DUFFY (*slowly*). Woman, I have nothing to give you.

EILISH. Nothing you *dare* give. (*takes off her wedding ring*) On the word of a self-seeking woman, you took that in your hand and called it holy. But it too belongs to Caesar. (*Emotionally, laying it on the bracket*). Take it, then, Sacred Heart, and bury it in the hell you made for wicked things. . . . And now I am free – to find my way.

The incompatibles remain incompatible, with an equal voice.

Carroll's tinkering with the conclusion is a pointer to some indecisiveness. The outcome, either way, does not really enshrine the point. Whether Eilish escapes or remains bound the society which enforces the choice remains intact. Carroll later asserted that Fr Duffy's was an admirable point of view.[20] He is allowed a humane, rational patience:

FR DUFFY. We exist of each other and never of ourselves alone. Union with others is concord, and aloofness is discord. You are fond of Shakespeare. Do you remember that exquisite picture of his on the harmony of the heavenly bodies? – 'There's not the smallest orb that thou beholdest, but in his motion like an angel sings.' There's concord for you. 'Twas Satan began the discord when he said, 'I will not serve.' And Cain followed him up with his defiant, 'Am I my brother's keeper?' Are these two fit apostles for you, Eilish?

EILISH. (*slowly*). You are hardly fair, Father. Satan was a – demon.

FR DUFFY. He was the brightest angel in Heaven. (*There is a pause*). A man the other day called you the loveliest girl in my parish.

Father Duffy is not a caricature, yet our final sense of him is of a dogma insisting on its tyrannical enactment, easier with condemnation than forgiveness.

The central character in the play is the society within whose corruptions, and the oppositions they excite, Father Duffy arbitrates. The play's power is its evocation of hypocrisy, worldliness, and affectations revealed in their inadvertent self-betrayals. Carroll is very good on the defining atmosphere of genteel vulgarity. 'Just as much', says a friend of Julia, offered a whiskey, 'as would conveniently fall off your smallest fingernail.' And Julia herself, steadily declining into drink, hectors the maid who has brought her a small measure: 'And you call that a half? (*She flings it off and gives glass to Alice.*) Here, take it. I never even tasted it. It got lost in the tube leadin' to me ear.'

Peter Kavanagh has said of Carroll: 'He had said everything in *Things That Are Caesar's*, and each subsequent play was but a repetition. The brilliance of his technique was not enough to disguise the superficiality of his thinking . . . Even Carroll's characters never varied from play to play, and those who were unable to recognize the sterility of thought did at least tire of looking at his Canon.'[21] Kavanagh's judgment is severe, but it does seize upon weaknesses in Carroll's imagination. In *Shadow and Substance*, Canon Skerritt is a portrait, intended to be impressive, of a learned, cultured priest, contemptuous of his servant Brigid's visions, and of their credulous acceptance by his curates. Finally, the Canon's care of souls is incapacitated by the very quality of mind, a cold and self-regarding erudition, which is supposedly his distinction. But Canon Skerritt is also a pompous ass, and Carroll never makes us feel that he is essentially anything more, never registers in him a true intellectual substance to mitigate his posturings. Faced with Brigid's demand for understanding, no one comes off well; and the play never focusses the various failures into a set of choices each with its own dynamic power – though that is its attempt. Intellect, pious superstition, sceptical questioning – none of them comes fully to life in its representatives. *Shadow and Substance* sets out to insist upon, and then sidesteps, judgments.

The White Steed further romanticises its satire. The White Steed is that of Ossian, returning after 300 years in Tír na nOg to find his father in an Ireland with 'all the great heroes dead, and swarming with priests and little black men';[22] touching its soil, he dies. It is a dispiriting tale, which Carroll takes as a parable of contemporary Ireland.

The little black men are Father Shaughnessy and the parishioners he recruits as a vigilante squad to enforce his hell-fire morality. There is resistance, some ineffectual as from Denis Dillon, the schoolteacher, enfeebled not only by his spinelessness but by his hypersensitive awareness of it. Father Shaughnessy's real antagonists are Inspector Toomy, spokesman for 'the secular independence I shot men down for and hid in haystacks for, and blew lorries of British soldiers sky-high for'; and Nora Fintry, with her contemptuous, 'No damned generation of clerics will hunt me down. I am a daughter of what was here before you all and a mother of what will be here after you are all gone.'

Nora, child of Ossian, holds to her faith. In the end she vitalises Denis. Shaughnessy's defeat, however, is brought about by Canon Matt Lavelle, restored from the paralysis which had given Shaughnessy his chance and dispensing benevolence and rebuke – 'simple as a dove, but as wise as a serpent'. Canon Matt is a great deal too good to be true, a picture of unshadowed virtue whose inactivity during Shaughnessy's rampaging prepares implausibly for the dénouement. Shaughnessy remains in the mind, a little black man who in the play's fable seems much more likely to oust the Ossian-spirit – as in the original legend – than to be summarily subdued into a happy ending and a utopian vision of 'a wiser and finer Ireland'.

The White Steed has scenes of an ugly intensity, bringing to life the passionate contentions of the characters. Father Shaughnessy, without rant, has a sinister credibility. The disappointment is that Carroll does not realise the latent suggestiveness of these figures in the Europe of 1939. Unlike *The Moon in the Yellow River*, equally and authentically local, *The White Steed* exorcises its demons with a wand facilely waved in a small Irish town. The authoritarian, triumphalist Church and its self-seeking adherents are the centre, which Carroll never wholly displaces, of a 'farewell to greatness';[23] its opponents advocates of a secularised individualism which he never wholly accepts.

Carroll is honourably enough in the line of descent from Colum and Murray, looking at his new Ireland as did they, theirs changing, his consolidating post-revolutionary orthodoxies. Like them, he dramatises scenes of provincial life which at their best enact profound disturbances of spirit. Unlike them, Carroll's most effective line is savage attack, too often confounded by abandoning strong positions. The tensions between, on the one hand, the characters, and on the other between the characters and the developing action slacken. Carroll's people become the creatures of a narrative imposed upon them: in *The White Steed* Nora's union with Denis

139

is unquestionably 'respectable' and the real conflict, between Nora and Father Shaughnessy, is manoeuvred out of sight. Formally, apart from some tentative exercises in fantasy, Carroll is a realist, a craftsman whose stage designs firmly solidify the transparent fourth wall. Beyond it, while we see much that is interesting happen, it casts none of the enlarging shadows of Synge and O'Casey, projected beyond the containing dimensions of the set.

Carroll epitomises, one might say, the best of the kind of self-enclosing realism at which the Abbey had arrived. It is prosaic, documentary, taking place on a stage whose curtains open on a measurable world, quite precisely fitted to the world which it is modelling. Its spaces are occupied by words and movements that ask to be judged by fidelity to their originals in life. The speech is accurately transcribed rather than imaginatively transfigured. Carroll's is not a prose, and in this it is typical, which echoes into a poetic spaciousness. Verse by now, with one interesting exception, was not being attempted. The exception was Austin Clarke. Unlike Gordon Bottomley (1874–1948) the English poet, whose verse plays he admired, Clarke was a considerable poet. Like Yeats – for the most part – he did not transfer his talent to a stageable verse. As dramatic prose was too close to its colloquial origins, verse was too far removed.

Clarke was born in Dublin in 1896 and had a typical enough Irish boyhood of the time, tormented by corporal punishment at school, and in adolescence by sexual guilt. In 1916 he graduated from University College Dublin and the next year was appointed Assistant Lecturer. His first marriage, in 1920, lasted ten days and on the discovery that it had taken place in a registry office, lost him his post at UCD. From 1923 until 1937 Clarke lived mainly in England, reviewing for literary periodicals and acquiring the minor cachet of having two of his novels banned in Ireland. Not until the nineteen-sixties did more substantial recognitions acknowledge his position as a modern poet. He died in 1974, the year in which his Collected Poems was published. The shadow of Yeats, who omitted Clarke from his Oxford Book of Modern Verse, was a long time diminishing over his career. Yet Yeats, and particularly Yeats's plays, fascinated and challenged him from the time of his first visit to the Abbey in 1913.

To re-animate the work begun by Yeats, he with his fellow-poet Robert Farren founded the Dublin Verse-Speaking Society in 1940. Up to 1953 it gave frequent performances of dramatic poems – by Browning, Chesterton, Vachel Lindsay – on Radio Eireann; and between 1941 and 1943 presented three seasons of verse plays, mainly by Clarke and Bottomley, at the Peacock. In 1944 he founded the Lyric Theatre Company entirely for stage performances. Without its own theatre or regular company, it presented bi-annual evenings at the Abbey until 1951 when the Abbey burnt down. Of the twenty-six plays put on by the Lyric, nine were by Clarke, two repeated. The Company also revived Fitzmaurice and gave five plays by Yeats – including first performances of *The Death of Cuchulain* and *The Herne's Egg* – T. S. Eliot's *Sweeney Agonistes*, Laurence Binyon's *Brief Candles*, and Donagh MacDonagh's *Happy as Larry*.[24]

The emphasis was plainly on verse drama. Welcome though it was as an occasional alternative to the Abbey and the Gate, it stimulated no revival beyond itself. The enterprise has a rather fustily revivalist air (Robert Browning, Chesterton, Sturge Moore, Douglas Hyde, Colum's *The Miracle of the Corn*), as of a well-meaning reprise of Yeats's intentions for the Abbey, with no generative power of its own, although Clarke, despite his regard for Yeats's aspirations, was no idolator. His opponent was the ritualism and the solemnity which he discerned as deadening both Yeats's treatment of his subjects and, in their less and less frequent occurrence, Abbey productions of the plays.[25] For both, the problem was to devise a verse at once poetic and dramatic.

In 1957 Robert Frost asked Clarke what kind of verse he wrote. 'I load myself with chains and I try to get out of them', answered Clarke. 'Good Lord', said Frost, 'you can't have many readers.' Clarke's celebrated reply is not a bad description of the intricate knottiness of his poetry, which, among much else, 're-enacts in living English forms the craft and temper of Gaelic poetry'.[26] It is a less promising formula for dramatic verse, in which, as Maurice Harmon has noted, Clarke ignored 'the emphasis in Eliot's plays . . . being essentially a verse dramatist whose lines are meant to read like poetry and not to be disguised as something else'.[27]

Clarke's plays, publication dates and settings are: *The Son of Learning* (1927) – re-named *The Hunger Demon*: a monastery, the Middle Ages; *The Flame* (1930): a convent, the Middle Ages; *Sister Eucharia* (1938): a convent, the present; *Black Fast* (1941): a castle, seventh century; *The Kiss* (1942): a wood, 'last May' – but the piece is a timeless harlequinade; *As the Crow Flies* (1943): the Shannon, seventh century; *The Viscount of Blarney* (1944): peasant dwellings, 'seventy years ago', but only nominally; *The Moment Next to Nothing* (1953): the River Boyne, the time of St Patrick. Typically, Clarke's plays are set in the Celtic Romanesque past, the period from the coming of Christianity to the Norman invasion, roughly the sixth to the twelfth century. They were the great years of the Irish Church, taken by Clarke to represent a nostalgic contrast between 'the Christian, medieval past and the dogmatic, Catholic present'.[28]

Often his plays deal with the mysteries and controversies, sometimes comic, of theological debate, of faith, saintliness, of a pagan and a Christian world. The time, the setting, the matter, as in Eliot's *Murder in the Cathedral*, establish a distance in which the artifice of verse may more easily

Modern Irish drama

win over an audience's normal expectations. It also skirts the problem of a verse which will make itself part of immediate contemporary scenes, though Roger McHugh claims that Clarke is 'especially adept in drawing upon Irish mediaeval material for themes as well as for "objective correlatives" for contemporary problems'.[29]

The Son of Learning: Cathal, King of Munster, betrothed to Ligach, is afflicted by her brother with a hunger-demon whose insatiable appetite ravages the kingdom. The monks of Cork fail to exorcise it. Anier MacConglinne, wandering scholar–poet, arrives at the monastery, runs foul of the Abbot, flirts for no clear reason with Ligach, tempts the demon from Cathal's body and vanishes with it – to Purgatory, according to the Abbot, certainly bearing with him the King's gold collar. A Chorus of beggars and cripples conducts a slow and broken exposition. Farcical monks go about their duties. With the arrival of MacConglinne, the play turns to the disputes between the poet and the monks, traditional enemies, leading in Act III to the centre of the play, a long time in coming, the antics by which MacConglinne expels the demon.

Clarke thought of the play as an exuberant 'throng of merry events'[30] a rebuke to Yeats's solemnity. The Scholar capers around amidst the monks, picks the Abbot's pocket, and there is business with laying tables and serving food. A Fat Brother and a Thin Brother have patter speeches – 'to toast / to roast, to boil, to broil, to baste, to braze, to stew, to simmer, to grill' – which fail because they are not sufficiently inventive. Altogether, the very ordinary jokes and pantomime do not make up for the funereal progress to the climax, which peters out into a series of enigmatic couplets from the beggars. The play must depend, in fact, not on character and action but on words which will beguile the audience into the clash of attitudes between the poet and the monks. Clarke's blank verse, nimble-footed enough in itself, too often derives its momentum by taking off along a side-track. So MacConglinne's account of his intentions becomes a poem on Mannanaun. So too his tempting the King with food and drink is distracted into a tortuous conceit:

> Aye, calving milk that blobs and blubbers down
> The gullet till the first drop cries to the last:
> 'Stop, cur, for by my doggedness I swear,
> O speckled mongrel, that if you come down
> I will come up, for there's no share for two
> Such dogs as us in this dark puppery.'

The serious plays – despite Clarke's objectives replete with ritual – are dramas of belief, of communal discipline against the solitary conscience. In *The Flame*, a novice neglects her tending of the holy flame, both tempted by

142

and distrustful of her own beauty. By re-kindling itself the flame perhaps approves her sexuality – or, it may be, the Abbess's condemnation of it. There are evocatively lyrical moments:

> Never
> To look across Kildare in sun and know
> The far flocks move along the mountain slope
> Before soft cries that drive them until grass
> Is hushed with cloud.

But merely fanciful images clot the movement; 'my sight / has but this flame to lean upon', 'but idle thought is an unknotted thread / forgetful of the needle'. Their purpose is presumably to archaise, to solemnise, the language; their effect is to arrest a situation in moments which have nothing to do with it.

Sister Eucharia, being contemporary, more pressingly invites a response to the demand outlined by Eliot: for a verse compatible with 'people dressed like ourselves, living in houses and apartments like ours, and using telephones and motorcars and radio sets'.[31] However, the subject and the convent setting again insulate the verse against contact with a socially wider vernacular. Sister Eucharia, fasting and predicting her death, converses with souls in Purgatory: delusion, excessive piety, or saintliness? The blandly cautious Father Sheridan, consulted by the Reverend Mother, refuses to hear Sister Eucharia's last confession, and, her arms torn by penitential chains, she dies in the Chapel. How, the play is asking, are the otherworldly claims of spiritual life best to be satisfied nowadays?

The verse has to entertain the anguish of Sister Eucharia's vision. Here and there it does:

> Fear, fear, not faith still holds me down
> With iron arm and pincer, heats the pitch
> Of frenzy, strips me for the martyrdom
> Of shame. The saints are their own example
> And when we die in thought, the senses are
> Our executioners.

It also has to place this idiom in a hostile present of preoccupations and language more mundane, the nowadays:

> Last night, thinking that I had never been
> Professed, that I was still Elizabeth
> O'Connor . . . I hurried from street to street, in coat
> And skirt, with high-heeled shoes.

It is revealing of a failure to create a language that would permit easy transitions from world to world that Father Sheridan, emissary from the life of practicalities, speaks almost entirely in prose.

Clarke experimented widely. In *The Kiss* Pierrot's embrace transforms
Uirgeal from an ugly crone into a beautiful young girl. When the fairy world
reclaims her he thinks of suicide, but contents himself with carving their
names on a tree. Clarke darkens the pastoral with, it would seem, shadows
from the global savagery of 1942, when the play was first produced:

> airmen, flying past the sun
> Through icicles, before the lever drops
> The high explosive, whiteness that never stops,
> Whiteness from which the moon is shining back,
> Although the clouded skies we know – are black
> With horror.

We cannot, however, take those realities with the seriousness they affect in
Pierrot's limpid world of wittily rhymed heroic couplets, where life goes
elegantly on.

Cauth, the orphan girl of *The Viscount of Blarney*, wins a home after
tribulations both real and fantastic, including encounters with the Pooka,
Jack O'Lantern, and a pandering eighteenth-century gallant – 'the Devil
Himself'. As Clarke notes, 'rhyme and end-assonance are used in the play',
prosodic tricks which here he keeps in hand. Cauth is a charming heroine
whose adventures move to song, dance, moonlight, lamplight, the red glow
enveloping the devil, and stop short of authentic nightmare. *The Viscount of
Blarney* is a fast-paced, entertaining trifle, somewhere on the fringes of
Fitzmaurice country, eradicating Fitzmaurice's terrors:

> You're safe now. The lantern went out.
> You were gone but a tick when herself heard you calling.
> I caught up the candlestick, came out to look.
> Don't cry, child. Don't cry. Sure it's nothing at all.

Observing the long interruption of Clarke's poetic career from 1938
(*Night and Morning*), Thomas Kinsella remarks: 'Mr. Clarke would probably disagree . . . pointing perhaps to the continued appearance of his verse
dramas. But I think it has to be doubted if these will enter quite as seriously
into a final estimate of his work.'[32] Nor, one might add, into enhancing the
dismal record of twentieth-century verse drama. Kinsella says of Clarke's
poetry

that the world it deals with, though miniature, is complete . . . The best of the latter
poems – a sustained masterpiece like 'Martha Blake at Fifty-One', the tiny 'Japanese
Print' . . . some of the very latest narrative poems, are notable additions to modern
poetry. They do not stand alone, mere occasional unconnected successes. The body
of Clarke's poetry, flawed or not, constitutes one of the notable modern poetic
careers.[33]

This cohesive reality is absent from the plays. Their verse neither fully establishes their own claustrophobic universe, nor implies present analogies, nor effectively makes itself heard in modulations of common tongues. Despite its occasional successes, Clarke's dramatic verse reinforces the cautionary moral that on the modern stage, prose, not verse, is poetry's host.

This is not to argue that the use of prose is a warranty for the release of poetry, or of drama either. In this period, M. J. Molloy is the Irish dramatist whose work exemplified both the poetry which prose may attain and its dramatically enfeebling self-indulgences. 'Poetic', one asks of his plays, 'or quaintly colourful; theatrical, dramatic design or just conversation pieces'? Robert Hogan says of Molloy's prose that it 'stands midway between Shiels's thinning of the language and Synge's thickening of it . . . a tone lacking in Irish drama since the death of Synge and the early plays of Fitzmaurice'.[34] It is a fair description of Molloy's heredity and of the major enticement of his plays, their speech.

Like Clarke, Molloy has in his mind an historical period which he uses to reflect his image of contemporary Irish life. His best known and best play, *The King of Friday's Men* (1948), is set in 1787 'in the remote and hilly corner where the countries Mayo, Galway and Roscommon meet'. The period represents an idyll of land reclamation by bold pioneering, which savage customs disfigure by an internecine brutality among the peasants and by their subservience in the 'state of slavery'. A large part of the play's theme, in Molloy's words, is 'the feudal mentality'.[35] In the oral tradition of Molloy's own Ireland a rapidly attenuating residue of its ways and customs survived.

Molloy's region is County Galway, where he was born in 1917. Illness put an end to his training for the priesthood. He has spent his life working a small farm near his birthplace, closely attuned to its life, speech, and history. Molloy's is essentially a folk drama, circumscribed by an intense localism which he never makes more widely comprehensible. He is the least exportable of modern Irish playwrights. Synge and Fitzmaurice, to whom he is often compared, write from settings which, although in their origins equally parochial, burst through the constrictions of their time and place. The plays in which Molloy uses the contemporary or near-contemporary scene put him most clearly in difficulties; the nearer he is to the now, the less recoverable is the fascinating then which most fully excites his imagination.

The Visiting House (1946), for example, recaptures an institution now gone but within recent memory. The Master of a visiting house arranged evenings of song, dance, and story telling for the folk of remote country areas when neither cinema nor easy transport existed. In Molloy's play, Broc Heavy's house is the stage for situations dramatised to involve his audiences, amidst the real-life story of his daughter's indecision between marriage and her father's endlessly exciting entertainments. It is a backward look, melancholy and vivacious, authentically elegaic, relating its phantoms to the new circumstances which have robbed them of their being.

By contrast, *The Will and the Way* (1955), set 'in a West of Ireland countryside traditionally accustomed to fend for itself in the matter of entertainment', is at a loss to do much with its period, 'the present day'. It is with the past, as in *The King of Friday's Men*, that Molloy most fully claims his theme of loss and change. The play's opening words introduce the first verse of a graceful ballad, sung in its entirety in Act II, of the carefree union of two young lovers: 'Then we'll goodbye to all sorrow and care.' In the events of the play, love is thwarted, debased, put to dissembling ends.

Caesar French, landlord of Kilmacreena, has his pressgang in search of a new tallywoman, a concubine, among his peasants. They choose Una Brehony, just engaged to Owen Fennigan. Her uncle Gaisceen urges her to make up to Bartley Dowd, champion shillelagh fighter, who will protect her. Bartley is in Kilmacreena to lead its peasants in their murderous yearly battle against the peasants of Tulrahan. Still vigorous, still valiant in his barbaric skills, but scarred and aged beyond his years, Bartley longs for married peace. He believes Una's protestations of love and when the gang comes to seize her routs them in a bloody shillelagh fight. In Act II, Una begins to form a true attachment to Bartley, who leads Kilmacreena to victory. Caesar – in melodramatic terms – strikes again. His bailiff, Boorla, abducts Owen and Una; Caesar offers them and Bartley freedom – if Una will admit to pretending love for Bartley and choose between him and Owen. She chooses Owen. As they leave, Caesar breaks faith. Bartley and his shillelagh, to the rescue once again, free them from the pressgang. He kills Caesar and must flee to exile in the mountains, beyond French's lands.

For all its sensational plot, *The King of Friday's Men* compels acceptance of its strange, distant world of unsettling loyalties, surrounded by a pervasive violence, as the charming song accompanies the opening of the brutal shillelagh battle and Boorla's entrapment of Una. 'Tis a pity', says Boorla of Una's plight; 'still she's the flower of the flock', and ' 'tis the flower of the flock His Honour should get. None of us'd be in the world at all but for the land and goodness of the Frenches.' Gaisceen responds similarly to Una's appeal: 'Is it raise my hand against the Frenches of Kilmacreena, that all belonging to me are serving since the foundation of the world?' However they may feel for Una, Gaisceen and Boorla honour a feudal bond.

Two cultures, of the peasants and of the landlord, reflecting each other's brutalities, are in collusion. Caesar's has been a life of whoring, hunting, duelling: now he suffers the gloomy consciousness of old age denying him the only pleasures he knows. His death is the death of a house, which will go to one of his bastards. The life of the peasants, with its own ferocious sports, is redeemed by song, dance, story-telling – as, according to Molloy, is Caesar's by the intensity of his despair, which 'almost ennobles him'.

Caesar's star declines. In the action of the play none rises to replace it. Bartley – to a lesser extent Owen – rebels, but is a victim of both cultures: subject to Caesar and in his own world caught between the lives of part-reluctant 'bullyboy' and aspiring bard/lover. An interesting sub-plot helps to define his exile, which offers a resolution of sorts. With him goes Rory, old son of blind Cormac Commons, last of the bards. Rory is cantankerous, free with the threat of his father's curses on anyone who refuses him favours, envious of his father's gift, promised as his inheritance. At the end, the two leave together:

BARTLEY. Rory, you have the same mistake made as me. 'Tisn't for good fortune God put our like in the world, but only to do odd jobs for Him. Yourself to give good minding to His composer that was blind, and myself to snatch a girl from the Pressgang . . . We can no way complain. Himself gave His life for us of a Friday.

GAISCEEN. It appears all right ye're picked amongst the King of Friday's men.

Rory is denied his father's gift but accepts guardianship of his work. Bartley, to be taught Cormac's songs and stories, is initiated as story-teller and warrior both, resigned to the loss of Una. Molloy's is a world as savage and grotesque as the worlds of Synge and Fitzmaurice. Like theirs, his language imitates an accent from its rural models; unlike theirs, it rarely vibrates, unpredictably, into higher registers of feeling. *The King of Friday's Men* is toughminded elegy, a powerfully imagined reconstruction of its world. The play draws us into that world, but is so close to it in sympathy that when the curtain falls the characters behind it remain fixed in their own time, their voices and destinies diminished in any but their own circumstances.

(III)

Molloy is important both in himself and in a representative way. He is the last at all remarkable exponent of the folk-drama of Synge and Fitzmaurice. These genealogies have their truth: Clarke in the line of Yeats; Carroll in that of Colum/Murray; Molloy in that of Synge/Fitzmaurice. The dramatists of the nineteen-thirties and forties were picking up their ways mainly from the first (Yeats, Synge, Colum) and second (Murray, Fitzmaurice) generations of Abbey writers. O'Casey and Johnston (1923–9) entered a different set of possibilities, which certainly up to 1955, when we see new developments, had not attracted a practising discipleship. The truth of the genealogies is an approximate one. We are regarding inheritances clearly in decline and, also, variously broken and shared. Molloy, with a solidly recognisable individuality, worked a vein both of subject and style in which the Abbey's early audiences would have been entirely at home. He explores no new direction, no shaping towards contemporary landscapes and a means of viewing their forms. While he was by no means the last to write folk-drama, Molloy's plays embody the sense of an ending, the final utterance of a line.

The fire which on 18 July 1951 burnt down the Abbey was almost a symbol, as has been often remarked, of that decline. Fifteen years of exile followed, mainly in the decrepit Queen's Theatre. The Abbey did not have enough popular plays to maintain, for this larger auditorium, its practice of a succession of short runs. It had to depend on long runs of popular new plays, and of the few revivals that would draw audiences. Hence it came close to being a commercial theatre for Irish playwrights. As Hugh Hunt notes,[36] between 1940 and 1955 there was a diminishing number of new plays, many of those by the established writers. Partly this was because of the economics of staging after the move to the Queen's; partly it was because there was no renewed creative flourish.

A few new playwrights did appear. Their work, decently competent and much like the run of their aboriginal forebears, satisfied its audiences. The theatre was fortunate enough to sustain that level. Some plays achieved at least the passing fame of trenchant presentation of some popularly controversial issue. Seamus Byrne's *Design for a Headstone* (1950) is a 'strong' treatment of the conflict, provoked by a hunger strike, between Church doctrine and IRA principle. It fails to make us link it to its many past and present analogies of dissent, even to the Northern Ireland of 1982. Louis D'Alton's *This Other Eden* (1953) is a debate on romantic Irish and romantic English notions about Ireland. Wittily conducted, it is enclosed within satire that is only circumspectly daring. Alan Simpson had reason in his ambition when he and Carolyn Swift opened the tiny Pike Theatre in 1953, 'to stir up the theatrical lethargy of post-war Ireland'.[37]

There were stirrings in the North of Ireland, but amongst much enthusiastic dedication to theatre and a small group of playwrights, no sabotage of the Abbey moulds. The Ulster Group Theatre was founded in the winter of 1939–40 by the informal amalgamation of three amateur companies, unifying in late 1940 under a board of directors that included Harold Goldblatt and Joseph Tomelty. Although the group presented Ibsen, Sheridan, Chekhov and Odets, its stage was given primarily to Ulster plays: by Shiels and Ervine; and by its own writer Joseph Tomelty, a versatile man.

Born in 1911 in the seaside village of Portaferry, Co. Down, Tomelty has had a distinguished acting career and has written some thirteen plays. The best known are *The End House* (1944), *All Souls' Night* (1949), *Is the Priest at Home?* (1954). They have in common both the sardonic temper of the Ulster dialect and a more lyrical use of it than either Shiels's or Ervine's. The Northern Ireland of the plays is more evocative of the sardonic. Urban or rural, it is a ravenous land: the political and economic impositions of Belfast in the thirties bring a Catholic family to grief – though an accumulation of chance disasters weakens the theme (*The End House*); the two sons of a family of fisherfolk, drowned through their mother's greed, return as ghosts (*All Souls' Night*); a priest meditates on his uneasy role in the peculiar Catholicism of the 'Church Hibernicus' (*Is the Priest at Home?*). Tomelty does not stray further from the familiar ground of realism than the device of the interpolated episodes which illustrate the priest's speculations. He is wholly at ease in the manner, in conveying 'how things are'.[38] The conveying is full of echoes: in *The End House* of Ervine's *Mixed Marriage* and O'Casey's *Juno*; in *All Souls' Night* of Cousins's *The Racing Lug*.

The demise of the Ulster Group Theatre was brought about by the usual financial difficulties, and by internal argument over Sam Thompson's politically embarrassing *Over the Bridge* (1958), first accepted, then after a demand for cuts withdrawn by its author. Despite Tomelty, and Jack Loudan, who gave the Company four plays between 1941 and 1953, the Group never became a playwrights' theatre – though the local accent it solicited was in time to find itself fully. Like the Gate in Dublin, it concentrated, apart from its Ulster emphasis, on standards of acting and production and on a representation of international drama. Much the same is true of two other ventures. The Belfast Arts Theatre, formed by Hubert Wilmot in the late forties, had until the fifties a varied, ambitious repertoire of classic and contemporary plays; and did not particularly seek out new local works. With its occupation of the attractive theatre specially built in 1961, the box office has dictated its offerings: musicals, thrillers, farces. Mary O'Malley's Lyric Theatre, founded in Belfast in 1951, envisaged itself as a home for poetic drama, Yeats's specifically, and world classics, not as a nursery for fledgling dramatists. More recently, however, the Lyric has actively encouraged new writers – Martin Lynch (*The Interrogation of Ambrose Fogarty*, 1982, *Castles in the Air*, 1983) and Christina Reid (*Tea in a China Cup*, 1983).

These endeavours instigated no dramatic upheaval in the early fifties, no break in the theatre's marking time. Nor did the two events which, ending this period in exciting promise, proved for different reasons to be, at least immediately, ends in themselves. In 1954 Brendon Behan's *The Quare Fellow* went on in the Pike Theatre; and in 1955 the same theatre, simultaneously with the Arts Theatre in London, presented the English language première of Beckett's *Waiting for Godot* (French version 1953).

(IV)

Brendan Behan was born in Dublin on 9 February 1923, a child of the tenements, and died there after a rambunctiously alcoholic life on 20 March 1964. His father was a house painter, as was Brendan Behan himself, and the family had strong connections both with Republicanism and Dublin Theatre.

Behan once remarked, 'When Samuel Beckett was in Trinity College listening to lectures, I was in the Queen's Theatre, my uncle's music hall. That is why my plays are music hall and his are university lectures.' Behan's judgment is very partial. Beckett's fantastics are at times songsters, and they can juggle with hats, ladders, and knick-knacks as elaborately as Laurel and Hardy. Referring to his own affinity with Joan Littlewood's sense of theatre, Behan said that 'the thing to aim for is to amuse people and any time they get bored, divert them with a song or a dance'. Yet Behan could organise his music hall beyond self-indulgent song and dance. Written originally in Irish (*Casadh Sugáin Eile – The Twisting of Another Rope*), *The Quare Fellow*'s English version was rejected by the Abbey, then by Hilton Edwards – partly because of Behan's own dilatoriness. Alan Simpson was more patient. In its final shape *The Quare Fellow* is in debt to him, though he claims only that 'we rearranged rather then rewrote some of the play'. It entirely avoids the wasteful 'turns' of *The Hostage* (1958), the result largely of Joan Littlewood's Theatre Workshop production at Stratford East.

Before curtain rise on *The Quare Fellow*, a prisoner's sardonic song gives human voice to the stage set's images of confinement: the severe lines of cell doors and the administrative circle, the women's section visible but beyond reach, the notice in Victorian lettering which says, 'SILENCE'. All except the voice is institutional, correctional. The play, like the voice, challenges the restraints: morning stand-to, the line-up for inspection, the filing out to dig the grave for the condemned man. These dreary rituals, to which the inmates pay mocking observance, stand against the antic caperings of the two Young Prisoners, who 'samba out with their brushes humming the Wedding Samba'. Like the choreographed coal-stealing in Wesker's *Chips with Everything* (1962), the parade drill in McGrath's *Events While Guarding the Bofors Gun* (1966), *The Quare Fellow*'s chores and disciplines evade the intentions of their supervisors. 'By the left, laugh', as Dunlavin says.

The one song, 'that old triangle', sounds the play's strict chronology, from 'To begin the morning / The warder bawling' through 'On a fine spring evening / The lag lay dreaming' to 'The day was dying / And the wind was sighing.' Apart from this there are a few snatches of song only. Thus discreetly used, the song generalises on the passage of time, which is the main 'action' of the play. The prisoners return obsessively to it – particularly the coming hour of execution, but generally as the focus of their lives: 'Healey is coming up today', 'the small hours of this morning', 'long months here', 'out again this day week', 'three days of No. 1', 'the death watch coming on at twelve o'clock'. Hardly a page lacks such a confining definition by hours, days, years. Time and space impose their restrictions, brought together in the final song:

> In the female prison
> There are seventy women
> I wish it was with them that I did dwell,
> Then that old triangle
> Could jingle jangle
> Along the banks of the Royal Canal.

The crude pun, in the diminuendo after the hanging, revives the sexual antithesis to death.

For the prisoners the Quare Fellow is not a Cause. He is a victim, a sacrifice, the ceremonies of his death detailed in their minds. Only through them has the audience access to the condemned cell and to knowledge of its occupant, whom we never see, and who is deprived of individuality. He is all the Quare Fellows who have met this death.

Much of the conversation about the Quare Fellow is in the past tense. It refers to him only indirectly, through prison lore of the gruesome mechanics of hanging and of the hours before it. Warders and prisoners agree on its messiness. What do we learn about it? The duty warders make futile attempts to conceal the passage of time. The washer is put beneath the condemned man's ear, the hood is donned. The prisoner's weight and build may be wrongly estimated: decapitation or strangulation – 'his head was all twisted and his face black, but the two eyes were the worst, like a rabbit's; it was fear that had done it'. The prisoners' view is unsentimental, almost clinical, with a colouring of macabre fascination. Most feel some compassion. But the compassion is for a man seen as his own executioner – 'Begod, he's not being topped for nothing – to cut his own brother up and butcher him like a pig.'

These responses are far from the absolutes of reformist opinion. Their power is the greater for an anguish – and an appetite – which does not come from any sense of Virtue Crucified. The personification is not to suggest any symbolic association between the Quare Fellow and Christ. Christ, however, did share his crucifixion with two outcasts more of the Quare Fellow's persuasion. Without urging, Behan's play hints at some such extension.

As the Quare Fellow's superior last meal is taken to him, the other prisoners crowd the yard in an antiphonal chorus:

PRISONER A. Pork Chops
PRISONER B. Pig's feet.
PRISONER A. Salmon.
NEIGHBOUR. Fish and chips.
MICKSER. Jelly and custard.
NEIGHBOUR. Roast lamb.
PRISONER A. Plum pudding.
PRISONER B. Turkey.
NEIGHBOUR. Goose.
PRISONERS A., B., AND NEIGHBOUR. Rashers and eggs.
ALL. Rashers and eggs, rashers and eggs, and eggs and rashers and eggs and rashers
     it is.

The hangman and his sober attendant deliver a litany which tastelessly but formally solemnises the soul and body of the Quare Fellow:

JENKINSON (sings). My brother, sit and think
                While yet some time is left to thee
                Kneel to thy God who from thee does not shrink
                And lay thy sins on Him who died for thee.
HANGMAN. Take a fourteen stone man as a basis and giving him a drop of eight
     foot. . . .

Finally, the prisoners enter the rite. Their wordless howling at the moment of execution, and Mickser's parody of a race-course commentator determine their presence at a mystery, not a demonstration against capital punishment.

Structurally, as Colbert Kearney has remarked, the play is subtly made. We observe the prisoners, who are observing 'the externals of the closet drama',[39] luring us to experience the condition of the outcast and the pressure of the social defences against him. The play represents the psychological defences which people set up against violent death, and at an even deeper level its fascination. The emotions which welcome barbaric revenge in whatever form – execution, feud, assassination, war – enter the play's ambit, recorded with remarkable neutrality of tone. Even Warder Regan who comes closest to explicit condemnation of the whole process, never fully interrogates its motives. One of his speeches, towards the end, refers to the pandering to a lust for death and spectacle, now hypocritically muted with the hanging removed from public to private view, from mass audience to its secular and ecclesiastical representatives. Almost shouting, Regan says, 'I think the whole show should be put on in Croke Park; after all, it's at the public expense and they let it go on. They should have something more for their money than a bit of paper stuck up on a gate.' But he continues in his office.

The Quare Fellow epitomises – almost *is* – Behan's achievement in the theatre. It is localised by language, and through language escapes to its wider applications. The music-hall styles are there, but refined to subtle purposes. The play has a message, but the message is not the play. It is entertainment, but entertainment is not its substance. *The Quare Fellow*, classically restricted to one day's action, disturbs in its audience's imagination longer scopes of time and experience. It takes us into the presence of individuals who merge into a voice beyond their individualities.

The Hostage is an altogether more erratic performance. It began as *An Giall* (*The Hostage*), a one-act play in Irish commissioned by Gael-Linn and performed in 1958. Behan then wrote the three-act English version, the number of characters also increased by Joan Littlewood for her London production.[40] The matter on which Behan's imagination fastens is how large, public occasions – wars, campaigns, causes – reduce the individual – the hostage here – to an object; and on the need to resist this diminishment. His play, he said, 'is basically about the ordinariness of people – which is an extraordinary thing at such times . . . All that I am trying to show in my play is that one man's death can be more significant than the issues involved.'[41] A programme note to *The Quare Fellow* re-affirms the point: 'this is not a play about prisons, but a play about people'.

The Hostage forsakes *The Quare Fellow*'s (relatively) documentary soberness for a jumble of styles. It is partly the patchwork that gives it verve. In Joan Littlewood's production, the stage vibrated with alternations of movement and inertia. The script was a diagram for elaboration – improvisations of dance, song, topical references, even of dialogue. The danger of the method is its potential for indiscipline. Comedy and pathos are not given time to reach into each other. Behan/Littlewood manipulates the characters and situations to sudden reversals of effect as unfeelingly as Public Good, National Security, The Cause – the play's targets – manipulate their real-life counterparts.

As a character, scene or mood begins to take hold, an easy notion of 'good theatre' subverts it, removes it from unfulfilled possibilities. This can disable the comedy as readily as the pathos. The strange homosexual sequence in Act III never stabilises its variations on comic and sinister. *The Hostage* takes place between 'a wild Irish jig' and a mock dirge – 'The bells of hell go ting-a-ling-a-ling.' None of the abandon, the mockery, or the lament determines a governing style. Judging the play by the high standards

Behan can demand, it remains a kind of glorification of the popular music-hall diversion, the medley.

Behan had a short life and wrote only two plays of value. Nevertheless he deserves attention. Around the time of his first play Dubliners were seeing Shaw (*St Joan*, *The Doctor's Dilemma*), a Eugene O'Neill (*Anna Christie*), an Elmer Rice (*Not for Children*); from the home dramatists Lady Longford's *The Hill of Quirke*, and at the Abbey, Tomelty's *Is The Priest at Home?*, Molloy's *The Will and the Way*, and *Twenty Years A-Wooing* by John McCann, a prolific and successful writer of soap operas: revivals, safe new works, potboilers. *The Quare Fellow* is of a superior order. It is basically realistic, yet with chorus, song, mime, a language that transforms the vernacular it draws on, redeems realism from hand-me-down imitation; and is genuinely continuous with a tradition, the urban drama of O'Casey, because it is re-phrasing, not merely aping, a style. Nothing, of course, immediately came of the example. Behan himself was destroyed by financial

13 Brendan Behan's *The Hostage*, Abbey, 1970

success and personal excess. Dublin theatre was inattentive to him. Alan Simpson remembers that 'respectable' managements were dubious about Behan.[42] The Abbey did not stage *The Quare Fellow* until 1958, after its acclaim in London; nor *The Hostage*, which Ernest Blythe considered filthy rubbish, until 1970. But even though his native city did not take him up, Behan's work remained a standing intimation of theatrical alternatives to the 'grim, grey similarity', as Tomas MacAnna called it, 'of the plays that went on at the Queen's'.[43]

Where Behan, a vociferous presence, was disreputable, the reticent and absentee Beckett was riskily *avant-garde*. Though he is unquestionably Irish, born in Dublin in 1906, of a social background resembling Denis Johnston's, he has spent most of his life in France. His plays might seem to belong more to a placeless Waste Land than to Ireland, unlike his early fiction, where Dublin is the scene. *More Pricks Than Kicks* (1934) is an exuberantly nihilistic *Dubliners*. *Murphy* (1938) is intellectual grotesque, set in England but with a cast of macabre Irish. In *Molloy* (1948) the Irish landscapes of Bally melt into a phantasmagoric Beckettstate. Of the plays O hAodha says that the Irish references are 'tentative, tangential'. Beckett is an 'outsider', 'writing first in French and later translating into English, with faint undertones of Dublin middle-class usage'.[44] Steadily, Beckett loses touch not only with Ireland but with any place other than the terrifyingly comic world he invents, with characters too – *Breath* (1966) – and with words – *Breath, Ghost Trio* (1977).

Alec Reid, on the other hand, says of the actor Jack McGowran's stage presentation of Beckett pieces that it ' "realised" the Beckett Man in every shambling movement, every helpless gesture, in his gravel-like lower class Dublin voice'. Vivian Mercier, more guardedly, is prepared to call Beckett 'an Irishman, but to call him an Irish writer involves some semantic sleight of hand'. On his literary inheritance Thomas Kilroy speaks of 'the private, asocial theatre of Yeats and Beckett'; and Seamus Deane of Ireland's operating for both Beckett and Synge 'as an image of the universe'.[45] Beckett himself has indicated a preference for Yeats, Synge, and O'Casey over Shaw; 'What I would do is give the whole unupsettable applecart for a sup of the Hawk's Well, or the Saints', or a whiff of Juno, to go no further.'[46] Equally, he has asserted, in 'Hommage à Jack B. Yeats', 'L'artiste qui joue son être est de nulle part.' Beckett's Irishness remains an open, or half-open, question, which will be taken up later. Here, for the moment anyway, he is to be regarded as giving at least a backward glance at the Ireland he has left.

In *Waiting for Godot* certainly, a simple test suggests some Irish heredity, or the affectation of it. 'Ah stop blatherin', says Estragon, and, 'Excuse me, Mister, the bones, you won't be wanting the bones'; Pozzo: 'He wants to cod me', and Vladimir, 'Then we'd be bollocksed.' Contrariwise, Estragon also says, 'I find this really most extraordinarily interesting.' The switching of idioms may be affectation, part of the game-playing, and at one with Beckett's use of the physical stage as a measurable version of incomprehensible life: maybe, reassuringly, just manageable.

Estragon and Vladimir know 'the limit of the stage'. They use its spaces and its boundaries. It can admit, at whim, 'The pantomime/the music-hall', a bit of dialogue which isn't 'a bad little canter'. It is a refuge: 'Off you go. Quick! . . . You won't? (*He contemplates the auditorium*). Well, I can understand that.' On stage, one can be what one wants: 'We could play at Lucky and Pozzo'; 'Let's just do the tree, for the balance. (*Vladimir does the tree, staggering about on one leg*).' 'Outside', when the curtain closes, is threatening, beyond control: 'Certainly they beat me.' Such assaults on customary understandings of how theatre and reality combine constitute one of Beckett's eerie powers. The stage in *Godot* is, so far as its properties go, in its sparse way realistic enough, undistorted by dissolves or intricate divisions of its space. It is unsettling because it seems to be offering itself not as a reflection, but as an alternative to, or displacement of, reality.

Godot is Beckett's first exercise in the dramatic and mythic possibilities of farce, patter, meticulously symmetrical structure, even the bait of the 'problem play' (who is Godot?), when they are put on a stage which nonchalantly assumes that it is 'real' and at the same time admits, indeed insists upon, its very theatricality. Nothing could have been further from expectations built up on the drama customarily playing in Dublin. It is true that any lesson Beckett might have had for the Irish playwright did not depend on his being presented in Dublin. His work – and Behan's – was accessible elsewhere. Simpson's productions have more a symbolic than a practical importance.

They represent the quickening of an emigrant imagination, discontented with the ruling local pieties. One should remember, too, while acknowledging the period's vapidity, that Denis Johnston was writing, and Shiels's ambiguous moralities continued, however brash the Abbey's treatment of them. There was something of a resurgence in the North. The Pike was an adventure larger than its minute theatre suggested. The barren land, in fact, secreted germinal soil. Its crop was not to be a single figure, an O'Casey. The imminent revival – still in full flower today – was an astonishingly multiple growth. Shortly to emerge were, amongst others, Hugh Leonard (*The Big Birthday* 1956, *A Leap in the Dark* 1957); Brian Friel (*The Francophile* 1958, *The Enemy Within* 1962, *Philadelphia, Here I Come!* 1964); Thomas Murphy (*A Whistle in the Dark* 1961, *Famine* 1968); Thomas Kilroy (*The Death and Resurrection of Mr Roche* 1968).[47] It is not an extravagant claim for the work of these writers and their contemporaries that, apart from the heights it reaches, the quality of its achievement generally is unprecedented in Irish theatre, and comparable to the revival of British theatre in the fifties and sixties. Something, as Clov says in *Endgame*, is taking its course.

9. Explorations 1956–1982

(1)

The Queen's Theatre might stand, during the years when the Abbey occupied it, as an image of the Ireland of that period. It was a somewhat rundown structure with an entirely orthodox nineteenth-century stage. In it the Abbey Board managed with unimaginative conservatism a self-perpetuating repertoire of realist plays – 'parish-pump Ibsenism', Hugh Leonard called it. Continuity with the earliest 'dreams and responsibilities', though piously proclaimed, had diminished to vanishing-point. As to the state, its neutrality in the Second World War had secured in the minds of its people a sense of its genuine independence. Within that wellnigh unanimously supported declaration of political autonomy, over 50,000 Irish citizens served in the British armed forces. Nevertheless, for all that paradoxical combining of an asserted diplomatic impartiality with mass individual participation, the twenty-six-county state confirmed in itself over the postwar years the strongly isolationist tendencies apparent in government policies of the nineteen-thirties.

As the poet Patrick Kavanagh wrote in 1942, 'All Ireland . . . froze for the want of Europe.' Culturally there had long been a tradition, at least a sub-tradition, of traffic between Europe and Ireland. In the twentieth century, James Joyce wrote his major works in European exile, as did his most famous successor, Samuel Beckett. Lesser known young writers – Thomas McGreevy, Denis Devlin, Brian Coffey – followed the same path. Their work had no acknowledgment in the officially approved culture and small recognition of any sort in their native land.

By and large, in the nineteen-fifties official ideology, supported by a rigorous literary censorship, enforced the dogma of a Gaelic Catholic society and culture. It asserted a supposedly unbroken inheritance of identity between medieval and modern Ireland – while making play with England's destruction of the old Irish civilization. It extolled the virtue of the peasantry, and in the national identification with Catholicism an almost imperialist destiny of spiritual mission throughout the world. The economy continued to stagnate, emigration to rise. Not until 1959, when the more empirically minded Sean Lemass succeeded de Valera as Taoiseach (Prime Minister) of the Fianna Fail government, did more adventurous policies inaugurate a remarkable economic revival and generally a more outward-looking vision. The nineteen-sixties was a period of economic reconstruction. Probably beyond the intentions of its planners, it questioned the entire social and political ethos which had been ossifying, pretty much without regard to changing circumstances, over the three decades since independence. A freshness of thought at least animated new possibilities.

Lemass's programmes were not, of course, a wholly unheralded development. Tremors of change need time to register their impact. So it was in theatre too. As we have seen, younger dramatists were having their work produced at the Abbey and Queen's, however inadequately they saw their intentions realised. There as well the tremors of change were at work, a pervasively philistine and repressive set of attitudes conceding slow defeats. In 1957 when Alan Simpson presented Tennessee Williams's *The Rose Tattoo* he was arrested and charged with 'presenting for gain an indecent and profane performance'.[1] The Dublin District Court, after an anxious year of complex legal argument, cleared him of the charge. The verdict abated police zeal and encouraged a greater daring in theatrical managements. Also in 1957 the Dublin International Theatre Festival was inaugurated. Its purpose was – and remains – to have plays by Irish and foreign dramatists staged by local and imported companies. The Festival ran into trouble in its second year. The Catholic Archbishop of Dublin's disapproval of O'Casey's *The Drums of Father Ned* and a dramatisation of Joyce's *Ulysses* led to its cancellation for that year. But the Festival survived, and from the nineteen-sixties has included many notable first productions of plays by Irish dramatists.

From outside Ireland one development, beyond the censors' prohibitions, was radically influential, the growing accessibility of BBC television. Until 1953 it had been received in Ireland only in chance pockets along the east coast. In that year however, with the establishment of the Divis transmitter in Northern Ireland, it began to be picked up much more widely and reliably. Then on New Year's Eve 1961 Radio-Telefís Eirann – RTE – started transmissions, heavily dependent on British and American imports. Its first programme was *The Cisco Kid*.

One can only speculate on the extent to which the new medium influenced aspiring dramatists. Certainly they turned with increasing frequency to writing television plays; and stage design in the sixties reflects the fluidity of imaginative television camera work. Where the cinema, oddly, has left its impression only on isolated works like Denis Johnston's *Old Lady* and *Dreaming Dust*, television more pervasively suborned the assumptions of a fossilising realist theatre. Formally it questioned the standardised sets and lighting, as in content it did the timidity of subject matter and treatment. In Britain, the origin of the questioning was the work of the new wave of dramatists and directors – John Osborne, Arnold Wesker, Peter Brook. Television promulgated their dissent.

A concrete theatrical embodiment of the altering times in Ireland, to anticipate briefly by a few years, was the new Abbey, constructed on the site of the old. It opened on 18 July 1966. Hugh Hunt describes its main features:

Its fan-shaped auditorium – sixty feet from stage to back wall – has a seating capacity of 628 of which ninety-seven are located in a shallow balcony . . . The open stage, with its forestage mounted on two lifts that descend to form an orchestra pit, can extend forward to a total of fourteen feet from the curtain line, and provides a sense of intimacy between players and audience. The stage itself has a full complement of counterweights for flying scenery, and three large lifts extending across its full width make the stage floor adaptable to various levels. Lighting and sound desks are housed in control rooms located at the rear of the auditorium commanding a view of the stage. The lighting console with its 120-way dimmer-bank controls some 200 outlets of which a generous proportion are located in the front of the house, concealed in wall recesses in the auditorium and in the movable ceiling flaps.[2]

Under the same roof is the Peacock, which opened a year later, a little theatre seating 157, also of sophisticated design.

The Abbey chose to open with *Recall the Years*, a retrospective look at itself. The nature of this new production displeased the critics. Instead of a re-hash of its history, the new theatre demanded the work of one of the new dramatists, set into the flexible stage and calling on its manifold lighting resources – in short, an indication of a clear break with the naturalistic inheritance. It was not until the next year that the new Abbey began to come into its own. Paradoxically, the work one might take as the true debut was by a dead writer and not originally written for the stage – the enormously successful adaptation of Brendan Behan's autobiographical *Borstal Boy*.

The play was a triumph of production by Tomas MacAnna, appointed 'artistic adviser' in 1966 and associated with the Abbey ever since. MacAnna is an exhilaratingly inventive director and *Borstal Boy* showed him at his best. He conceived the playing of Behan by two actors, Niall Toibín as an astonishingly life-like representation of the older Behan, commenting on the experiences of his younger self, played by Frank Grimes. Brilliant use of the Abbey's lighting transported a bare stage through multiple shifts of place, time, and mood, honouring both a new theatrical style and a dramatist who was one of the earliest harbingers of the revival. It was the early sixties which consolidated the renaissance, in ways like this, from James Douglas's *North City Traffic Straight Ahead*:

HARRY (*Recites*). Little moon, little moon of Alban. It's lonesome you'll – (*Emmie cries louder*) – be this night and tomorrow night and many's the long night after – (*Suddenly, off right back, there is a burst of laughter. Harry stops. Again the laughter.*

Donal's timorous laughter and the street whore's cackle of Anna. Harry turns slowly around to face the sound. Emmie hears the laughter.)

EMMIE. Who – who is laughing, Henry?

HARRY. Laughing. . .

EMMIE. A woman is laughing? Some woman? Who – who is the woman? That woman?

(*The laughter comes up again, Anna's predominant. Harry stands helplessly without movement.*)

EMMIE. Henry, I'm coming down there! I'm coming down!

(11)

The quotation is from the first play written by James Douglas, born in Bray in 1929. It was presented at the Gaiety, directed by Alan Simpson, for the 1961 Theatre Festival. In the dialogue quoted above, the couple on the telephone are the husband and wife of a middle-class and childless Dublin marriage. Harry is in the office, back of stage, of the United News, an agency of which he is manager, where Donal works. Emmie is in the hallway of their home, right stage. Between them, front stage, a raised dais represents a city footpath, linking and dividing them and occasionally peopled, mainly by Anna and an aged flower seller, Janie. Lighting brings the three parts into being, as a composition and separately as required.

North City Traffic is an urban play about failed bourgeois lives. Harry's quotation from Synge's *Deirdre* enters a lyricism and an heroically tragic love to which Douglas's play is a modern, waste-land equivalent. Unlike Deirdre and Naoise, Harry's present time regards not any tragic destiny but memories of whose truth, as he reconstructs his past, we can never be wholly certain. What are the relative truths of experiences recalled?: the aura of romance in this –

HARRY. The grass is long and golden. And there are daisies, way up as high as your head in the ditches. Dog daisies with great brown hearts and white, fluffy petals. A girl is sitting among the flowers. She's young, this girl. Very young. If you look at her, she'll smile and look away. . .

or the more frequent reminiscence of confined, petty, emotionally squalid family backgrounds? Such verbal flights as in the quotation above are rare. The dialogue is for the most part spare, echoing between the speakers:

EMMIE. But you didn't put a hand on her, Henry.

HARRY. I told you, Emmie, and it's true.

EMMIE. You told me, Henry. You told me.

HARRY. It was you I kissed.

EMMIE. Then you came home again.

HARRY. I came home again.

EMMIE. You asked me to marry you. Begged me.

HARRY. We got married, Emmie. I married you.

EMMIE. You kept begging me, Henry.

HARRY. We were very happy, Emmie. Weren't we very happy? Weren't we?

From this tapestry of conversation we are to infer a way to the collapse of feeling between Harry and Emmie. Until the very end, when Emmie visits the office, the couple talk entirely by phone, Emmie's voice amplified over the agency's sound system. In United News, despite its supposed function, the words received from life outside are domestic, declaring a private and a public isolation. A possible moment of communion, as Harry and Emmie face each other, passes unfulfilled. The play closes with the signboard, 'North City Traffic Straight Ahead', which has led Emmie to the office, starkly illuminated – 'a white-hot visible scream', Harry alone, crouched in silhouette.

Douglas has written a number of other plays, including *The Ice Goddess* (1964), *A Day Out of School*, and *The Savages* (1968). His *The Painting of Babbi Joe* was presented off-off Broadway in 1978. He also writes short stories and is a prolific contributor to Irish television, for which he created the long-running serial *The Riordans*. His short television play *The Bomb* renders an affecting encounter between youth and age. A young boy, bullied by a friend, throws a celluloid and paper 'bomb' into the rooms of an old lady living in genteel poverty. In its brief span the play encompasses a vista of her decline from the comforts of an affluent Protestant family, the death of her fiancé in the First World War, real as opposed to mock violence. A faded life mirrors great social shifts. For the boy it is an initiation moving him to defy his friend, whose vicious spirit has its sadness too. Yet television, and particularly long stints of serial scripting, may perhaps deplete as much as stimulate creativity. None of Douglas's later work for the theatre has quite the force of *North City Traffic*.

The year of *North City Traffic*, 1961, also saw Joan Littlewood's production of Thomas Murphy's major first play, *A Whistle in the Dark*, at Stratford East, described by Kenneth Tynan as an 'uninhibited display of brutality'. Murphy was born in Tuam, Co. Galway in 1935. After *A Whistle* he did a great deal of television scriptwriting in London, returning to Ireland in 1970. Outstanding among his later plays are *Famine* (1968), *The Fooleen*, later, *A Crucial Week in the Life of a Grocer's Assistant* (1969), *The Morning After Optimism* (1971), *The Sanctuary Lamp* (1975) and *The Blue Macushla* (1980), all produced at the Abbey. Murphy is a dramatist of sustained and considerable power. From *A Whistle's* deployment of an essentially realist stage, he has explored various theatrical shapes to express the collisions between savage actualities of failure and despair and the solace

or defence offered by human faiths, rituals, fantasies – most often their
incapacities. The very title of his first play suggests – as Murphy's titles
commonly do – the respective fragility and strength of the opposites, the
'whistle' inaudible and ineffective in the oppressive 'dark'. Usually but not
invariably Irish in setting, Murphy's plays, without sacrificing their local
identity, carry their scenes and characters into the emotional landscape,
universally recognisable, of the twentieth century.

A Whistle is set in the living room of a council house in Coventry occupied
by Michael Carney and his English wife, Betty. His brothers, Hugo, Iggy,
and Harry, are unwelcome lodgers. 'Dada' Carney and Des, the father and
youngest brother, are arriving on a visit from Ireland. The emotional action
of the play pivots on the swirls of antagonism and an urge for love between
Dada and Michael, slightly better educated than his brothers. He is revolted
by the brutal violence which for Dada and his other sons is an ennobling
manliness, and is bent on preserving Des from it. Almost all the physical

14 Thomas Murphy's *The Sanctuary Lamp* at the Abbey, 1975

violence is off stage, in a brawl, much encouraged by Dada and waged with fists and feet, clubs and chains, between the Carneys and the Mulryans. Dada evades it, and at the drunken victory celebration tells a mendacious Falstaff-like tale of his own prowess when set upon on his way to join his sons.

Violence is in the air throughout. It is in the choreography of the opening preparations to meet Dada and Des, confused, abrupt, abusive, and in a mock cowboy gunfight where one of the party 'dies'. It is electric in the dialogue and the flickering tension between Michael and the rest:

HARRY. Naw-naw. A bottle is better than a fist. A broken bottle is better than two fists. See the fear of God into them when they start backin' away from you.

IGGY. I seen fellas fightin' better because of the fear of God.

HARRY. Naw, not with the spikey glass in front of their eyes. They don't know what to do they're so frightened. And he tries to save himself with his hands, and they get bleeding first –

MICHAEL. (*Entering with some tea things.*) Take it easy, Harry.

The brutality of words and feeling inevitably brings viciousness to its embodiment on stage. Family alliances fluctuate in the spacing of groups. Betty – 'which comes first . . . me or your brothers?' – walks out on Michael. Des, now belligerently confident, taunts and punches him. Michael, also drunk, strikes him dead with a bottle, his own self-betrayal. The curtain drops on the maundering self-justifications of Dada, isolated in a corner of the stage.

Failures all, and on an edge of society; Harry a ponce, Iggy bribed to hire men on a building site. Dada is a failed policeman, failed salesman, failed husband, vulnerable in supports which at times he cannot keep from crumbling: his bravery, the respect he is held in, his important friends, his pedantically incorrect grammar – 'And whom should judge that?' – and cultural pretensions – 'I bet you never read "Ulysses"? Hah? Wha'? Did you? No. A Dublin lad an all wrote "Ulysses". Great book. Famous book. All about how . . . how . . . Yeah . . . Can't be got at all now. All classic books like them I have.'

Yet the play is not judging a simple conflict between brutishness reproved and higher aspirations applauded. Michael's and Dada's overtures to each other are tentative and come to nothing, but both grope towards companionship. Even of Iggy's violence, 'an innate part of his character', we are told that 'it is not without nobility in his case': 'They wasn't expecting the chain. It's not the same winning that way.' Most important, the play very delicately pushes the characters' linguistic boundaries to a tightly strung vernacular poetry, articulating feelings in them of want and deprivation for which their lives have no consolation nor they any normal utterance but aggression:

DADA. Yas, yas, yas, that's him all right! That's –

HARRY. No! Not *you*! I'm talking for a while now . . . I'm talking. (*To* MICHAEL) Hah? . . . Yes! Yes! You're right there too! I did salute McQuaide once. But I'm not still tearing the head off myself, pulling off my cap to salute them shams. They kick, you salute, and then they pray for you. Oh yes! One fella come up to me one day and told me he prays for me. He's praying with false teeth now. They're praying for me, inside, indoors, they're praying. That's right. Pray for the poor dirty pigs, now and at the hour of our death.

DADA. Amen.

HUGO. Amen.

HARRY. . . . Amen.

DADA. Ignatius?

IGGY (*Quietly*). I know what he's talking about.

Harry's is a world of first and last things. Murphy observes it in a way that lets us see Harry both as he appears to the outside, drunken, menacingly venomous, and as the man inside too, wounded, anguished, despairing.

Another doubleness is at work in *The Fooleen*, between the waking life of John Joe Moran, the grocer's assistant, and passages from his nightly dreams. The unreality of the latter is suggested by 'unreal' lighting and a stylised speech, complemented by stylised delivery and movement. Though 'unreal', the interior life of the dreams, as we shall see, isolates and sharpens the bewilderments of John Joe's waking hours. A brother in America is doing badly. A friend has gone to England, where he makes good money, but as John Joe asks him, 'if it's that good, what are you so bitter about?' The emigrants did not want to emigrate. They are victims of Ireland's population haemorrhage – ironically, the salvation of its stagnant economy – driven abroad by unemployment and poverty, against the strong Irish sense of local *pietas*. The *pietas*, however, is not idolatrous. It may be for a place clearly seen to have betrayed an ideal of community. Thus the actual circumstances of John Joe's life are a travesty of such a community. In this failed or failing home he moons about late and idle at the shop; to abandon the home or, somehow, to create it?

The town's inhabitants are either doing well for themselves or like John Joe's parents just making do – 'feeding on this corpse of a street'. Private affairs are public and maliciously judged. John Joe's courtship of Mona – it is more hers of him – scandalises the sanctimonious. His splendidly sardonic proclamation of rumour and gossip, shouted at the sleeping houses, cauterises their wound in him and brings him to a decision. He will stay. Quite brutally rejecting Mona – her world is not his – he says, 'It's not just a case of staying or going. It's something to do with Frank. And Pakey. And others like me who left. And others like Miko and Mullins and me who stayed. It's something to do with that.' Having transformed his quiet into vocal rebellion John Joe may by staying discover the 'something to do with that', which has certainly to do with the ties of place and history. Murphy says of John Joe's mother – 'a product of Irish history – poverty and ignorance; but something great about her' – that she might be called heroic 'if it were the nineteenth century we were dealing with'. So too might John Joe's hard-won settlement.

His dreams are all of escape, embarked on and thwarted: to start the play, a dream-elopement with Mona; later, a dream-soliloquy on a weird *mélange* of America, England, and his native countryside. The last dream is of Mona's imploring him to ask her father, played by John Joe's employer, for her hand. Its tight, surrealistic structure, full of Joycean word-games and Swiftian lists, makes quotation difficult. The opening gives an idea of its verve:

MONA. Abscond!

JOHN JOE. Let me think.

FR DALY. Congratulations for being the great christian and holy-moreover people that we are.

MONA. Well, will you marry me?

MR BROWN. I remember the time –

FR DALY. Ever since four thirty two –

MR BROWN. And not so long ago at all –

FR DALY. A.D., I'm talking about –

MONA. Please! Will you? Please?

FR DALY. Since St Patrick came to Ireland, look at all the things that's happened. Look at all the people called Paddy today.

Thereafter come the patter-catechism by the employer/father:

Any priests in your kin? Maynooth men or foreign mission types? Any doctors, lawyers, teachers, vagabonds, blackguards, idiots, jailbirds, fiddlers? I say, any jailbirds? Have you been to uni, oony, bo-bo-bing, or West Point? How many letters have you after your name? Have you a gas cigarette lighter? Did you shoot Patrick Pearse? Do you know what à la carte means?

and the priest's patter-homily on emigration:

But woe, says he, to the fooleen that goes Holyhead way-woe and leaves himself behind . . . For, merrily, I would say unto that man: verily, watch me, look, and behold! I have a bag here for his soul. Woel! Cause he'll have to leave it behind him! We insist on that. Hand it in. I have a few nice ones in it already. Aw yes. The soul is not a thing to be bandied about in any way, or in any old place. Manchester for instance.

Wakened from the importunings of this final comic nightmare, John Joe resolves, 'We have to do something', and he does.

The like of John Joe's town we have encountered in earlier plays. Murphy's version of it is of his own time, seen along the fractured lines of twentieth-century vision. The social issues, obliquely there, are an emblem of a spiritual crisis, beckoning to exile or renewal. Among Murphy's plays, *The Fooleen* has the most gently cadenced resolution.

In *The Sanctuary Lamp*, derelicts again people the stage: Harry, ex-strong man; Francisco, a juggler, his partner in a defunct circus act; and Maudie, a sixteen-year-old child of the streets. Behind these living characters are the dead: Olga, Harry's wife, a contortionist, Francisco's lover; Harry's daughter, Teresa; Maudie's illegitimate son. The scene is a church in a city which might be Dublin. The action stretches from dawn one day until after 3 a.m. the next. The events, the conversational reconstruction of the characters' pasts and speculation on their future, constitute a kind of Passion. Indeed, the duration of the main block of the play, chimes marking the hours, recalls that of the Crucifixion, in a parody conflation with the Last Supper, as Francisco drinks the altar wine, and Harry and Maudie share fish and chips. The furnishings of the church where they doss down are desecrated: the pulpit when Harry lifts it as the sacrilegious Francisco is delivering a mock sermon; a confessional, placed horizontally, in which the trio lie together.

The subject of Francisco's sermon is 'the thing in Harry's mind' from the beginning, at least in its human embodiment, his desertion by Olga and the torn fabric of relationships between them and Francisco. The 'sermon' is a grotesquely comic account of her last performance, with Francisco and a dwarf, in a private house, prelude to sexual encounters and to her death two days later from an overdose of drugs, hinted at all through the sermon. Harry makes no direct response to the disclosure, but expounds his theory of souls merging in union as silhouettes after death:

Stack them, softly, like clouds, in a corner of space, where they must wait for a time. Until they are needed . . . And if a hole comes in one of the silhouettes already in that outer wall, a new one is called for and implanted on the damaged one. And whose silhouette is the new one? The father's. The father of the damaged one. Or the mother's sometimes. Or a brother's, or a sweetheart's. Loved ones. That's it. And one is implanted on the other. And the merging – y'know? Merging? – merging of the silhouettes is true union. Union forever of loved ones, actually.

As a theory, says Francisco, 'it's certainly as good, better, than anything they've come up with'. 'They', constantly so referred to, is the church, remote, bureaucratic, inhumane.

The characters are groping not just within the web of purely human relationships. They 'are obsessed with Innocence and Forgiveness and Guilt and Perfectibility',[3] with a divine solace or illumination, not the torments of the church's God. 'What a poxy con!' says Francisco. 'All Christianity!':

. . . the only thing that babies feared was the hand of God, that could hold your little baby body in his fist, before dipping you into the red hot coals of hell. Then take you out again and hold you up before his unshaved and slobbering chin, before dipping you again, this time into the damp black heat of purgatory. Experimenting. Playing with Himself. Wondering which type of heat to cook you on.

Nor is the secular human world, shifting and shifty, any more of a sanctuary. By the end of Act I Harry and Maudie have come into some ground of fellow feeling. The dialogue of Act II juggles Harry's jealousy and resentment as Francisco usurps their intimacy.

The world of Murphy's plays is a Limbo of frustrated search. It is the work of an imagination 'antic, bleak, agitated, bewildered, capable of great cruelty and great compassion',[4] realised in a language whose complexity remains true to its theatrical function. Contemporary Irish drama in general is at home in this territory of quest and loss and moments of vulnerable union, though not always in the metaphysical dimensions into which Murphy reaches. The plays of John B. Keane, for instance, widely popular with the amateur drama groups which began to burgeon in the nineteen-fifties,[5] occupy a scene as violently dispossessed as Murphy's but confined to its social deprivations.

Keane was born in 1928, son of a local teacher in Listowel, Co. Kerry, where he now owns a pub. Apart from a couple of years as a labourer in England, from where he returned in 1953, he has spent his life there. He is a prolific writer: journalism, essays, fiction, and over a dozen plays. Of the last, produced mostly by the Southern Theatre Company, the most notable are *Sive* (1959), *Many Young Men of Twenty* (1961), *Hut 42* (Abbey, 1962), *The Man from Clare* (1962), *The Year of the Hiker* (1963), *The Field* (1966), *Big Maggie* (1970). Geographically but not imaginatively, their locale is George Fitzmaurice's countryside, no longer so evocative of demonic dolls.

Like M. J. Molloy, Keane writes in the main line of Irish peasant drama. Unlike Molloy, he has not turned to historical subjects, though his plays never come wholly to terms with contemporary Irish life and the erosion, if not the loss, of old customs. During a crucial scene in *The Field* a jet plane is heard flying by, perhaps to contrast with the community, or enclave, beneath it, where the feuding land hunger of the nineteenth century persists. The play certainly has nothing to do with jet planes, nor with the myriad psychological implications they might represent. In it, an outsider who has bought a field over the rival claims of a local farmer is murdered. Though known, the murderer is never charged, a bullying victory in which he is subtly aware of a defeat. The play is an authentic enough portrayal of the speech, the close-mouthed privacies and parochial defensiveness of 'a small village in the southwest of Ireland'. The central character, 'Bull' McCabe, emanates a brooding physical menace, but the play never brings him, its story, and the telling of its story, into 'The Present'. The aircraft, the electricity and television, the talk of women as 'birds' remain trappings.

In *Hut 42*, set on a building site in the north of England, much of the chat of the characters – essentially the joke trio, an Englishman, an Irishman and a Welshman – is easy listening. They do their 'turns' while – the simple plot unrolls – a bad Irishman disgraces his nation and is put down. Though *Hut 42* sentimentalises the exile, his drunken heart of gold and 'love of a small home in Ireland', it has a promise which Keane's writing since his plays returned to Irish settings has not realised. He takes up urgent themes whose Irish forms, fully expressed, are comprehensible beyond their locality: exile, loss of faith, dead or dying folkways and their often garish replacements. Keane's Kerry is an indecisive fiction which falls short of wider identifications. A closer approach to them is Eugene McCabe's Co. Leitrim in his *King of the Castle*, presented at the 1964 Dublin Theatre Festival.

McCabe was born in Glasgow in 1930 and educated in Ireland. After graduating from University College Cork he dairy-farmed for ten years, turning to writing in 1962. His dramatic talent is undeniable, best represented in his more recent work by a trilogy of television plays written for RTE on the Northern Irish troubles (*Cancer* 1976). *King of the Castle*, to which McCabe has not written a comparable successor for the stage, brings contemporary rural Ireland into a perturbed view of its past.

The King is Scober (Barney) MacAdam, the Castle his home, once a Big House, surrounded by his farmlands, painfully and rapaciously acquired. The public hard man, feared and admired, is in private gossip the ageing husband, childless, sexually impotent with his young wife, Tressa. Taunted to folly, Scober chooses a stud from his labourers:

LYNCH. Maguire?
SCOBER. (*nods*). He finds the weak spot and turns the knife till you act or go mad. An hour ago – after the grub – he went back – to talk to her . . .
LYNCH. Above?
SCOBER (*nods*). To her face he said – 'Take me, I'm a man, I'll put a belly on you.'
LYNCH. She told you this? (*Scober nods*)
I'd kill a man for that.
SCOBER. Not clever . . . It's her *time* – so I said – to myself (*long pause*) Why not *a man* – the right man . . . (*long pause*) A man I'll pick . . . (*long pause*)
LYNCH. I'm not your man, Scober.
SCOBER. You are.

Eventually he is, though in accidental passion, not as Scober intended.

'You've lost', Tressa tells him, '. . . it's over. We're not yesterday people
. . . We're alone.' Yesterday is the previous day, when they had some
understanding of each other, whatever its frustrations. It is other yesterdays
too. The vanished Big House – 'Truly hideous, I'd rather see it empty, open
to the sky', Tressa reports a visitor's remarks on Scober's 'improvements' –
a ghostly peasantry whose heirs we see: these preside over a domestic
tragedy in which Scober's barren successes speak of a countryside embittered by change. Maguire sees it:

In the auld days it was the flail across a plank . . . the winter long and plenty of talk
. . . now it's this thing howlin' chaff and dust . . . combines, groups and co-ops . . .
All for Scober and the go go men, and we're the corn they'll fatten on, we're the chaff
they'll blow to Birmingham, for good if they get their way. There'll be nothin' here
soon but Scobers, tinkers and tourists.

The dialogue, stammeringly oblique, tense with pauses, conveys the lesions
at home and in the community at large.

The new talents of the 1960s take their subjects from an Ireland still
essentially rural and small town. Its frustrations, immobility, hypocrisy – or
stability and loyalty to old pieties – are familiar. We know them from
Colum, Murray, Shiels, Carroll. The sixties, particularly in matters of
sexual conduct, treat them much more explicitly. The twentieth-century
allure of other places has become more strident, more persistent, with its
siren cries of the gracious life of television commercials, new sets of make-
believe, and, far from fairy-tale, distant wars imposing international
commitments.[6]

The escapes, to Douglas's Dublin, Murphy's Coventry, are to new dead-
ends, different settings for an internal, psychic limbo. One can see in these
dramatists, apart from their common use of Irish subjects, a division where
realism shades into fantasy and a neutral other-land: Keane and McCabe
occupy the former, Murphy and to some extent Douglas the latter. At its
most extreme, in Murphy's *The Morning after Optimism*, fantasy takes us to
a debased, twentieth-century Forest of Arden where a whore and her pimp
are the shadows and finally the murderers of two idealised lovers. In its
wholly independent way this is an eloquently stated parable reminiscent of
Tom Stoppard's *Rosencrantz and Guildenstern are Dead*, much less directly
alluding to a Shakespearean antecedent. Where Ireland is the location it is
accidentally so, exemplary, not interesting just because it is Irish. *A
Streetcar Named Desire* (1953) and *The Glass Menagerie* (1945) are in the
same region. Nearer home, it is in touch with the desperate wastes of
Pinter's *The Caretaker* (1960), *The Homecoming* (1965); Edward Bond's *The
Pope's Wedding* (1962) and *Saved* (1965); John McGrath's *Events while
Guarding the Bofors Gun* (1966); Peter Nichols's *A Day in the Death of Joe*

Egg (1967): violent, rootless, secular yet at least glimpsing a basic spirituality in human experience.

An interesting name from the same period is that of David Rudkin. Born in 1936 of an English father and an Irish mother, he grew up outside Armagh. He was educated in England, where he lives, and has a title somewhere along the border of Irish/English drama. His first play, *Afore Night Come*, was staged by the Royal Shakespeare Company in 1961.

Rudkin's work aims very high. It insists upon acceptance of its epic, mythological worlds of prodigious events and characters. Occasional sideslips into more recognisable normalities of discourse and feeling are subordinate to the overshadowing legend-like adventures. In *The Sons of Light* (1976) a pastor and his three sons free a remote Scottish island from its lord's demonic spell and a labyrinthine underworld of psychologically induced mass slavery. *The Triumph of Death* (1981), ranging from the Children's Crusade to the present, surveys the human search for spiritual vision and its contingent brutalities. From the stage, light and sound play upon the senses, in Rudkin's words 'monumental, operatic, hallucinatory'. The action is as savage as in Edward Bond, the language full of scatological images and images of degrading violence.

Rudkin's language is unique, and perhaps the conclusive test of the claims he makes. It calls British and Northern Irish local inflections into a dialect of Rudkin's own creation. Clipped and elliptical, expansive and magniloquent, abstruse, it is a fusion – or, according to one's viewpoint, a confusion – of the archaic, the regional, the contemporary colloquial and the stately. It is a difficult, highly mannered style, in my judgment overreaching, but in that of *The Times Literary Supplement* 'the finest language to be heard in the theatre today'.

The two Irish plays by Rudkin are *Cries from Casement as his Bones Are Brought to Dublin* (BBC radio, Royal Shakespeare Company, 1973) and *Ashes* (1974). The subject of the latter is the present Northern Irish troubles, and it confronts the central difficulty of finding a dramatic metaphor for them. Rudkin's is the demeaning attempts of an infertile couple to conceive. It is obtrusively worked and its application not entirely lucid. Nonetheless, Rudkin is a playwright of uncommon imagination. The bold assertion of his dramatic rites goes a long way towards justifying his obstinate demands.

Irish drama more often remarks in rural than in urban places the social and spiritual violence observed by Rudkin. However, the lives of middle-class city dwellers and suburbanites have increasingly become a subject. The slums of Dublin and its inner-city flats are the fallen world of Thomas Kilroy's plays. Its essence is a legacy, whatever the cruelties of its making, of 'Tall house, tall windows, tall doors with steps to every door' and the indignities brought upon it by its sad, lost inheritors.

Kilroy was born in Callan, Co. Kilkenny in 1934. He took his MA at University College Dublin, where he became a lecturer in the Department of English. He has been a visiting professor at various American universities and in 1978 was appointed Professor of English at University College Galway. His novel *The Big Chapel* (1971) won a number of Irish and English awards, but outside his academic work Kilroy has been mainly a dramatist: *The Death and Resurrection of Mr Roche*, a success at the 1968 Dublin Theatre Festival and later at the Hampstead Theatre Club; *The O'Neill* (1969); *Tea and Sex and Shakespeare* (1976); and *Talbot's Box* (1977). Of these the first and the last are unquestionably the most impressive.

The scene of *Mr Roche* is a Dublin flat, part of a Georgian house, in the Ireland of Sean Lemass's economic miracle and suggestive also of a miracle more cryptic. The participants in the depressing Irish celebration, the all-male drinking party, are white-collar workers in various stages of drunkenness and personal insecurity. Behind them is a Dublin declined from any former grandeur and a now romanticised memory of the rural poverty from which intelligence has uprooted them. Those pasts have led to the Civil Service (Kelly), schoolteaching and a dissatisfied marriage (Seamus), a car salesman's job (Myles) and failure to qualify as a doctor ('Doc'). Myles, clearly not either the executive or the womaniser he suggests, speaks for the ideals of his times: 'The country is on the move, man. On the up and up. For those that are on the move, that is. Fellows that dig. Fellows with savvy. Get me? You got to be moving too or you'll be left behind. It's the lad with the go that's going to get the gravy, Kelly.'

An aspect of Irish society in the late sixties is firmly in the play's groundwork, its pretensions and promises satirised, belied, by dialogue in which the characters conceal the reality of their lives, and visually by the bachelor squalor of Kelly's basement flat. The layout of the flat, however, is also made fit for a Mystery which transcends the actualities of time and place.

Kelly, approaching his front door, cannot find his keys. The door opens. 'This tomb! Look at this tomb!' cries Myles. It has a cellar, called the holy hole by Kelly. While Kelly sings his song his surroundings recede and a piano unaccountably accompanies him. Unobtrusively, the real allows for the insubstantial. Enter Mr Roche.

He is a middle-aged homosexual, Jewish. The party baits him and ultimately immures him in the cellar in which, apparently, he dies. Act II, 'The Disposal of the Body and a Requiem', is also a confessional, of sexual misgivings and a vanished companionship, between Seamus and Kelly. Mr Roche's resurrection, if dead he was, a Jesus or a mistaken diagnosis by

'Doc', reasserts in a luminous dawn – 'Breaking up over the rooftops into particles of silver and gold' – a tender humanity:

MR ROCHE. I also have sympathy for collectors of old letters, oddments of jewellery and faded photographs that have ceased to mean anything except the memory of happiness.

KELLY. Are you going home or not?

MR ROCHE. No, I don't think so.

KELLY. You'd better shift yourself. Real quick . . . I could sling you out on your ear this minute –

MR ROCHE. Oh, go away –

KELLY. I mean it –

MR ROCHE. Go away. Go off and pray. Pray for the dead. For all the dead and the living dead. Isn't that what you have your book for? Requiescent in Pacem. A consolation for the dead. How to die.

For his tormentors it is a doubtful epiphany, self-revelations that they will

15   Thomas Kilroy's *Talbot's Box* at the Abbey, 1977

again conceal, Mr Roche, alone on stage at the end, saying 'hello' on a dead phone.

Mr Roche delicately implies the loss of meaning in the religious symbolism which for its characters is an empty observance of forms: 'The Carmelites . . . I go up there regularly myself on a Sunday when it's too late to go to bed.' *Talbot's Box* turns to the material of sainthood, obsessive mystical belief, its demands on the will and courage of the individual, and the relationship of that uncompromising self-realisation/self-surrender to the claims of society.

A large box takes up most of the stage, opening to disclose the body of Matt Talbot, the scars of penitential chains grotesquely painted, a Priest Figure, A First Man, a Second, a Woman. It is an arresting image, the four satellites enclosed in Talbot's stage within a stage, beyond them the audience. In kaleidoscopic, stylised scenes the four enact parts, mainly depersonalised, emblematic, in the life of Matt Talbot, Dublin working-man, a carpenter – by one account a scab in the Great Lock-out of 1913 – and Christian mystic. Born in 1856, Talbot turned at the age of twenty-eight from alcoholism to a life of the severest physical penance, fasting and prayer. After his death in 1925 – a simple case, for the autopsy, of 'myocardial degeneration' – he became a cult – 'the workers' saint'.

The movement to canonise him, as the play represents it, would have left him indifferent, scornful. His was a private way, ritual observances given meaning by his tormented vision, his own road to God, not a path blazed for others: 'Would anywan need another to copy if they were able to make themselves inta what they be? If ya'll excuse me, father, I've not time for the Church devotions when 'tis only people runnin' from themselves.' It is a solitary, at times heretical, quest. 'That's your darkness, Matthew', a priest tells him, 'the absence of God', and Talbot replies, 'Beggin' your pardon, father, I think meself the darkness is Gawd.' Frustrated by the words that will not express an ecstasy of suffering, Talbot endures in the deprivations of his self-sufficiency. The supreme, isolated egoism is conveyed in a conflux of blinding light and wailing cries of human agony which is 'of physical discomfort to the audience'. In the lock-out sequence the off-stage noises of marching, slogans, warnings, the police attack leave Talbot immune, reciting his ambiguous beatitudes: 'Blessed be the body, / For its pain is the message o' the spirit. / Blessed be the starvin' peoples of the earth, / For they bring down the castles of the mighty.'

Around Talbot's frenzy, interchanging parts, are the manipulators, the interpreters, asserting their claims to Talbot and his myth, brilliantly evoked by the bare stage and the protean quartet. In a sardonically comic scene, the coarsest metaphor of exploitation, a sports commentator describes Talbot's final agonised round of devotions. Women, family, the

Union, politicians, employers, the priesthood – the community – seek to translate the mystical into comprehensible, usable forms, to put it to ends which it would not condone – a saint for Ireland, a model for recalcitrant workers. *Talbot's Box* is about power, the enticements of power achieved, Talbot's demonic, interior force, which nourishes him, and could be born of possession by any faith. Talbot is left with a kind of unspoilt glory – 'he could hear them, the sound of the hammers 'n they batin' the timbers inta the shape o' the cross'; and also with both the legacy of that glory in its vulgarised modern observances and the legitimate appeal of its mundane alternatives.

'The kind of texture which the play has', Kilroy comments, 'derives from the idiom of the Dublin streets.' In *Talbot's Box*, oscillating between realism and moral allegory, solid and evanescent, the ground of strikes and streets, the hand-to-mouth of daily life, is also the ground of the rival apologetics, Illusion or Higher Truth, which aver that human suffering and happiness all make sense. Near the same streets Hugh Leonard's suburban families, affluent or hanging on, in quieter ways as desperate, aspire only to the deceptions of (mainly) polite, domestic armistices.

Hugh Leonard is the pseudonym of John Byrne, born in 1926 in Dalkey, Co. Dublin. After fourteen years in the Irish Civil Service, and some recognition for his early plays, in 1959 he left Ireland to work as a contract writer for Granada Television. His best-known contribution was a low-farce series, *Me Mammy*. He also adapted for television works by Emily Brontë, Dickens, Flaubert, and Maugham. His *Silent Song* won the 1976 Italia Award. Leonard's early stage plays were succeeded by adaptations, of Joyce's *Portrait of the Artist* (*Stephen D*, 1962) and Flann O'Brien's *The Dalkey Archive* (*When the Saints Go Cycling In*, 1965). He has an informed fascination with farce, adapting Labiche's *Célimare*. His *The Patrick Pearse Motel* (1971) uses farce to burlesque the manners of his favourite subject, the well-to-do and other inhabitants of such fashionable outer Dublin suburbs as Dalkey and Killiney – 'the folks', he has called them, 'that live on the Pill'.

Journalist, scriptwriter, adapter, Leonard is an enormously prolific writer, unfailingly a witty entertainer. He consequently invites the suspicion that he constructs his plays – with great skill – around good lines. The good lines are memorably funny; their occasion and their deliverers are more likely to fade from recollection. Take this, from *Time Was* (1976):

JOHN. No, my theory is: those people have gone back to a single remembered moment in time. And they're caught inside of it, like a pea in a deep-freeze.
P.J. Like a . . . ?
JOHN. No, a garden pea . . . P-E-A.

P.J. Oh.

JOHN. Poor devils. Stuck there . . . watching themselves holding a first-born, winning a prize at school, making love.

P.J. And it's permanent?

JOHN. Forever is a better word.

P.J. The world's longest orgasm . . . my God.

The jokes work on their own, though they are in fact part of an ingenious fantasy. A pandemic longing for the good old days is transporting people back into them. Conversely, idols from the past are being willed into the present, including a prostitute who had captivated P.J. in youth, various film stars, and a very pukka Englishman, the original of Beau Geste. Individual sequences have a beautiful absurdity but lack the sustained zaniness that would hold them together and conceal inconsistencies in the 'theory'. The play has too many possible centres: spoofing fictional heroes, social satire, P.J.'s romance of his wife as, or as he thinks, she was when they first met.

The suspicion of facility is neither unfounded nor wholly fair. Two plays, highly acclaimed in Ireland and the United States, which Leonard wrote after his return to Ireland in 1970 are the test cases: *Da* (1973) and *A Life* (1976). 'Stop it', says Charlie to his dead foster-father in *Da*, 'it's not then any more, it's now.' Now a successful writer, Charlie has come back to Dalkey to clear up his father's few relics. Unwillingly, he conjures up *revenants*: Da at various ages, Mother, Young Charlie, the cynical Mr Drumm, who found him his first, menial job. Moving around a stage in whose space lighting isolates scenes from his past, its 'womb' the kitchen at home, they re-enact the growth of their relationships.

The earliest 'then' is Charlie's childhood – 'Da, I love you' – its 'now' Charlie's sardonic, 'When I was seven. You were an Einstein in those days.' Young Charlie too, gauche, resentful of his circumstances, is both derided by his alter ego – 'that little prick' – and re-possessed. 'I listened, faint with shame', Charlie takes over from him in one episode. The scorn he cultivates wilts under Da's placid acquiescence, his stock jokes, his proverbial opiates, his total incomprehension of Charlie's doing well by him:

DA. And after that you had me put into the Union.

CHARLIE. Into the what?

DA. You know . . . the . . . the . . . the poorhouse.

CHARLIE. Oh, you malignant, lop-sided old liar. It was a private room in a psychiatric hospital.

DA. I know, I know.

CHARLIE. A hospital.

DA. Yis.

CHARLIE. Poorhouse!

DA. Sure it's greatly improved since I was a young lad. You wouldn't know a bit of
it.

At the end, Da will not be banished, irreducibly a part of Charlie, following
him as he exits with a song that recalls his blundering on Young Charlie's
first inept effort at seduction.

A Life picks Mr Drumm out of *Da* and places his desiccated married life
against his self-conscious adolescence. Here, the two adult couples are
unaware, apart from two intrusions by Drumm, of their past being
recapitulated around them. The doubling of times and parts achieves some
moving effects. It does little more, however, than corroborate our knowledge of the grown selves, much as they were, and their quite faithful
reminiscences. Our sight of the past requires no adjustment of our focus on
the present, though it seems to hint at a disturbance of the single view. In
the present action the centre is an autocratic attempt by Drumm, who has
been told he is fatally ill, at reconciliation with his wife and oldest friends.
Perhaps he moves towards it. 'Make a start', is his curtain line. He is telling
his wife to set off for home, but may mean more than that. That, however, is
another story, and again, time remembered does not significantly comment
on it.

Though the transitions of time in *A Life* are cunningly stitched, by Act II
one is aware more of the stitching than of a garment taking shape. The
device is a trick that ends up by drawing attention to itself. Without it the
drama of Drumm's acrid defensiveness, crumbling in his mature years and
station, would have been better served. *Da*, a superior piece of work, is
made coherent by Charlie, who is the reason for the form it takes, a subject
of the play and its medium, where times and feelings intersect. Both plays
are set in the location that may inspire in Leonard the work that would
finally still the reservations.

In a 1970 interview Leonard gave a perversely disparaging account of the
state of Irish drama – 'still copying Murray and Robinson . . . They do not
realise what the playwrights of other countries are trying to say . . . still
dribbling on about the aunt's farm and the marriage broker.'[7] Leonard is
clearly wrongheaded. The aunt's farm and the marriage broker are now far
to seek. The contemporary dramatists still work their home ground. It is
increasingly submissive to an amorphous, supra-national world.[8]

No doubt a play of a documentary kind might be written on the social
mutations thus brought about – off-shore oil rigs, factories in rural areas,
urban re-development – some successor to *The Mineral Workers* by William
Boyle. The plays of the sixties and seventies, among the same place and
family names as their predecessors used, witness the psychic effects of these
displacements of the familiar. Their need is for dramatic parables – in the
inhabitants of Douglas's news agency, Murphy's church or rural town,

Kilroy's flat, Leonard's suburban homes – which will condense the changed realities to their human essentials.

The more honestly they record their part of the small Irish canvas the more probably will its lines reach beyond the exits, blind alleys, havens of the local frame, into their analogues elsewhere, into feelings that are not, basically, restricted by place and time. In Brian Friel's *Philadelphia, Here I Come!*, for example, a young man is about to emigrate from Ballybeg, Co. Donegal, to America. The play's concern is not the problem of Irish emigration. As Friel has said, its concern is 'a kind of love: the love between a father and a son and between a son and his birthplace'[9] – to which one should add that for Friel, love is a complex and often acrid emotion. Here, as we shall see in the fuller consideration of Friel's plays, an unmistakably parochial accent, idiom, landscape, translate themselves into images of estrangement, loneliness, hopes (and their frustration) of understanding and intimacy. Their effective home is an Irish village.

In its imaginative development of such local themes, Irish writers are in at least one respect unique in the English-speaking world. As Thomas Murphy has put it – he is speaking of Catholics, the national majority – 'An Irishman is baptised by a priest, educated by priests or brothers and nursed in hospitals by nuns.'[10] Practising or lapsed, the Irish Catholic writer, and to a large extent his Protestant fellow countryman, still has from his upbringing a natural access to the Christian symbolism of faith, disbelief, guilt, expiation. Among the plays discussed here, Murphy's and Kilroy's most fully absorb it into a secular world, about whose rejection or indifference it is one way of talking – not, as once it might have been, a dependable orthodoxy of solace or solution.

As a once accepted faith is questioned yet still supplies an imagery, so too the realist theatre remains an influence. The extreme stylisation of *Talbot's Box* and *The Morning After Optimism* is unusual. Although many of these plays use the transitions of multiple area lighting to break the enclosure of a single, fixed set, and often identify place by suggestion rather than elaborate furnishings, they are by these means modifying an essentially realist presentation. These variants, imaginatively used, not just tricks, are important. Like forms of any kind, they must be totally in union with an informing vision, a sense of place, people, of a situation dictating its deployment on the stage. The unconventionality of contemporary Irish drama is renewing its tradition.

(III)

Neither the city, nor violence, nor the Northern counties are new subjects in Irish theatre. The three fused for the first time in St John Ervine's *Mixed*

Marriage (1911). Not until Sam Thompson's *Over the Bridge*, a popular success at the Empire Theatre, Belfast, in 1960, and later in Dublin, did the subject emerge again, and to an extent that makes it almost a sub-genre.

Thompson was born in Belfast in 1916. Like Behan he was a house painter, encouraged to write by the BBC producer and novelist, Sam Hanna Bell. *Over the Bridge*, his first stage play, written in the mid-fifties, was in rehearsal at the Ulster Group Theatre when the directors withdrew it, allegedly because it might 'offend or affront the religious or political beliefs or sensibilities of the man in the street'. It was in fact offensive to the Unionist establishment. Partly retrospective – Rabbie White recalls the shipyard barbarities of the twenties – *Over the Bridge* is a prophetic miniature of the seventies and eighties.

Its people exist within the institutions of their days and ways: pubs, football pools, fundamentalist sects, lodges, unions. Thompson is adroit in animating, for example, what might easily be the dreary protocols of trade-unionism. It is a political play that goes beyond merely sectarian definitions. A shop steward himself, Thompson does not wink at trade-unionism's Bumbledom, stupidities, and, in the dilemmas with which the play presents it, equivocations and ultimately impotence.

This is not just incidental. Thompson very fully grasped the Belfast proletarian background, and the wider-than-sectarian miseries of its industrial workers. Nonetheless, the play does turn largely upon sectarian passions. After a supposed IRA bombing, rumour excites the almost ritualised emotions of suspicion, fear, revenge. Peter O'Boyle, because he is a Catholic and won't quit work, is battered by the mob; Davey Mitchell, for standing by him, is beaten to death.

The mob leader feeds only upon the platitudes of his fanaticism: 'Popehead', 'defiant bastard', 'good Prod'. As he is the only unnamed he is the only one-dimensional character, his appearance compelling because single and brief. Reason, perhaps humdrum, perhaps defeated, is at least functioning in the Union disputes. The final events, by any rational standard, take place in an absolute political wasteland. A play's testimony is not to be found in isolated quotation. But the closing lines of *Over the Bridge* convey something of the reticence of its manner and the implication of its content:

A man told me yesterday that when that mob went into action he walked away, and so did hundreds of his so-called respectable workmates because they said it was none of their business. None of their business, Rabbie, that's what they said. Then they walked away, and that's what frightens me, they walked away!

Sam Thompson never again quite fused subject, theme, and form, as he did in *Over the Bridge*. *The Evangelist*, his second play, misses its butt, the crippling tightness of the Bible belt, and its release in the emotional orgasm of public confession. The play wavers between broad farce and on the whole soberly observed realities, Thompson's strength. Unlike Sean O'Casey, Thompson takes purposefully the hard tack of Labour politics. It is partly that kind of solidity that makes *Under the Bridge* so suggestive a model for dramatising the sociology of violence in Ulster.

The evidence of Thompson's example in more recent drama is inescapable, for instance in the plays of John Boyd. Boyd was born in Belfast in 1912, and was a producer for BBC radio. He is literary adviser to the Lyric Theatre, and is known primarily as a dramatist, his continuing interest being the North and the outcroppings of its violent disunities. He works from the local language common to the adherents of the warring faiths. Each can understand the idiom, though not sharing the belief, of the other. Boyd's plays draw on this common idiom for his dramatic statement of the origins and manifestations of factional hatreds. His *The Assassin* (Dublin Theatre Festival, 1969) makes a much more consequential figure of its clerical demagogue than Thompson managed. Thompson burlesques the religious hysteria. Boyd anatomises its passage into populist fascism and the aggressions of private armies. Boyd's characters appear creatures of a society impersonally shaping human beings who in adult life consolidate, by political action, the social forces which have conditioned them. Formally too, it has a more elaborate backstitch construction. In one flashback, Freudian bogies, as well as social duress, corrupt the leader's past, and dispose of his future. Nevertheless, *The Assassin* adopts, as do Thompson's plays, a basically documentary method, and works through the argot of the Belfast streets. His *The Flats* (Lyric Theatre, 1971) is altogether realist in manner, recording its self-perpetuating cycle of upheaval in rigorously matter-of-fact language. It places domestic tragedy in the midst of collective violence on the streets of Belfast, slogans translated into action which vitiates any genuine political discourse. These naturalistic plays, together with *The Farm* (Lyric, 1972) and *The Street* (Lyric, 1977) speak to the local immediacies of tribal dispossession, and to Boyd's sense of the gulf between the truth of circumstances and its partisan interpretations.

Between Two Shadows (Lyric; Royal Court, London, 1972), by Wilson John Haire, born in Belfast in 1932, son of a working-class mixed marriage, executes further arabesques on a realist base. It is far from flawless. The squabbling family of its mixed marriage, the McGreevys, has a low flashpoint, but even so, some of their brawls spring from immediate causes that the dialogue doesn't identify, and the play does not relate the family's private anguish to the hysteria around it – the bullying Orange parades, and eventually the riots and shootings: it closes still in the period of Protestant attacks on Catholic districts, before the IRA became a real force. Finally, the raw material of the language is the Belfast vernacular, drawing on its vogue expressions: 'This'll keep your belly from thinkin' your throat's cut.' Haire, though, initiates another process, to distance the language quite considerably from the purely naturalistic.

He is allowing to feeling an eloquence appropriate to its intensity; instead of homespun simplicity and reticence, embellishments and vehemence. Even quite mundane matters evoke images, as Lily on her son, late in learning to walk: 'One and a half calendars spent and not the flutter of a half step out of him.' Or more heightened, after her husband has again invoked, as evidence of his liberalism, the shade of Wolfe Tone, 'a man of Protestant proportions':

Don't dig up bare Protestant bones to build a bridge to me. Eighteenth century bones makes a brittle bridge. You won't recognize me – your livin' wife and mother of your five livin' children – yet, you offer me dead Protestants . . . A dead Protestant United Irishman leader . . . Do youse think I'm goin' to sur-render for a bag of old bones? You better go and rattle them somewhere else.

The language, full of bones, flesh, rocks, ashes, is enacting the disputes, the antagonisms, the rancours, of this divided family. Haire's purpose is not political analysis, nor a revelation of causes; nor need it be. He is dramatis-ing the consequences of a given state of affairs in a particular family; and glancing at counterparts in society at large. As he suggests in a programme note 'the bombings, the murders, the nihilism, are the militant expression of those fears, hatreds and wasted lives', which the afflictions of the McGreevys epitomise. Since *Between Two Shadows* Haire has written *Bloom of the Diamond Stone*, which, set in a Belfast factory, is on the same theme, but does not add to his first treatment of it.

The means to deepen a simple recording of documentary detail are literary and dramatic, not tolerance or political wisdom or sociological research. When the imagination has fully assimilated it, the present violence may be seen as an outlet for stresses of which it is not the cause, which find expression in politically motivated campaigns for reasons which do not originate in politics at all.

A Southern writer, Tom MacIntyre, born in Co. Cavan in 1933, has developed the subject in this way. His more recent work, from the seventies, has turned increasingly to mime, gesture, groupings of move-ment, as in his adaptation of Patrick Kavanagh's *The Great Hunger* (Peacock, 1983). MacIntyre's earlier plays kept language at their centre. His *Eye Winker, Tom Tinker* (Peacock, 1972) concerns the successful re-organisation of a demoralised revolutionary group for a campaign of violence, constantly delayed. MacIntyre is not particularly interested in explaining how the politics of violence has rooted itself in Ireland, nor in articulating its aims and consequences. The play's debates barely touch upon the morality, the demands, and the tactics, of violence as a political expedient. Neither its vacillating hero, Shooks, nor his activist comrade argue ideology. The play of rhetoric, from the bluntly colloquial to Shooks's increasingly self-absorbed word-spinning, in itself debates his retreat from action, in an episodic development recalling at least the structure of the Moralities. It happens to be a political entanglement that exposes Shooks. It might equally, for all the play says about politics, be a domestic or a commercial one. Its major interest is Shooks's gaudy psychology, the deceptions of self-betrayal, the illusions of commitment, the misconceptions of motive and purpose. Shooks's predicament, by accident of time and circumstance, works itself out in revolutionary politics. *Eye Winker, Tom Tinker* is most suggestive about the immediate situation in proposing behind the slogans, press-releases, manifestos, the normal human tensions, miseries, aspirations, disabilities.

MacIntyre's protagonists are the superintendents of violence. Most of these plays move through the suffering of their victims, so commonly a feature of newscasts that its factual pictures carry no assurance of theatrical shock. The play must in a sense reduce the familiarity, displace its emotional numbing. Three Northern dramatists have arrived at distinctive transferences of the same reality: Bill Morrison's *Flying Blind* (Everyman Theatre, Liverpool, 1977), Stewart Parker's *Catchpenny Twist* (Peacock, 1977), and Graham Reid's *The Death of Humpty Dumpty* (Peacock, 1979).

Bill Morrison, born in Ballymoney, Co. Antrim, in 1940, is a law graduate of Queen's University, Belfast. Since leaving Queen's he has worked entirely in drama, acting, directing, and writing, the last including radio plays, adaptations for theatre and television, and original stage plays. His treatment of intimidation and murder is daringly farcical, the social territory of *Flying Blind* a Belfast equivalent of Leonard's Dublin. It presents us with a dissatisfied married couple, Dan and Liz Poots; Bertha, a dissatisfied wife from next door; Michael and Boyd, two old friends visiting the Poots; and an attractive baby-sitter. Circumstances lead to the traditional buffoonery, much of it designed for laughs, of inopportune entrances, eavesdropping, concealments, seductions, undressings. The buffoonery is deeply ironic, the cross-purposes are not amenable to a farcical *coup de théâtre*. In the sexual bouts all the men are impotent, pathetically, not comically so. We see that it has to do with an other than sexual abdication, with power and with defeat. Poots has withdrawn from the daily brutalities, listening through earphones to Charlie Parker, 'who simply found the terms of membership unacceptable'. Boyd has abandoned his political activities. Their surrender appals Michael, vainly convinced that 'the working class must get together here, that any solution must come from them'. 'What am I going to say to this fellow?' a repairman asks him. 'This is a radical political action I have here pointed at you, drop your gun?'

Two sets of young hoodlums actualise the argument, first Protestants, hijacking Dan's car for an assassination, then Catholics bent on revenge. A *danse macabre* takes over from the harlequinades of farce. Entering from the kitchen, where in Act I a pop-up toaster had alarmed Michael and the repairmen, Boyd, his dressing-gown flapping open, is shot in the back. So is the Protestant leader as he rises from behind the couch which earlier had hidden the wantoning of Bertha and Dan. Farce, which makes sport of humanity, here edges from human folly to human mortality:

BOYD. Look at the skin. What a pathetic envelope.
DAN. It is waterproof.
BOYD. You're not likely to get licked to death.
DAN. True. (*Goes on dressing.*)
BOYD. What a piece of work. Hair pulls out. One speck in your eye is enough. Did you ever get hit on the nose? Incapacitates you . . . Liver and kidneys exposed to one sharp dig. And as for his balls, one good squeeze and he'd sing a high C that would crack glasses.

Flying Blind is in part a commentary on the possibilities of farce. Morrison skilfully manipulates it into unstrained reversals of its conventional effects. He halts stock responses to his subject and leaves his characters in the final tableau – a gun, two corpses, a bucket of piss, an embracing couple – of a world where the laws of farce and tragedy are interchangeable.

Stewart Parker's *Catchpenny Twist*, similarly intentioned, is subtitled 'A Charade'. Parker, an East Belfast Protestant, was born in 1941 and is a graduate of Queen's University. He has written extensively for radio and television. His *Spokesong* was a hit of the 1975 Dublin Theatre Festival. In *Catchpenny Twist*, the words to be unriddled are presumably those of its title. The catchpenny people are Monagh, Martyn, and Roy, all sacked as teachers. Monagh, a little late in life, then seeks to be a pop singer. Roy and Martyn set to composing the instant balladry of Belfast's paramilitary exploits: 'But Ireland's sons will not forget / The name of Sean McVeagh' – and so on. They offend both factions and two live bullets in the post send them to refuge in Dublin, then London, ambitious for repute in the commerce of 'mass-produced catchpenny idiocies': 'Somebody out there loves you, sugar' – ending, ominously, 'Somebody out there'. Success eludes them, they shed Monagh, and at the airport after a disastrous European song contest open a parcel which explodes in their faces. Monagh's final song supplies the curtain line: 'You know that loving is really something / Money can't buy.'

The narrative also involves Marie Kyle, former colleague, now a Republican sworn to force of arms; and an English television reporter gallivanting with Monagh (who is attached to Roy as well), and gunned down in Belfast. The plot, complicated enough for a problem play, is not, deliberately one supposes, made a direct narrative concern. It flickers in the background, only at times held steadily to the fore. *Catchpenny Twist* is like a sketch for a melodrama going on as a backdrop to second-rate cabaret acts. Its scenes are multifarious and volatile: the school, city streets, Monagh's down-at-heel clubs, a prison, Roy and Martyn's flat, where they try out their lyrics and melodies, sharing their performance with Monagh, though in fact she is not with them.

If this play is in any line, it is that of the Auden/Isherwood borrowings from Brecht in the nineteen-thirties. It shares the same problems: are the songs good enough to listen to and bad enough to be parodies? the ballad-mongering, the pop scene, the private and public anguish – how do they

16   Graham Reid's *The Death of Humpty Dumpty* at the Peacock Theatre, 1979

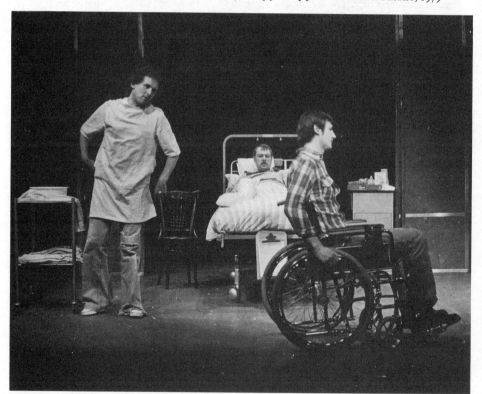

connect? *Catchpenny Twist* faces these difficulties. It settles for a series of entertaining diversions without a unifying likeness. Parker's *Nightshade* (1980) draws fairy tale, mystery story, political satire, legerdemain into an ambitiously philosophical parable. Again Parker is overreaching, tempted, though in beguiling ways, by theatre as an expression, in his own words, of 'the instinct for play itself . . . a quintessentially ludicrous theatre'.[11] The object of a game, however, while its beauty is in movement, is, if this does not seem over-solemn, to score points.

Graham Reid's work, pungent with what Parker calls the 'thick and acrid' air of Belfast, is more soberly mounted. Reid was born in Belfast in 1945 and having left school at fifteen returned to full-time studies when he was twenty-six, graduating from Queen's University in 1976. *The Death of Humpty Dumpty*, his first play, is set in one of the Belfast hospitals whose experience has been that 'people who had been injured in civil disturbances found it more difficult to adjust. There was often the question "Why me? I am innocent." '[12] Reid's innocent is George Sampson, a school teacher, unfaithful to his wife, shot because he may be able to bear witness to a sectarian assault, in consequence paralysed from the neck down.

The play's contact with terrorism is peripheral. Its regard is on the sequel to crippling disaster brought on by chance, and the widening circle of victimised bystanders. Taking place mostly in Sampson's ward, where a chillingly sadistic orderly torments him, and punctuated by flashbacks – Sampson as he vigorously was – the action traces his physical humiliations and deteriorating will. Fleeting moments of resolve yield to fretful complaint and ruinous emotional tyranny over his family. At the last, his two children smother him in his bed. There has been a transmission of violence, of government by terror, from the original perpetrators to their victim, to his household, all in the end injured and injuring, a fate like that of Shakespeare's appetite, the 'universal wolf that last eats up itself'.

Reid's second play, *The Closed Door* (Peacock, 1980), moves a similar moral canvassing to the low life of the illegal, paramilitary drinking dens of Belfast: a hanger-on, brutally beaten up, tests the strength of neighbourly obligations. Both works comment eloquently on a society whose ethic solicits violence. They do not 'adjudicate between agony and injustice',[13] but record their local insignia.

It would be wrong to see the Northern Irish situation as the unique catalyst of an imaginative urge. But in 1982, thirteen years of continuing violence are always at least on the fringe of local consciousness. These seven playwrights testify to its imaginative allure. Heartlessly, it presents an emotional and technical problem: how to distance oneself from the widespread suffering to which one is intimately witness, and to contain it within the stage. Formally, the answers vary from straightforward realism to degrees of fantasy. Common to them is reductive comedy. As a simple instance, in *Over the Bridge* one potential monster is called 'Archie Boyne Water for he's living in 1690'. In *Humpty Dumpty* the loathsome orderly entertains, dancing about, full of chatter, rebuked by the matron. Threats become jokes which the threat outlives, another whistling in the dark. Raillery, flyting, cross-talk, forms of theatre imitated – farce, social comedy, cabaret, pantomime – catch the audience between easy judgments.

The particular subject has become almost the figurative type of the society in which it originates, and of its equivalents in societies elsewhere:

> the rough field
>   of the universe
> growing, changing
>   a net of energies[14]

The situation which sets the playwrights to devising expressive metaphors is itself a metaphor of, as Bill Morrison rather too bleakly puts it, 'our morose, separate, and possibly doomed Northern society'.[15] The nativeness of that society is the natural and perhaps the necessary ground for the dramatists of the region. Stewart Parker has argued for 'plays that confront the central issues of Western society, rather than those peculiar only to Crossmaglen or Connemara or Rathfarnham' – adding that these 'sets of issues are not mutually exclusive'.[16]

Such possibilities in the efflorescence of Northern drama arrive at their fullest realisation in the plays of Brian Friel, which constitute the most comprehensive body of work in contemporary Irish drama. He has written one play on the Northern violence. *The Freedom of the City* (1973) translates the events of Bloody Sunday in Derry City in 1972 into a fiction of the dehumanising apparatus of the modern state. This generalising power has its source in Friel's intense awareness of the genius of place and of the language peculiar to its being. That language may joyfully declare, stubbornly protect, cry down, or satirise the decay of the culture of which it is the voice. Friel's plays invent fables of lives whose destinies interpret the community which is a part of their shaping, and in which the interpretations, in turn, are amending agents.

It was to encourage such imaginative excursions, to consolidate them on a regional base, to secure a local stage and audience that Friel, with the actor Stephen Rea, founded the Field Day Theatre Company. It opened with his own *Translations* in 1980. Field Day has no theatre of its own, and assembles its cast from play to play. Its practice has been to open in Derry, then to tour, first in the North, then the South. Although its three productions so far have all been of works by Friel – *Translations*; a translation of *The Three Sisters* (1981); *The Communication Cord* (1982) – its ideal is choric. It hopes to be host to a cluster of writers, each with an independent way – and it is proper to quote Yeats on his venture – 'of expression for an impulse that was in the people themselves', and addressing that people as its first enabling audience.

A unifying intention, suggestive not prescriptive, is to entertain theatrical fictions intimate with the actual, releasing from it, to quote Yeats again, 'a memory and a prophecy'.[17] The Field Day Company is looking towards, in the words of a character in *Translations*, the utterance of a region's '*desiderium nostrorum* – the need of our own', statements locally heard, and if so pitched that they carry, more broadly overheard. Unlike the Lyric in Belfast it has no commitment to represent the range of existing drama, nor anything like the obligation of the Lyric's charter to present Yeats plays annually. Field Day is an act of faith, with the hazards entailed, encouraged by a theatrical environment of lively promise.

10. The honour of naming: Samuel Beckett and Brian Friel

(1)

MARTIN. I was the like of the little children do be listening to the stories of an old woman, and do be dreaming after in the dark night it's in grand houses of gold they are, with speckled horses to ride, and do be waking again, in a short while, and they destroyed with the cold, and the thatch dripping maybe, and the starved ass braying in the yard.

The Well of the Saints

ESTRAGON. You and your landscapes! Tell me about the worms!
VLADIMIR. All the same, you can't tell me that this (*gesture*) bears any resemblance to . . . (*he hesitates*) . . . to the Macon country for example. You can't deny there's a big difference.

Waiting for Godot

In the late nineteen-twenties in Paris, when he was an *assistant* at the Ecole Normale Supérieure, Beckett championed Joyce's *Work in Progress* and at times helped him by taking dictation. Beckett's literary way, however, does not imitate Joyce's. The two are complementary. Joyce might be seen, in a rather simplifying view, as moving from the linguistic drab of *Dubliners* to the neological fertility of *Ulysses* and in *Finnegans Wake* to the invention of a language. Drawing the distinction between the two, Beckett said, 'The more Joyce knew, the more he could. He's tending towards omniscience and omnipotence as an artist. I'm working with impotence, ignorance.'[1] Beckett's early fiction is verbally lavish, yoking vernacular and abstruse, intellectually gamesome, riddling its audience with coinages, and oddities often drawn from technical vocabularies: triorchous, strangury, syzygy, apnoea, marasmus, genustuprations, asthenia, nosonomy. This particular obscurity diminishes. *Molloy* (French version, 1950), like the trilogy (completed by *Malone Dies* (1952) and *The Unnamable* (1953)) it begins, presents its enigmas in plainer words, in evasive narrative and a mysteriously echoing structure. The plays continue the process, language reduced to simplicity, experimenting with muteness. The favourite directions – *Pause, Silence* – become governors, and as in *Ghost Trio III* (1976) words may cease entirely and even human movement give way to that of a television camera.

The use of technical vocabulary, though Beckett dropped it, is significant of a persistent idea: that all one can certainly know about human beings and their environment, and the only confidence they can have in themselves, is

188

in the physically diagnosable, quantifiable: one can try that, at any rate. Beckett's characters convert the metaphysical problems which surround them into soluble conundrums. So Murphy is delighted that, if he rejects a couple of prejudices, his assortment of five biscuits 'would spring to life before him, dancing the radiant measure of its total permutability, edible in a hundred and twenty ways!' So Molloy organises the 'mode of circulation' which will ensure the sucking of his sixteen stones turn and turn about, only to decide after six pages of permuting, 'deep down I didn't give a fiddler's curse'; and so he establishes by number and frequency that he hardly farts at all: 'Extraordinary how mathematics help you to know yourself.'

These are all ploys to avoid the entrapment implied in Hamm's nervous question in *Endgame* (1956): 'We're not beginning to . . . to . . . mean something?' In the plays the stage is a territory at least partly governable which can be practically surveyed: 'ten feet by ten feet by ten feet', Clov says of his kitchen, 'Nice dimensions, nice proportions'. The audience is the world beyond, regarded in *Waiting for Godot* with horror, in *Endgame* with derision: '[Clov:] (*picks up the telescope, turns it on auditorium*) I see . . . a multitude . . . in transports . . . of joy. (*Pause*) That's what I call a magnifier.' A scattering of objects may sub-divide the stage and define rôles: in *Godot* boots, bowler hats, a bag, a stool, a basket, a watch; in *Endgame* a step-ladder, a whistle, a telescope, a toy dog, a gaff, an alarm clock. The *Endgame* miscellany even invites a flurry of ambitious action:

HAMM. What are you doing?
CLOV. Putting things in order. (*He straightens up. Fervently.*) I'm going to clear everything away! (*He starts picking up again.*)
HAMM. Order!
CLOV. (*straightening up*). I love order. It's my dream. A world where all would be silent and still and each thing in its last place, under the last dust.

It comes to nothing. At the end the stage is more littered with the objects than a Shakespearean tragedy's with corpses, and Nell and Nagg, dead or alive – 'The dead go fast' / 'Life goes on' – belong with them. Still, the measuring, the observations, the properties are a hypothetical sustainment, a tangible equivalent of the variants on Hamm's reply to Clov:

CLOV. Why this farce, day after day?
HAMM. Routine.

The 'routines', some visual, are mainly verbal. Vladimir and Estragon incite each other to follow a conversational line, often with rhetorically powerful consequences, whether the haunting 'wings/leaves/sand/feathers/ashes' or the comic 'family/friends/agents/correspondents . . .' Pozzo exercises lyrical/prosaic and Hamm narrative/normal tones. The dialogue calls our attention to the stage forms used – aside, soliloquy, exit. The story Hamm tells is

CLOV. The one you've been telling yourself all your . . . days.
HAMM. Ah you mean my chronicle?
CLOV. That's the one. (*Pause*)
HAMM. (*angrily*). Keep going, can't you, keep going.
CLOV. You've got on with it, I hope.
HAMM. Oh not very far, not very far. (*He sighs.*) There are days like that, one isn't inspired. (*Pause*) Nothing you can do about it, just wait for it to come. (*Pause*) No forcing, no forcing, its fatal. (*Pause*) I've got on with it a little all the same. (*Pause*) Technique, you know.

A fiction where language is allowed to deal only with a set of circumstances imposed by its user is more scrutable than life. When language threatens to escape the limitations either there is silence or a new routine takes over.

Yet the fictions constantly allude to past times and places, perhaps objective, recoverable, perhaps tricks of memory, involuntary fictions. Agreement is rare, either on the meaning of phrases calling on the past or on memories supposedly held in common. Nell's sentimental, 'Ah yesterday!' is Clov's 'that bloody awful day, long ago, before this bloody awful day'. His use of the pleasurably reminiscent 'God be with the days' refers to the time before he was 'in the land of the living'. Repetition, changing contexts reduce words to ironic precision: 'naturally' in *Endgame* comes to apply to the passing of life; 'once' – 'You loved me once. / Once! – 'It was sawdust once. / Once!' – to mean 'never again'. Vladimir's 'fullness of time' is synonymous with his 'for the time being', and Lucky's sermon offers 'time without extension'. Durations – a day, fifty years – are indifferent. Pozzo, to determine 'That was nearly sixty years ago', consults his watch. When Vladimir tries to recall 'this evening', Estragon retorts, 'I'm not a historian'. Of the only memory the two seem to share – though perhaps Estragon is just 'returning the ball, once in a way' – Vladimir says, 'no use harking back to that'.

Beckett's tatterdemalions are trying to discover where to be in time and place, both equally indeterminate: 'I feel too old, and too far', Clov declares. If we are to take at all literally the clues in *Godot* – 'in the nineties', 'fifty years perhaps', 'half a century' before – they place the action in the nineteen-forties. Vladimir and Estragon are living at the time of the underground French resistance movement, in which Beckett served, against German occupation. The play vibrates, in its own underground way, with the fear, strain, and distress of that time: claustrophobic but relatively safe enclosure, waiting for agents who fail to appear, interrogation ('let's ask each other questions'), beatings to extract information unknown to the victim ('why did they beat you? – I don't know'), hidden loyalties:

ESTRAGON. (*laughing noisily*). He wants to know if we are friends!

VLADIMIR. No, he means friends of his.

Documentary facts are secreted far beneath the dolours of Vladimir and Estragon. Macon and Cackon (in the French version Vaucluse, where Beckett lived for part of the war, and its scatalogical complement Merdecluse) are not real places. They are names which Vladimir remembers, Estragon dismisses. Places, like times, are hardly worth differentiating, even were it possible – 'the light gleams an instant, then it's night once more'.

Despite the skeletal topography, a vanished – or banished – knowledge of district, of parish, flutters in details of Hamm's memories – 'Kov, beyond the gulf' – in the intimately idiomatic tone of Estragon's 'We're not from these parts', Vladimir's 'Are you a native of these parts?' Beckett's scenes are zones of the mind. The landscapes of their origin are a blur, a mumble, abstracted into their essential nature – much as the wartime experience is in *Godot* an echo of distant echoes. Beckett's subjugation of his characters' personal biography, 'scenes of my childhood', the outward singularities of region, of existence defined by those realities, recalls us to Synge's sabotage of the world of facts.

Beckett's family, like Synge's, was affluent Protestant, his mother evangelically pious, also like Synge's. Though Synge returned from France to Ireland and Beckett made France his home, both men were equally exiles from the faith of their upbringing. However, certain Protestant lessons, secularised, persist. In Catholic practice, confession leads to absolution given by a priest. Protestantism exalts the self-enquiry of private conscience, not clerical, authoritarian mediation. In Protestantism which has lost God, the final recourse, shriving, is less the prosecution of an end than an absorption in the process of trial. Hugh Kenner has called it 'the issueless Protestant confrontation with conscience'. In Synge and Beckett the confrontation certainly bulks large. Issue, however, there may be.

From their similar legacies, the worlds of Beckett and Synge work on evidently different teleologies. Synge, in the end, is a shriver. His man-as-god – the tramp of *In the Shadow*, Christy Mahon, Deirdre, Martin Doul – creates a saving grace by interior energy, facing out the oppression of grief, melancholy, acquiescence. Beckett, on the other hand, is the pure inquisitor, pure because doubtful of any premisses, refusing conclusions or interpretation: 'You think so? – I don't know. – You may be right.' His man-as-god travels the 'perilous zones in the life of the individual: dangerous, precarious, painful, mysterious and fertile, when for a moment the boredom of living is replaced by the suffering of being'.[2] This would apply precisely to Synge were we to substitute 'affirmation' for 'suffering'. The dramatic method of both writers is to molest by words a limited,

17 Beckett's *Waiting for Godot* at the Pike Theatre Club, Dublin, 1955

explicable reality. Beckett's stage parodies any such concept. His characters cannot sustain the necessary contraction and evasions, though they keep trying; and that may be all that's possible for them. Synge engulfs the same reality in imaginative expansions of its boundaries.

The language of Synge's plays, as we have seen, holds physical reality close in its gaze: rocks, sky, lakes, rivers, hills, sloughs, paths, trees, birds,

192

animals – all in their local shades. Nature is hazardously benign or ruinous. Human nature, as the plays regard it, is not an honouring of mystical peasant innocence. Appetite works its selfish way, impure motives mis-represent their ends. Physical realities, material and swarming in the plays, have no impregnable right of dominion. Imagination and its force of words may, with its own concessions, hold sway, diverting and finally subduing fact. The words in Synge are heroic.

The places in which Synge's people will events and feelings to their ends are of Wicklow, West Kerry and the Aran Islands. Beckett's characters may seem in contrast playboys of a worldless west, represented by a country road and interiors that could be anywhere. Topography, landscape, region, reliable memory and report of place have been eliminated. Clov relates his observations: 'zero . . . zero . . . and zero . . . All gone. . . . Zero . . . Grey. Grey! GRREY!' Like the stage, the surroundings – if we are to believe Clov, and we have no objective testimony – are featureless, delocalised. They leave 'unaccommodated man' to make what he can of them by sports and words: 'Say you are, even if it's not true.' The small, ephemeral triumphs, achieved as are Synge's larger victories, by words, hold at bay

18   Synge's *Riders to the Sea* at the Abbey, 1971

menace, insecurity, an incomprehensible universe, so that one may say, 'Well I never! In spite of everything you were able to get on with it!', or 'We always find something eh Didi, to give us the impression we exist?' They are to no lasting purpose. The rare, hard-won laugh dies: 'I couldn't guffaw again today'; a moment of friendship vanishes: 'It'd be better if we parted.' Those moments perish too. A reluctance to exist competes with the desire. The desire requires a history, a memory of time and place, to authenticate a chronicle of the self: memories are evaded, tentatively sought; an item is achieved, evaded . . . always continuing.

Whatever the landscape (in its broadest sense) or the lack of it, Synge's and Beckett's characters use language, their primary agent, respectively in Synge to dislodge it from its mundane restrictiveness and in Beckett to secure temporary lodgings for pretences that it may be safely ignored: 'Go on, I'm saying', says Christy. 'Not a word out of you'; and Vladimir: 'Yes, but now we'll have to find something else.' In both writers landscape is to be taken as more than the details of its physical cast. It is a storehouse of geological change, historically and architecturally of its culture. Synge's ambitious intention was to raise from it the ancient Gaelic identity, buried by colonisation. Believing that the Gaelic language was effectively dead, he turned for his medium to an English that spoke, or could be made to speak, for a sensibility not native to it. He was happy in his time, perhaps the last point at which an attempt of this magnitude had any prospect of so marvellously concluded a success.

A colonised people has a profound desire to restore its native lineage undeformed by the colonial impositions. The energy required diminishes. In one view of the industrial present, that energy is expended, any such flourish as Synge achieved now impossible. Beckett's landscapes are a sighting of that disinheritance. The past now submerged under its colonial overlay, its times and places are irrecoverable. The deprivation of Vladimir and the rest is in part a racial or historical consequence, an image of a colonised post-colonial imagination making do with dispossession: 'the earth is extinguished, though I never saw it lit'.

In Beckett's debauched landscapes it is possible to make out shadows of their native geography. In *Krapp's Last Tape* (1958) – Krapp in brilliant light, the rest of the stage dark – Miss McGlome is 'from Connaught, I fancy' ('fancy', of course, from the dark). Krapp's later memory of 'Croghan' echoes Yeats's Cruachan, pronounced 'Crockan' as Yeats tells us, the ancient capital of Connaught, the probable burial place of Maeve, and the site of Hell Mouth. It is the scene of Yeats's 'The Hour Before Dawn' (*Responsibilities*), in which, with Maeve a ghostly presence, a crippled beggar and a lumpish youth quarrel about tranced sleep, immortality, and death, when blessedly 'flesh and bone may disappear'. 'The Dancer at

Cruachan and Cro-Patrick' (*Words for Music Perhaps*) immediately precedes the Tom the Lunatic poems: the voice of 'The Dancer' is St Cellach's, of the Tom poems one of Yeats's wise fools, speaking in reply, yet in the debate fool and Christian mystic are not wholly distinguishable. The *dramatis personae* are forerunners of the down-at-heels in Beckett, who strips their landscape of its wondrous figures: in Yeats still invoked to share the domain, in Beckett their explusion acknowledged.

As Vivian Mercier has demonstrated, we can disinter from *Happy Days* (1961) sufficient evidence of Winnie's descent from the bygone Anglo-Irish gentry.[3] In the play Winnie endures in a world amputated from that or any other past, a private Hell/Limbo/Purgatory; or the result, we are allowed to infer, of some unspecified calamity. The 'last human kind' have passed by. Even the natural laws are doubtful. Winnie wonders if the earth has lost its atmosphere. The violated past, 'the sweet old style', persists in fragments, a yellowed newspaper, in Winnie's memories, her usually mutilated quo-

19   Beckett's *Happy Days* at the Peacock Theatre, 1975

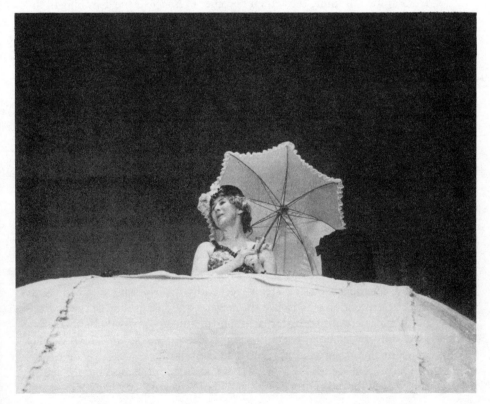

tations – 'one's classics' – from Shakespeare and Milton. Among them, and coherent, is, 'I call to the eye of the mind.' Perhaps an in-joke: Winnie's only audience, Willie, shares his name with its author, Yeats. It is from *At the Hawk's Well*: another of Beckett's sly reminders to the larger audience that they are watching a play and quite possibly judging it, in Shower's or Cooker's words, the 'usual drivel'.

The very presence of these allusions admits an inheritance. More interesting is the understanding and the use made of them. Although Beckett was suspicious of a showy romanticism in the Irish Literary Revival, and in Yeats, of 'high laughter, loveliness and ease', he is able in 'Recent Irish Poetry' to write of Cuchulain, Maeve, and the Tain.[4] It was a tradition known to him and for all his scepticism not wholly refused, even if to be treated reductively. As we have seen in Chapter 8, 'a sup of the Hawk's Well' is more palatable than Shaw's 'whole unupsettable applecart'. Beckett turns to an adjacent but distinctive well. His plays clearly diminish Yeats's heroic personages caught up in heroic destinies. Formally too he burlesques Yeats's ritualising stagecraft. The folding and unfolding of the cloth in *The Hawk's Well*, framing the action, becomes in *Endgame* the disrobing of the dustbins and to close, Hamm's enveloping his face in his handkerchief. In *Krapp's Last Tape* Krapp peels (unfolds) two large bananas; at the end the tape ceaselessly unreels. *Happy Days* opens with a ringing bell and an unspoken prayer. It finishes with the bell again, signal that, in the hymn which is in Winnie's mind, and which Krapp sings, 'Now the day is over, / Night is drawing nigh': in the Protestant experience of Beckett's generation deeply evocative of evensong, closings. Reverence and farce collaborate.

Beckett, in other words, gives the inheritance a combative reception. He transmutes all his borrowings, and to a single end, as Thomas Kilroy observes in his perceptive analogy between 'the dramatisation of myth in Yeats and the use of vaudeville-type routines in Beckett'.[5] However, as Beckett debases Yeats's stage rituals, so he reconstructs vaudeville usage. *Happy Days*, for instance, is related to the classic music-hall routine of the straight man bent on singing or reciting and being constantly thwarted. Here, Winnie herself delays her song, her interlocutor is largely mute, and in fact the first to sing the song, though partially. Kilroy argues that the attraction of both examples, Yeats/Noh and music-hall, is their effect of closing off the stage as an area governed by its own self-contained rules. Beckett's intention is to isolate the stage as 'the sole ground of the action', not 'a miniature of some external ground of human activity'.[6] His characters exist only by right of their playing in certain ways with their various impedimenta, their present scene, and their past.

The present scene of *Happy Days* is a landscape of 'hellish light', 'hellish sun', earth 'the old extinguisher', and in prospect the – perhaps comforting

196

– happy days when 'flesh melts at so many degrees'. To cope with it Winnie has the familiar sort of trappings: toothbrush, toothpaste, medicine bottle; lipstick, nailfile, hat and handkerchief; music box; spectacles, mirror, magnifying glass; and the revolver. Between them they at least confirm the senses of her physical being: taste, touch, smell, hearing, and sight. In the second act, however, while their receptacle and the combustible parasol are restored, she is deprived, buried to the neck, of their solace.

Things have a life, Winnie says. Her possessions are a welcome reassurance in her hellish condition, part of the inuring habits which are a diversion from suffering and doubts. In his *Proust* Beckett calls them 'the countless treaties concluded between the countless subjects that constitute the individual and their countless correlative objects': a screen against reality. Along with memory, habits give a semblance of unity to the indeterminate flux which is the individual, composed, again according to *Proust*, of the ceaseless flow of its future into its past. So Winnie's trifling with her oddments, her solicitous, repetitive bantering with Willie, the recollections of her prelapsarian experiences are all attempts to assert a stable identity and a relationship with Willie. They keep her going, though they are not altogether trustworthy – when Willie fails to play along, or very powerfully in the strange, riddling end when his expression terrifies Winnie as he tries and fails to reach the revolver. She recovers, to sing, rightly or wrongly, 'It's true, it's true, / You love me so.'

Willie, Winnie tells us, has 'no interest in life'. It could mean either that he has nothing to occupy him or that he is indifferent to life itself. The former is more probable, in view of the grand gesture of his final appearance, dressed to the nines. Winnie certainly is keeping up her spirits and finding 'great mercies' in her situation, for all its horror. She proposes, with an irony of which she may or may not be aware, to 'magnify the Almighty'. In practice she magnifies, with her glass, the two-dimensional obscene postcard and the progress of an ant over the sand which imbeds her. The visual/verbal pun again reduces the already reduced landscape to a part of its area, as does Clov with his telescope, and in a way Krapp too, with his switching tape segments. The audience watches Winnie – 'someone is looking at me' – and in her mirror, which she shatters, Winnie watches herself. These devices confirm the whole recessive scheme: world made over to stage set, stage set circumscribed by telescope, magnifying glass, reflected image. Thus curtailed, Winnie does as good a job of holding her own as the Beckett world permits.

Beckett's first four main plays are in part about surrounding landscapes. Within their precisely delimited compass the characters try to locate themselves/their selves. The time in which they exist is less determinate. How long passes between the two acts of *Godot*? – time enough for the tree to blossom sparsely; between the two acts of *Happy Days*? – enough for Winnie to tell us that she no longer prays. In neither do we know the duration. We are told in *Krapp's Last Tape* that the tape is a record of events made thirty years earlier. But as the old Krapp listens to the young, the young looks back at an even younger in a time manipulated by Krapp as he erases parts by switching back and forward, changes the tape to record himself, and reverts to the first tape.

The most unsettling common feature is that while stage time equals 'actual' time, the circling recurrences of speech, the elaborately annotated and enacted pantomime distort or retard any normal sense of time's progress. The characters undergo their torments in a kind of *perpetuum stabile*. It is not altogether frivolous to think of the answer of the Irish linguist asked if there is an Irish equivalent to the Spanish *mañana*. He replied that there is, adding that the Irish word does not have the same pressing urgency as the Spanish. Beckett's characters exist in some such leisurely, meditative time of agonised crisis. Krapp, quite apart from his juggling with temporal sequence, lives with the others in that continuum, engaged in the same exercise of reconstruction.

Contemplation and memory define it for Krapp in Yeats's dilemma of committal to 'perfection of the life or of the work' – however imperfect either may be: the women remembered by the multiple Krapp, in grossly sexual relationships and one idyllic encounter, the younger Krapp rejected in favour of 'the opus . . . magnum'. Krapp recurs most often to the tender concord with the girl on the lake, opening her eyes to let him in – as Vivian Mercier points out, a spiritual not a meanly sexual union.[7] There is a great deal more to it than a wiser old Krapp's chastising his youthful folly. At sixty-nine his memory has dismantled experiences, like his mother's death, once alive with feeling. Bitter, shifting from attitude to attitude, Krapp nonetheless preserves an episode of love briefly shared. Movingly, he is at once incapable and capable of devotion. One should not make too much of the sparingly lyrical memory. The painful recognition of a reality is as always subject to the enticement of footling substitutes: Krapp's lengthy preparations, his drinks off in the dark, his consulting the dictionary, and general fiddling.

Comparing Beckett's *Watt* to *Gulliver's Travels*, Hugh Kenner observes in Swift's narrator his host of 'inventories and numerical estimates'. It is a fictional device to characterise a mind 'devoid of moral resources', imprisoned in a systematising, narrowly phenomenal perception. Joyce similarly designates the lost mind of Leopold Bloom by loading it 'to the eyes in quantifiable matter'. Objects are 'not a background for human identity but a densely compacted substitute'.

Beckett's plays set him with these 'great Irish nihilists . . . the persistent reformers of the fictional imagination'.[8] His characters try to limit themselves to definition by their portable odds and ends, the measured stage, by words which in a dance of their own stand in for a reality too fearful to inhabit. Glimpses of it breach the defences. The stage then seeks to neutralise their revelation, consoling or discouraging, in its own games. Beckett's version of human suffering is in the end one of human endurance, imaged in a theatrical form. Its painfulness is mitigated by the 'gallows humour' which Beckett shares with O'Casey, pervasive to the temperament of Irish writing in English. In its own way Beckett's world is kin to Murphy's or Kilroy's, where God is an unlikely, or grimly laughable, hypothesis. These shapings are a strain of the relatively brief Irish dramatic tradition. The brevity, however, has its opportunities. There is a strong Irish inclination to the solo performance. This virtuosity, a kind of imaginative self-genesis, can fall flat, but it is the effective energy through the whole of Synge, in O'Casey's Dublin trilogy and his later plays spasmodically, in Beckett at least up to *Happy Days* (1961).

We are aware in them all of an autocratic willing of one's own art into being. Both Synge and Beckett keep 'the reality' of their stage, its words, its characters and action, at a carefully maintained distance from the world outside it. O'Casey, in his bent, creates a tumbling, absurdist metropolis whose heirs, when its communes finally fail, might be Beckett's Vladimirs and Estragons. 'Tradition' is perhaps a presumptuous word to apply to this grouping. Certainly it enfolds a cluster of likenesses enough to suggest their presence together in and constituting a common imaginative heredity. Humour is a consequential part of it. Of these three dramatists, Beckett has most consciously diminished, though never extinguished, it. Even with the least cordial possibilities, the sequence of interrogation and torture in *Radio II* (1960), the bureaucratisation of suffering, mordantly and grotesquely comic, intercepts the anguish and holds it to the view.

This is obviously not an exhaustive account of Beckett's work, even of his work for the stage. Its emphasis, too, is much more on a manner of seeing than on themes or subjects. It is profoundly true of Beckett that the manner is very close to being the matter. Whatever may be lurking as detachable theme or meaning is almost inextricably part of the way it is perceived and presented, or more usually, masked. Godot fails to arrive. A boy, different (he says) in each act, does turn up, but is of no help. In *Endgame* a boy appears, prodigiously, from the blighted world of Clov's description. So, at least, Clov tells us, and he prepares to depart. At the end of the play he remains on stage, bondage to Hamm perhaps unbroken – if bondage is all it is.

The only absolute is uncertainty, and it is individuals, in whatever certainties they may pretend, who must make the most of that. Beckett's desolate landscape, if it is lit up at all, is lit by lingering tenacities of friendship and loyalty – a shared despair. In *Godot*, Vladimir and Estragon, having agreed, 'let's go', do not move. Nor do they part. 'The light gleams an instant, then it's night once more.' Débris, bits and pieces, ends and odds never achieve the self-annihilation which it is their function to represent. Beckett's honour is to have re-named a local hinterland of actuality into its metaphysical constituencies.

(II)

SCENE: A 'RESTORED' PEASANT COTTAGE IN CO. DONEGAL –

Tim signals frantically to Claire to go back up. She sees his gestures but keeps coming down. Donovan is crouching down at the [cattle] posts.

DONOVAN. My God, Tim, that's wonderful, that's really wonderful! I haven't seen these for – my God, it must be over fifty years! And you've incorporated them into the kitchen as of course it should be because that is exactly as it was! Oh, you're no amateur at this, Tim! You know your heritage! Oh, you and I are going to have a lot to say to each other! Marvellous! Just marvellous!

Claire is now at the bottom of the stairs and is approaching them. As she approaches, Tim's panic rises. He scarcely knows what he is saying.

TIM. This is where we all come from.

DONOVAN. Indeed.

TIM. This is our first cathedral.

DONOVAN. Amen to that.

TIM. This shaped all our souls. This determined our first pieties. This is a friend of mine.

The Communication Cord

In contrast to Beckett's, all Brian Friel's plays are unmistakably Irish in setting. Friel was born in Omagh in 1929 and has spent his life in Ireland. In 1939 the family moved to Derry City, where his father had been appointed a teacher at the Long Tower School. Friel was educated there and at St Columb's College. From 1945 to 1948 he attended Maynooth College, the Catholic seminary, leaving it with a BA, but not for the priesthood. He taught for some years in Derry, writing, as an after-hours activity, short stories which appeared regularly in the *New Yorker* in the mid-fifties. In 1960 he began to work full time as a writer. By then the BBC had accepted two radio plays from him, and in 1962 the Abbey presented his *The Enemy Within*, the earliest play he is still prepared to acknowledge. The first wide recognition of his work came with *Philadelphia, Here I Come!*, produced at the Dublin Theatre Festival of 1964, in 1966 in New York, and in London in 1967.

Over the eighteen years from 1964, Friel has written the most substantial and impressive body of work in contemporary Irish drama. Its variety, from the late seventies taking on new strengths, is to be seen in *Philadelphia, Lovers* (1967), *Crystal and Fox* (1968), *The Freedom of the City* (1973), *Aristocrats* (1979), *Faith Healer* (1979), *Translations* (1980) and *The Communication Cord* (1982). While they constitute a pattern, the integrity of its design eludes prediction, confirmed in the re-casting imposed by each succeeding play. *Faith Healer*, for example, to consider a particular theme, by adopting unexpected forms and applications, makes us see Friel's earlier plays in a different though still coherent way.

Friel has always been absorbed in the figments of memory: in *Philadelphia* a day in a rowing boat, a song, remembered differently by father and son. In *Crystal and Fox*, Fox, the proprietor of a travelling show, methodically destroys his present situation because of its incongruity with the past of his recollection. In *Aristocrats*, Casimir's fables of the patrician dignity of the Catholic Big House of his childhood break into the ruin of its decline confirmed. The characters persuade us to accept their views of what may have been or happened. Its actuality is perhaps irreclaimable, a re-creation of fond memory, which may comfort, or equally, destroy. *Faith Healer* is similarly concerned with the apparitions of memory, now shifted to different outlines.

'But that's another story', says Frank Hardy, faith healer, early in the play. It is made up of stories and other stories, a riddling account of the lives of its three characters – the faith healer himself, his wife (or mistress) Grace, and Teddy, Frank's manager and warm-up man. In structure it consists of four monologues: by Frank, who we gradually learn is dead, at the beginning and end; by Grace, also now dead, and Teddy in between – a boldly demanding form. Inconsistently, the monologues reconstruct the itinerary of Frank's career through Welsh and Scottish villages until his killing (never directly so named) outside an Irish pub by the four drunken friends of a cripple whom, we infer, he has failed to heal. That is the major tale that is told, or partly told. From what it tells us we may compose answers for its riddles, or leave them as perfectly articulated questions. Some of them tease us with matters of plain fact. What is the 'truth' of the episode at Kinlochbervie? All three speakers evoke it in solid and often brutal physical detail, converting it, however, each into his own version of an event. Is the reality the cruel birth of Grace's stillborn child, or that Frank heard there of his mother's death; the idyllic weather in Teddy's mind, 'all blue and white and golden', or Grace's 'heavy wet mist'? Or have the memories a validity of their own?

Between Frank, Grace and Teddy, psychological recognitions and misapprehensions, a flux of dependences and rejections, divulge themselves to us. They do not emerge from minds insulated within their own fantasies. The characters have dealings with a social world and its demands. Grace's father is a judge, 'obsessed with order', with his 'family profession and his formal Japanese gardens'. Frank's father says of his son, 'it'll be hard for him to beat his oul fella'. A policeman and a city gent, in Teddy's monologue, outrage his grief. Above all are 'the crippled and the blind and the disfigured and the deaf and the barren', unseen worshippers of Frank's 'ministry without responsibility, a vocation without a ministry'. They enter the tatty halls to be healed, or for confirmation of their despair.

Frank's gift is real but fickle, independent of his will. 'Was it all chance?' he asks, '– or skill? – or illusion? – or delusion?' In the end he confronts savagery, the menace of an axe, a crowbar, a mallet, a hayfork. Approaching the cripple in the pub yard, sure that he will fail, warned 'if you do nothing for him, Mister, they'll kill you', he is submitting to his gift in a mortal test which becomes a kind of sacrificial victory:

20   Brian Friel's *Philadelphia, Here I Come!* at the Abbey, 1981

And as I moved across that yard towards them and offered myself to them, then for the first time I had a simple and genuine sense of home-coming. Then for the first time there was no atrophying terror; and the maddening questions were silent.

After Frank's triumphant performance in Llanbethian an old farmer whom he has cured pays tribute, 'and whatever way he said Glamorgan', says Teddy, 'it sounded like the whole world'. The remark applies to *Faith Healer*. It solidly establishes its immediate occasion. Its words create the three lives at issue, their soul-fearings, their squalid surroundings – their battered van, its primus stove, the wet kindling, the bottles. It also disengages them from the particular histories. They enter a limbo where life, reviewed by an act of imagination, may declare some meaning.

The meaning proposed by *Faith Healer* is a harsh one, but gestured by language into an elevation of feeling. Both the comic and the sombre spirits are observers. Friel has never written more splendidly comic prose than in Teddy's monologue, modulating with total assurance into grief and loss. We move from the grotesquely funny account of Rob Roy the Piping Dog as Dedicated Artist – 'Morning, noon and night he'd sit there blowing the bloody thing and working them bellows with his back leg' – to Kinlochbervie and Grace's child, 'that little wet thing with the black face and the black body, a tiny little thing, no size at all – a boy it was'. Comic or tragic, memory tries to come to terms with the past. Reality, both malleable and stubborn, as of the three of them Frank Harvey most clearly and consciously sees, is the material with which faith and imagination live, remembering and re-creating, and, if they work, changing. Frank is an image of the artist, the mystery of his enhancing powers and their capricious release.

As a parable of the artist, Frank Harvey makes explicit that particular expression of the allure of make-believe. Throughout Friel's plays the characters are interpreting the reality of their situation by imagining it into other possibilities, or supplying alternatives to it. What might be, or might have been, is being asked to put its pressure on, and perhaps alter, actuality; or at least to relieve, to displace, facts which have become intolerable. That exercise too, conscious fantasy or illusion, is in its way a creative act.

These metaphors of the imaginative operations which lead to art are recurrent in Friel's plays. They do not, however, at all make the plays a dramatised discourse on aesthetics. The characters and their predicaments are urgent with entirely human distresses and desires. Frank Harvey is latently a symbol of the artist. Primarily he is Frank Harvey, faith healer, in the suffering of choice, indecision, self-indulgence.

In *Philadelphia* a young man, Gar O'Donnell is about to emigrate from Ballybeg, Co. Donegal. The play's concern is not 'the problem of Irish emigration'. Its concern, in Friel's words, 'is a kind of love, the love between a father and a son and between a son and his birthplace'. Gar despises, tolerates, disregards, loves his father, S.B., and mocks him. The mockery is voiced, in the play's striking technical device, by Private Gar, present on stage with his Public *alter ego*, unseen, unheard by the other actors. He comments, for instance, on S.B. as he enters from his shop and prepares to take his evening meal:

The pert little apron is detachable – (*S.B. removes apron.*) – Thank you, Marie Celeste – and underneath we have the tapered Italian-line slacks in ocelot. I would draw your attention to the large collar stud which is highly decorative and can be purchased separately at our boutique. We call this seductive outfit 'Indiscretion.' It can be worn six days a week, in or out of bed. (*In polite tone*) Have a seat Screwballs. (*S.B. sits down at the table.*) Thank you. Remove the hat. (*S.B. takes off the hat to say grace. He blesses himself.*) On again (*Hat on*) Perfectly trained

and so into the deadly familiar nightly conversation.

The guying does not, of course, summarise the relationship. Friel's lyricism is sparing, but when the scene demands, responsive, as love fractures into a past where memories never quite coincide. S.B. and the local Canon are playing chess. 'I had you cornered', says the Canon, setting Private off into a popsong parody. Then, Mendelssohn's violin concerto on his gramophone, he thrusts his face between the two players:

D'you know what the music says? It says that once upon a time a boy and his father sat in a blue boat on a lake on an afternoon in May, and on that afternoon a great beauty happened that has haunted the boy ever since, because he wonders now did it really take place or did he imagine it? There are only the two of us, he says; each of us is all the other has; and why can we not even look at each other?

Brought into the open by Public, it elicits no memory from S.B.

The Public/Private bond is an involved one. They are convincingly a single person, sharing both their sardonic humour and their vulnerable affections. The Private Gar, at times amenable to the Public's buffoonery, ready on occasion to divert his misgivings, at other times forces into the open feelings of which the composite Gar fights shy. The deeper searching comes gradually. The audience is at first engrossed by brilliantly comic exchanges.

Public and Private between them, with S.B. at the centre, assemble the circle of Gar's relationships. The schoolmaster, once a suitor of Gar's mother, now a seedy mountebank, pays a moving farewell, reaching into emotions not even alluded to by the words. Gar surrenders his sweetheart to her father's notion of a better prospect, as Gar's 'present' time of kitchen and bedroom fades, leaving empty space to the young lovers. Gar retreats, demoralised, from his buoyant proposals of marriage and family – 'very well preserved for a father of fourteen children', says Private.

Different aspects of the present and another possible future press their claims. Gar is waiting for 'the boys' to come and say goodbye. When they do, they open another of Ballybeg's confined perspectives. Their endless reminiscences of imaginary seductions conceals a reality of futile street wanderings, of cold, of locked doors, of drawn blinds. But their faulty camaraderie, with its cadences of silence, embarrassed by Gar's leave-taking, calls on Gar's uncertain loyalties with something that memory may 'distil of all its coarseness'. The future represented in the re-enacted visit by his childless, tippling Irish-American aunt arouses in Private dread of an oppressive motherliness as claustrophobic as Ballybeg. The vistas forebode blind alleys.

Philadelphia is in part generalising a statement about Ireland, the Ireland of religious and sexual frigidity, of overbearing old age, of joyless, close-mouthed rural puritanism; and of their opposites seeking release. More broadly, the play is talking about estrangement, loneliness, hopes (and their frustration) of understanding and intimacy, translated from a parochial accent, idiom and scene.

Private Gar tells S.B. to make an unpredictable remark, say, 'I like to walk across the White Strand when there's a misty rain falling', or, 'stick it out here with me for it's not such a bad aul' bugger of a place': possibilities that remain unenacted, a chance of union not realised. In *Crystal and Fox*, Fox remembers when he and Crystal 'raced across the wet fields in our bare feet'. The sense is of transient moments, actual or desired, which epitomise the enhancing ideal of a life: a longing for, or an experience, past or fated to pass, of love, friendship, shared observances. In the first play of *Lovers*, during the one day we see of the young couple, ending in their death by drowning, Joe and Mag banter, quarrel, make their peace. Early death frustrates the insinuations of bitterness to be. They are the 'Winners' of the play's title. The 'Losers' of the second play, married in middle age, lapse from real, though less ardent, love into sardonic self-containment. It is something like Joe and Mag's still healing responsiveness to each other that Fox wants to re-possess from his and Crystal's past.

In order to return, Fox sets out to destroy what is, his dying show. Hearing his showman's patter, one might almost forget his theatre's broken seats, holey roof, and the run-down truck. His poise is infirm, under it weariness and bafflement. Gradually he rids himself of the insignia of failure. Offensively heedless of El Cid's pretensions, he drives him away. He wonders if, at a sudden moment of moonlight, Pedro's performing dog might not prefer 'to all the sugar cubes in the world just one little saucer of arsenic'; and if he did, whether Pedro would love him enough to supply it. Fox does. His son, a fugitive, does not quite understand Fox's privacy:

GABRIEL. You're full of hate – that's what's wrong with you – you hate everybody!
FOX. No.
GABRIEL. Even Crystal.
FOX. What about Crystal?
GABRIEL. She'll be the next. You'll ditch her too.

Finally Crystal leaves after Fox tells her, falsely, that he has informed on Gabriel for a reward. Vilifying himself he is believed and rejected, his own last victim.

Fox destroys, neither through hatred nor love, but because of a bewildering groping to understand them, and what may become of them, what happens to youth when its hopes have gone and 'love alone isn't enough – not nearly enough'. Fox's quest is not just a death-wish. It has a desperate hope in view – 'I want to live like a child. I want to die and wake up in heaven with Crystal' – but it leaves him, loving still, denied the human ruses for dissembling reality. In his small community, Fox sees through the simple-hearted panaceas for human discontents. In the world at large, of which Fox's might be a microcosm, universal brotherhood and selfless love have to work through recalcitrant agents. Fox is an itinerant showman who proves that he would rather not believe; in part, the old Adam of Everyman.

Philadelphia, Lovers, Crystal and Fox are inspecting some of the popular concepts of love – family, romantic, Christian – and the expectations that reality is unlikely to gratify. *The Freedom of the City* consolidates a shift, apparent in *The Gentle Island* (1971), to a broader than household placing of, as they nevertheless remain, private lives. It took shape during the late sixties, the years of renewed civil dissent in Northern Ireland, though its origins go further back. As a play set in Derry City in 1970 it engages the problem of maintaining the prismatic individuality of character in a situation – that is, the real-life situation – readier to assume the simplicities of dogma.

Michael, Lily, and Skinner are dead to begin with, identified, as soldiers drag their bodies from the stage, to the Judge conducting the enquiry into their deaths. The stage is fluid. Judge and witnesses make episodic appearances on the wall battlements above the main scene. The Tribunal is literally a framework for the main action. This covers the day when, as rumour and official account agree, a gang of armed subversives occupied Derry Guildhall, headquarters of the City administration, after the army had broken up a Civil Rights demonstration. Hence a basic irony: events as they were; events as the enquiry elicits and pronounces on them. But we are to be wary of taking such an irony as anything like the whole story. Outside, the army marshals; people feed on word of insurrection and atrocity; television interprets, a ballad singer mythologises, the events. All the external accounts are entirely at odds with what we see happen in the Mayor's Parlour.

Finally emerging from the Guildhall, unarmed, Michael, Lily, and Skinner are shot down. Their funerals, heavily graced by dignitaries from the Republic, almost immediately institutionalise their deaths as National Monuments. For the TV commentator, they are notably 'dignified', a mirror image of the Civil Rights marches derided by Skinner. The Tribunal has deliberated conflicting eyewitness testimony, and expert evidence, much of it gruesomely clinical. The judge, on legally sufficient evidence, finds that the three carried arms and used them; he exonerates the army. The victims, as in their funerals, have become objects, the individuality we have seen of no account.

Michael appears a little pompous, his eyes on the middle class, half out of the slums, full of Civil Rights doctrine. He regrets the vanished 'dignity' of the earliest marches, when the presence of 'doctors, teachers, accountants', impressed him. 'Shite', says Skinner, impatient of respectability as he pours the Civic drink. Michael is in part what Skinner mocks, an easy butt. Yet he has an appealingly bewildered honesty, touchingly uncertain. The circumstances that supplied his answers, he uneasily suspects, have gone.

Lily, ignorant and artless, forty-three years old, with eleven children, is most fully of her background, spokeswoman for ghetto miseries she hardly sees as injuries. Her world is the streets around her, their life her conversation, indifferently of suffering, brutality, high spirits. It is entirely from such facts that Lily articulates her being. The demands of Civil Rights – 'wan man, wan vote', 'no more gerrymandering' – though she marches for them, are exotic abstractions in her life. So Skinner, over her protests, tells her.

Lily marches, Skinner says, because she's obscurely aware of outrage at the hardships so vividly expressed in her uncalculating chronicles; because, 'in a vague groping way', she has awakened to 'hundreds, thousands, millions of us all over the world . . . It's about us – the poor – the majority – stirring in our sleep. And if that's not what it's all about, then it has nothing to do with us.' His statement is liable to be taken as the play's point of view. It is not, like Michael's, undermined by mockery.

Yet how valid does the play make it appear? For Skinner, at that moment, a vision of the unified poor is the only motive with any reality. But those are not Lily's terms, though some response to them may crystallize her own moving formulation:

SKINNER. Where did you hide the brandy?
LILY. I told a lie about our Declan. That's what Declan is. He's not just shy, our Declan. He's a mongol.
(*She finds the brandy bottle and hands it to him.*) And it's for him I go on all the civil

rights marches . . . Isn't that the stupidest thing you ever heard? Sure I could
march and protest from here to Dublin and sure what good would it do Declan?
But I still march – every Saturday I still march. Isn't that the stupidest thing you
ever heard?

SKINNER. No.

We are in the presence of a culture that is breaking up. However miserable,
ghetto life had for Lily its reassuring familiarities. Ambitions such as
Michael's, ideas like Skinner's, threaten its vehemently local integrity and
domestic loyalties. Would they survive Skinner's internationalism; and by
what, without them, would that be supported? The world in which Lily
suffered sustained her too, and is collapsing into problematical shapes.

Through these lives Friel observes an urban face – and catches the urban
as accurately as the rural voice – of the society familiar in his work. He has
observed in it its 'peculiar spiritual, and indeed material, flux'. The imprint
of that we may identify, for example, in Gar or in Fox; as we may,

21 Brian Friel's *Translations* at the Abbey, 1980

differently manifested, in *The Freedom of the City*, the same individual search for some covenant with dissolving, although once familiar, prospects. Its methods too – the recurrent dissolves of scene, the forceful management of shifting viewpoints, the commentaries – are revisions of technique appropriate to the new subject and setting. The play is recording tremors of a social mutation.

Like *The Freedom*, *The Gentle Island* expresses a sense – or the loss of a sense – of possessing and of belonging – to farm, region, culture. Its point of departure is the peculiarly regional one of the depopulated offshore western islands. More broadly, it is a parable of human searching after communion and permanence, and the rupture of contact, as the islanders abandon Inishkeen, between a people and their untenable home, its places and their legends. The theme has increasingly occupied Friel, reaching full statement in *Translations*.

The year is 1833. The occasion is the exercise in which the British army, compiling the first systematic mapping of Ireland, is assigning to the Gaelic place-names either a roughly accurate English transliteration or an English translation as exact as may be. Within the closeness of its characters' private experiences, *Translations* enshrines the wasting of a local being, which is in the end a national being, usurped by the comprehensive re-naming/un-naming of its localities. The setting is Hugh's hedge-school in, again, Ballybeg, where a contingent of sappers (two of their horses reported missing as the play opens) is at work on the survey; and where all the Irish speak Irish and are assumed to be doing so on stage. They have in various degrees, from their schooling, a knowledge of Latin and Greek. Generally, they have no English. The world of Jimmy Jack Cassie, the sixty-year-old 'Infant Prodigy', is one in which Homeric deities, Diarmuid and Grania, the Donnelly twins (also, ominously, missing) live together in a union of fact and legend.

Not all the locals have Jimmy's and Hugh's devotion. Maire wants to learn English and urges Manus, Hugh's son, to apply for a post in the new national school. Owen, Hugh's other son, works for the army as a translator. Loyalties, linguistic and emotional, divide. Maire falls in love with Lieutenant Yolland, who is bewitched not only by her but by a place, and a language he can no more understand than she can his. In a beautifully hesitant scene the obstacle of language dissolves, the place-names become their entrance to communion:

MAIRE. Carraig an Phoill
YOLLAND. Carraig na Ri
      Loch na nEan.
MAIRE. Loch an Iubhair
      Machaire Buidhe. . . .

YOLLAND. . . . if you could understand me . . . I would tell you how I want to be here – to live here – always – with you – always, always.
MAIRE. 'Always'? What is that word – 'always'?
YOLLAND. Yes – yes; always.
MAIRE. You're trembling.
YOLLAND. Yes, I'm trembling because of you.
MAIRE. I'm trembling, too.
She holds his face in her hands.
YOLLAND. I've made up my mind –
MAIRE. Shhh.
YOLLAND. I'm not going to leave here.
MAIRE. Shhh – listen to me. I want you, too, soldier.
YOLLAND. Don't stop – I know what you're saying.
MAIRE. I want to live with you – anywhere – anywhere at all – always – always.
YOLLAND. 'Always'? What is that word – 'always'?

The private liturgy of names is profaned when, Yolland missing, Captain Lancey announces his reprisals through Owen: evictions, houses razed 'in the following selected areas' –

LANCEY. Swinefort.
OWEN. Lis na Muc.
LANCEY. Burnfoot.
OWEN. Bun na hAbhann.
LANCEY. Drumduff.
OWEN. Druim Dubh.
LANCEY. Whiteplains.
OWEN. Machaire Ban.

The play ends in that tone of dying affirmation. Jimmy, drunk, announces his coming marriage – to Pallas Athene, though it will be 'exogamous', 'outside the tribe'. The next day he is to meet her father, Zeus. Hugh, as the lights dim, drunkenly salutes Juno, who 'discovered that a race was springing from Trojan blood to overthrow some day these Tyrian towers – a people kings of broad realms and proud in war who would come forth for Lybia's downfall'. Sarah, the mute girl who had been learning to speak, reverts to silence.

Baile Beag is an imperfect Eden, the corrupt smell of potato blight portending its other disasters. Its inhabitants are themselves not wholly certain of their civil being, 'imprisoned in a linguistic contour which no longer matches the landscape of . . . fact'. The fact that was is now being reduced by the deletion of its familiarising names. The Anglicised names and their originals echo through all the play in a litany of lament for the Gaelic topography – the *'desiderium nostrorum* – the need of our own. Our *pietas'*. The loss of names figures and pre-figures the loss of the language itself:

Yes, it is a rich language, Lieutenant, full of the mythologies of fantasy and hope and self-deception. A syntax opulent with tomorrows. It is our response to mud-cabins and a diet of potatoes; our only method of replying to . . . inevitabilities.

Architecturally identical, the set of *The Communication Cord* parodies that of *Translations*. It is a 'traditional' Irish cottage interior, 'an artifact of today making obeisance to a home of yesterday', a painstaking but in the end phoney restoration. The play itself boldly diminishes the tragic burden of its predecessor to farce. The characters embroil themselves in the predicaments of the convention: mistaken identities (with fake and genuine foreign accents), embarrassing entrances, past *affaires* re-asserted, girls and underclothing to be concealed or explained away, machinations of seduction or personal advantage. Haplessly caught in the intrigue is Tim Gallagher, junior lecturer without tenure in linguistics, expert on 'communicational structures', lost for words when he needs them. He is to impress Senator Donovan, vulgarian enthusiast for 'the Gaelic inheritance', but with both a nubile daughter and university influence, that Tim's roots are in genuinely peasant soil.

Tim achieves none of his purposes, lost in a linguistic and physical fog. The cottage door is given to springing open, extinguishing the lamp and enveloping the scene in smoke from the turf fire. Objects, malign and untrustworthy as language, are traps. Irish idiom baffles a German (taken by Tim to be his friend Jack imitating the German). The Senator locks himself in the cattle posts, humiliatingly trapped and mocked by the past he so espouses. The relics, so insensitively restored in the cottage, are in a state of collapse and language cannot keep up with the mad onrush of complications. In the end Tim gets a girl, though not Susan Donovan. As he kisses her, leaning against the supporting upright, Jack now imprisoned in the posts, the lamp dying, the building falls apart:

NORA. Jesus, Mary and Joseph, the house is falling in!
SUSAN. Jack, the place is . . . Ooogh!
JACK. O my God.
The lamp dies. Total darkness.

Tim's unfinished thesis is on 'response cries – an involuntary response to what you've just heard' – as 'O my God' – which may cover a whole range of reactions, genuine or pretended. *The Communication Cord* is itself a richly elaborate response cry: primarily to Senator Donovan's affectations, a sham nostalgia, the trifling society which indulges it, and its conversational flights. 'This is what I need – this silence, this peace, the restorative power of that landscape . . . This is the touchstone. That landscape, that sea, this house – this is the apotheosis.' To which Tim replies, 'Yes'. The past – heroic, its landscape seen by instinct as the abode of gods and men – can no longer perpetuate its myth-making powers. Its present heirs, in this view of them, can see it only in coarsened perceptions, whether pseudo-anti-quarianism or commercialising indifference. In the play the cottage is widely desired – as love-nest, property, miniature museum. In the society of *The Communication Cord* the past, mourned in *Translations*, is caricatured, a home for the cavortings of farce. It is a very funny play. Its laughter alleviates by liberating truths, however discomfiting.

The Communication Cord might also be seen as a tilt against all the Abbey kitchens, match-makings and disputed inheritances, the wily and amiable peasants. The workings of art, its varied ways of naming, contribute to Friel's possessing of his realities. In the development of his theatre considerable formal variety contains a unity of themes and of attitudes to human affairs. There is a clustering around experiences of love, the traffic between present and past, personal and national, the shaky armistices with suffering that illusion, art or dream, may negotiate. 'I would like', he has said, 'to write a play that would capture the peculiar spiritual, and indeed material, flux that this country is in at the moment. This has got to be done, for me anyway, at a local, parochial level, and hopefully this will have meaning for people in other countries.' This describes the plays Friel has already written, regarded as a composite, a single, continuing testimony. They find the dramatic forms which generalise, with humour and com-passion, on his particular and regional veracities, where art begins.

Friel's work is entirely compatible with that of his contemporaries considered here. With them and with Beckett it falls into a recognisable line of descent. Of the writers whose images are in their origin directly of Ireland, Friel most fully identifies a landscape whose parts, in their naming, translate to other regions. The logic of the landscape, clear and concrete in its references, is different from – even, like Synge's, the reverse of – Beckett's. Each, however, has rights of passage into the others. Yeats the theorist, Synge, O'Casey, Johnston, Beckett, Friel, assembling with the other dramatists, irradiate realist theatre with a diverse dramatic poetry. The work of the present generation is fertile with new possibilities.

Notes

INTRODUCTION

1. This and the movement's early years are documented in Lady Gregory's *Our Irish Theatre*.
2. Boyd, *The Contemporary Drama of Ireland*, p. 4.
3. Malone, *The Irish Drama*, pp. 14–15.
4. *Ibid.*, pp. 2–12.
5. See William Smith Clarke, *The Irish Stage in the Country Towns, 1720–1800*.
6. Kavanagh, *The Story of the Abbey Theatre*, p. 184.
7. Ellis-Fermor, *The Irish Dramatic Movement*, p. 115.
8. Hogan, *After the Irish Renaissance*, pp. 147–51.
9. Flannery, *W. B. Yeats and the Idea of a Theatre*.
10. Yeats, *Explorations*, p. 250.
11. Preface to the first edition of *John M. Synge's Poems and Translations*, ed. Yeats, *The Cutting of an Agate*, p. 124.
12. Yeats, *Explorations*, p. 257.
13. *Ibid.*, p. 183.
14. *Ibid.*, p. 167.
15. Patrick Collins in *Ireland Today*, 994 (1983), 5.
16. Yeats, *Autobiographies*, p. 571.

1. DREAMS AND RESPONSIBILITIES: 1891–1904

1. Lady Gregory, *Our Irish Theatre*, pp. 8–9.
2. Moore, *Ave* 1911; *Salve* 1912; *Vale* 1914. Later published together as *Hail and Farewell*.
3. Yeats, *Autobiographies*, pp. 280, 413.
4. *Ibid.*, p. 428.
5. *Ibid.*, p. 401.
6. For an entertaining account of Dublin's staple theatrical fare see R. Hogan and J. Kilroy, *The Irish Literary Theatre*, pp. 9–22.
7. They were jointly the inspiration of the Independent Theatre founded by J. T. Grein in London in 1891. Designed to advance the cause of Ibsen, it survived without much distinction for seven years, though it did give Shaw his first production – *Widowers Houses*.
8. *Beltaine: The Organ of the Irish Literary Theatre*, an occasional publication, May 1899–April 1900.
9. *Beltaine*, 2, 1900, pp. 9–13; *Samhain* (1901–5, 1908; the successor to *Beltaine*), 1901, pp. 14–15. The Theatre's third occasional periodical was *The Arrow*, 1906–9.

10. Yeats, *Autobiographies*, pp. 348–9; letter to Frank Fay, 26 August 1904, quoted in Gerard Fay, *The Abbey Theatre*, p. 86. The general question of Yeats's attitude to Continental theatre is for later remark (pp. 29–30). Briefly, however, it may be said here that he drew upon it, as was his habit, in a selective and individual way. While violently experimental work like Jarry's disturbed him, he found in the French theatre's use of 'symbolic and decorative scenery' (Yeats, *Letters*, p. 280), in aspects of Maeterlinck's drama, and above all in Villiers de l'Isle Adam's *Axël*, suggestions of dramatic style adaptable to the kind of play he was imagining for himself.
11. Yeats, *Autobiographies*, p. 279.
12. Lady Gregory, *Our Irish Theatre*, p. 17.
13. Yeats, *Autobiographies*, p. 283.
14. George Moore, 'Introduction' to Martyn's *'The Heather Field' and 'Maeve'*, p. ix.
15. Yeats, *Explorations*, pp. 109, 128.
16. Yeats, *Autobiographies*, p. 280.
17. Interview, *Freeman's Journal*, 13 November 1901.
18. Frank J. Fay, *Towards a National Theatre*, ed. R. Hogan, pp. 51–76.
19. Denis Gwynn, *Edward Martyn and the Irish Revival*, pp. 142–3, Martyn quoted.
20. Joyce, 'Ibsen's New Drama', in *The Critical Writings of James Joyce*, ed. Ellsworth Mason and Richard Ellmann, p. 67.
21. Joyce, 'The Day of the Rabblement', *ibid.*, p. 67.
22. Martyn, *Beltaine*, 2, 1900; Yeats, *Samhain*, 1901; Moore, *Freeman's Journal*, 23 February 1900.
23. Yeats, *Explorations*, p. 96.
24. Gerard Fay, *The Abbey Theatre*, p. 90.
25. Yeats, *Autobiographies*, p. 349.
26. Yeats, *Explorations*, p. 88.
27. *Ibid.*, p. 86.
28. See Yeats, *Explorations*, pp. 108–9. 171–4; and James Flannery, *W.B. Yeats and the Idea of a Theatre*, pp. 196ff.
29. Frank Fay, *Towards a National Theatre*, pp. 77–8.
30. Max Beerbohm, *Saturday Review*, 9 April 1904.
31. A. B. Walkley, *Drama and Life*, 1907, p. 311.
32. Yeats, *Letters*, p. 405.
33. Gerard Fay, *The Abbey Theatre*, p. 60.
34. *Ibid.*, p. 89.
35. Yeats, *Uncollected Prose*, II, ed. John P. Frayne and Colton Johnson, p. 375.
36. Sam Hanna Bell, *The Theatre in Ulster*, pp. 2–3.
37. Yeats, *Explorations*, p. 76.
38. Yeats, 'The Controversy over the Playboy', *The Arrow*, 1907.
39. *United Irishman*, 29 October 1904; reprinted in *Lost Plays of the Irish Renaissance*, ed. R. Hogan and J. Kilroy 1970.
40. *United Irishman*, 24 October 1903.
41. *Ibid.*, 17 October 1903.
42. Yeats, *Autobiographies*, pp. 213, 209.

43. Frank Fay, *Towards a National Theatre*, pp. 50, 56.
44. Yeats, *Uncollected Prose*, II, p. 289.
45. John Eglinton, 'The de-Davisisation of Irish Literature', *United Irishman*, 31 March 1902.
46. Yeats, *Uncollected Prose*, I, ed. John P. Frayne, pp. 90, 158.
47. *Ibid.*, I, p. 408; II, p. 37.

2. POSSIBLE FORMS: THE EARLY PLAYS

1. See Synge's account of the occasion, *Collected Works*, II, ed. Alan Price, pp. 381–2.
2. Yeats, *Uncollected Prose*, II, ed. John P. Frayne and Colton Johnson, p. 202.
3. Yeats, 'Preface' to *Poems 1899–1905*, 1906.
4. Yeats, *Plays in Prose and Verse*, p. 430.
5. J. M. Synge, *Collected Works*, II, p. 384.
6. Malone, *The Irish Drama*, p. 56.
7. Ann Saddlemyer, *In Defence of Lady Gregory*, p. 30.
8. Lady Gregory, *Collected Plays*, ed. Ann Saddlemyer I, p. 253.
9. *Ibid.*, p. 262.
10. Quoted in Ann Saddlemyer, *Theatre Business*, pp. 164–80.
11. Una Ellis-Fermor, *The Irish Dramatic Movement*, p. 132.
12. *United Irishman*, 19 December 1903.
13. Yeats, *Explorations*, p. 183.
14. Katherine Worth, on the other hand, speaking mainly of the revised version, puts the play with *Everyman* and the last scene of Marlowe's *Dr Faustus* (*The Irish Drama of Europe from Yeats to Beckett*, pp. 53–8). James Flannery, who directed the revised version at the Project Arts Centre in Dublin in 1976, says that the poetic version is 'superior . . . in the expression of its tragic theme' (*W. B. Yeats and the Idea of a Theatre*, p. 307).
15. S. B. Bushrui, *Yeats's Verse Plays: The Revisions 1900–10*, 1965, p. 28.
16. *Irish Times*, 13 January 1911.
17. Katherine Worth, *The Irish Drama of Europe*, pp. 52, 58.
18. Yeats, *Uncollected Prose*, I, pp. 324–5; *Autobiographies*, p. 320.
19. Yeats, *Essays and Introductions*, p. 195; *Uncollected Prose*, II, pp. 52–3.
20. Yeats, *Letters*, ed. Allan Wade, pp. 255–80.
21. Maeterlinck, *Treasury of the Humble*, pp. 98–111.
22. Micheál MacLiammóir, *Theatre in Ireland*, p. 15.
23. See David H. Greene and Edward M. Stephens, *J. M. Synge 1871–1909*, p. 121.
24. Synge, *Collected Works*, II, p. 350.
25. Yeats, 'J. M. Synge and the Ireland of his Time', *Essays and Introductions*, p. 341.

3. DIFFICULT, IRRELEVANT WORDS: W. B. YEATS AND J. M. SYNGE

1. Yeats, introduction to *Fighting the Waves*, the prose version of *The Only Jealousy of Emer, Explorations*, p. 370; Synge, letter to Stephen MacKenna, January 1904.
2. See, for example, F. A. C. Wilson, *Yeats's Iconography*, 1960; Peter Ure, *Yeats the Playwright*, 1963; James Rees Moore, *Masks of Love and Death*, 1971; Thomas Kilroy, 'Two Playwrights: Yeats and Beckett' in *Myth and Reality in Irish Theatre*, ed. J. Ronsley, 1977; James Flannery, *W. B. Yeats and the Idea of a Theatre*, 1976; Katherine Worth, *The Irish Drama of Europe*, 1978. Denis Donoghue, *The Third Voice* 1959; *Yeats*, 1971, is more reserved. Helen Vendler, *Yeats's Vision and the Later Plays*, 1963, discounts the plays as drama. There is considerable argument on interpretation of detail. I have chosen to carry out my own discussion without reference to it, though I am indebted to all the commentators.
3. Yeats, *Essays and Introductions*, p. 170; *Samhain* in *Explorations*, p. 108.
4. Yeats, *Essays and Introductions*, p. 224; elsewhere (p. 165), he speaks in more Aristotelian terms of 'the purification that comes with pity and terror to the imagination'.
5. Yeats, *Essays and Introductions*, pp. 521–2.
6. Yeats, *Explorations*, p. 194. Yeats's example was T. W. Robertson's *Caste*, New York, De Witts Acting Plays, 1868.
7. *Explorations*, p. 173.
8. *Ibid.*, p. 255.
9. Yeats, *Essays and Introductions*, p. 528.
10. Yeats, *Explorations*, p. 178.
11. *Ibid.*, p. 258.
12. Referring to his experiments with scenic design, Yeats notes that 'With every simplification the voice has recovered something of its importance' *Essays and Introductions*, p. 222.
13. Richard Ellmann, *Yeats: The Man and the Masks*, 1978, p. 216.
14. Yeats, *Autobiographies*, p. 503.
15. Yeats, *Essays and Introductions*, pp. 122, 123.
16. *Ibid.*, p. 235.
17. Yeats, *Explorations*, p. 184.
18. *Ibid.*, pp. 429, 336.
19. *Ibid.*, p. 375.
20. Yeats, *Autobiographies*, p. 524.
21. Yeats, *Memoirs*, pp. 184, 223.
22. See Seamus Deane, 'Irish Poetry and Irish Nationalism' in *Two Decades of Irish Writing*, ed. D. Dunn, 1975, p. 7.
23. Yeats, *Autobiographies*, p. 471; *Explorations*, pp. 153–4.
24. Quoted in Joseph Hone, *The Life of W. B. Yeats*, p. 225.
25. There are similarities of setting, possibly accidental, between this play and

Beckett's, *Waiting for Godot*, where Vladimir and Estragon lament: 'They make a noise like feathers. / Like leaves. / Like ashes. / Like leaves.'

26. Donoghue, *Yeats*, p. 16.
27. T. S. Eliot's notorious 'objective correlative', in 'Hamlet', in *Selected Essays* (3rd edn), 1951, is not, though it is often taken to be, a point of reference, a symbol, outside the work of art. It is the imagined circumstances exterior to a character in a play, which must account adequately for his feelings.
28. Eliot, 'Yeats', *On Poetry and Poets*.
29. Yeats, *Essays and Introductions*, p. 517.
30. *Ibid.*, p. 243.
31. Yeats, *Plays and Controversies*, London, 1923, p. 122; *Explorations*, pp. 154–5.
32. Synge, *Collected Works*, IV, ed. Ann Saddlemyer, p. 394; *Collected Works*, II, ed. Alan Price p. 384.
33. Synge's *Collected Works*, II, p. 29.
34. Yeats, *Uncollected Prose*, II, ed. John P. Frayne and Colton Johnson, p. 494.
35. Synge, notebook, 18 March 1907; Preface to *The Playboy*.
36. David H. Greene and Edward M. Stephens, *J. M. Synge*, p. 126; Ann Saddlemyer, 'Deirdre of the Sorrows' in *J. M. Synge. Centenary Papers 1971*, ed. M. Harmon, p. 107.
37. Ann Saddlemyer, Introduction, *J. M. Synge: Plays*, volume IV of *Collected Works*, p. xi.
38. Greene and Stephens *J. M. Synge*, p. 80. Van Hamel's article appeared in *Englische Studien* XLV in 1912.
39. Padraic Colum, *The Road Round Ireland*, 1926, p. 82.
40. Alan J. Bliss, 'The Language of Synge' in *J. M. Synge. Centenary Papers*, p. 44.
41. *Ibid.*, p. 54.
42. Yeats, *Explorations*, pp. 236, 253; *Essays and Introductions*, p. 339.
43. Thomas Kilroy, *Irish Times*, 26 April 1971; also Kilroy, 'Synge and Modernism' in *J. M. Synge. Centenary Papers*.
44. Synge, *Collected Works*, II, p. 14.
45. Quoted in Greene and Stephens, *J. M. Synge*, p. 296.
46. Synge, *Collected Works*, II, p. 384.
47. Eliot, *On Poetry and Poets*, p. 77.

4. AN ART OF COMMON THINGS: 1905–1910

1. Yeats to John Quinn, 16 September 1905, Yeats, *Letters*, ed. A. Wade, p. 461. The Russell referred to is George Russell (1867–1935), who wrote under the pseudonym AE. A poet, essayist, painter, and economist, he was active in the Irish literary revival and for a while in the early stages of the dramatic movement.
2. See the account in R. Hogan and J. Kilroy, *The Abbey Theatre*, pp. 123–62; and J. Kilroy, *The 'Playboy' Riots*.
3. Synge's Abbey Theatre programme note, 26 January 1907.
4. 'The Drama in Dublin', *Evening Telegraph*, 11 February 1908.
5. Yeats, *Explorations*, p. 243.

6. Synge, letter to *The Irish Times*, 31 January 1907.
7. Synge's Abbey Theatre programme note.
8. *London Sunday Sun*, 3 December 1905.
9. *Northern Whig*, 5 December 1906.
10. J. W. Good, in *Uladh*, May 1905.
11. Joseph Holloway, *Impressions of a Dublin Playgoer*, MS 1803, National Library of Ireland.
12. Carol Gelderman in *Eire-Ireland*, VIII: 2, pp. 62–70; 'Austin Clarke and Yeats's Alleged Jealousy of George Fitzmaurice'.
13. *Manchester Guardian*, quoted in *Freeman's Journal*, February 1909.
14. Yeats, letter of 30 December 1907, Microfilm 5380, National Library of Ireland.
15. *Dublin Evening Mail*, 4 October 1907; *Evening Telegraph*, 4 October 1907.
16. *The Plays of George Fitzmaurice*, I, *Dramatic Fantasies*, Introduction by Austin Clarke, pp. xi, xiv.
17. *Evening Telegraph*, 20 May 1911.
18. Yeats, *Explorations*, p. 250.
19. Robinson, *Curtain Up*, p. 22.
20. *The Dramatic Works of Denis Johnston*, I, p. 15.
21. Archer, *The Old Drama and the New*, 1923, p. 370.
22. For a discussion of expressionism in Irish Drama see Chapter 5 pp. 89–92.
23. Denis Johnston, quoted in Michael J. O'Neill, *Lennox Robinson*, p. 2.
24. Quoted in Joseph Hone, *The Life of W. B. Yeats*, p. 320.
25. W. B. Yeats, *Collected Poems*, p. 107.

5. A PAINTED STAGE: 1911–1929

1. W. B. Yeats, interviewed on the use of Gordon Craig's screens, *Evening Telegraph*, 9 January 1911.
2. An objection which had not deterred it from staging *The Shewing-Up of Blanco Posnet* in 1909. Earlier, Shaw had been a victim of the theory when in 1905 the Abbey refused *John Bull's Other Island* on the grounds that it had no actor capable of playing Broadbent.
3. *At The Hawk's Well*, for example, was first performed in March 1916 in Lady Cunard's London home.
4. St John Ervine, *The Orangeman* in *Four Irish Plays*.
5. Andre Barsacq, *Cambridge Opinion* 21, 1960.
6. Quoted in Sam Hanna Bell, *The Theatre in Ulster*, p. 80.
7. Foreword by George Shiels to *Tenants at Will*.
8. David Kennedy, 'George Shiels: Playwright at Work', *Threshold* 25, p. 57.
9. Shiels's Note to *Tenants at Will*.
10. Kennedy, 'George Shiels'.
11. It was also undertaking extensive American tours which were securing its reputation abroad and were on the whole financially profitable. To keep the Dublin theatre operating during these absences a second company was formed in 1912, based upon the Abbey School of Acting.

12. Walter Mennloch, 'Dramatic Values', *The Irish Review*, I, 1911–12, September 1911, pp. 325–9; G. Hamilton Gunning, 'The Decline of the Abbey Theatre Drama', *ibid.*, February 1912, pp. 606–9.

13. Gabriel Fallon, who acted in the Abbey in the early twenties, appeared in O'Casey's first plays, and eventually became a director, looks back on the period with equal asperity, though for quite different reasons. Fallon considers that a '"Literary theatre" . . . is, in plain terms just bosh. Plays that are not plays can never, by any stretch of imagination, be plays that are literature . . . a literary theatre is a monstrosity in theatres.' According to Fallon, the glory of the Abbey had been entirely the work of the Fays. With their departure the excitement of 'primal dramatic qualities' vanished too. The 'dramatic venture disintegrated' into careless production and acting and pretentious notions that a play's essence is in its written, extra-theatrical being. ('The Ageing Abbey', *The Irish Monthly* LXVI, April 1938, pp. 265–72.) Fallon grossly overstates his case both against the importance of the playwrights and against Yeats's indifference to stage techniques: Yeats, demonstrably, was fascinated by them. But others shared Fallon's sense of a self-satisfied carelessness in the Abbey. See also Ernest A. Boyd, 'The Irish National Theatre', *The Irish Times*, 27 December 1912.

14. 'J. M. Synge and the Ireland of His Time', Yeats, *Essays and Introductions*, p. 340.

15. Christopher Innes, *Piscator's Political Theatre*, p. 162.

16. *Ibid.*, p. 20.

17. W. B. Yeats, 'The Circus Animals' Desertion', *Collected Poems*, p. 392.

18. Kennedy, 'George Shiels', p. 56.

19. Robinson, *Curtain Up*, pp. 119–20.

20. According to B. K. Clarke and H. Ferrar, *The Dublin Drama League 1919–41*, p. 16.

21. Quoted in Lander McClintock, *The Age of Pirandello*, 1951.

22. Blythe joined the Abbey directorate in 1935 and in 1941 became managing director, resigning in 1972 at the age of eighty-six. He was politically astute, a ruthless administrator, as dictatorial as Yeats, and entirely lacking Yeats's imaginative sweep.

23. A flamboyant, old-style actor-manager, McMaster, who died in 1962, and his company were almost legendary figures to their audiences throughout the Irish countryside.

24. Micheál MacLiammóir, *Theatre in Ireland*, pp. 23–4, 28.

25. MacLiammóir, *All for Hecuba*, p. 82.

6. PLAYS AND CONTROVERSIES: SEAN O'CASEY

1. *The Plough and the Stars, Selected Plays*, 1956, p. 193 – an ironic rendering of some of Padraic Pearse's oratory.

2. Letter of Sean O'Casey to David Krause, quoted in Krause, *Sean O'Casey: The Man and His Work*, p. 36.

3. There are echoes of this in Ayomonn's rehearsing his lines from Shakespeare in Act I of *Red Roses for Me*; perhaps of Othello's account of Desdemona's love for

him when in *The Shadow of a Gunman* Seamus Shields says to Davoren, 'You think a lot about her simply because she thinks a lot about you because she looks upon you as a hero.' Or in Othello's words, 'she lov'd me for the dangers I had pass'd / And I lov'd her that she did pity them.'

4. O hAodha, *Theatre in Ireland*, p. 115.
5. Ronald Ayling, 'Popular Tradition and Individual Talent in Sean O'Casey's Trilogy', *Journal of Modern Literature*, II, no. 4, pp. 491–504.
6. Hogan, 'In Sean O'Casey's Golden Days', *The Dubliner*, v, no. 3/4.
7. Beckett, *Molloy*, pp. 73–9.
8. 'The Essential and the Incidental', a review of O'Casey's *Windfalls*, reprinted from *The Bookman*, 1934, lxxxvi, in *Sean O'Casey: A Collection of Critical Essays*, ed. Thomas Kilroy.
9. Krause, *Sean O'Casey: The Man and His Work*, p. 67.
10. *Ibid.*, p. 70; O hAodha, *Theatre in Ireland*, p. 109.
11. James Simmons, 'The Dramatic Vision of Sean O'Casey', lecture given at the Yeats International Summer School, Sligo, Ireland, August 1981.
12. Reported in Lady Gregory, *Journals*, p. 99.
13. Krutch in *The Nation*, 21 December 1927; Krutch, *Modernism in Modern Drama*, p. 99.
14. Deane, 'Irish Politics and O'Casey's Theatre', *Threshold*, no. 24, Spring 1973, pp. 5–16.
15. Thomas Kilroy also cites their sharing 'sheer fertility . . . the melodrama, the quality of the humour, the sympathy for the downtrodden, the detail of physical life in the writing'; adding that this kind of comparison ignores 'the differences between the two writers, and between the two modes of fictional narrative'; Introduction, *Sean O'Casey: A Collection of Critical Essays*, p. 8.
16. *Ibid.*, pp. 61–76.
17. Abbey Theatre programme note, 75th Anniversary Celebrations production of *Juno and the Paycock*, 27 December 1979.
18. *Ibid.*
19. McHugh 'The Legacy of Sean O'Casey', *Texas Quarterly*, Spring 1965, pp. 123–37.
20. Bernard Benstock, *Sean O'Casey*, 1970.
21. Yeats, *Letters*, ed. Allan Wade, pp. 740–2.
22. The tenements were still lively enough in 1952 to inspire Brendan Behan's little radio play, 'Moving Out'. It concerns a father's bitter resentment at having to leave the tenements for a Crumlin housing estate.
23. Jack Lindsay, Abbey Theatre programme note to *Juno and the Paycock*, 27 December 1979.
24. Samuel Beckett, 'The Essential and the Incidental', a review of *Windfalls*, *The Bookman*, LXXXCI, 1934.
25. Lady Gregory, *Journals*, 15 April 1923, 8 March 1924, 14 May 1928.
26. Fielding, Preface to *Joseph Andrews*.
27. Lady Gregory, *Journals*, 20 September 1925.
28. Bentley, *The Life of the Drama*, pp. 346–7.

7. THE MILL OF THE MIND: DENIS JOHNSTON

1. *The Dramatic Works of Denis Johnston*, I, pp. 16, 76, where Johnston records Lady Gregory's response.
2. *Ibid*, p. 17.
3. *Ibid*, p. 81.
4. *Ibid*, p. 79.
5. *Ibid*, pp. 17–18.
6. Harold Ferrar, *Denis Johnston's Irish Theatre*, p. 46.
7. Johnston is a copious and drastic reviser. His revisions are a study in themselves. Some of them, aimed at keeping up with contemporary usage, are hardly worth the labour – like the introduction of 'partisans' to mean rebel groups in *The Old Lady*, or the conversion of pounds, shillings and pence to decimal currency. Other revisions are more fundamental. The earlier versions of *Unicorn* made more direct and fuller use of the theories expounded by J. W. Dunne in *An Experiment with Time* (1928). Its reduction is unquestionably an improvement. The discussion of Johnston's plays in this chapter is based on the most recent texts, in *The Dramatic Works*.
8. J. Ronsley, 'A humane and well-intentioned piece of gallantry', in *Denis Johnston A Retrospective*, ed. Ronsley, p. 146.
9. Johnston, *Dramatic Works*, II, p. 166.
10. Kilroy, '*The Moon in the Yellow River*: Denis Johnston's Shavianism', in *Denis Johnston A Retrospective*, ed. Ronsley p. 51.
11. Vivian Mercier, 'Perfection of the life or of the work,' in *ibid*. See also Hilton Edwards in *The Bell*, February 1942, pp. 359–60, where he attributes Johnston's re-writings to 'what at first appears to be infinite patience, until one discovers that it is infinite impatience'.
12. Substantiation of these large statements is to be found in Terence Brown, *Ireland: A Social and Cultural History 1922–79*.

8. THE PLAYS, THE PLAYERS AND THE SCENES: 1930–1955

1. Micheál MacLiammóir, *All for Hecuba*, p. 318.
2. *Ibid.*, p. 231.
3. *Ibid.*, p. 367. Although the comment applies to 1939 it speaks truly enough of the earlier years.
4. Holloway, *Joseph Holloway's Irish Theatre*, ed. R. Hogan and Michael J. O'Neill, II, p. 33.
5. MacLiammóir, *All for Hecuba*, p. 267.
6. *Ibid.*, pp. 107–8.
7. R. Hogan, *After the Irish Renaissance*, p. 117.
8. Lady Gregory, *Our Irish Theatre*, p. 78.
9. Micheál O hAodha, *Theatre in Ireland*, p. 134.
10. Holloway, *Joseph Holloway's Irish Theatre*, p. 48.
11. O'Connor and O'Faolain, *Irish Times*, 25 February 1934.

12. O hAodha, *Theatre in Ireland*, p. 133.
13. Hunt, *The Abbey, Ireland's National Theatre*, p. 159.
14. Yeats's phrase, quoted in Hunt, *ibid.*, p. 148.
15. Succeeded in 1939 by Anne Yeats, the poet's daughter.
16. Quoted in *The Story of the Abbey Theatre*, ed. Sean McCann, p. 156.
17. For an account of her work see Hogan, *After the Irish Renaissance*, pp. 39–43.
18. Carroll, 'Reforming a Reformer', *New York Times*, 13 February 1935.
19. Carroll, 'The Substance of Paul Vincent Carroll', *New York Times*, 30 January 1938.
20. Hogan, *After the Irish Renaissance*, p. 54.
21. Quoted in *The Story of the Abbey Theatre*, p. 166.
22. Carroll's 'Note' on the play.
23. The title of Carroll's play about Swift, Stella, and Vanessa.
24. After the Second World War, Christopher Fry's *The Lady's Not for Burning* (1949) and T. S. Eliot's *The Cocktail Party* (1950) were widely and mistakenly proclaimed as heralds of a re-birth of verse drama. In that false dawn, Donagh MacDonagh (1912–68) had a popular success in Dublin and London with *Happy as Larry* (1946). His other plays are *God's Gentry* (1951) and *Step-in-the-Hollow* (1957). *Happy as Larry* is a linguistically spirited romp. Somewhat in the manner of John Gay's *The Beggars Opera* it draws upon street songs and ballads, filling the stage with music and spectacle. The language glitters, sinks to doggerel, keeps the audience aware of strong and varied patterns of verse which sacrifices metaphorical density, though not always an extravagance of words, to clarity of meaning. Clarke and Yeats manoeuvre around a rich but static lyricism; MacDonagh's verse, readily speakable and intelligible, has a thinness that does not long survive its performance.
25. Yeats apparently felt that Hugh Hunt's 1936 production of *Deirdre* flouted his ideas on the speaking of verse, though he raised no objection to the 1938 *Purgatory*, which he specifically asked Hunt to direct. See Hunt *The Abbey, Ireland's National Theatre*, pp. 155–63.
26. Robert Welch, 'Austin Clarke and Gaelic Poetic Tradition', *Irish University Review*, ed. Maurice Harmon, Austin Clarke special issue, IV, no. 1, p. 41.
27. *Ibid.*, 'Introduction.' p. 10.
28. *Ibid.*
29. Roger McHugh, 'The Plays of Austin Clarke,' in *Irish University Review*, IV, no. 1, p. 134.
30. Clarke, *Collected Plays*, p. 398.
31. For Eliot's views on the matter see *Poetry and Drama*, pp. 22–4.
32. Thomas Kinsella, 'The Poetic Career of Austin Clarke', in *Irish University Review*, II, no. 1, p. 134.
33. *Ibid.*, p. 131.
34. Hogan, *After the Irish Renaissance*, pp. 87, 96.
35. *Ibid.*, p. 90.
36. Hunt, *The Abbey, Ireland's National Theatre*, p. 169.
37. Simpson, *Beckett and Behan and a Theatre in Dublin*, p. 1.
38. Tomelty, quoted in Sam Hanna Bell, *Theatre in Ulster*, p. 85.

39. Kearney, *The Writings of Brendan Behan*, p. 71.
40. Alan Simpson, 'Behan: the Last Laugh', in *A Paler Shade of Green*, ed. Des Hickey and Gus Smith, 1972, p. 214.
41. Rae Jeffs, *Brendan Behan; Man and Showman*, p. 35.
42. Simpson, *Beckett and Behan and a Theatre in Dublin*, pp. 55–6.
43. MacAnna, 'New Abbeys for Old', *Irish Times*, 4 September 1969.
44. O hAodha, *Theatre in Ireland* pp. 152–3.
45. Alec Reid, 'Beckett, the Camera, and Jack McGowran', in *Myth and Reality in Irish Literature*, ed. J. Ronsley, p. 224; Vivian Mercier, *Beckett/Beckett*, p. 21; Thomas Kilroy, 'Yeats and Beckett', in *Myth and Reality*, p. 187; Seamus Deane, 'Synge's Western Worlds', *Threshold*, no. 28, p. 39.
46. *Samuel Beckett: An Exhibition*, ed. James Knowlson, London, 1971, p. 23; letter from Beckett to Cyril Cusack.
47. Both Leonard plays were repeated at the Abbey. The Group Theatre Belfast produced *The Francophile*, the Abbey *The Enemy Within*; Edwards/MacLiammóir *Philadelphia* at the 1964 Dublin Theatre Festival. *A Whistle in the Dark* was first produced at the Theatre Royal, Stratford East. *Mr Roche* was presented at the 1968 Dublin Theatre Festival.

9. EXPLORATIONS 1956–1982

1. Simpson's *Beckett and Behan and a Theatre in Dublin* gives a full account of the episode.
2. Hunt, *The Abbey, Ireland's National Theatre*, p. 196.
3. Brian Friel, Abbey Theatre programme note to *The Blue Macushla*, 6 March 1980.
4. *Ibid.*
5. T. Brown, *Ireland: A Social and Cultural History*, pp. 178–9.
6. An early play by Brian Friel, *The Blind Mice* (1963), concerns the return to Ireland of a priest brainwashed in Korea. His *Living Quarters* (1977) re-casts the Phèdre legend into the domestic tragedy of an army officer back from heroic service with a UN force in Africa. The hero of James Douglas's *The Savages* (1968) is killed, and his death commercialised at home, on a similar expedition.
7. Hugh Leonard in *A Paler Shade of Green*, ed. Des Hickey and Gus Smith, 1972, p. 201.
8. Robert Hogan writes on the subject in 'Where Have All the Shamrocks Gone?', in *Aspects of the Irish Theatre*, Paris, 1974, pp. 261–71; and Brian Friel has said, 'We are no longer even West Britons; we are East Americans' – in *A Paler Shade of Green*, ed., p. 224.
9. *Ibid.*, p. 222.
10. *Ibid.*, p. 227.
11. Parker, 'State of Play', *The Canadian Journal of Irish Studies*, June 1981, pp. 9–10.
12. Abbey programme note, 3 December 1979.
13. Seamus Heaney, quoted in T. Kearney, 'Befitting Emblems of Adversity', *Threshold*, Winter 1982, p. 68.

14. John Montague, *The Rough Field*, Dublin, 1972, p. 71.
15. Morrison, programme note to his adaptation of Brian Moore's *The Emperor of Ice Cream*, Abbey, 1977.
16. Parker, 'State of Play', p. 11.
17. Yeats, *Explorations*, pp. 74, 255.

10. THE HONOUR OF NAMING: SAMUEL BECKETT AND BRIAN FRIEL

1. Interview with Israel Shenker, 'Moody Man of Letters', *New York Times*, 6 May 1956.
2. Samuel Beckett, *Proust*, p. 8.
3. Mercier, *Beckett/Beckett*, pp. 217–18.
4. 'Recent Irish Poetry', *Bookman*, 86, August 1934. Beckett under the pseudonym Andrew Belis.
5. 'Two Playwrights: Yeats and Beckett', in *Myth and Reality in Irish Literature*, ed. J. Ronsley, p. 188.
6. *Ibid.*, p. 190.
7. Mercier, *Beckett/Beckett*, p. 198.
8. Kenner, *Samuel Beckett*, pp. 70, 69.

Select Bibliography

INDIVIDUAL AUTHORS

(A) IRISH DRAMATISTS

Samuel Beckett (b. 1906)

The Collected Works of Samuel Beckett, New York, Grove Press 1970.
Special reference: Plays. *Waiting for Godot*, London, Faber & Faber, 1956.
Endgame, London, Faber & Faber 1958; *Krapp's Last Tape*, London, Faber &
Faber 1959. *Happy Days*, New York, Grove Press, 1961.
Other work: *Proust*, London, Chatto & Windus, 1931. *More Pricks Than Kicks*,
London, Chatto & Windus, 1934. *Murphy*, London, Routledge, 1938. *Molloy* (in
French, Paris, Editions de Minuit, 1951) London, Calder & Boyars, 1966.
Malone Dies, (*Malone Meurt*, Editions de Minuit, 1951) London, Calder &
Boyars, 1958. *The Unnamable* (*L'Innomable*, Editions de Minuit, 1953); New
York, Grove, 1958.
Studies of: Deirdre Bair, *Samuel Beckett: A Biography*, New York, Harcourt
Brace Jovanovich; London, Jonathan Cape, 1978; *Journal of Modern Literature*,
VI, no. 1, guest ed. E. Brater, Philadelphia, Temple University, February 1977. A
Beckett number; John Calder, ed., *Beckett at Sixty: a Festschrift*, London, Calder
& Boyars, 1967. Ruby Cohn, *Samuel Beckett, The Comic Gamut*, New Brunswick,
Rutgers University Press, 1962; *Back to Beckett*, Princeton University Press,
1973; *Just Play: Beckett's Theatre*, Princeton University Press, 1980; *Samuel
Beckett: a Collection of Criticism*, New York, McGraw-Hill, 1975; Hugh Kenner,
Samuel Beckett, Berkeley & Los Angeles, University of California Press, 1968; *A
Reader's Guide to Samuel Beckett*, New York, Farrar, Straus, and Giroux, 1973.
Journal of Beckett Studies, ed. J. Knowlson, New York, Humanities Press, 1976.
Vivian Mercier, *Beckett/Beckett*, Oxford University Press, 1977.

Brendan Behan (1923–64)

The Complete Plays (Introduction by Alan Simpson), London, Eyre Methuen, 1978.
Contains *The Quare Fellow*, *The Hostage*, *Richard's Cork Leg*, and three radio
plays, 'Moving Out', 'The Garden Party', 'The Big House'.
Special reference: Plays. *The Quare Fellow*, London, Methuen, 1956. *The
Hostage*, London, Methuen, 1958.
Other work: *Borstal Boy*, London, Hutchinson, 1958.
Studies of: Beatrice Behan, with Des Hickey and Gus Smith, *My Life with
Brendan*, London, Leslie Frewin, 1973. Rae Jeffs, *Brendan Behan: Man and*

Select bibliography

Showman, London, Hutchinson, 1968. Colbert Kearney, *The Writings of Brendan Behan*, Dublin, Gill & Macmillan, 1977. E. H. Mikhail ed. *The Art of Brendan Behan*, New York, Barnes & Noble, 1979. Ulick O'Connor, *Brendan Behan*, London, Hamish Hamilton, 1970. Raymond J. Porter, *Brendan Behan*, Columbia Essays on Modern Writers, no. 66, 1973.

John Boyd (b. 1912)

The Collected Plays, vol. I *The Flats, The Farm, Guests*, Introduction by Daniel J. Casey; vol. II *The Street, Facing North*; Introduction by John Boyd. Belfast, Blackstaff Press, 1981, 1982.
Special reference: Play. *The Flats*, Belfast, Blackstaff Press, 1973.

William Boyle (1853–1923)

The Building Fund, Dublin, Maunsel, 1905; *The Eloquent Dempsey*, Dublin, Maunsel, 1906; *The Mineral Workers*, Dublin, Maunsel, 1907.

Seamus Byrne (1904–68)

Design for a Headstone, Dublin, Progress House, 1956; also in R. Hogan, ed., *Seven Irish Plays*, Minneapolis, University of Minnesota Press, 1967.

Paul Vincent Carroll (1900–68)

Shadow and Substance, New York, Random House, 1937; *The White Steed*, in *Three Plays* (with *Things That Are Caesar's* and *The Strings, My Lord, Are False*), London, Macmillan, 1944; *Farewell to Greatness*, ed. R. Hogan, Dixon, Proscenium Press, 1966.

Austin Clarke (1896–1974)

Collected Plays, Dublin, Dolmen, 1963: *The Son of Learning, The Flame, The Viscount of Blarney, The Second Kiss, The Plot Succeeds, The Moment Next to Nothing*.
Special reference: Plays. *The Son of Learning*, London, Allen & Unwin, 1927; *The Flame*, London, Allen & Unwin, 1930; *Sister Eucharia*, London, Williams & Norgate, 1939; *The Viscount of Blarney*, London, Williams & Norgate, 1944.
Other work: *Collected Poems*, Dublin, Dolmen, 1974.
Studies of: Susan Halpern, *Austin Clarke, His Life and Works*, Dublin, Dolmen, 1975. *Irish University Review*, ed. M. Harmon, vol. IV, Spring 1974. An Austin Clarke special issue.

Padraic Colum (1881–1972)

Three Plays: The Land, The Fiddler's House, Thomas Muskerry, Dublin, Allen Figgis, 1963.

226

Select bibliography

Special reference: Plays. *The Land*, Dublin, Maunsel, 1905. *The Fiddler's House*, Dublin, Maunsel, 1907. *Thomas Muskerry*, Dublin, Maunsel, 1910.
Studies of: Zack Bowen, *Padraic Colum*, Carbondale, Southern Illinois University Press, 1970; *Journal of Irish Literature*, 2 January 1973, Proscenium Press. A Colum number.

James Cousins (1873–1956)

The Racing Lug, United Irishman 5 July 1902; also in R. Hogan and J. Kilroy, eds., *Lost Plays of the Irish Renaissance*, Dixon, Proscenium Press, 1970. *The Sleep of the King* and *The Sword of Dermot*, ed. W. Feeney, Introduction by W. A. Dumbleton, vol. III, The Irish Drama Series, Chicago, DePaul, 1973.
Study of: William Dumbleton, *James Cousins*, Boston, Twayne, 1980.

Louis D'Alton (1900–51)

This Other Eden, Dublin, P. J. Bourke, 1954; *They Got What They Wanted*, Dundalk, Dundalgan Press, 1962.

Teresa Deevy (? –1963)

Three Plays: Katie Roche, The King of Spain's Daughter, The Wild Goose, London, Macmillan, 1939.

James Douglas (b. 1929)

North City Traffic Straight Ahead, Dixon, Proscenium Press, 1968; *The Ice Goddess*, in R. Hogan, ed., *Seven Irish Plays*, Minneapolis, University of Minnesota Press, 1967; *The Savages*, Newark, Proscenium Press, 1979.

St John Ervine (1883–1971)

Four Irish Plays: The Critics, Jane Clegg, The Orangeman, Mixed Marriage, New York, Macmillan, 1911; Dublin, Maunsel, 1914.
Special reference: Plays. *Jane Clegg*, London, Sidgwick & Jackson, 1914. *Mixed Marriage*, Dublin, Maunsell, 1911. *John Ferguson*, Dublin, Maunsel; London, Allen & Unwin; New York, Macmillan: 1915; and with Introduction by Ervine, New York, Macmillan, 1920. *Boyd's Shop*, London, Allen & Unwin, 1947.

George Fitzmaurice (1877–1963)

The Plays of George Fitzmaurice, vol. I, *Dramatic Fantasies*, Introduction by Austin Clarke, Dublin, Dolmen Press; Chester Springs, Dufour Editions: 1967. Vol. I contains *The Magic Glasses, The Dandy Dolls, The Linnaun Shee, The Green Stone, The Enchanted Land, The Waves of the Sea.* Vol. II *Folk Plays*, Introduction by Howard K. Slaughter, Dublin, Dolmen Press; Chester Springs, Dufour Edi-

tions: 1970. Vol. II contains *The Ointment Blue*, *The Pie-Dish*, *The Terrible Baisht*, *There Are Tragedies and Tragedies*, *The Moonlighter*. Vol. III *Realistic Plays*, Introduction by Howard K. Slaughter, Dublin, Dolmen Press; Chester Springs, Dufour Editions: 1970. Vol. III contains *The Toothache*, *The Country Dressmaker*, *One Evening Gleam*, *'Twixt the Giltinans and the Carmodys*, *The Simple Hanrahans*, *The Coming of Ewan Anzdale*.
Special reference: Plays. *Five Plays*, London and Dublin, Maunsel, 1914; Boston, Little Brown, 1917: *The Country Dressmaker*, *The Moonlighter*, *The Pie-Dish*, *The Magic Glasses*, *The Dandy Dolls*.
Studies of: Carol Gelderman, *George Fitzmaurice*, Lewisburg, Bucknell University Press, 1975; Nora Kelley, *George Fitzmaurice*, 1877–1963, New York, David H. Greene, 1973.

Brian Friel (b. 1929)

Philadelphia, Here I Come! London, Faber & Faber, 1965; New York, Farrar Straus, 1966; *The Loves of Cass Maguire*, London, Faber & Faber; New York Farrar Straus; 1967; *Lovers*, New York, Farrar Straus, 1968; London, Faber & Faber, 1969; *Crystal and Fox*, London, Faber & Faber, 1970; also included in *Two Plays*, New York, Farrar Straus, 1970; *The Mundy* Scheme in *Two Plays*; *The Gentle Island*, London, Davis Poynter, 1973; *The Freedom of the City*, London, Faber & Faber, 1974; *The Enemy Within, Journal of Irish Literature*, May 1975; also in *The Irish Play Series*, Newark, Proscenium Press, 1975 (produced Abbey Theatre, 1962); *Living Quarters*, London and Boston, Faber & Faber, 1978; *Volunteers*, London, Faber & Faber, 1980; *Aristocrats*, Dublin, Gallery Books, 1980; *Faith Healer*, London and Boston, Faber & Faber, 1980; *Translations*, London, Faber & Faber, 1981; *The Communication Cord*, London, Faber & Faber, 1983.
Other work: short stories *Selected Stories* (Introduction by Seamus Deane), Dublin, Gallery Books, 1979.
Study of: D. E. S. Maxwell, *Brian Friel*, Lewisburg, Bucknell University Press, 1973.

Augusta, Lady Gregory (1852–1932)

The Coole Edition of Lady Gregory's Writings, Colin Smythe and T. R. Henn general editors, Gerrards Cross, Colin Smythe, 1970 – vol I of the *Collected Plays* contains the Comedies, II Tragedies and Tragi-Comedies, III Wonder and Supernatural, IV Translations, Adaptations and Collaborations: all edited and with introductions by Ann Saddlemyer.
Special reference: Plays. *Twenty-five* (in Saddlemyer, ed, *Collected Plays*, I)
Spreading the News, Dublin, Maunsel, 1909. *The Rising of the Moon*, London, Putnam, 1907.
Other works: *Cuchulain of Muirthemne*, London, John Murray, 1902. *Gods and Fighting Men*, London, John Murray, 1904. *Visions and Beliefs in the West of Ireland* (with two essays and notes by W. B. Yeats), 2 vols. London, Putnam,

1920; *Our Irish Theatre*, London, Putnam, 1913; also New York, Oxford University Press, 1972; Gerrards Cross, Colin Smythe, 1973. *Lady Gregory's Journals 1916–30*, ed. Lennox Robinson, London, Putnam, 1946.
Study of: Ann Saddlemyer, *In Defence of Lady Gregory, Playwright*, Dublin, Dolmen, 1966.

Wilson John Haire (b. 1932)

Between Two Shadows, Plays and Players, 19, 9 June 1972.

Douglas Hyde (1860–1949)

Casadh an tSugáin: or, the Twisting of the Rope, translated by Lady Gregory. Irish and English, Dublin, Cló-Chumann, 1905.
Other work: *Love Songs of Connacht*, Dublin, Gill, 1893.

Denis Johnston (b. 1901)

The Dramatic Works of Denis Johnston, vol. I (General Introduction; *The Old Lady Says 'No!'*; *A Note on what happened; The Scythe and the Sunset; Storm Song; The Dreaming Dust; Strange Occurrence on Ireland's Eye*); Vol. II (Preface; *A Bride for the Unicorn; The Moon in the Yellow River; A Fourth for Bridge; The Golden Cuckoo; The Tain – a Pageant;* 'Introducing the enigmatic Dean Swift'); Gerrards Cross, Colin Smythe, 1977, 1979. Johnston contributes the General Introduction, 'Note', Preface, and prefatory remarks on each play.
Special reference: Plays. *The Old Lady Says 'No!'*, *The Moon in the Yellow River*, *Two Plays*, London, Jonathan Cape, 1932; *Storm Song and A Bride for the Unicorn*, London, Jonathan Cape, 1935; *The Golden Cuckoo and other plays*, London, Jonathan Cape, 1954.
Other works: *Nine Rivers from Jordan*, London, Derek Verschoyle, 1953; *In Search of Swift*, Dublin, Allen Figgis, 1959, *The Brazen Horn*, Dublin, Dolmen, 1977.
Studies of: Harold Ferrar, *Denis Johnston's Irish Theatre*, Dublin, Dolmen, 1973; J. Ronsley, ed., *Denis Johnston A Retrospective*, Gerrards Cross, Colin Smythe, 1981.

John B. Keane (b. 1928)

Sive (staged Listowel, Co. Kerry 1951; London 1961), Dublin, Progressive House, 1959; *The Man from Clare*, Cork, Mercier Press, 1963; *Hut 42* (Abbey 1963), Dixon, Proscenium Press, 1963; *The Year of the Hiker* (staged Cork and Chicago 1964), Cork, Mercier Press, 1964; *The Field* (staged Dublin 1965, New York 1976), Cork, Mercier Press, 1966; *Big Maggie*, Cork, Mercier Press, 1969.

Select bibliography

Thomas Kilroy (b. 1934)

The Death and Resurrection of Mr Roche, London, Faber & Faber; New York, Grove Press: 1968; *Talbot's Box*, Dublin, Gallery Books, 1979; *The Seagull*: a new version. Introduction by Rob Ritchie, London, Methuen, 1981.
Other work: Novel *The Big Chapel*, London, Faber & Faber; Pan Books: 1971.

Hugh Leonard (b. 1926)
(pseudonym of John Keyes Byrne)

Three Plays (*Da, A Life, Time Was*), Harmondsworth, Penguin Books, 1981.
Other works: Plays. *The Poker Session*, London, Evans, 1963; *The Patrick Pearse Motel*, London, *Plays and Players*, 18 May 1971, and Samuel French, 1972. Adaptations *Stephen D*. (from *A Portrait of the Artist as a Young Man* and *Stephen Hero*), London, Evans, 1962; 'Some of My Best Friends Are Husbands' (after Eugene Labiche) not published. Autobiographical memoir: *Home Before Night*, London, Deutsch, 1979.

Christine, Countess Longford (b. 1900)

Mr Jiggins of Jigginstown in Curtis Canfield, ed., *Plays of Changing Ireland*, New York, Macmillan, 1936; *The United Brothers*, Dublin, Hodges Figgis, 1942; *Tankardstown*, Dublin, P. J. Bourke, no date.

Edward, Lord Longford (1902–61)

Yahoo, Dublin, Hodges Figgis, 1934, also in Curtis Canfield, ed., *Plays of Changing Ireland*, New York, Macmillan, 1936; *The Vineyard*, Dublin, Hodges Figgis, 1943.

Eugene McCabe (b. 1930)

King of the Castle, Dublin, Gallery Books, 1979.

Micheál MacLiammóir (1899–1978)

Ill Met by Moonlight, Dublin, James Duffy, 1954; *Where Stars Walk*, Dublin, Progress House, 1962; *Diarmuid agus Grainne*, Dublin, Oifig Dialta Foillseachain Rialtais, 1935.
Other works: *All for Hecuba* (autobiographical memoir), London, Methuen, 1946, revised, Dublin, Progress House, 1961; *Theatre in Ireland*, 2nd edition with sequel, Dublin, Three Candles, 1964.
Studies of: Bulmer Hobson, *The Gate Theatre, Dublin*, Dublin, Gate Theatre, 1934; Peter Luke, ed., *Enter Certain Players: Edwards–MacLiammóir and the Gate*, Dublin, Dolmen, 1978.

Select bibliography

Brinsley MacNamara (1890–1963)

Look at the Heffernans!, Dublin, Talbot Press, 1929; *The Glorious Uncertainty*, Dublin, P. J. Bourke, 1957.

Gerald MacNamara (1866–1938)
(pseudonym of Harry Morrow)

Thompson in Tir-na-nOg, Dublin, Talbot, 1918.

Edward Martyn (1859–1923)

'The Heather Field' and 'Maeve': Two Plays, Introduction by George Moore, London, Duckworth, 1899; *The Tale of a Town and An Enchanted Sea*, Kilkenny, 1902.
Studies of: Denis Gwynn, *Edward Martyn and the Irish Revival*, London, Jonathan Cape, 1930; Sister Marie-Thérèse Courtney, *Edward Martyn and the Irish Theatre*, New York, Vantage, 1956.

Rutherford Mayne (1878–1967)
(pseudonym of Samuel Waddell)

The Turn of the Road, Dublin, Maunsel, 1907, reprinted Dublin, James Duffy, 1950; *The Drone*, Dublin, Maunsel, 1909; *Bridgehead*, London, Constable, 1939, also in Curtis Canfield, ed., *Plays of Changing Ireland*, New York, Macmillan, 1936.

Alice Milligan (1866–1953)

The Last Feast of the Fianna, Dublin, *The Daily Express*, 1899, reprinted Chicago, DePaul University, 1967; *Brian of Banba*, United Irishman, 1904; *Oisin in Tir-nan-Oig*, *The Daily Express*, 1899.

M. J. Molloy (b. 1917)

The King of Friday's Men, Dublin, James Duffy, 1954, also in J. C. Trewin, ed., *Plays of the Year*, London, P. Elek, 1949; *The Wood of the Whispering*, Dublin, Progress House, 1961; *The Visiting House* in R. Hogan, ed., *Seven Irish Plays*, Minneapolis, University of Minnesota Press, 1967; *The Paddy Pedlar*, Dublin, James Duffy, 1954.

George Moore (1852–1933)

Works, uniform edition, London, Heinemann, 1924–33.
Special reference: Plays. *The Strike at Arlingford*, London, Walter Scott, 1893; *Diarmuid and Grania* ed. Anthony Forran, Chicago, DePaul, 1974.

Select bibliography

Other work: Novel, *Hail and Farewell*, London, Heinemann, 1947, reprint of
1933 edition.
Studies of: Joseph Hone, *The Life of George Moore*, New York, Macmillan, 1936;
A Norman Jeffares, *George Moore*, London, Longmans Green, 1965; Jean C.
Noel, *George Moore: L'Homme et l'oeuvre*, Paris, Didier, 1966.

Bill Morrison (b. 1940)

Flying Blind, London, Faber & Faber, 1978.

Thomas Murphy (b. 1935)

The Fooleen (an early version of *A Crucial Week in the Life of a Grocer's Assistant*),
Dixon, Proscenium, 1968; *A Whistle in the Dark*, New York, Samuel French,
1970. *The Morning After Optimism*, Cork, Mercier Press, 1973; *The Orphans*,
Newark, Proscenium Press, 1974; *The Sanctuary Lamp*, Dublin, Poolbeg Press,
1976; *On the Outside/On the Inside*, Dublin, Gallery Books, 1976; *Famine*,
Dublin, Gallery Books; Newark, Proscenium Press, 1978.

T. C. Murray (1873–1959)

Birthright, Dublin, Maunsel, 1911; *Maurice Harte*, Dublin, Maunsel, 1912; *Aftermath*, Dublin, Talbot, 1922; *Autumn Fire*, London, Allen & Unwin, 1925, Boston
& New York, Houghton Mifflin, 1926; *Michaelmas Eve*, London, Allen & Unwin
1932.

Sean O'Casey (1880–1964)

Collected Plays, 4 vols., London, Macmillan, New York, St Martin's Press, 1949–
51; *Three Plays* (*The Shadow of a Gunman, Juno and the Paycock, The Plough and
the Stars*), London, Macmillan, 1957.
Special reference: Plays. *The Shadow of a Gunman*, New York and London,
Samuel French, 1932; *Juno and the Paycock*, London, Macmillan, 1930; *The
Plough and the Stars*, London, Macmillan, 1926; *The Silver Tassie*, London and
New York, Macmillan, 1928; *The Star Turns Red*, London, Macmillan, 1940;
Purple Dust, London, Macmillan, 1940; *Red Roses for Me*, London, Macmillan,
1942; *Oak Leaves and Lavender*, London and New York, Macmillan, 1946; *Cock-
a-Doodle-Dandy*, London and New York, Macmillan, 1949; *The Bishop's Bonfire*,
London and New York, Macmillan, 1955; *The Drums of Father Ned*, London and
New York, Macmillan, 1960.
Other works: *Autobiographies*, 2 vols., London, Macmillan, 1963; *Feathers from
the Green Crow*, ed. R. Hogan, London, Macmillan, 1963; *Blasts and Benedictions*,
ed. Ron Ayling, London and New York, Macmillan, 1967; *The Letters of Sean
O'Casey*, vol. I, *1910–41*, ed. D. Krause, London, Cassell, 1975.
Studies of: Ron Ayling, ed. *Sean O'Casey*, London, Macmillan, 1968; Ron Ayling
and Michael J. Durkin, *Sean O'Casey, a Bibliography*, London, Macmillan, 1978.

Select bibliography

M. Harmon, ed., *Irish University Review*, x, no. 1 Dublin, Wolfhound Press, 1980; Robert Hogan, *The Experiments of Sean O'Casey*, New York, St Martin's, 1960; Hugh Hunt, *Sean O'Casey*, Dublin, Gill and Macmillan, 1980; Thomas Kilroy, ed., *Sean O'Casey. A Collection of Critical Essays*, Englewood Cliffs, Prentice-Hall, 1975; David Krause, *Sean O'Casey: The Man and His Work*, London, McGibbon & Kee; New York, Macmillan: 1960; David Krause and Robert Lowery, eds., *Sean O'Casey Centenary Essays*, Gerrards Cross, Colin Smythe, 1980; Michael O hAodha, *The O'Casey Enigma*, Dublin and Cork, Mercier Press, 1980; Eileen O'Casey, *Sean*, ed. J. C. Trewin, London, Macmillan, 1971; James Scrimgeour, *Sean O'Casey*, Boston, Twayne, 1978.

Seamus O'Kelly (1875–1918)

The Matchmakers, Dublin, Gill, 1908; *The Shuiler's Child*, Dublin, Maunsel, 1908 (bound with Thomas MacDonagh, *When the Dawn is Come*); *Meadowsweet* Dublin, Talbot, no date.
Study of: George Brandon Saul, *Seamus O'Kelly*, Lewisburg, Bucknell University Press, 1971.

Stewart Parker (b. 1941)

Nightshade, Dublin Co-op Books, 1980; *Catchpenny Twist*, Dublin, Gallery Books, 1980.

J. Graham Reid (b. 1945)

The Death of Humpty-Dumpty, Dublin Co-op Books, 1980.

Lennox Robinson (1886–1958)

Two Plays (*The Clancy Name* and *Harvest*), Dublin, Maunsel, 1911; *The Lost Leader*, Dublin, Eigas Press, 1918; *The Whiteheaded Boy*, London, Putnam, 1921; *Ever the Twain*, London, Macmillan, 1930; *Drama at Inish*, London, Macmillan, 1933; *Church Street*, London, Macmillan, 1935.
Other work: *Ireland's Abbey Theatre: a History 1899–1951*, London, Sidgwick & Jackson, 1951; *Curtain Up*, London, Michael Joseph, 1942.
Study of: Michael O'Neill, *Lennox Robinson*, New York, Twayne, 1964.

George Russell (AE) (1867–1935)

Deirdre, Dublin, Maunsel, 1907.
Other works: *Selected Poems*, London, Macmillan, 1935; ed. *The Irish Statesman*, 1923–30.
Studies of: Robert Davis, *George William Russell – 'AE'*, Boston, Twayne, 1977; Richard Kain and James O'Brien, *George Russell (A.E.)*, Lewisburg, Bucknell University Press, 1976.

Select bibliography

G. B. Shaw (1856–1950)

The Bodley Head Bernard Shaw Collected Plays with their Prefaces, ed. Dan H. Laurence, London, Max Reinhardt, The Bodley Head, 1970–4.
Other works: *Major Critical Essays* (includes *The Quintessence of Ibsenism*), London, Constable, 1932; *Our Theatres in the Nineties*, 3 vols., London, Constable, 1932.
Special reference: Norma Jenckes, 'The Rejection of Shaw's Irish Play, *John Bull's Other Island*', *Eire-Ireland*, x, Spring, 1975.

George Shiels (1886–1949)

Two Irish Plays: Mountain Dew, Cartney and Kevney, London, Macmillan, 1930; *The Rugged Path, The Summit*, London, Macmillan, 1942; *Three Plays: Professor Tim, Paul Twyning, The New Gossoon*, London, Macmillan, 1945; *The Fort Field*, Dublin, Golden Eagle Books, 1947; *The Old Broom*, Dublin, Golden Eagle Books, 1947; *Tenants At Will*, Dublin, Golden Eagle Books, 1947; *The Caretakers*, Dublin, Golden Eagle Books, 1948.
Study of: David Kennedy, 'George Shiels: A Playwright at Work', *Threshold*, xxv, Summer, 1974.

J. M. Synge (1871–1909)

Collected Works (general editor Robin Skelton), vol. I: *Poems*, ed. R. Skelton, London, Oxford University Press, 1962; vol. I: *Prose*, ed. Alan Price, Oxford University Press, 1966; vols. III and IV: *Plays*, ed. Ann Saddlemyer, Oxford University Press, 1968.
Special reference: *The Shadow of the Glen, Riders to the Sea*, London, Elkin Matthews, 1905; *The Well of the Saints*, London, A. H. Bullen, 1905; *The Playboy of the Western World*, Dublin, Maunsel, 1907; *Deirdre of the Sorrows*, Dundrum, Cuala Press, 1910.
Studies of: S. B. Bushrui, ed. *Sunshine and the Moon's Delight*, Gerrards Cross, Colin Smythe, 1972; David H. Greene and Edward M. Stephens, *J. M. Synge 1871–1909*, New York, Macmillan, 1959; Maurice Harmon, ed., *J. M. Synge. Centenary Papers 1971*, Dublin, Dolmen, 1972; Declan Kiberd, *Synge and the Irish Language*, London, Macmillan, 1979; James Kilroy, *The 'Playboy' Riots*, Dublin, Dolmen, 1971; Ann Saddlemyer, *J. M. Synge and Modern Comedy*, Dublin, Dolman Press, 1968; Robin Skelton, *The Writings of J. M. Synge*, New York, Bobbs-Merrill; London, Thames & Hudson, 1971.

Sam Thompson (1916–1965)

Over the Bridge, ed. and introduction by Stewart Parker, Dublin, Gill & Macmillan, 1970.

Select bibliography

Joseph Tomelty (b. 1911)

Is the Priest at Home?, Belfast, H. R. Carter, 1954; *All Souls Night*, Belfast H. R. Carter, 1955; *The End House*, Dublin, James Duffy, 1962.

Oscar Wilde (1854–1900)

Complete Works of Oscar Wilde, ed. Vyvyan Holland, London and Glasgow, Collins, 1948; new edn, 1966.

W. B. Yeats (1865–1939)

Collected Plays, London and New York, Macmillan, 1952; *The Variorum Edition of the Plays of W. B. Yeats*, ed., Russell K. Alspach, London and New York, Macmillan, corrected second printing 1966; *Collected Poems*, London and New York, Macmillan, 1956; *The Variorum Editions of the Poems of W. B. Yeats*, ed., Peter Allt and Russell Alspach, London and New York, Macmillan, corrected third printing 1966.

Special reference: 'The Countess Cathleen', London, T. Fisher Unwin, 1892; 'The Shadowy Waters', London, Hodder & Stoughton, 1900; 'Cathleen ni Houlihan', London, A. H. Bullen, 1902; 'The Hour Glass', London, Heinemann, 1903; *'The King's Threshold'* and *'On Baile's Strand'*, London, A. H. Bullen, 1904; *Deirdre*, London, A. H. Bullen; Dublin, Maunsel: 1907; 'At the Hawk's Well' in *The Wild Swans at Coole*, Dundrum, Cuala Press, 1917; *Two Plays for Dancers* ('The Dreaming of the Bones', 'The Only Jealousy of Emer'), Dublin, Cuala Press, 1919; *Plays in Prose and Verse*, New York, Macmillan 1928; 'The Words upon the Windowpane', Dublin, Cuala Press, 1934; 'Fighting the Waves', in *Wheels and Butterflies*, London, Macmillan, 1934; *Last Poems and Two Plays* ('Purgatory', 'The Death of Cuchulain'), Dublin, Cuala Press, 1939.

Other works: *Autobiographies*, London, Macmillan, 1956; *Essays and Introductions*, London, Macmillan, 1961; *Explorations*, London, Macmillan, 1962; *Memoirs*, ed. Denis Donoghue, London, Macmillan, 1972; ed. *Poems and Translations by J. M. Synge*, Dundrum, Cuala Press, 1909; *Uncollected Prose*, I, ed. John P. Frayne; II, ed. John P. Frayne and Colton Johnson, London, Macmillan, 1970, 1975: *Letters*, ed. Allan Wade, London, Macmillan, 1954.

Studies of: Denis Donoghue, *Yeats*, London, Collins, 1971. Richard Ellmann, *Yeats: the Man and the Masks*, New York, Norton, 1978; James Flannery, *W. B. Yeats and the Idea of a Theatre*, New Haven, Yale University Press, 1976; Joseph Hone, *The Life of W. B. Yeats*, New York, 1943; Richard M. Kain, *Dublin in the Age of W. B. Yeats and James Joyce*, Norman, University of Oklahoma Press, 1962; Frank Kermode, *Romantic Image*, London, Routledge & Kegan Paul, 1957; James Rees Moore, *Masks of Love and Death: Yeats as Dramatist*, Ithaca, Cornell University, 1971; George Brandon Saul, *Prolegomena to the Study of Yeats's Plays*, Philadelphia, University of Pennsylvania Press, 1958; Donald Torchiana, *W. B. Yeats and Georgian Ireland*, Evanston, Northwestern, 1966; Peter Ure, *Yeats the Playwright*, New York, Barnes & Noble, 1963; Helen

235

Select bibliography

Vendler, *Yeats's Vision and The Later Plays*, Cambridge, Mass., Harvard University Press, 1963.

(B) OTHER DRAMATISTS

John Arden: *Serjeant Musgrave's Dance*, London, Eyre Methuen, 1977.

Edward Bond: *The Pope's Wedding*, London, Methuen, 1961; *Lear*, London, Eyre Methuen, 1972.

Josef Capek: *The Land of Many Names*, translation by Paul Selver, London, Allen & Unwin, 1965.

T. S. Eliot: *Sweeney Agonistes*, London, Faber & Faber, 1932; *Murder in the Cathedral*, London, Faber & Faber, 1939; *The Cocktail Party*, London, Faber & Faber, 1950.

Henrik Ibsen: *The Oxford Ibsen*, translated and edited by James W. McFarlane and others, New York, Oxford University Press, 8 vols., 1960–77.

Alfred Jarry: *Tout Ubu*, Paris, Livre de Poche, 1962.

Georg Kaiser: *The Coral*, vol. 1 of a trilogy, the second of which is *Gas I*, the third *Gas II*, New York, Ungar, 1963.

John McGrath: *Events While Guarding the Bofors Gun*, London, Methuen, 1966.

Maurice Maeterlinck: *L'Oiseau Bleu*, Paris, Fasquelle, 1950; *Pelléas et Mélisande*, Paris, Fasquelle, 1963; *The Treasury of the Humble*, translated by Alfred Sutro, London, Allen, 1897.

Peter Nichols: *A Day in the Death of Joe Egg*, New York, French, 1967.

Clifford Odets: *Six Plays of Clifford Odets* (includes *Golden Boy* and *Waiting for Lefty*), New York, Random House, 1939.

Eugene O'Neill: *The Hairy Ape*, London, Cape, 1923; *Three Plays* (including *Desire under the Elms*), London, Cape, 1925; *Strange Interlude*, London, Cape, 1928.

John Osborne: *Look Back in Anger*, London, Faber & Faber, 1957; *The Entertainer*, London, Faber & Faber, 1957; *Luther*, London, Faber & Faber, 1961.

Harold Pinter: *The Room* and *The Dumb Waiter*, London, Methuen, 1960; *The Birthday Party*, London, Methuen, 1960; *The Homecoming*, London, Methuen, 1965.

Tom Stoppard: *Rosencrantz and Guildernstern Are Dead*, London, Faber & Faber, 1967; *The Real Inspector Hound*, London, 1970.

August Strindberg: *The Plays*, introduction and translation by Michael Meyer, London, Secker & Warburg, 2 vols. 1975.

Count August Villiers de l'Isle Adam: *Axël*, Paris, La Colombe, 1960.

Arnold Wesker: *Chips with Everything*, London, Cape, 1962; *The Wesker Trilogy* (*Chiken Soup with Barley*, *Roots*, *I'm Talking about Jerusalem*), Harmondsworth, Penguin, 1960.

Tennessee Williams: *The Glass Menagerie*, New York, Random House, 1945; *A Streetcar Named Desire*, New York, Dramatists' Play Service, 1953.

GENERAL WORKS

(A) LITERARY/HISTORICAL STUDIES

André Antoine, *Mes Souvenirs sur le Théâtre Libre*, Paris, Anthème–Fayarde, 1929.

Sam Hanna Bell, *The Theatre in Ulster*, Dublin, Gill & Macmillan, 1972.

Eric Bentley, *The Life of the Drama*, New York, Athenaeum, 1967.

Ernest A. Boyd, *Ireland's Literary Renaissance*, Dublin, Maunsel, 1916; Dublin, Allen Figgis, 1969.

The Contemporary Drama of Ireland, Dublin, Talbot Press, 1918.

Malcolm Brown, *The Politics of Irish Literature: from Thomas Davis to W. B. Yeats*, Seattle, University of Washington Press, 1972.

Robert Brustein, *The Theatre of Revolt*, London, Methuen, 1965; *The Third Theatre*, London, Jonathan Cape, 1970.

William S. Clarke, *The Irish Stage in the Country Towns, 1720–1800*, Oxford, Clarendon Press, 1965.

B. K. Clarke and Harold Ferrar, *The Dublin Drama League 1919–1941*, Dublin, Dolmen; New York Humanities Press: 1979.

Denis Donoghue, *The Third Voice: Modern British and American Verse Drama*, London, Oxford University Press, 1959.

T. S. Eliot, *Poetry and Drama*, London, Faber & Faber, 1951.

On Poetry and Poets, London, Faber & Faber, 1957.

Una Ellis-Fermor, *The Irish Dramatic Movement*, London, Methuen, 1939; revised 1954.

Martin Esslin, *The Theatre of the Absurd*, London, Eyre & Spottiswoode, 1962; revised edn Woodstock, New York, Overlook Press, 1973.

Brief Chronicles: Essays on Modern Theatre, London, Temple Smith, 1970.

Richard Fallis, *The Irish Renaissance*, Syracuse, Syracuse University Press, 1977.

Frank Fay, *Towards a National Theatre: Dramatic Criticism*, edited and introduction by Robert Hogan, Dublin, Dolmen, 1970.

Gerard Fay, *The Abbey Theatre*, London, Hollis & Carter, 1958.

Richard J. Finneran, ed., *Anglo-Irish Literature: A Review of Research*, New York, Modern Language Association of America, 1976; *Supplement*, 1982.

James Flannery, *W. B. Yeats and the Idea of a Theatre*, Toronto, Macmillan of Canada, 1976;

Miss Annie F. Horniman and the Abbey Theatre, Dublin, Dolmen 1970.

Bamber Gascoigne, *Twentieth-Century Drama*, London, Hutchinson, 1962.

Lady Augusta Gregory, *Our Irish Theatre*, Gerrards Cross, Colin Smythe, 1973.

Stephen Gwynne, *Irish Literature and Drama*, New York, Nelson, 1936.

Maurice Harmon, *Select Bibliography for the Study of Anglo-Irish Literature and its Backgrounds*, Port Credit, P. D. Meany, 1977.

Robert Hogan, *After the Irish Renaissance*, London, Macmillan, 1968.

Robert Hogan, ed., *Modern Irish Drama*, 4 vols.:

I: *The Irish Literary Theatre, 1899–1901*, with James Kilroy, Dublin, Dolmen Press, 1975.

II: *Laying the Foundations, 1903–4*, Dublin, Dolmen Press, 1976.

Select bibliography

III: *The Abbey Theatre: The years of Synge, 1905–9*, with Richard Burnham and Daniel Poteet, Dublin, Dolmen Press, 1978.

IV: *The Rise of the Realists, 1910–15*, Dublin, Dolmen Press, 1979.

Joseph Holloway, *Joseph Holloway's Irish Theatre*, 3 vols., ed. R. Hogan and Michael J. O'Neill, Dixon, Proscenium Press, 1968–70.

Herbert Howarth, *The Irish Writers 1880–1940*, London, Rockcliff, 1958.

Hugh Hunt, *The Abbey, Ireland's National Theatre, 1904–1979*, Dublin, Gill & Macmillan, 1979.

Douglas Hyde, *A Literary History of Ireland*, New York, Barnes & Noble, 1967,

Christopher Innes, *Erwin Piscator's Political Theatre*, Cambridge University Press, 1972.

Peter Kavanagh, *The Story of the Abbey Theatre*, New York, Devin-Adair, 1950.

James Kilroy, *The 'Playboy' Riots*, Dublin, Dolmen Press, 1971.

Kimball King, *Ten Modern Irish Playwrights: a Bibliography*, Garland, 1979.

Heinz Kosok, ed. *Studies in Anglo-Irish Literature*, Bonn, Bouvier Verlag, Herbert Grundmann, 1982.

J. W. Krutch, *Modernism in Modern Drama*, Ithaca, Cornell University Press, 1953.

Sean McCann, ed. *The Story of the Abbey*, London, New English Library, 1967.

Micheál MacLiammóir, *Theatre in Ireland*, Dublin, Cultural Relations Committee, 1964.

All for Hecuba, London, Methuen, 1946.

A. E. Malone, *The Irish Drama*, London, Constable, 1929.

E. H. Mikhail, *A Bibliography of Modern Irish Drama 1899–1970*, London, Macmillan, 1972.

Contemporary British Drama 1950–1976: a Bibliography, London, Macmillan, 1976.

Allardyce Nicoll, *A History of English Drama*, 5 vols. Cambridge University Press, 1952–9, V: *Late Nineteenth-Century Drama*.

English Drama 1900–1930, Cambridge University Press, 1973.

Máire Nic Shiubhlaigh and Edward Kenny, *The Splendid Years*, Dublin, Duffy, 1955.

Frank O'Connor, *The Backward Look*, London, Macmillan, 1967.

Micheál O hAodha, *Theatre in Ireland*, Oxford, Basil Blackwell, 1974.

Mary O'Malley and John Boyd, eds., *A Needle's Eye* (a record of the Lyric Players Theatre, Belfast), Belfast, Lyric Players Theatre, 1979.

Lennox Robinson, *Ireland's Abbey Theatre: A History 1899–1951*, London, Sidgwick & Jackson, 1951.

J. Ronsley, ed., *Myth and Reality in Irish Literature*, Waterloo, Wilfred Laurier Press, 1977.

Ann Saddlemyer, *Theatre Business, Management of Men, the Letters of the First Abbey Theatre Directors*, New York, New York Public Library, 1971.

Alan Simpson, *Beckett and Behan and a Theatre in Dublin*, London, Routledge & Kegan Paul, 1962.

J. L. Styan, *The Dark Comedy; the Development of Modern Comic Tragedy*, Cambridge University Press, 1968.

Select bibliography

John Russell Taylor, *Anger and After; a Guide to the New British Drama*, London, Methuen, 1969.
The Second Wave; British Drama for the Seventies, London, Methuen, 1971.
Raymond Williams, *Drama from Ibsen to Eliot*, London, Chatto & Windus, 1968.
Katherine Worth, *The Irish Drama of Europe from Yeats to Beckett*, Atlantic Highlands, Humanities Press, 1978.

(B) BACKGROUND

J. C. Beckett, *The Making of Modern Ireland*, New York, Knopf, 1966.
Terence Brown, *Ireland: A Social and Cultural History 1922–1979*, London, Collins, 1981.
J. T. Carroll, *Ireland in the War Years, 1939–45*, New York, Crane, Russak, 1975.
Robert Fisk, *In Time of War, a study of the Free State and Northern Ireland 1939–45*, London, Deutsch, 1983.
Robert Kee, *The Green Flag; a History of Irish Nationalism*, New York, Delacorte, 1972.
F. S. L. Lyons, *Ireland Since the Famine*, London, Weidenfeld & Nicolson, 1971.
Charles Stewart Parnell, London, Collins, 1977.
Conor Cruise O'Brien, *States of Ireland*, London, Hutchinson, 1972.
Sean O Faolain, *The Irish*, West Drayton, Penguin, 1947.

PERIODICALS

The Arrow: an occasional publication of the National Theatre Society, ed. W. B. Yeats, vol. 1, nos. 1–5, 1906–9; Yeats commemoration no. 1939.
The Bell, ed. Sean O'Faolain and Peadar O'Donnell, vols. 1–19, 1940–54.
Beltaine, an occasional publication, organ of the Irish Literary Theatre 1899–1900, reprint London, Cass, 1970.
The Dublin Magazine, ed. Seamus O'Sullivan, old series vols. 1–3, 1923/4–1925; new series vols. 1–33, 1926–58.
The Dublin Magazine (formerly *The Dubliner*, 1961–4) ed. Rivers Carew and others, Dublin, 1965–9.
Eire-Ireland, ed. Eoin McKiernan, vol. 1 no. 1. 1966, St Paul, Minnesota.
Irish University Review, ed. Maurice Harmon, vol. 1, 1970– .
Motley, the Dublin Gate Theatre Magazine, ed. Mary Manning, nos. 1–19, 1932–4.
The Nation, ed. Thomas Davis, vol. 1–vol. 10, Dublin, 1846–96.
Samhain, an occasional publication, organ of the National Theatre Society, ed. W. B. Yeats, Dublin and London 1901–5, 1908.
Theatre Ireland, Belfast and Dublin, Theatre Ireland Ltd, 1982– .
Threshold ed. Mary O'Malley, John Boyd, vol. 1 no. 1, Belfast 1957, Lyric Players Theatre Company.
Uladh, ed. Bulmer Hobson and Joseph Campbell, nos. 1–4, Belfast 1904–5.
United Irishman, ed. Arthur Griffith, Dublin, 1899–1906.

Index

Abbey Theatre x, xi, xii, xiii, xiv, 1,
  3–4, 6–7, 16, 32, 51, 58, 61, 62–3,
  80, 92–5, 131, 133–6, 140, 148, 155,
  160, 212, 218
Abercrombie, Lascelles 4
AE (George Russell) ix, x, 60
Allgood, Sara 61, 66
Andreyev, Leonid 92
Anglo-Irish Treaty xi, 79, 96
Anglo-Irish War xi, 79, 96
Antient Concert Rooms ix
Antoine, André 11, 13
Archer, William 11, 73, 218
Arden, John 105, 108
Arrow, The 17, 213, 214
Arts Theatre Club (London) xiii
Arts Theatre Studio (Belfast) xiii, 149
Ayling, Ron 97, 220

Bauhaus 89
BBC Radio xv, 171, 180, 200
BBC Television xv, 159
Beckett, Samuel xiii, xiv, xv, 2–3, 4,
  6, 37, 45, 58, 78, 98, 99, 111, 155–7,
  158, 188–200, 212, 217, 220, 223.
  PLAYS: *Breath* xiv, 155; *Endgame*
  xiii, 157, 189–91; *Film* xiv, 37;
  Footfalls xv; *Ghost Trio* xv, 155, 188;
  Happy Days xiii, 195–7, 198, 199;
  Krapp's Last Tape xiii, 194, 196,
  198; *Not I* xiv; *That Time* xv; *Radio
  II* xv, 199; *Waiting for Godot* xiii,
  150, 155–6, 189–91, 197–8, 200,
  217. OTHER WORKS: *Malone Dies*
  188; *Molloy* 155, 188, 189; *More
  Pricks Than Kicks* 155; *Murphy* 155,
  189; *The Unnamable* 188; *Watt* 198;
  Proust 197, 224
Beerbohm, Max 14, 214
Beggar on Horseback (Kaufman/
  Connelly) 118–19

Behan, Brendan xiii, 150–4, 160,
  220, 223. PLAYS: *The Hostage (An
  Giall)* xiii, 153, 155; 'Moving Out'
  220; *The Quare Fellow* xiii, 149,
  150–5. OTHER WORK: *Borstal Boy* 160
Bell, Sam Hanna 16, 84, 214, 218,
  222
Beltaine 11, 12, 213, 214
Benstock, Bernard 107, 220
Bentley, Eric 112, 220
Binyon, Laurence 141
Bliss, Alan 48, 217
Blythe, Ernest xii, 93, 134, 155, 219
Bond, Edward 4, 170. PLAYS: *The
  Pope's Wedding* 170; *Saved* 170
Bottomley, Gordon 140
Boucicault, Dion 3, 10, 96. PLAYS:
  Arrah na Pogue 3; *The Colleen Bawn*
  3; *The Shaughran* 3
Boyd, Ernest 1, 213
Boyd, John xiv, 180. PLAYS: *The
  Assassin* 180; *The Farm* 180; *The
  Flats* 180; *Guests* 180
Boyle, William x, 5, 6, 66, 71–2, 73,
  78, 88, 93, 177. PLAYS: *The Building
  Fund* x, 71–2; *The Eloquent Dempsey*
  71; *The Mineral Workers* x, 71
Brahms, Otto 11
Brecht, Berthold 54, 90, 97, 184.
  PLAY: *Baal* 90
Brook, Peter 159
Brown, Terence 221, 223
Browning, Robert 140, 141
Brustein, Robert 37
Bunyan, John 105
Burns, Robert 107, 108
Bushrui, S. B. 28, 215
Byrne, Seamus xiii, 148. PLAY:
  Design for a Headstone xiii, 148

Canadian Journal of Irish Studies 223

Index

Capek, Josef 118. PLAY: *The Land of Many Names* 118
Capek, Karel 94, PLAY: *R.U.R.* 94
Carroll, Paul Vincent xii, 135, 136–40, 147, 170, 222. PLAYS: *Shadow and Substance* xii, 135, 138; *Things That Are Caesar's* xii, 137–8; *The White Steed* 135, 138–40
Casey, Michael 96
Chekhov, Anton 46, 92, 131, 133, 148. PLAY: *The Three Sisters* 186
Chesterton, G. K. 55, 140, 141
Clarke, Austin xi, xii, xiv, 66, 79, 132, 134, 140–5, 147, 218, 222. PLAYS: *As the Crow Flies* 141; *Black Fast* 141; *The Flame* 141, 142–3; *The Kiss* 141, 144; *The Moment Next to Nothing* 141; *Sister Eucharia* 141, 142; *The Son of Learning (The Hunger Demon)* xi, 79, 132, 141–2; *The Viscount of Blarney* 141, 144. OTHER WORKS: *Collected Poems* 140; *Night and Morning* 144
Clarke, William Smith 213
Claudel, Paul 92
Coffey, Brian 158
Collins, Patrick 7, 213
Colum, Padraic x, 4, 6, 7, 14, 25–7, 48, 60, 66, 69–71, 72, 78, 81, 88, 89, 93, 139, 141, 147, 170, 217. PLAYS: *Broken Soil* x, 14, 25, 26; *The Fiddler's House* x, 25–6, 71; *The Land* x, 69–70, 71; *The Saxon Shillin'* 14; *Thomas Muskerry* x, 70, 72. OTHER WORK: *The Road Round Ireland* 217
Conder, Charles Edward 13
Congreve, William 1
Conrad, Joseph 57
Cork National Theatre Society 64–5
Cousins, James ix, 14, 15, 20. PLAYS: *The Racing Lug* ix, 14, 16, 20–1, 81, 149; *The Sleep of the King* ix
Craig, Gordon 16, 29, 218
Crowe, Eileen 92
Cummings, E. E. 90, 91. PLAY: *Him* 90, 91
Cusack, Cyril xiii, 109, 223

D'Alton, Louis 148. PLAY: *The Other Eden* 148
Dante, Alighieri 58
Davis, Thomas 18–19
Davitt, Michael ix
Deane, Seamus 102–4, 155, 216, 220, 223
Deevy, Teresa 136. PLAYS: *Katie Roche* 136; *The King of Spain's Daughter* 136; *The Reapers* 136
de Valera, Eamonn xi, xii, 158
Devlin, Denis 158
Dickens, Charles 103, 111, 175
Digges, Dudley 15, 16
Donoghue, Denis 43, 216, 217
Dos Passos, John 91. PLAYS: *Airways Inc.* 91; *The Moon Is a Gong* 91
Douglas, James xiii, 160–2, 170, 177, 223. PLAYS: *North City Traffic Straight Ahead* xiii, 160–2; *The Savages* 162, 223; *A Day Out of School* 162; *The Bomb* 162; *The Ice Goddess* 162; *The Painting of Babbi Joe* 162; *The Riordans* 162
Drinkwater, John 4
Dublin Drama League xi, xii, 91–2, 94, 219
Dubliner, The 220
Dublin Evening Mail 218
Dublin Theatre Festival xiii, xiv, xv, 109, 159, 172, 180, 200, 223
Dublin Verse-Speaking Society xii, 140

Easter Rising xi, 79, 80, 94, 96, 97, 101, 130
Edwards, Hilton xi, 94, 131–3, 150, 221, 223
Eglinton, John (W. K. Magee) ix, 18, 215
Eire-Ireland 218
Eliot, T. S. 4, 45, 54, 58, 89, 118, 141, 143, 217, 222. PLAYS: *The Cocktail Party* 222; *Murder in the Cathedral* 141; *Sweeney Agonistes* 58, 141. OTHER WORKS: *On Poetry and Poets* 45, 47, 217; *Poetry and Drama*

143, 222; *Selected Essays* 217; *The Waste Land* 89
Ellis-Fermor, Una   4, 24, 213, 215
Ellman, Richard   214, 216
Emmet, Robert   18, 73, 115, 116, 117
Empire Theatre (Belfast)   179
Ervine, St John   xi, 80–4, 88, 93, 136, 148, 149, 178–9, 218. PLAYS: *Boyd's Shop* 81, 136; *Friends and Relations* 81; *Jane Clegg* 80; *John Ferguson* xi, 81, 82–4; *The Magnanimous Lover* xi, 80; *Mixed Marriage* xi, 80–2; *The Orangeman* 80, 218; *William John Mawhinney* 81, 136
Euripides   92
Evening Telegraph   217, 218
Evreinov, Nikolai   94, 118. PLAY: *Theatre of the Soul* 94

Fallon, Gabriel   219
Farquhar, George   1
Farr, Florence   9
Farren, Robert   xii, 140
Faulkner, William   48
Fay, Frank   x, 12–14, 16, 18, 60–1, 214
Fay, Gerard   3, 13, 14, 16, 214
Fay, W. G.   ix, x, 12, 14, 16, 60–1, 62
Ferrar, Harold   121, 219, 221
Fianna Fail   xi, xii, xiii, 158
Field Day Theatre Company   xv, 186–7
Fielding, Henry   112, 220
Fitzgerald, Barry   92
Fitzmaurice, George   x, xi, 5, 66–9, 78, 141, 144, 145, 147, 168, 218. PLAYS: *The Country Dressmaker* x, 67; *The Dandy Dolls* 67–8; *The Magic Glasses* xi, 67–8; *The Pie-Dish* x, 66, 67
Flannery, James   4, 213, 214, 215, 216
Frayne, John P.   214, 215
Freeman's Journal   214, 218
Free Stage Society   11
Friel, Brian   xiii, xiv, xv, 6, 91, 105–6, 155, 178, 186, 200–11, 212, 223.

PLAYS: *Aristocrats* xv, 201; *The Blind Mice* 223; *The Communication Cord* 186, 200, 201, 211–12; *Crystal and Fox* xiv, 201, 205–6; *The Enemy Within* xiii, 156, 200, 223; *Faith Healer* 201–3; *The Francophile* 156, 223; *The Freedom of the City* xiv, 186, 201, 206–9; *The Gentle Island* xiv, 209; *Living Quarters* xiv, 223; *Lovers* xiv, 201; *The Loves of Cass Maguire* xiv; *The Mundy Scheme* xiv; *Philadelphia, Here I Come!* xiv, 156, 178, 200, 201, 203–5, 223; *The Three Sisters* (translation) 186; *Translations* xv, 186, 187, 201, 209–11, 212; *Volunteers* xiv
Frost, Robert   141
Fry, Christopher   222

Gaelic League   ix, 15, 18, 96
Gaiety Theatre   ix, xii, xiv, 132
Garvey, Máire   60, 62
Gate Theatre   xi, xii, xiv, 10, 94–5, 115, 131–3, 141, 149
Gelderman, Carol   66, 218
Goethe, Johannes Wolfgang von   54, 131
Gogarty, St John   26
Goldsmith, Oliver   1
Gonne, Maud   x, 10, 14–15, 17–18, 128
Good, J. W.   65, 218
Greene, David   46, 48, 215, 217
Gregory, Augusta, Lady   ix, x, 1, 6, 8, 9, 10, 11, 14, 16, 19, 20, 21–3, 61, 62, 66, 72, 78, 92, 108, 111–12, 115, 134, 213, 214, 221. PLAYS: *Coats* 77; *Collected Plays* 215; *Dervorgilla* 66; *Hyacinth Halvey* 66; *Kincora* 66; *Spreading the News* x, 21–3; *Twenty-Five* x, 14, 22, 23; *The Unicorn from the Stars* (with W. B. Yeats) x, 61; *The Workhouse Ward* 66. OTHER WORKS: *Journals* 220; *Our Irish Theatre* 8–9, 134, 213, 214, 215, 221
Grein, J. T.   9, 213
Griffith, Arthur   ix, 14–15, 18
Grimes, Frank   160

Index

Gunning, G. Hamilton 89, 136, 219
Guthrie, Tyrone 88
Gwynn, Denis 214

Haire, John Wilson xiv, 180–1.
PLAYS: *Between Two Shadows* xiv,
180–1; *Bloom of the Diamond Stone*
xiv, 181
Harmon, Maurice 141, 217, 222
Heaney, Seamus 223
Helen Hayes Theatre xiv
Herford, C. H. 11
Hickey, Des 223
Higgins, F. R. xii, 134, 136
Hobson, Bulmer 16, 65. PLAY: *Brian
of Banba* 65
Hogan, Robert 4, 13, 88, 97, 132,
136, 145, 213, 214, 217, 220, 221,
222
Hogarth, William 112
Holloway, Joseph 66, 131, 134, 218,
221
Hone, Joseph 216, 218
Horniman, A. E. F. x, 15–16, 60–1
Hunt, Hugh xii, 3, 72, 135–6, 148,
160, 222, 223
Hyde, Douglas ix, x, xii, xiii, 8, 13,
17, 18, 19, 20, 141. PLAY: *Casadh an
tSugáin* (*The Twisting of the Rope*) ix,
13, 20, 30. OTHER WORKS: *Love
Songs of Connacht* ix, 19; 'The
Necessity for de-Anglicising Ireland'
ix, 8

Ibsen, Henrik 7, 10, 12, 24, 46, 48,
72–3, 96, 133, 148. PLAYS: *A Doll's
House* 11, 80; *An Enemy of the People*
11; *Ghosts* 24; *The Pillars of the
Community* 11
Independent Theatre 9, 213
Innes, C. 89–90, 219
Iremonger, Valentine 136
Irish Citizen Army xi, 96, 101
Irish Civil War xi, 79, 97, 101, 120
Irish Free State xi, xii, xiii, 79, 120,
130, 133, 134, 158–9
Irish Independent 84
Irish Literary Society ix, x, 8

Irish Literary Theatre ix, 1, 7, 8, 9,
10, 11, 12, 14, 88
Irish Monthly, The 219
Irish National Dramatic Company ix,
12–13
Irish National Literary Society ix, 8
Irish National Theatre Society x, 13,
14–16, 60
Irish Republican Brotherhood 17,
96
Irish Review, The 88–9, 219
Irish Times, The 17, 29, 133, 134,
215, 217, 218, 219, 221, 223
Irish University Review 222
Irish Volunteers xi

Jarry, Alfred 11, 13, 214. PLAY: *Ubu
Roi* 11, 13
Jeffs, Rae 223
Johnson, Colton 214, 215
Johnston, Denis xi, xii, xiii, 7, 73,
75, 79, 92, 114–30, 132, 139, 147,
155, 159, 212, 218, 221. PLAYS: *A
Bride for the Unicorn* xii, 114, 125,
221; *Blind Man's Buff* xii, 114, 123;
Dramatic Works 218, 221; *The
Dreaming Dust* xii, 114, 125–7, 159;
The Golden Cuckoo xii, 114, 123–4;
The Moon in the Yellow River xii,
114, 120–3, 129, 221; *The Old Lady
Says 'No!'* xii, 73, 79, 94, 114–20,
159, 221; *The Scythe and the Sunset*
xiii, 114, 127–9; *Storm Song* xii, 114;
Strange Occurrence on Ireland's Eye
xiii, 114, 123. OTHER WORKS: *The
Brazen Horn* 114; *In Search of Swift*
126; *Nine Rivers from Jordan* 114,
124
Jones, Henry Arthur 10. PLAY: *The
Silver King* 10
Jonson, Ben 48, 55
Journal of Modern Literature 220
Joyce, James xiii, 12, 24, 34, 39, 91,
93, 107, 118, 158, 159, 166, 175,
188, 198. WORKS: *The Critical
Writings of James Joyce* 214;
Dubliners 39, 93, 107, 155, 188;
Finnegans Wake 188; *Portrait of the*

Artist as a Young man 175; *Ulysses* 159, 188; *Work in Progress* 188

Kaiser, Georg 90, 120. PLAYS: *From Morn to Midnight* 90, 114, 118; *Gas* 90
Kavanagh, Patrick 158, 181
Kavanagh, Peter 3, 4, 138, 213
Keane, John B. xiii, 168–9, 170. PLAYS: *Big Maggie* 168; *The Field* 168–9; *Hut 42* xiii, 168, 169; *The Man from Clare* 168; *Many Young Men of Twenty* 168; *Sive* 168
Kearney, Colbert 152, 223
Keating, Sean 87
Kennedy, David 87, 88, 218, 219
Kenner, Hugh 191, 198–9, 224
Kilroy, James 217
Kilroy, Thomas xiv, xv, 54–5, 91, 106, 129, 155, 156, 171–5, 177, 178, 196, 199, 216, 217, 220, 221, 223. PLAYS: *The Death and Resurrection of Mr Roche* xiv, 156, 172–4, 223; *The O'Neill* 172; *Talbot's Box* xv, 172, 174–5, 178; *Tea and Sex and Shakespeare* 172. OTHER WORKS: *The Big Chapel* 172; *Sean O'Casey: A collection of Critical Essays* (ed.) 220
Kinsella, Thomas 144, 222
Knowlson, James 223
Krause, David 101, 219
Krutch, J. W. 102, 220

Larkin, Jim 96
Lemass, Sean xiv, 158–9, 172
Leonard, Hugh (J. K. Byrne) xiii, xiv, 156, 158, 175–8, 223. PLAYS: *A Leap in the Dark* xiii, 156; *A Life* 177; *The Big Birthday* 156; *Da* xiv, 176–7; *Me Mammy* 175; *The Patrick Pearse Motel* 175; *Silent Song* 175; *Stephen D* (adaptation) 175; *Time Was* xiv, 175–6; *When the Saints Go Cycling In* (adaptation) 175
Lincoln Centre xiv
Lindsay, Jack 220
Lindsay, Vachel 140
Littlewood, Joan 150, 153, 162

London Sunday Sun 218
Longford, Christine, Countess 133, 154. PLAYS: *The Hill of Quirke* 154; *Tankardstown* 133
Longford, Edward, Lord xii, 131–3
Longford Productions xii, 132–3
Loudan, Jack 149
Lugne-Poe, Aurélien 29–30
Lynch, Martin 149. PLAY: *The Interrogation of Ambrose Fogarty* 149
Lyric Theatre (Belfast) xiii, xiv, 109, 149, 180, 187
Lyric Theatre Company (Dublin) xii, 134, 140–1

MacAnna, Tomas 155, 160, 223
Macaulay, Thomas Babington, Lord 107
MacCathmaoil, Seosamh 65. PLAY: *The Little Cowherd of Slainge* 65
MacDonagh, Donagh 141, 222. PLAYS: *God's Gentry* 222; *Happy As Larry* 222; *Step-in-the-Hollow* 222
MacIntyre, Tom xiv, 181–2. PLAYS: *Eye Winker, Tom Tinker* xiv, 181–2; *The Great Hunger* (adaptation) 181
MacKenna, Stephen 47, 216
MacLiammóir, Micheál xi, 30, 94–5, 131–3, 215, 219, 221. PLAYS: *Diarmuid and Grania* 94; *Ill Met by Moonlight* 132; *Where Stars Walk* 132. OTHER WORKS: *All for Hecuba* 95, 219, 221; *Theatre in Ireland* 30, 94, 215, 219
MacManus, Seamus x, 20. PLAY: *The Townland of Tamney* 20
MacNamara, Brinsley 79, 84, 134. PLAY: *The Glorious Uncertainty* 79
MacNamara, Gerald (Harry Morrow) 16. PLAY: *Thompson in Tir-na-nOg* 16, 65
McCabe, Eugene xiv, 106, 169–70. PLAYS: *Cancer* 169; *King of the Castle* xiv, 169–70; *Swift* xiv
McCann, John 154. PLAY: *Twenty Years A-Wooing* 154
McCann, Sean 222

Index

McCormick, F. J. 92
McGinley, P. T. ix, 20. PLAY: *Lizzie and the Tinker* ix, 20
McGowran, Jack 155, 223
McGrath, John 150, 170. PLAY: *Events While Guarding the Bofors Gun* 150, 170
McGreevy, Thomas 158
McHugh, Roger 107, 136, 142, 220, 222
McMaster, Anew 94, 219
Maeterlinck, Maurice 4, 7, 29–30, 48, 214, 215. PLAY: *Pelléas et Mélisande* 29–30. OTHER WORK: *The Treasury of the Humble* 30, 215
Mallarmé, Stéphane 13, 48
Malone, A. E. 1, 2, 3, 22, 97, 213, 215
Manchester Guardian 218
Mangan, James Clarence 115, 117
Markiewicz, Con, Countess 128
Martyn, Edward ix, x, 1, 8, 9–10, 11, 12–13, 14, 15, 16, 24–5, 60, 131, 214. PLAYS: *An Enchanted Sea* 14; *The Heather Field* ix, 9, 14, 16, 214; *Maeve* ix, 16, 24, 214; *The Tale of a Town* 9
Marx, Karl 37, 58, 105, 106
Masefield, John 4
Mason, Ellsworth 214
Mayne, Rutherford (Samuel Waddell) x, xii, 16, 81. PLAYS: *Bridgehead* xii; *The Drone* x, 16, 65–6
Mennloch, Walter 88–9, 92, 219
Mercier, Vivian 155, 195, 198, 221, 223, 224
Miller, Arthur 91, PLAY: *Death of a Salesman* 91
Milligan, Alice 20. PLAY: *The Last Feast of the Fianna* 20–1
Moiseiwitch, Tanya 136
Molesworth Hall x
Molière (Jean Baptiste Poquelin) 12, 48. PLAY: *L'Avare* 48
Molloy, M. J. xiii, 145–7, 148. PLAYS: *The King of Friday's Men* xiii, 146–7; *The Visiting House* xiii, 145–6; *The Will and the Way* 146, 154
Monck, Nugent 135
Montague, John 224
Moore, Brian 224
Moore, George ix, xi, 1, 8, 9–10, 11–12, 14, 213, 214. PLAYS: *The Bending of the Bough* ix, 9, 16; *Diarmuid and Grania* (with W. B. Yeats) ix, 9, 20; *The Strike at Arlingford* 9. OTHER WORKS: *Hail and Farewell* xi, 9, 213; *Impressions and Opinions* 9
Moore, James Rees 216
Moore, Sturge 40, 141
Moore, Thomas 107, 115
Moreau, Gustave 13
Morrison, Bill 182, 186, 224. PLAY: *Flying Blind* 182–3
Murphy, Thomas xiii, xiv, 6, 91, 162–8, 170, 177, 178, 199. PLAYS: *A Whistle in the Dark* xiii, xiv, 156, 162–5, 223; *The Blue Macushla* 162, 223; *Famine* xiv, 156, 162; *The Fooleen (A Crucial Week in the Life of a Grocer's Assistant)* xiv, 162, 165–7; *The Morning after Optimism* xiv, 162, 170, 178; *The Sanctuary Lamp* xiv, 162, 167–8; *The White House* xiv
Murray, T. C. x, xi, 5, 65, 66, 75–7, 78, 79, 81, 88, 132, 136, 139, 147, 170, 177. PLAYS: *A Flutter of Wings* 132; *Aftermath* xi, 76; *Autumn Fire* xi, 76–7; *Birthright* x, 75–6; *Maurice Harte* xi; *Michaelmas Eve* xii, 76, 136; *Illumination* 136; *The Wheel of Fortune* 65

Nation, The 18
National Theatre Society Ltd x, 60
New Ireland 84
New York Times 222, 224
Nichols, Peter 170–1. PLAY: *A Day in the Death of Joe Egg* 170–1
Nic Shiubhlaigh, Máire (Mary Walker) 60
Noh plays 7, 36–7, 42
Northern Ireland xi, xiii, xiv, 79, 130, 159, 169, 171, 178, 185

246

Northern Whig 218

O'Casey, Sean xi, xii, xiii, xiv, xv, 3,
4, 7, 73, 79, 92, 93, 94, 95, 96–113,
114, 116, 127, 130, 134, 140, 147,
149, 155, 159, 199, 212, 219, 220.
PLAYS: *The Bishop's Bonfire* xiii, 97,
109; *Cock-a-Doodle-Dandy* xiii, xv,
97, 109; *The Drums of Father Ned*
xiii, 97, 109, 159; *Juno and the
Paycock* xi, 92, 94, 96–7, 99–100,
102, 108, 149, 220; *Oak Leaves and
Lavender* xiii, 97, 109; *The Plough
and the Stars* xi, 57, 73, 92, 96–7, 99,
100, 102, 108, 149, 220; *The Purple
Dust* xii, xiv, 97, 109; *Red Roses for
Me* xii, 97, 101–2, 105, 110–11, 219;
The Shadow of a Gunman xi, 92, 96,
97–8, 100, 101, 102, 108, 220; *The
Silver Tassie* xi, xii, 79, 94, 97, 99,
100, 105, 106–8, 134; *The Star Turns
Red* xii, 97, 109; *Within the Gates* xii,
97, 109
O'Connell, Daniel 86
O'Connor, Frank (O'Donovan) 86,
133–5, 221. PLAYS: *In the Train* 135;
The Invincibles 135
Odets, Clifford 148
O'Donovan, Fred 61
O'Faolain, Sean 134, 221
O'Grady, Standish ix, 19, 45
O hAodha, Micheál 97, 101, 134,
155, 220, 221
O'Leary, John 17–18
Olympia Theatre xiv
O'Malley, Mary xiii, 149
O'Malley, Pearse xiii
O'Neill, Eugene 91, 112, 114. PLAYS:
Anna Christie 94, 154; *Desire Under
the Elms* 91; *The Great God Brown*
91; *The Hairy Ape* 91, 94
O'Neill, Máire (Molly Allgood) 47,
55, 61
O'Neill, Michael J, 218, 221
Osborne, John 159
Oxford Playhouse xiv

Parker, Stewart xiv, xv, 183–5, 186,
223, 224. PLAYS: *Catchpenny Twist*
xv, 183–5; *Spokesong* xiv, 185
Parkhill, David 16
Parnell, Charles Stewart ix, 18, 39,
73, 82
Payne, Ben Iden 60–1
Peacock Theatre xi, xiv, 93, 94, 140,
160, 181
Peake, Bladon 135
Pearse, Padraig 101, 130, 219
People's Theatre 109
Pike Theatre xiii, 148, 149–50
Pinero, A. W. 10. PLAY: *The Second
Mrs Tanqueray* 10
Pinter, Harold 4, 6, 58. PLAYS: *The
Caretaker* 170; *The Homecoming* 170
Pirandello, Luigi 74, 92, 93, 114.
PLAYS: *The Game As He Played It*
92; *Henry IV* 90, 92; *Six Characters
in Search of an Author* 74, 90
Players' Club 14
Pound, Ezra 36
Price, Alan 217
Proust, Marcel 34
Purcell, Lewis 65. PLAY: *The Pagan*
65

Queen's Theatre 10, 148, 155, 158
Quinn, John 14
Quinn, Máire 15, 16

Racine, Jean 48. PLAY: *Phèdre* 48
Radio Eireann xi, 140
Radio Telefis Eireann (RTE) xiii,
159, 162, 169
Rae, Stephen xv, 186
Rains, Claude 114
Recall the Years 160
Reid, Alec 155, 233
Reid, Christina 149. PLAY: *Tea in a
China Cup* 149
Reid, J. Graham xv, 185. PLAYS: *The
Closed Door* xv, 185; *The Death of
Humpty-Dumpty* xv, 185, 186
Rice, Elmer 91, 154. PLAYS: *The
Adding Machine* 91, 94: *Not for
Children* 154
Roberts, George 60

Robertson, T. W. 216. PLAY:
Caste 216
Robinson, Lennox x, xi, xii, xiii, 3,
61, 65, 66, 72–5, 78, 79–80, 91–2,
135, 136, 177, 218, 219. PLAYS:
Church Street xii, 74–5, 136; The
Clancy Name x, 72–3; Crabbed Youth
and Age 75; The Cross Roads x;
Drama at Inish xii, 72, 75, 136; The
Dreamers 73; Ever the Twain 73; The
Far-Off Hills 75; Harvest x, 72; The
Lesson of Life 65; The Lost Leader xi,
73; The Lucky Finger 75; Patriots xi;
The Round Table 73; The
Whiteheaded Boy xi, 75. OTHER
WORKS: Curtain Up 19, 218, 219;
Ireland's Abbey Theatre 3
Ronsley, Joseph 216, 221, 223, 224
Royal Court Theatre xiii, xiv, xv, 180
Royal Shakespeare Company 171
Royal Theatre 10
Rudkin, David 171. PLAYS: Ashes
171; Cries from Casement as his Bones
Are Brought to Dublin 171; The Sons
of Light 171; The Triumph of Death
171
Ryan, Fred ix. PLAY: The Laying of
the Foundations ix, x

Saddlemyer, Ann 23, 48, 50, 215,
217
St Theresa's Hall ix
Samhain 11, 12, 13, 33, 34, 213, 214,
216
Shakespeare, William 5, 10, 12, 94,
96, 105, 111, 131, 133, 189, 196,
219–20. PLAY: King Lear 79, 128
Shaw, G. B. x, 1, 2, 3, 11, 96, 112,
129, 131, 133, 154, 155, 196, 213,
218. PLAYS: Androcles and the Lion
96; The Doctor's Dilemma 154;
Heartbreak House 129; John Bull's
Other Island x, 218; St Joan 154; The
Shewing-Up of Blanco Posnet x, 62,
64, 218
Sheridan, R. B. 1
Shields, Arthur 92
Shiels, George xi, xii, xiii, 79, 84–8,

91, 93, 145, 148, 170, 218. PLAYS:
Bedmates 84; The Caretakers 85;
Cartney and Kevney xi, 84; Felix
Reid and Bob (as George Morshiel)
84; Insurance Money 84; The New
Gossoon 93, 136; The Old Broom, xii,
85–6; The Passing Day xii, 88, 136;
Paul Twyning xi, 84; Professor Tim
xi, 84–5; The Rugged Path xii, 136;
Tenants at Will xiii, 86–8, 218; Under
the Moss (as George Morshiel) xi,
84
Simmons, James 101–2, 220
Simpson, Alan xiii, 148, 150, 155,
156, 159, 222, 223
Sinclair, Arthur 61
Sinn Fein x
Smith, Gus 223
Sophocles 5
Starkie, Walter 97
Stephens, Edward M. 215, 217
Stevenson, R. L. 55
Stoppard, Tom 91, PLAY: Rosencrantz
and Guildenstern Are Dead 91, 170
Strindberg, August 89, 92, 96, 114.
PLAYS: The Dream Play 89, The
Ghost Sonata 89, 92
Swift, Carolyn xiii, 148
Swift, Jonathan 1, 93, 125–6, 166,
198, 222
Symons, Arthur 29
Synge, J. M. x, 2, 5–6, 7, 14, 15, 17,
20, 21, 23–4, 25, 28, 30–2, 33, 35,
37–8, 46–59, 60, 61, 62–3, 66, 69,
77, 78, 84, 88, 89, 95, 117, 140, 145,
147, 155, 161, 188, 191–4, 199, 212,
215, 216, 217, 218, 219, 223. PLAYS:
Deirdre of the Sorrows x, 30, 46, 55–
7, 77, 161; In the Shadow of the Glen
x, 14, 15, 25–6, 30–1, 32, 46, 50, 52,
62, 191; The Playboy of the Western
World x, 46, 47–8, 49–51, 52, 55, 62,
63–4, 66, 94, 118, 217; Riders to the
Sea x, 20, 21, 31–2, 46, 47; The
Tinker's Wedding xiv, 46, 48, 51–2;
The Well of the Saints x, 35, 52–4,
62, 64, 188. OTHER WORKS: The Aran
Islands 31; Collected Works 46, 47,

Index

56, 58, 215, 217; *Poems and
Translations* 47

Théâtre de l'Oeuvre, Le 29
Théâtre Libre 11
Theatre of Ireland x, 25, 60–1
Theatre Royal, Stratford E. xiii, 150,
162
Thompson, Sam xiii, 149, 179–80.
PLAYS: *The Evangelist* 180; *Over the
Bridge* xiii, 149, 179–80, 186
Threshold 220, 223
Times, The 14
Times Literary Supplement 171
Toibín, Niall 160
Toller, Ernst 90, 114, 123. PLAYS:
The Blind Goddess 123; *Hoppla!* 92,
114; *Masses and Men* 92;
Transfiguration 90
Tolstoi, Count Leo 11, 94
Tomelty, Joseph 148–9, 222. PLAYS:
All Souls' Night 149; *The End House*
149; *Is the Priest at Home?* 149, 154
Tone, Wolfe 16, 18
Tree, Beerbohm 94
Tynan, Kenneth 162

Uladh 65, 218
Ulster Group Theatre xii, xiii, 85,
148–9, 179, 223
Ulster Literary Theatre x, xi, 16, 17,
65–6, 84
United Irishman, The ix, 12, 14, 17,
26, 28, 214, 215
Unity Theatre xii, 109
Ure, Peter 216

Vendler, Helen 216
Verlaine, Paul 13
Villiers de l'Isle Adam, Count
August 29, 214. PLAY: *Axël* 29, 214

Walker, Frank 60
Walkley, A. B. 214
Welch, Robert 222
Wesker, Arnold 150. PLAY: *Chips with
Everything* 150
Wilde, Oscar 1, 2, 49, 133. PLAYS:

The Importance of Being Earnest 49;
Salomé 94
Williams, Tennessee 91, 159, 170.
PLAYS: *A Streetcar Named Desire* 170;
The Glass Menagerie 91, 170; *The
Rose Tattoo* xiii, 159
Wilmot, Dorothy xiii
Wilmot, Hubert xiii, 149
Wilson, F. A. C. 216
Woolf, Virginia 34
Worth, Katherine 4, 29, 215, 216

Yeats, Jack B. 155
Yeats, W. B. ix, x, xi, xii, xiv, 1, 4–
6, 7, 8, 9, 10, 11, 12–13, 14, 15, 16,
17–19, 20–1, 23, 26–30, 32, 33–46,
47, 54–5, 58, 60–3, 66–7, 69, 72, 78,
79–80, 84, 89, 91, 92–3, 94, 107–8,
109, 112, 115, 123, 129, 133–4, 135,
140, 141, 147, 149, 155, 187, 195, 196,
212, 213, 214, 215, 216, 217, 218,
219, 222. PLAYS: *At the Hawk's Well*
xi, 34, 38–9, 40–2, 45, 92, 196, 218;
Calvary xi; *The Cat and the Moon* xi,
92, 134; *Cathleen ni Houlihan* ix, x,
16, 17, 27, 39, 62; *The Countess
Cathleen* ix, 8, 9, 10, 39; *The Death
of Cuchulain* xii, 45, 134, 141;
Deirdre x, 40, 61, 222; *Diarmuid and
Grania* (with George Moore) ix, 9,
20; *The Dreaming of the Bones* 45;
134; *Fighting the Waves* xii, 33, 79,
134, 216; *The Golden Helmet* x, 61;
The Green Helmet x, 61; *The Herne's
Egg* xii, 135; *The Hour Glass* x, xi,
11, 27–9, 36; *King Oedipus* xi, 79;
King of the Great Clock Tower xii;
The King's Threshold x, 14, 28, 39–
40, 50; *The Land of Heart's Desire* ix,
8; *Oedipus at Colonus* xi, 79; *On
Baile's Strand* x, 28–9, 36, 38–9, 43;
The Only Jealousy of Emer xi, 43–4,
92, 216; *The Player Queen* xi; *The
Pot of Broth* ix, x, 27; *Purgatory*, xii,
42, 45, 133; *Resurrection* xii; *The
Shadowy Waters* x, 28; *The Unicorn
from the Stars* (with Lady Gregory) x,
61; *The Words upon the Window Pane*

Yeats – *cont.*
xii, 134. COLLECTIONS: *Plays and Controversies* 217; *Plays in Prose and Verse* 215. PROSE WORKS QUOTED: *Autobiographies* 7, 9, 10, 11, 13, 18, 37, 40, 214, 216; *A Vision* 42; *The Cutting of an Agate* 5; *Essays and Introductions* 29, 32, 33–4, 35, 36, 37, 45, 54, 89, 215, 216, 217, 219; *Explorations* 5, 6, 11, 13, 17, 27, 33–4, 35, 37, 40, 46, 54, 62–3, 72, 213, 214, 215, 216, 217, 218, 224; *Letters* 14, 30, 214, 215, 217, 220; *Memoirs* 38, 216; *Uncollected Prose* 16, 18, 19, 20, 29, 47, 214, 215, 217. POETRY-COLLECTIONS: *Last Poems and Two Plays* xii; *Responsibilities* 27, 30, 194; *Words for Music Perhaps* 195. POEMS: 'A Coat' 30, 34; 'Byzantium', 37, 58; 'The Circus Animals' Desertion' 219; 'The Cold Heaven' 40, 42; 'The Curse of Cromwell' 54; 'The Dancer at Cruachan and Cro-Patrick' 194–5; 'Easter 1916' 105; 'The Hour Before Dawn' 194; 'Lapis Lazuli' 34; 'Meditations in Time of Civil War' 37; 'Sailing to Byzantium' 37, 42, 58; 'The Second Coming' 42; 'Tom the Lunatic' 195

Young Ireland 18

Zola, Emile 46, 48